GREEN LANTERN

RAGE OF THE RED LANTERNS

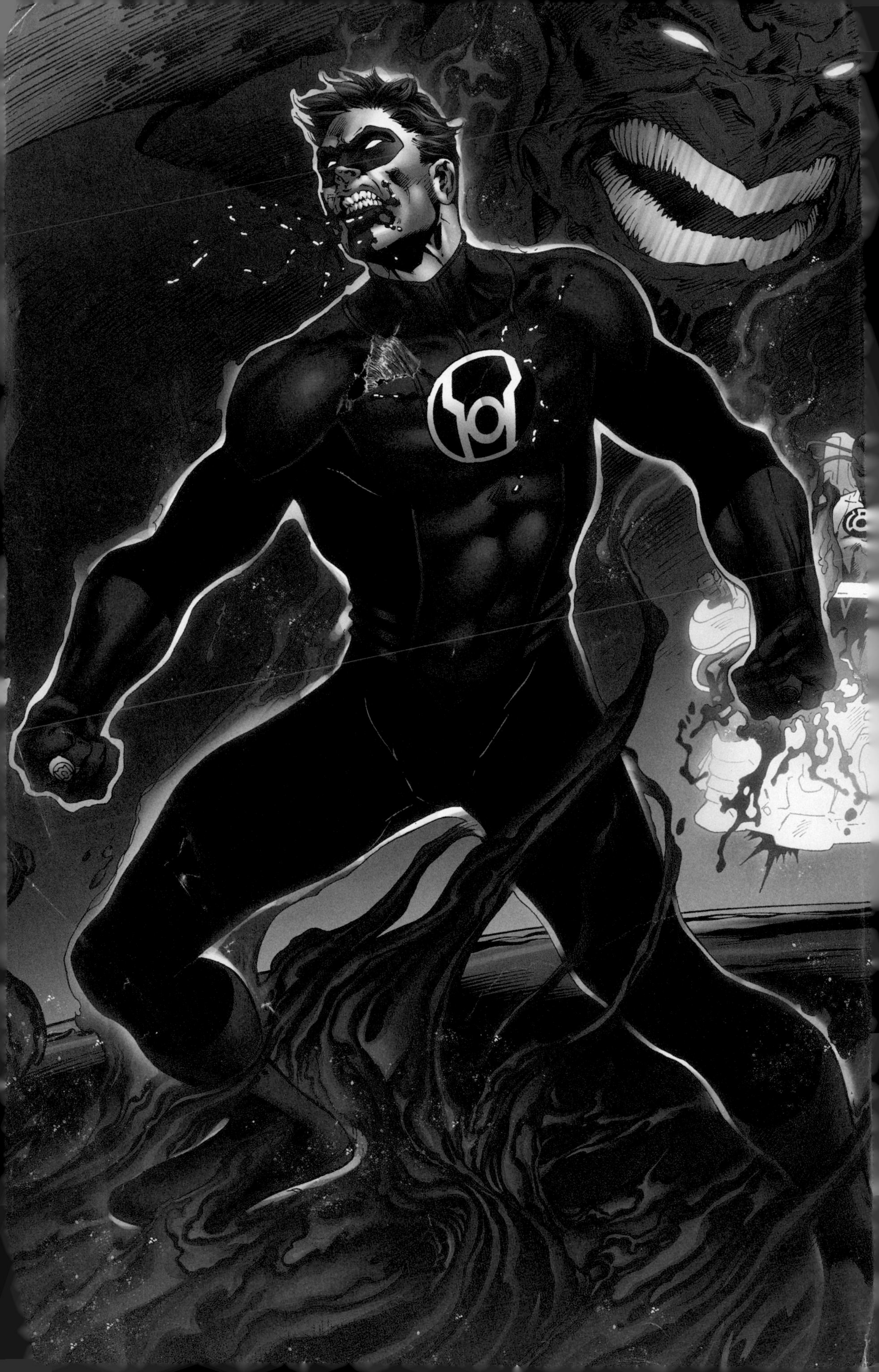

RAGE OF THE RED LANTERNS

Geoff Johns
Writer

Mike McKone   **Shane Davis**   **Ivan Reis**
Pencillers

Andy Lanning   **Marlo Alquiza**   **Cam Smith**
Mark Farmer   **Norm Rapmund**   **Sandra Hope**
Oclair Albert   **Julio Ferreira**
Inkers

JD Smith   **Nei Ruffino**
Colors

Rob Leigh   **Steve Wands**
Letters

DC COMICS

Dan DiDio Senior VP-Executive Editor
Eddie Berganza Editor-original series
Adam Schlagman Associate Editor-original series
Sean Mackiewicz Editor-collected edition
Robbin Brosterman Senior Art Director
Paul Levitz President & Publisher
Georg Brewer VP-Design & DC Direct Creative
Richard Bruning Senior VP-Creative Director
Patrick Caldon Executive VP-Finance & Operations
hris Caramalis VP-Finance
ohn Cunningham VP-Marketing
ri Cunningham VP-Managing Editor
y Genkins Senior VP-Business & Legal Affairs
on Gill VP-Manufacturing
d Hyde VP-Publicity
Kanalz VP-General Manager, WildStorm
ee Editorial Director-WildStorm
ry Noveck Senior VP-Creative Affairs
ohja VP-Book Trade Sales
Rotterdam Senior VP-Sales & Marketing
Rubin Senior VP-Brand Management
oll VP-Advertising & Custom Publishing
an VP-Business Development, DC Direct
ne VP-Sales

Cover by Shane Davis, Sandra Hope and Nei Ruffino

**GREEN LANTERN: RAGE OF THE
RED LANTERNS**

Published by DC Comics. Cover, text and compilation
Copyright © 2009 DC Comics. All Rights Reserved.

Originally published in single magazine form in
GREEN LANTERN 26-28, 36-38, FINAL CRISIS:
RAGE OF THE RED LANTERNS 1. Copyright © 2008,
2009 DC Comics. All Rights Reserved. All characters,
their distinctive likenesses and related elements featured
in this publication are trademarks of DC Comics.
The stories, characters and incidents featured in this
publication are entirely fictional. DC Comics does not
read or accept unsolicited submissions of ideas,
stories or artwork.

DC Comics, 1700 Broadway, New York, NY 10019
A Warner Bros. Entertainment Company
Printed by Quad/Graphics, Dubuque, IA, 11/17/10.
Second Printing.

ISBN: 978-1-4012-2302-1

SUSTAINABLE
FORESTRY
INITIATIVE
Certified Chain of Custody
Promoting Sustainable
Forest Management
www.sfiprogram.org
Fiber used in this product line meets the
sourcing requirements of the SFI program.
www.sfiprogram.org PWC-SFICOC-260

GREEN LANTERN 26 Cover by Mike McKone, Andy Lanning and Moose Baumann

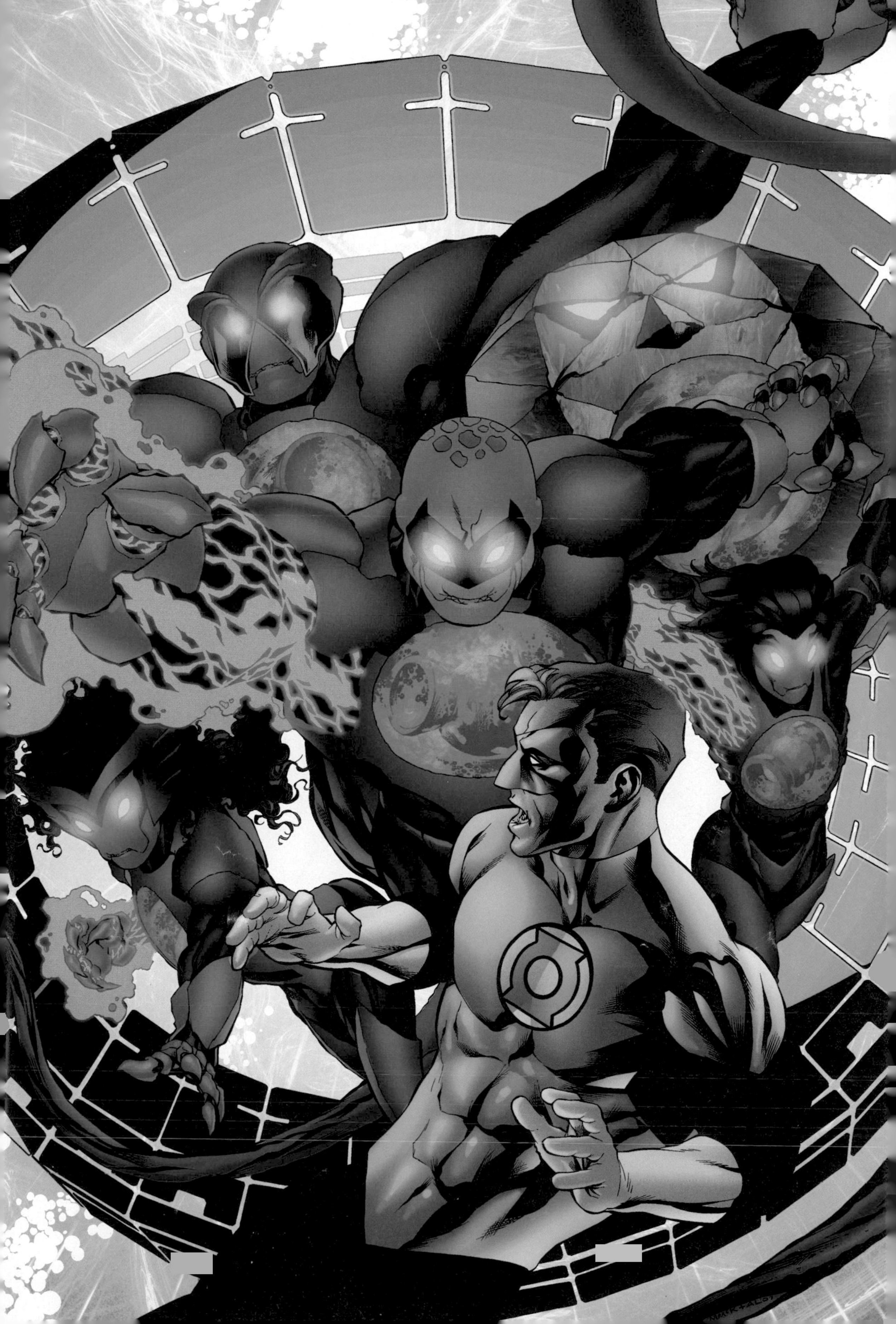

THE ALPHA LANTERNS
Part 1

Mike McKone Pencils
Andy Lanning **Marlo Alquiza** **Cam Smith** Inks
JD Smith Colors

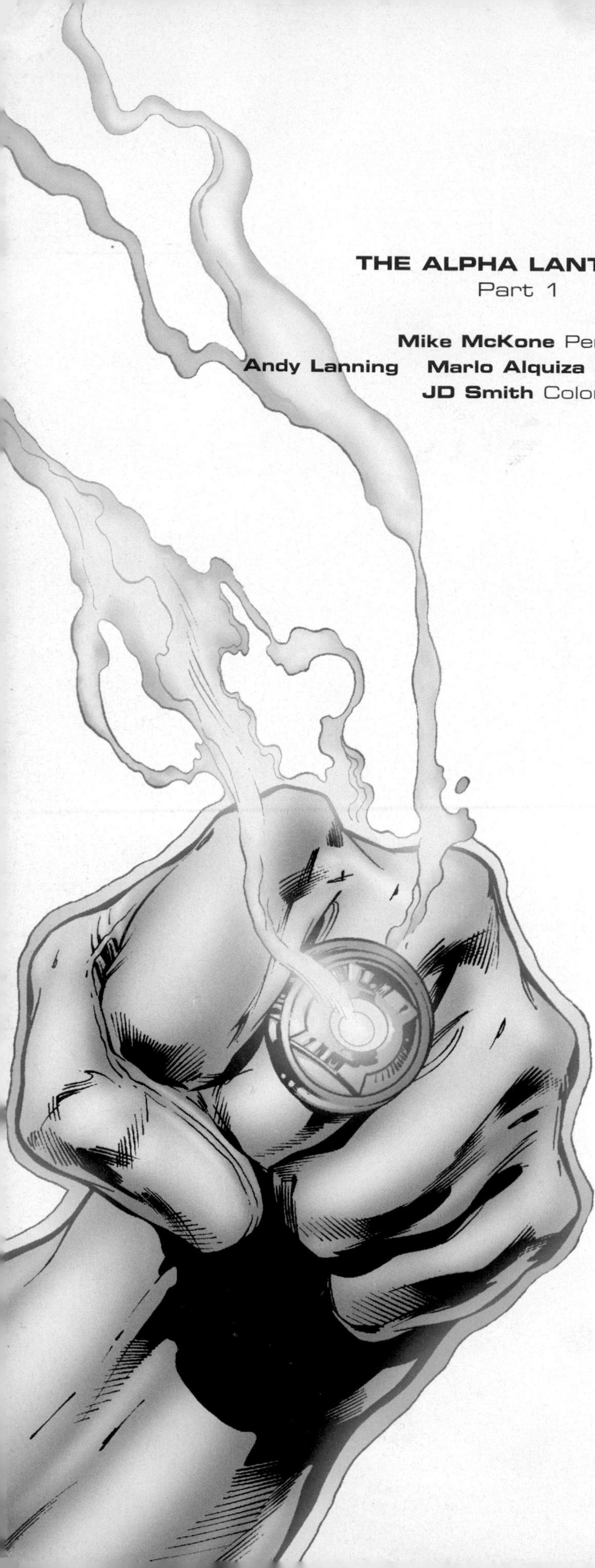

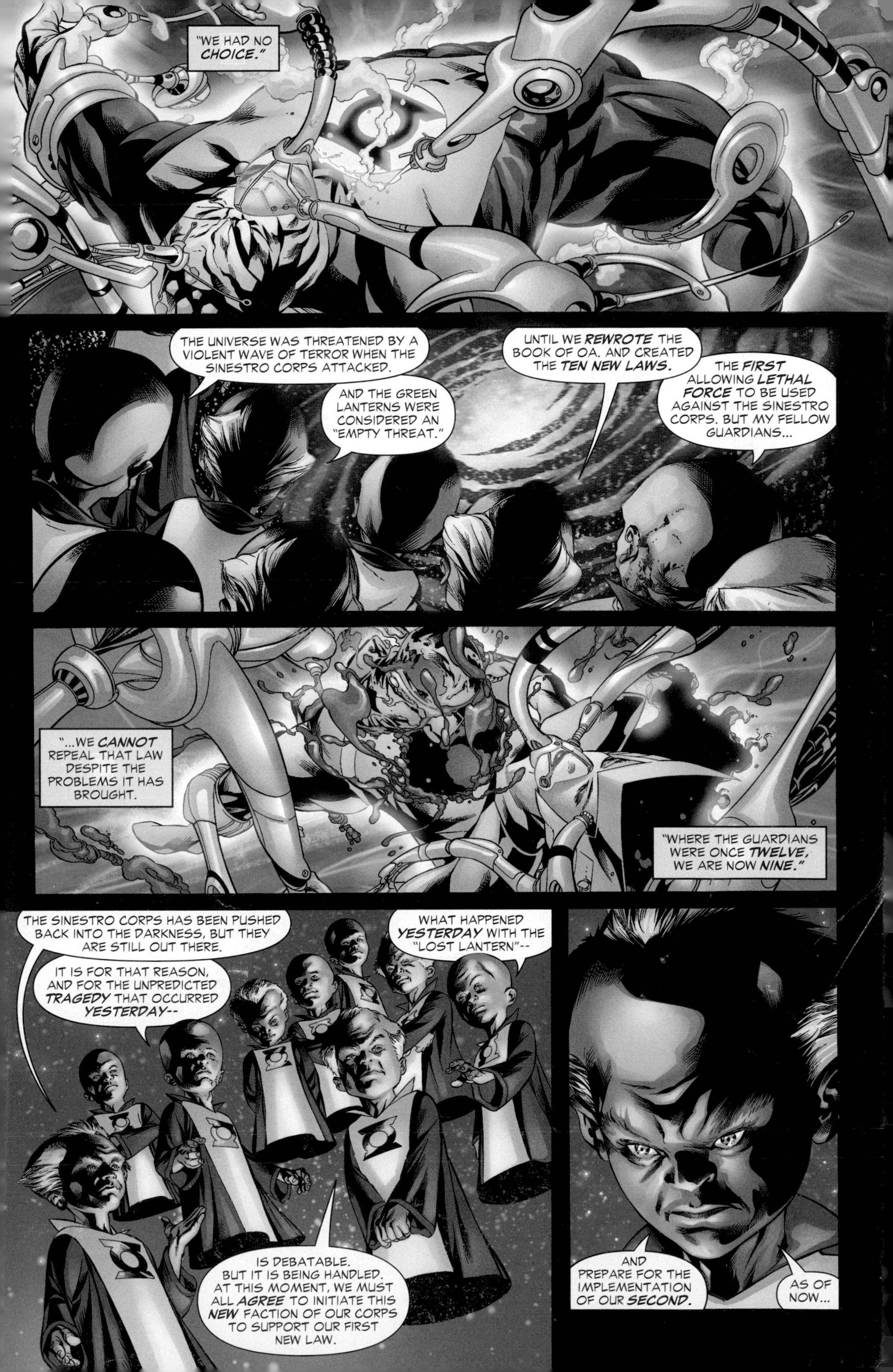

"WE HAD NO CHOICE."
THE UNIVERSE WAS THREATENED BY A VIOLENT WAVE OF TERROR WHEN THE SINESTRO CORPS ATTACKED.
AND THE GREEN LANTERNS WERE CONSIDERED AN "EMPTY THREAT."
UNTIL WE REWROTE THE BOOK OF OA. AND CREATED THE TEN NEW LAWS.
THE FIRST ALLOWING LETHAL FORCE TO BE USED AGAINST THE SINESTRO CORPS. BUT MY FELLOW GUARDIANS...
"...WE CANNOT REPEAL THAT LAW DESPITE THE PROBLEMS IT HAS BROUGHT.
"WHERE THE GUARDIANS WERE ONCE TWELVE, WE ARE NOW NINE."
THE SINESTRO CORPS HAS BEEN PUSHED BACK INTO THE DARKNESS, BUT THEY ARE STILL OUT THERE.
IT IS FOR THAT REASON, AND FOR THE UNPREDICTED TRAGEDY THAT OCCURRED YESTERDAY--
WHAT HAPPENED YESTERDAY WITH THE "LOST LANTERN"--
IS DEBATABLE. BUT IT IS BEING HANDLED. AT THIS MOMENT, WE MUST ALL AGREE TO INITIATE THIS NEW FACTION OF OUR CORPS TO SUPPORT OUR FIRST NEW LAW.
AS OF NOW...
AND PREPARE FOR THE IMPLEMENTATION OF OUR SECOND.

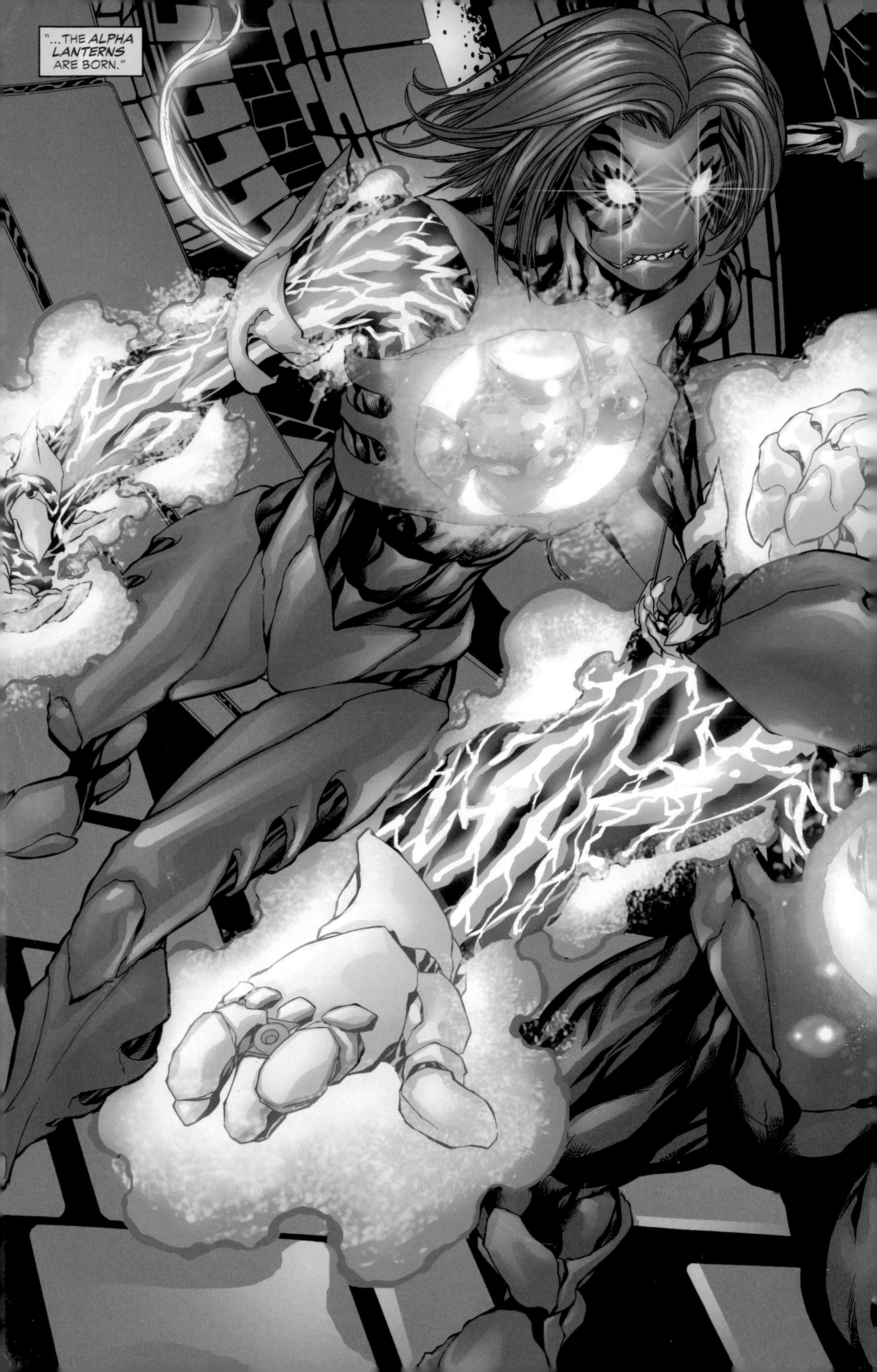
"...THE *ALPHA LANTERNS* ARE BORN."

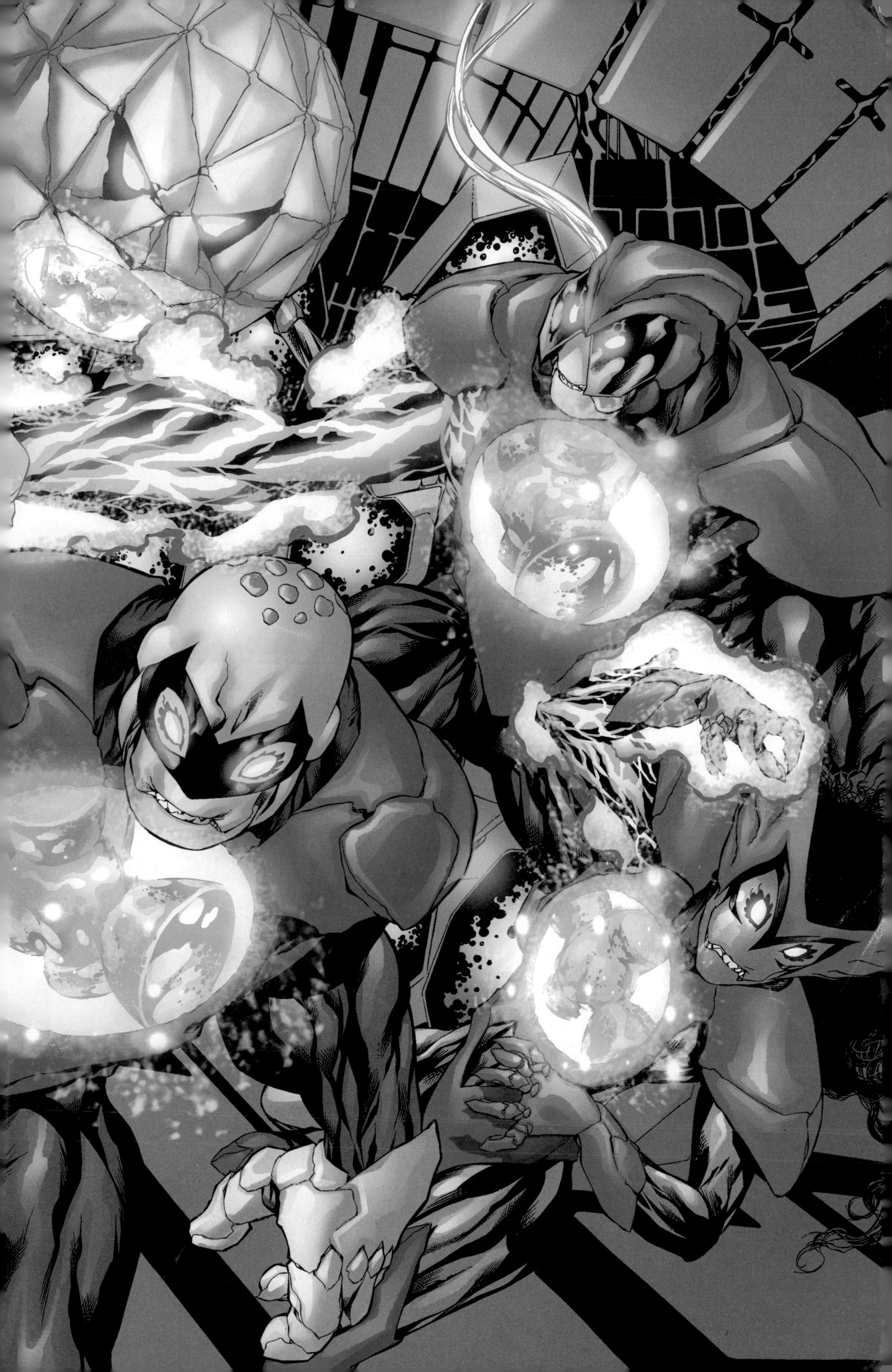

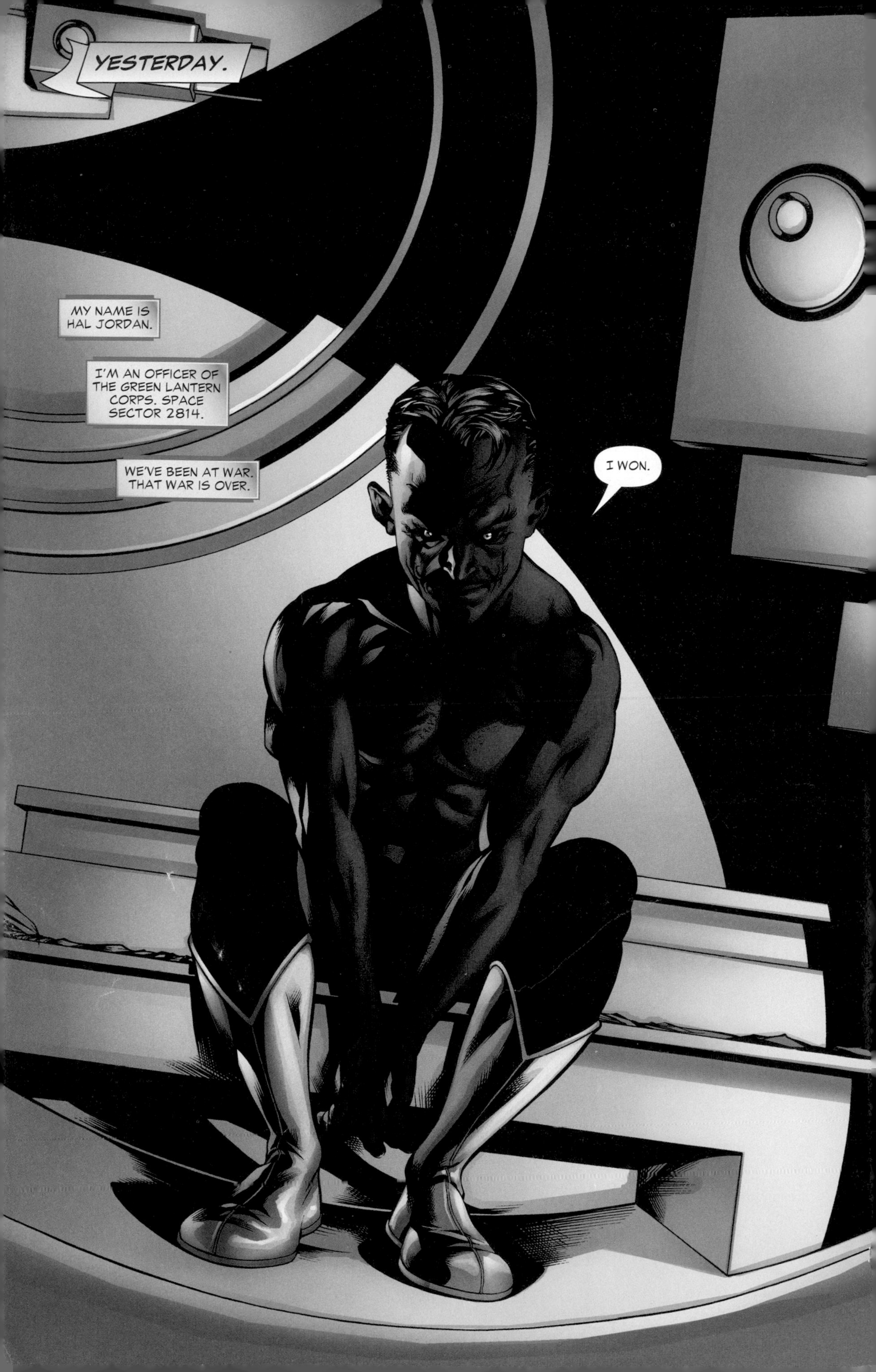
YESTERDAY.
MY NAME IS HAL JORDAN.
I'M AN OFFICER OF THE GREEN LANTERN CORPS. SPACE SECTOR 2814.
WE'VE BEEN AT WAR. THAT WAR IS OVER.
I WON.

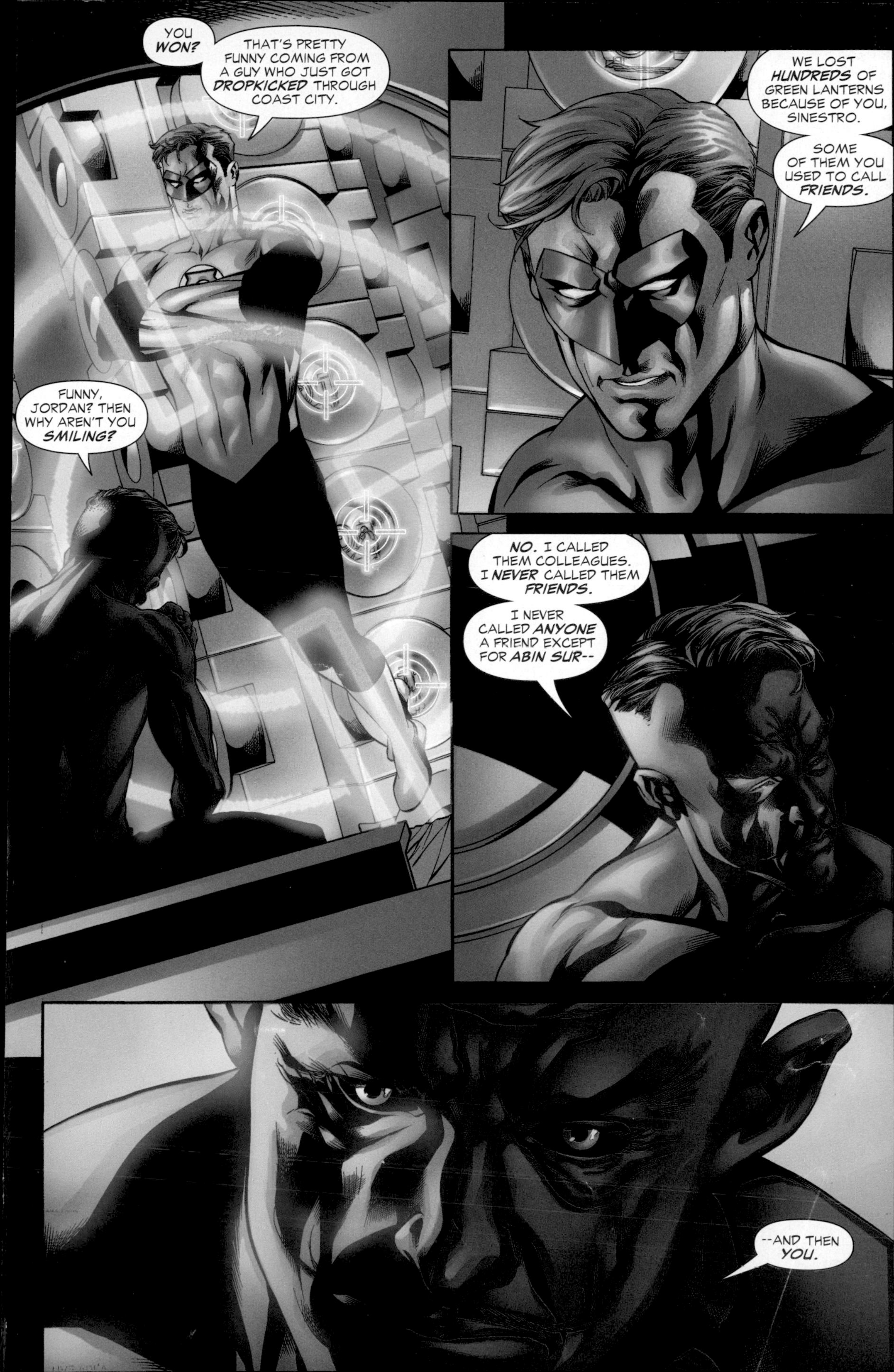

YOU WON?
THAT'S PRETTY FUNNY COMING FROM A GUY WHO JUST GOT DROPKICKED THROUGH COAST CITY.
FUNNY, JORDAN? THEN WHY AREN'T YOU SMILING?
WE LOST HUNDREDS OF GREEN LANTERNS BECAUSE OF YOU, SINESTRO.
SOME OF THEM YOU USED TO CALL FRIENDS.
NO. I CALLED THEM COLLEAGUES. I NEVER CALLED THEM FRIENDS.
I NEVER CALLED ANYONE A FRIEND EXCEPT FOR ABIN SUR--
--AND THEN YOU.

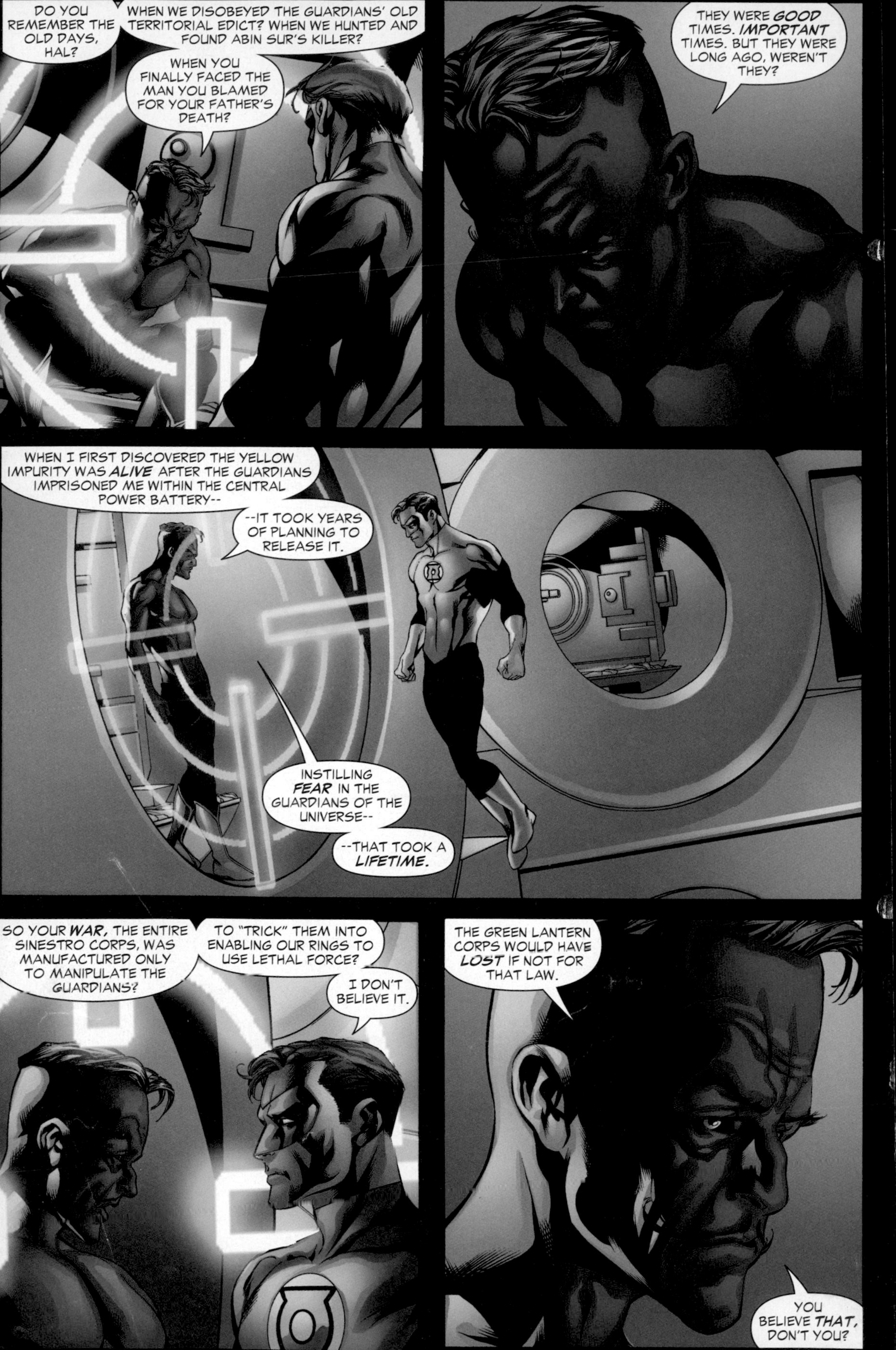
DO YOU REMEMBER THE OLD DAYS, HAL?
WHEN WE DISOBEYED THE GUARDIANS' OLD TERRITORIAL EDICT? WHEN WE HUNTED AND FOUND ABIN SUR'S KILLER?
WHEN YOU FINALLY FACED THE MAN YOU BLAMED FOR YOUR FATHER'S DEATH?
THEY WERE GOOD TIMES. IMPORTANT TIMES. BUT THEY WERE LONG AGO, WEREN'T THEY?
WHEN I FIRST DISCOVERED THE YELLOW IMPURITY WAS ALIVE AFTER THE GUARDIANS IMPRISONED ME WITHIN THE CENTRAL POWER BATTERY--
--IT TOOK YEARS OF PLANNING TO RELEASE IT.
INSTILLING FEAR IN THE GUARDIANS OF THE UNIVERSE--
--THAT TOOK A LIFETIME.
SO YOUR WAR, THE ENTIRE SINESTRO CORPS, WAS MANUFACTURED ONLY TO MANIPULATE THE GUARDIANS?
TO "TRICK" THEM INTO ENABLING OUR RINGS TO USE LETHAL FORCE?
I DON'T BELIEVE IT.
THE GREEN LANTERN CORPS WOULD HAVE LOST IF NOT FOR THAT LAW.
YOU BELIEVE THAT, DON'T YOU?

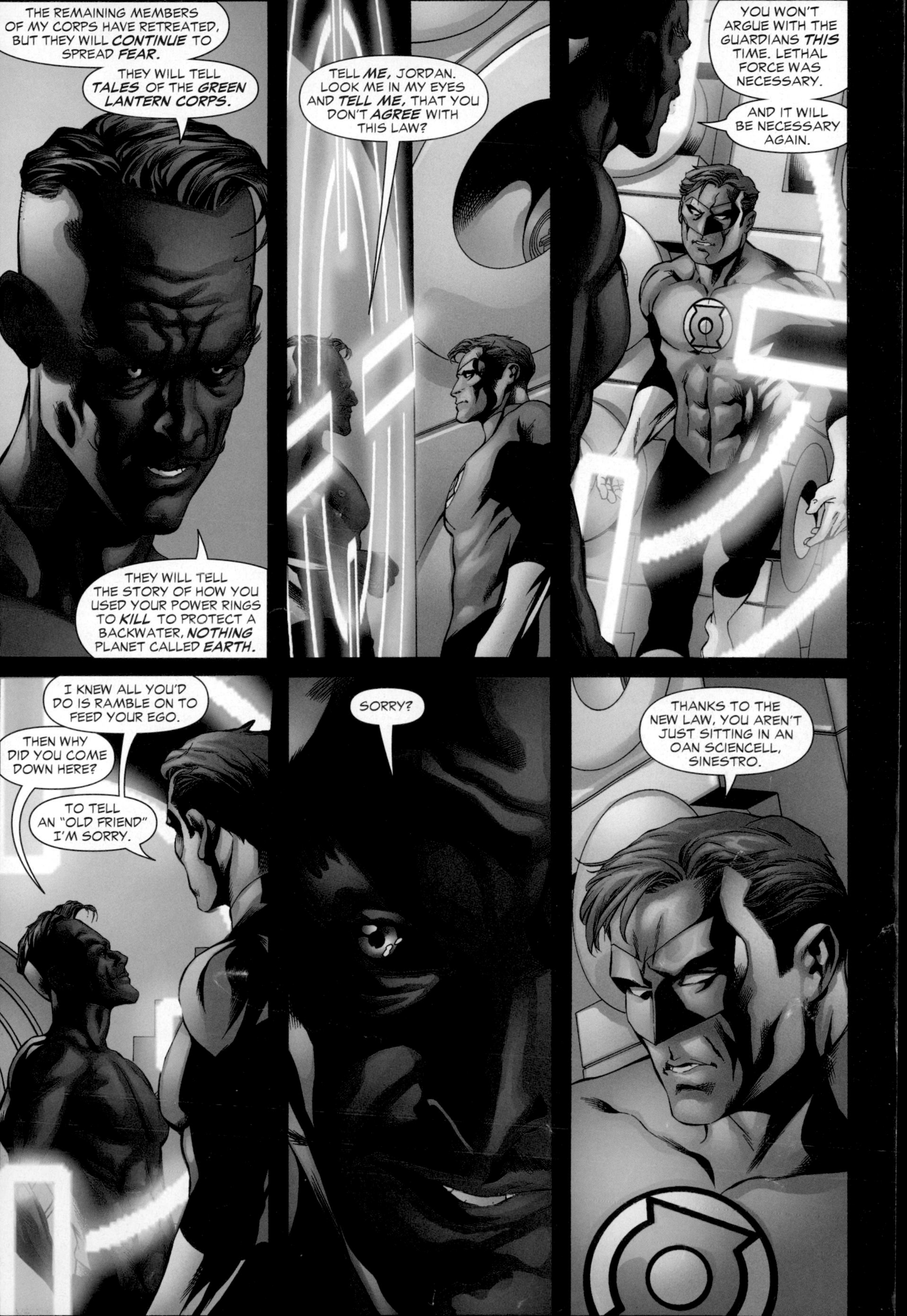

THE REMAINING MEMBERS OF MY CORPS HAVE RETREATED, BUT THEY WILL CONTINUE TO SPREAD FEAR.
THEY WILL TELL TALES OF THE GREEN LANTERN CORPS.
THEY WILL TELL THE STORY OF HOW YOU USED YOUR POWER RINGS TO KILL TO PROTECT A BACKWATER, NOTHING PLANET CALLED EARTH.
TELL ME, JORDAN. LOOK ME IN MY EYES AND TELL ME, THAT YOU DON'T AGREE WITH THIS LAW?
YOU WON'T ARGUE WITH THE GUARDIANS THIS TIME. LETHAL FORCE WAS NECESSARY.
AND IT WILL BE NECESSARY AGAIN.
I KNEW ALL YOU'D DO IS RAMBLE ON TO FEED YOUR EGO.
THEN WHY DID YOU COME DOWN HERE?
TO TELL AN "OLD FRIEND" I'M SORRY.
SORRY?
THANKS TO THE NEW LAW, YOU AREN'T JUST SITTING IN AN OAN SCIENCELL, SINESTRO.

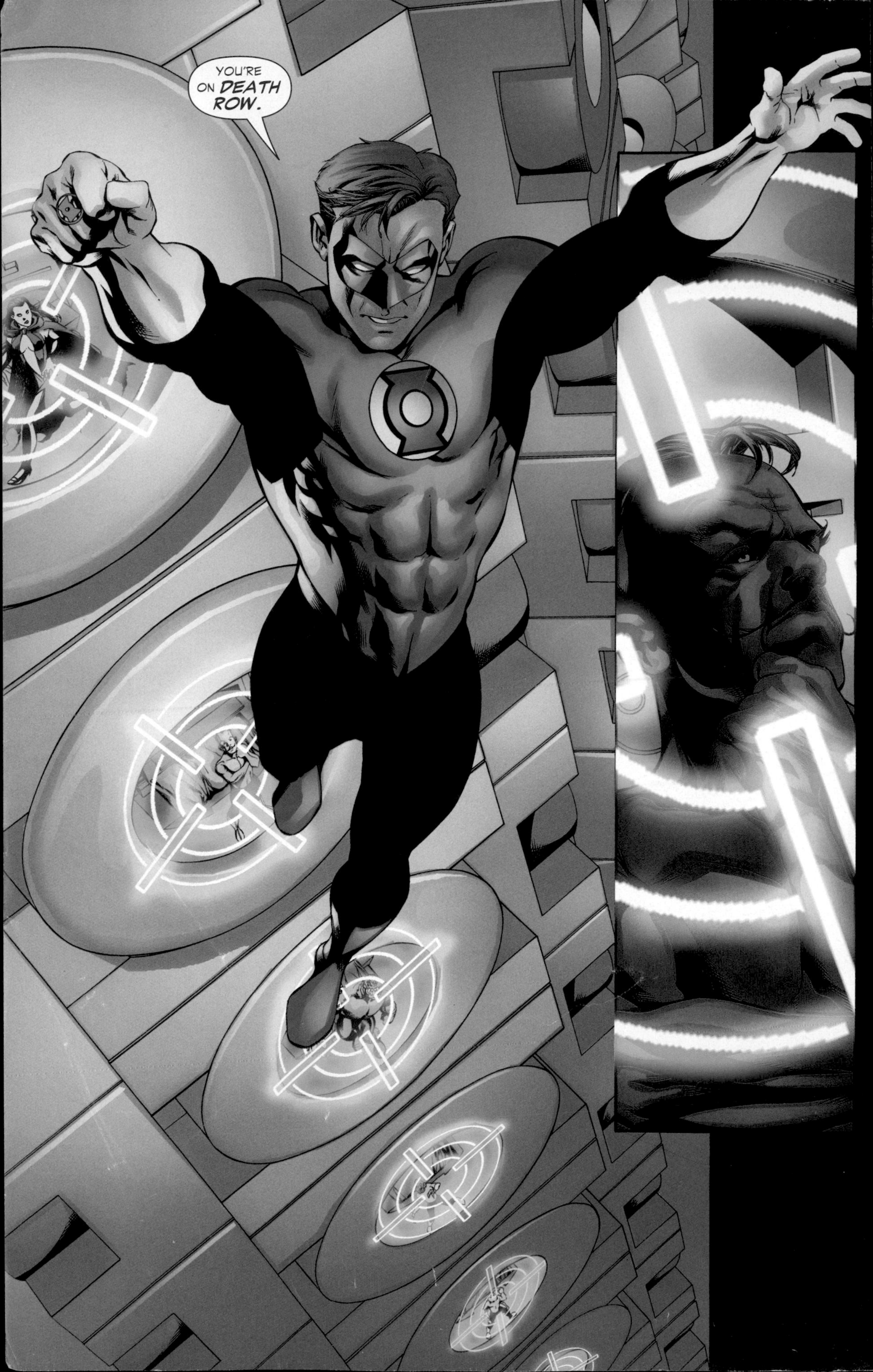
YOU'RE ON DEATH ROW.

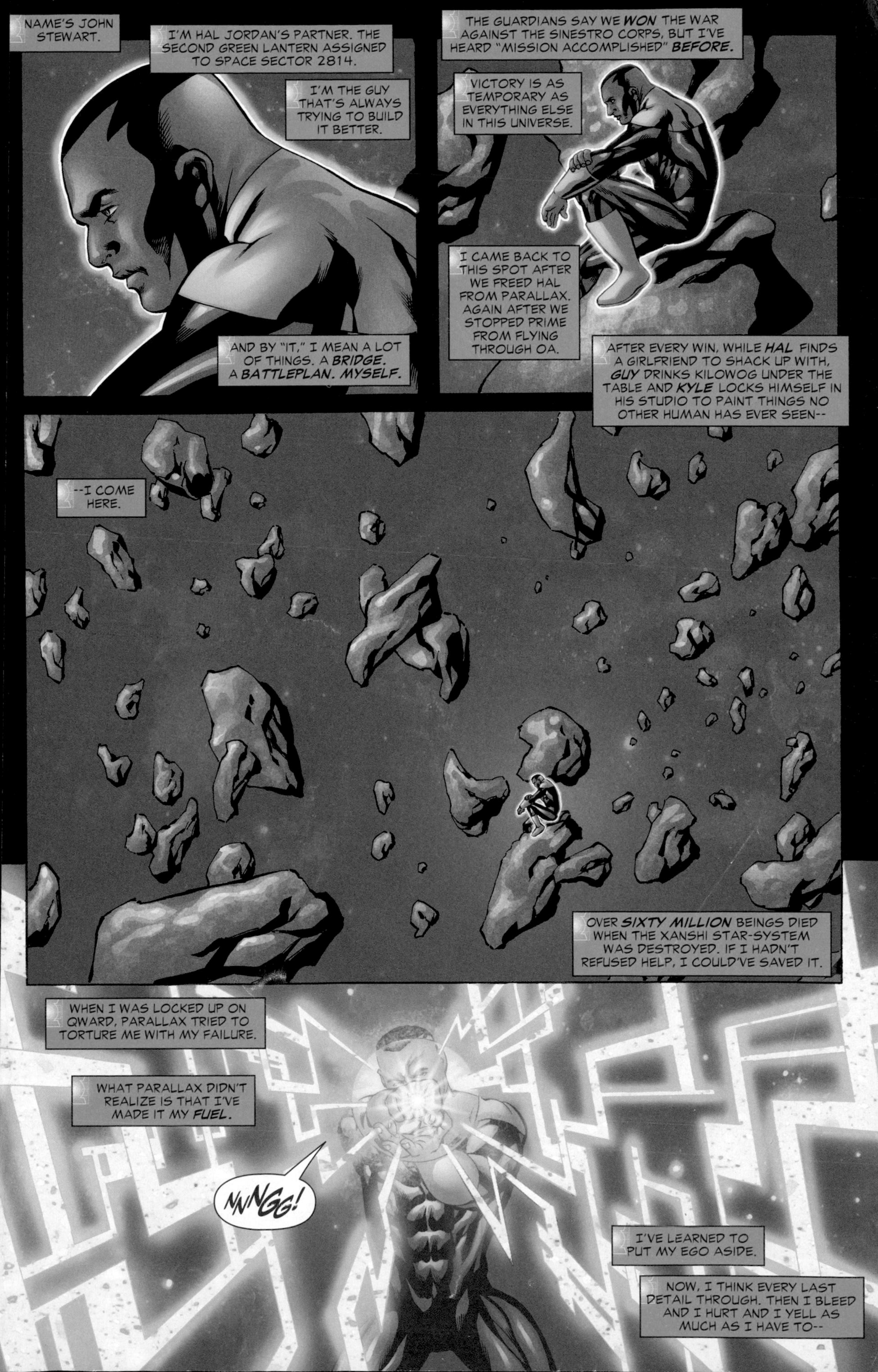

NAME'S JOHN STEWART.
I'M HAL JORDAN'S PARTNER. THE SECOND GREEN LANTERN ASSIGNED TO SPACE SECTOR 2814.
I'M THE GUY THAT'S ALWAYS TRYING TO BUILD IT BETTER.
AND BY "IT," I MEAN A LOT OF THINGS. A BRIDGE. A BATTLEPLAN. MYSELF.
THE GUARDIANS SAY WE WON THE WAR AGAINST THE SINESTRO CORPS, BUT I'VE HEARD "MISSION ACCOMPLISHED" BEFORE.
VICTORY IS AS TEMPORARY AS EVERYTHING ELSE IN THIS UNIVERSE.
I CAME BACK TO THIS SPOT AFTER WE FREED HAL FROM PARALLAX. AGAIN AFTER WE STOPPED PRIME FROM FLYING THROUGH OA.
AFTER EVERY WIN, WHILE HAL FINDS A GIRLFRIEND TO SHACK UP WITH, GUY DRINKS KILOWOG UNDER THE TABLE AND KYLE LOCKS HIMSELF IN HIS STUDIO TO PAINT THINGS NO OTHER HUMAN HAS EVER SEEN--
--I COME HERE.
OVER SIXTY MILLION BEINGS DIED WHEN THE XANSHI STAR-SYSTEM WAS DESTROYED. IF I HADN'T REFUSED HELP, I COULD'VE SAVED IT.
WHEN I WAS LOCKED UP ON QWARD, PARALLAX TRIED TO TORTURE ME WITH MY FAILURE.
WHAT PARALLAX DIDN'T REALIZE IS THAT I'VE MADE IT MY FUEL.
NNNGG!
I'VE LEARNED TO PUT MY EGO ASIDE.
NOW, I THINK EVERY LAST DETAIL THROUGH. THEN I BLEED AND I HURT AND I YELL AS MUCH AS I HAVE TO--

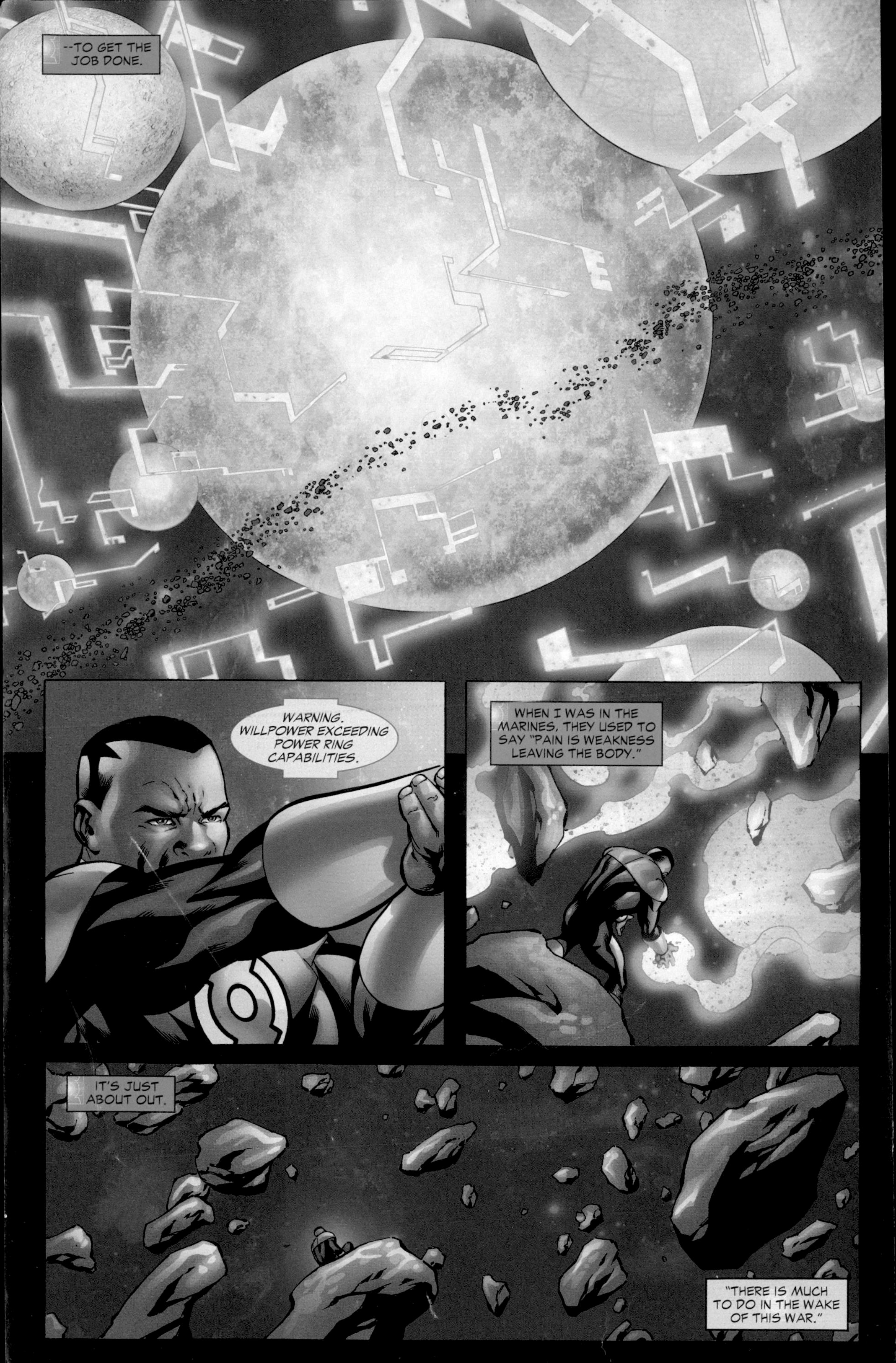
--TO GET THE JOB DONE.
WARNING. WILLPOWER EXCEEDING POWER RING CAPABILITIES.
WHEN I WAS IN THE MARINES, THEY USED TO SAY "PAIN IS WEAKNESS LEAVING THE BODY."
IT'S JUST ABOUT OUT.
"THERE IS MUCH TO DO IN THE WAKE OF THIS WAR."

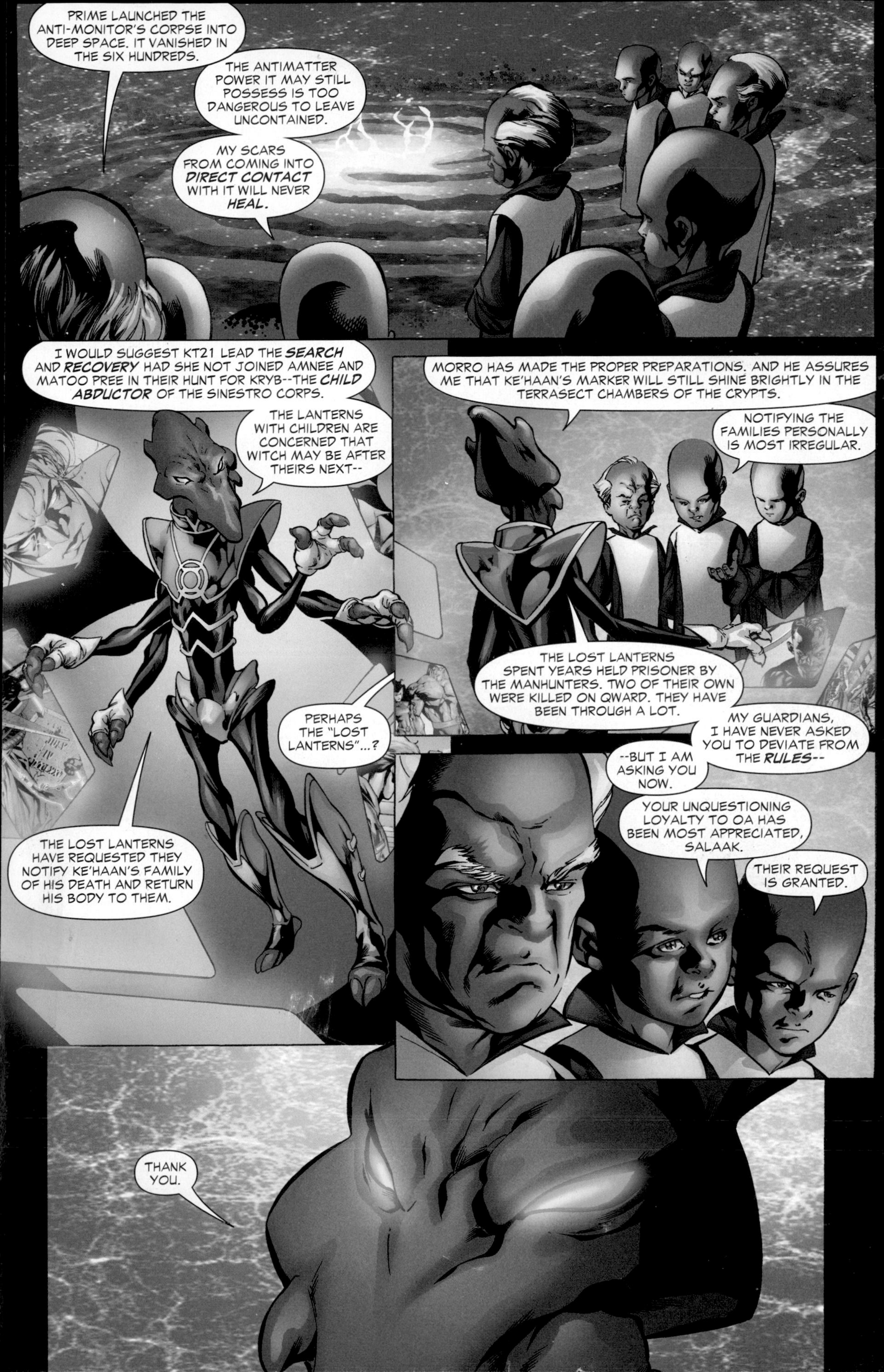
PRIME LAUNCHED THE ANTI-MONITOR'S CORPSE INTO DEEP SPACE. IT VANISHED IN THE SIX HUNDREDS.
THE ANTIMATTER POWER IT MAY STILL POSSESS IS TOO DANGEROUS TO LEAVE UNCONTAINED.
MY SCARS FROM COMING INTO DIRECT CONTACT WITH IT WILL NEVER HEAL.
I WOULD SUGGEST KT21 LEAD THE SEARCH AND RECOVERY HAD SHE NOT JOINED AMNEE AND MATOO PREE IN THEIR HUNT FOR KRYB--THE CHILD ABDUCTOR OF THE SINESTRO CORPS.
THE LANTERNS WITH CHILDREN ARE CONCERNED THAT WITCH MAY BE AFTER THEIRS NEXT--
PERHAPS THE "LOST LANTERNS"...?
THE LOST LANTERNS HAVE REQUESTED THEY NOTIFY KE'HAAN'S FAMILY OF HIS DEATH AND RETURN HIS BODY TO THEM.
MORRO HAS MADE THE PROPER PREPARATIONS. AND HE ASSURES ME THAT KE'HAAN'S MARKER WILL STILL SHINE BRIGHTLY IN THE TERRASECT CHAMBERS OF THE CRYPTS.
NOTIFYING THE FAMILIES PERSONALLY IS MOST IRREGULAR.
THE LOST LANTERNS SPENT YEARS HELD PRISONER BY THE MANHUNTERS. TWO OF THEIR OWN WERE KILLED ON QWARD. THEY HAVE BEEN THROUGH A LOT.
MY GUARDIANS, I HAVE NEVER ASKED YOU TO DEVIATE FROM THE RULES--
--BUT I AM ASKING YOU NOW.
YOUR UNQUESTIONING LOYALTY TO OA HAS BEEN MOST APPRECIATED, SALAAK.
THEIR REQUEST IS GRANTED.
THANK YOU.

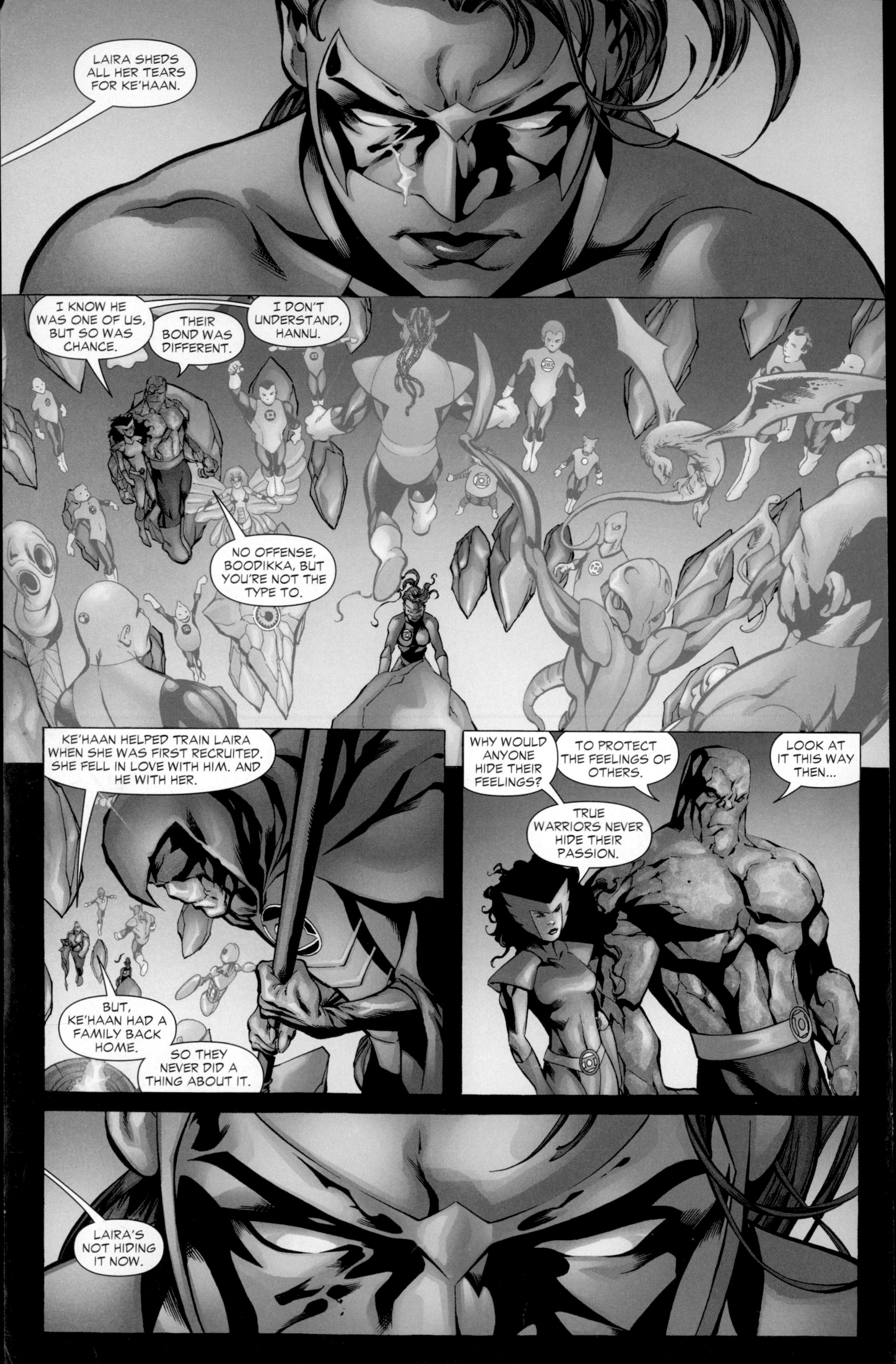
LAIRA SHEDS ALL HER TEARS FOR KE'HAAN.
I KNOW HE WAS ONE OF US, BUT SO WAS CHANCE.
THEIR BOND WAS DIFFERENT.
I DON'T UNDERSTAND, HANNU.
NO OFFENSE, BOODIKKA, BUT YOU'RE NOT THE TYPE TO.
KE'HAAN HELPED TRAIN LAIRA WHEN SHE WAS FIRST RECRUITED. SHE FELL IN LOVE WITH HIM. AND HE WITH HER.
BUT, KE'HAAN HAD A FAMILY BACK HOME.
SO THEY NEVER DID A THING ABOUT IT.
WHY WOULD ANYONE HIDE THEIR FEELINGS?
TO PROTECT THE FEELINGS OF OTHERS.
TRUE WARRIORS NEVER HIDE THEIR PASSION.
LOOK AT IT THIS WAY THEN...
LAIRA'S NOT HIDING IT NOW.

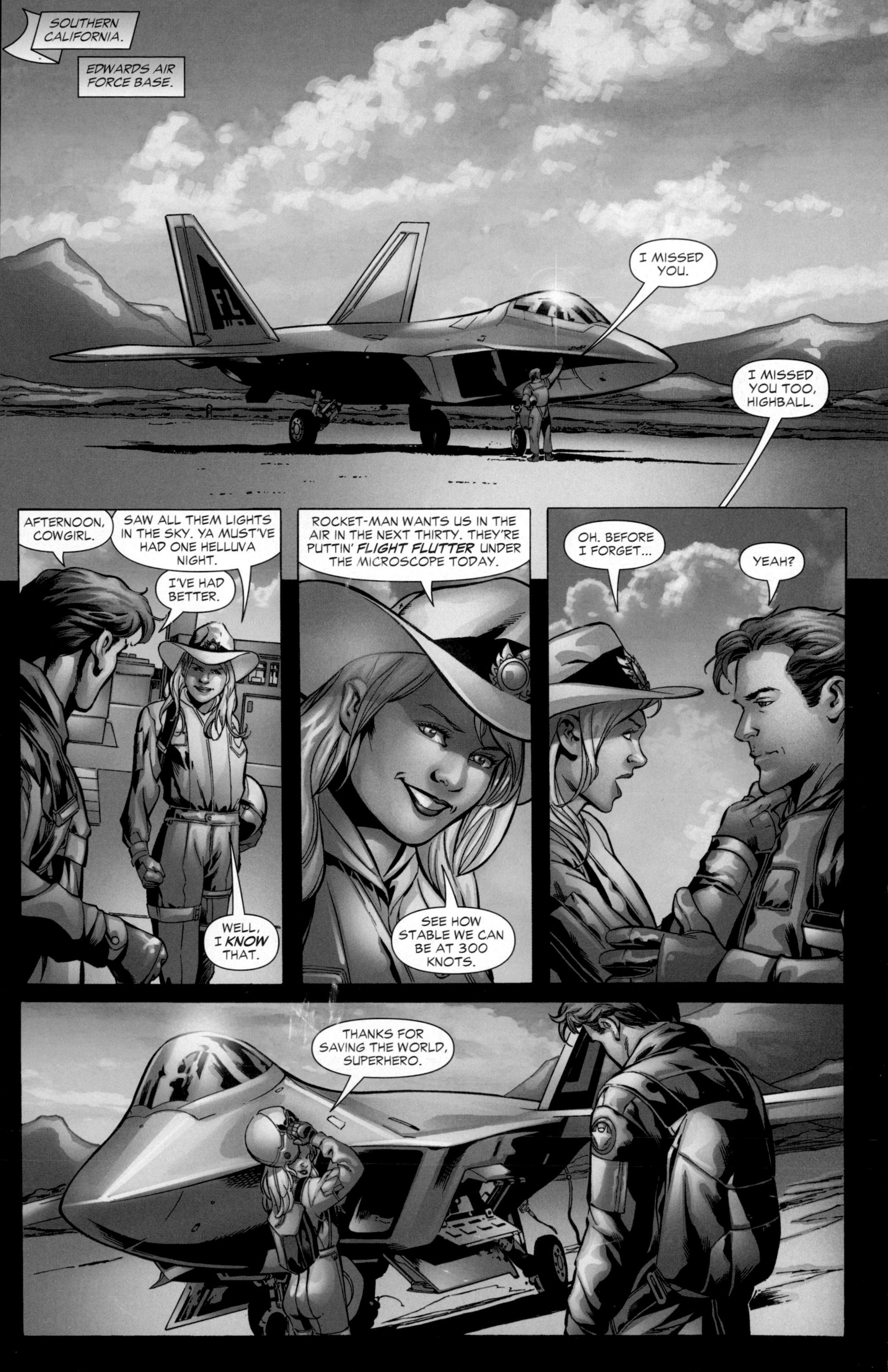
SOUTHERN CALIFORNIA.
EDWARDS AIR FORCE BASE.
I MISSED YOU.
I MISSED YOU TOO, HIGHBALL.
AFTERNOON, COWGIRL.
SAW ALL THEM LIGHTS IN THE SKY. YA MUST'VE HAD ONE HELLUVA NIGHT.
I'VE HAD BETTER.
WELL, I *KNOW* THAT.
ROCKET-MAN WANTS US IN THE AIR IN THE NEXT THIRTY. THEY'RE PUTTIN' *FLIGHT FLUTTER* UNDER THE MICROSCOPE TODAY.
SEE HOW STABLE WE CAN BE AT 300 KNOTS.
OH. BEFORE I FORGET...
YEAH?
THANKS FOR SAVING THE WORLD, SUPERHERO.

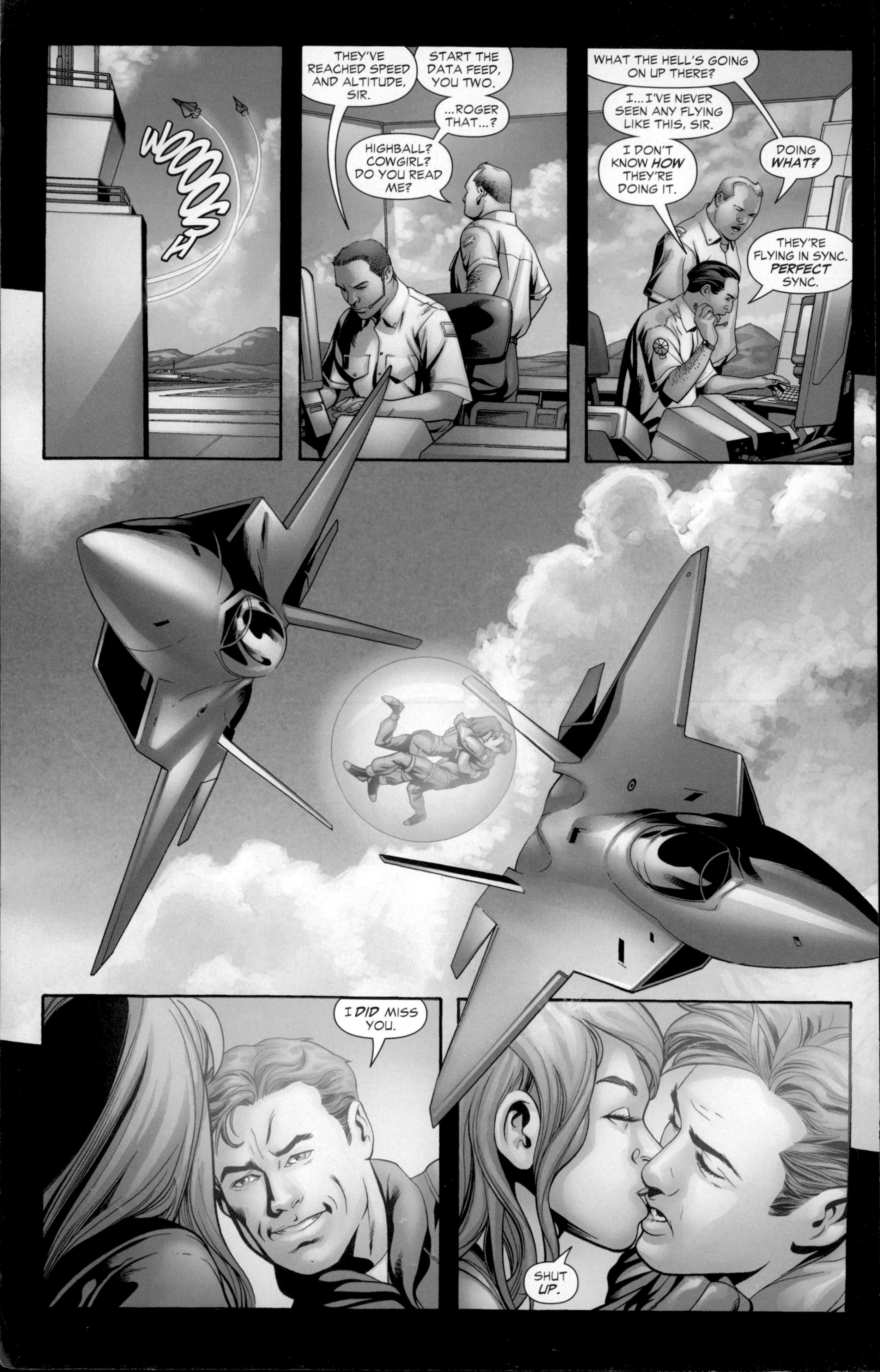
WOOOOSH
THEY'VE REACHED SPEED AND ALTITUDE, SIR.
START THE DATA FEED, YOU TWO.
HIGHBALL? COWGIRL? DO YOU READ ME?
...ROGER THAT...?
WHAT THE HELL'S GOING ON UP THERE?
I...I'VE NEVER SEEN ANY FLYING LIKE THIS, SIR.
I DON'T KNOW HOW THEY'RE DOING IT.
DOING WHAT?
THEY'RE FLYING IN SYNC. PERFECT SYNC.
I DID MISS YOU.
SHUT UP.

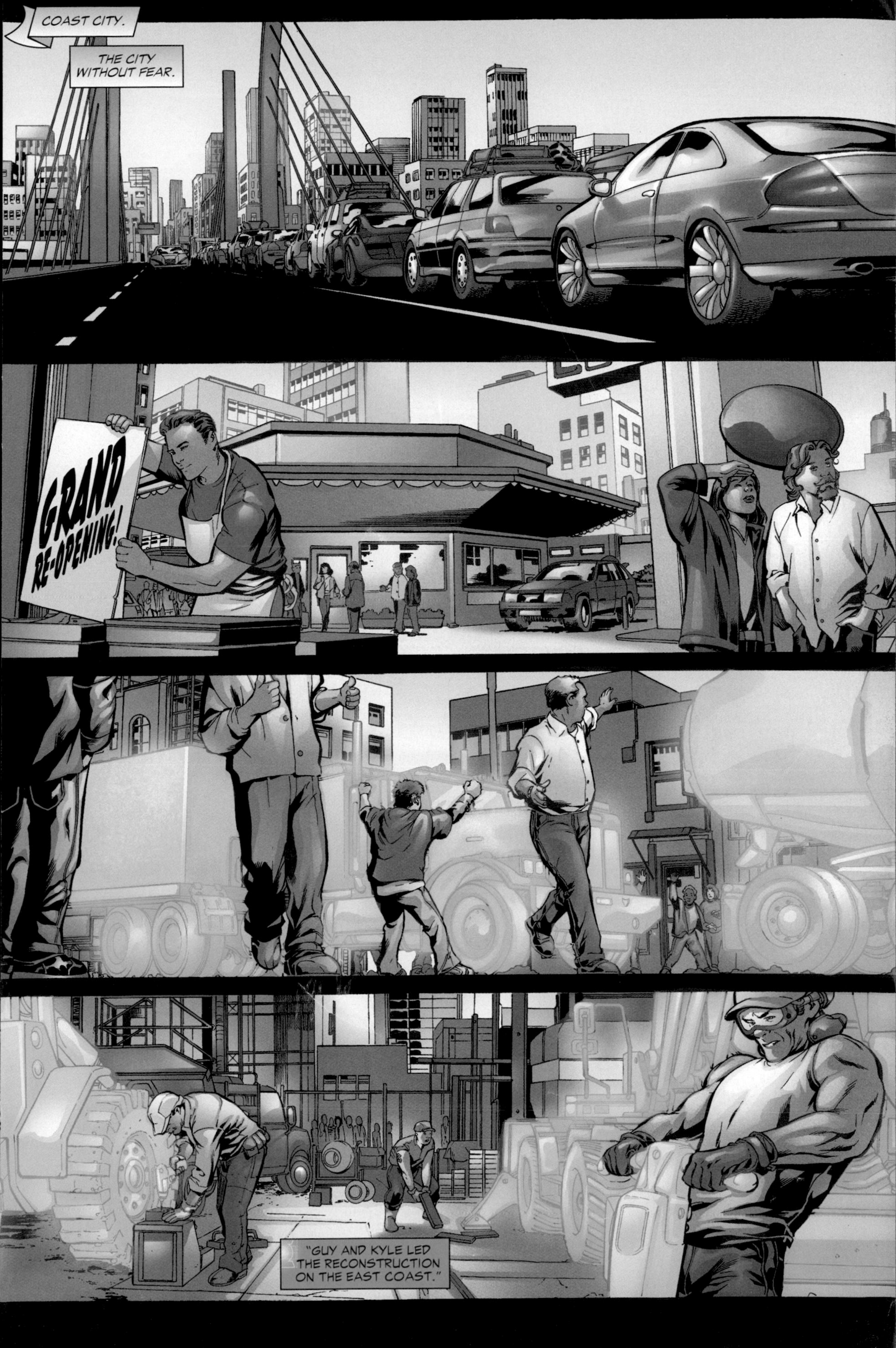
COAST CITY.
THE CITY WITHOUT FEAR.
GRAND RE-OPENING!
"GUY AND KYLE LED THE RECONSTRUCTION ON THE EAST COAST."

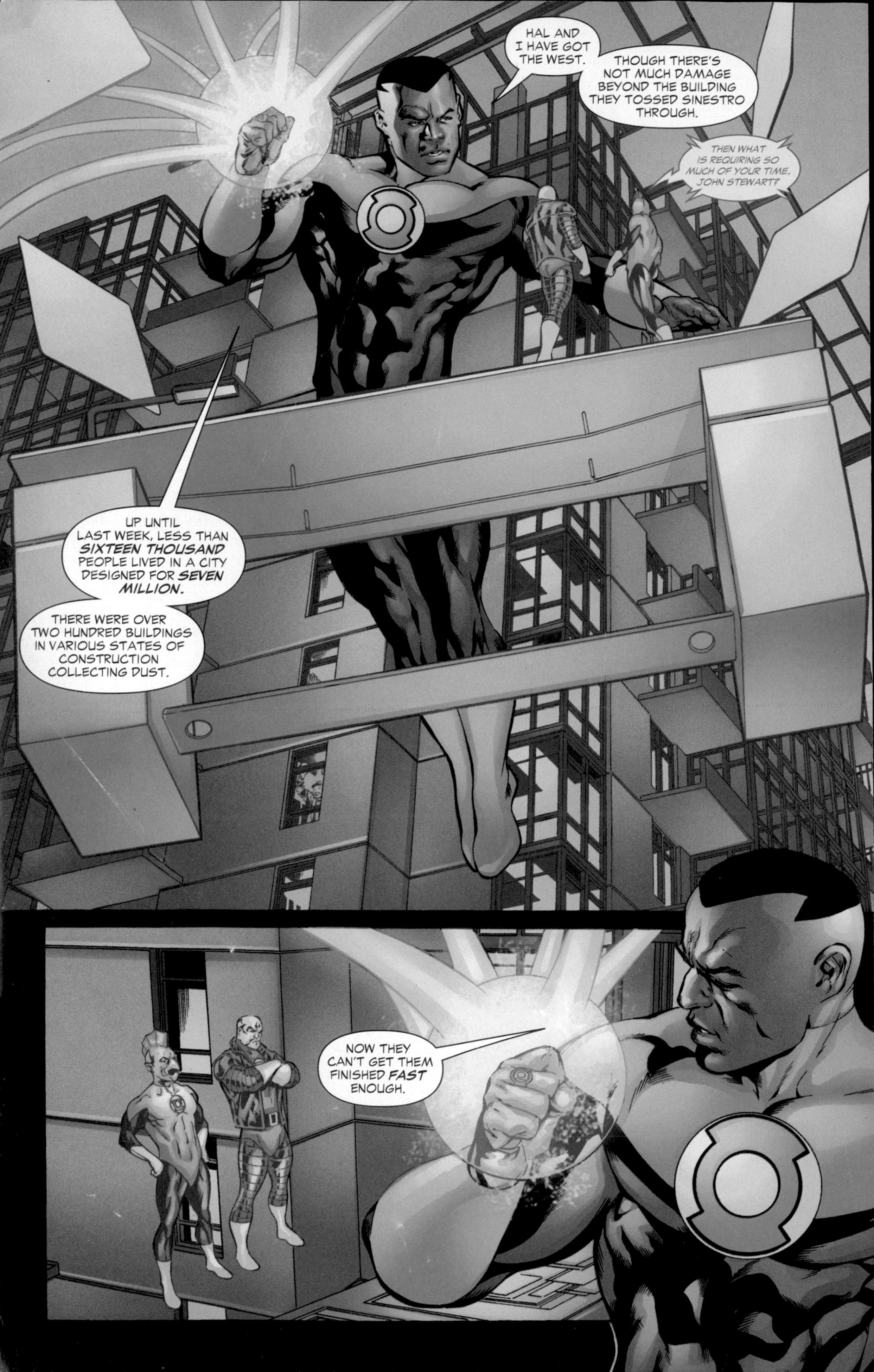
HAL AND I HAVE GOT THE WEST.
THOUGH THERE'S NOT MUCH DAMAGE BEYOND THE BUILDING THEY TOSSED SINESTRO THROUGH.
THEN WHAT IS REQUIRING SO MUCH OF YOUR TIME, JOHN STEWART?
UP UNTIL LAST WEEK, LESS THAN SIXTEEN THOUSAND PEOPLE LIVED IN A CITY DESIGNED FOR SEVEN MILLION.
THERE WERE OVER TWO HUNDRED BUILDINGS IN VARIOUS STATES OF CONSTRUCTION COLLECTING DUST.
NOW THEY CAN'T GET THEM FINISHED FAST ENOUGH.

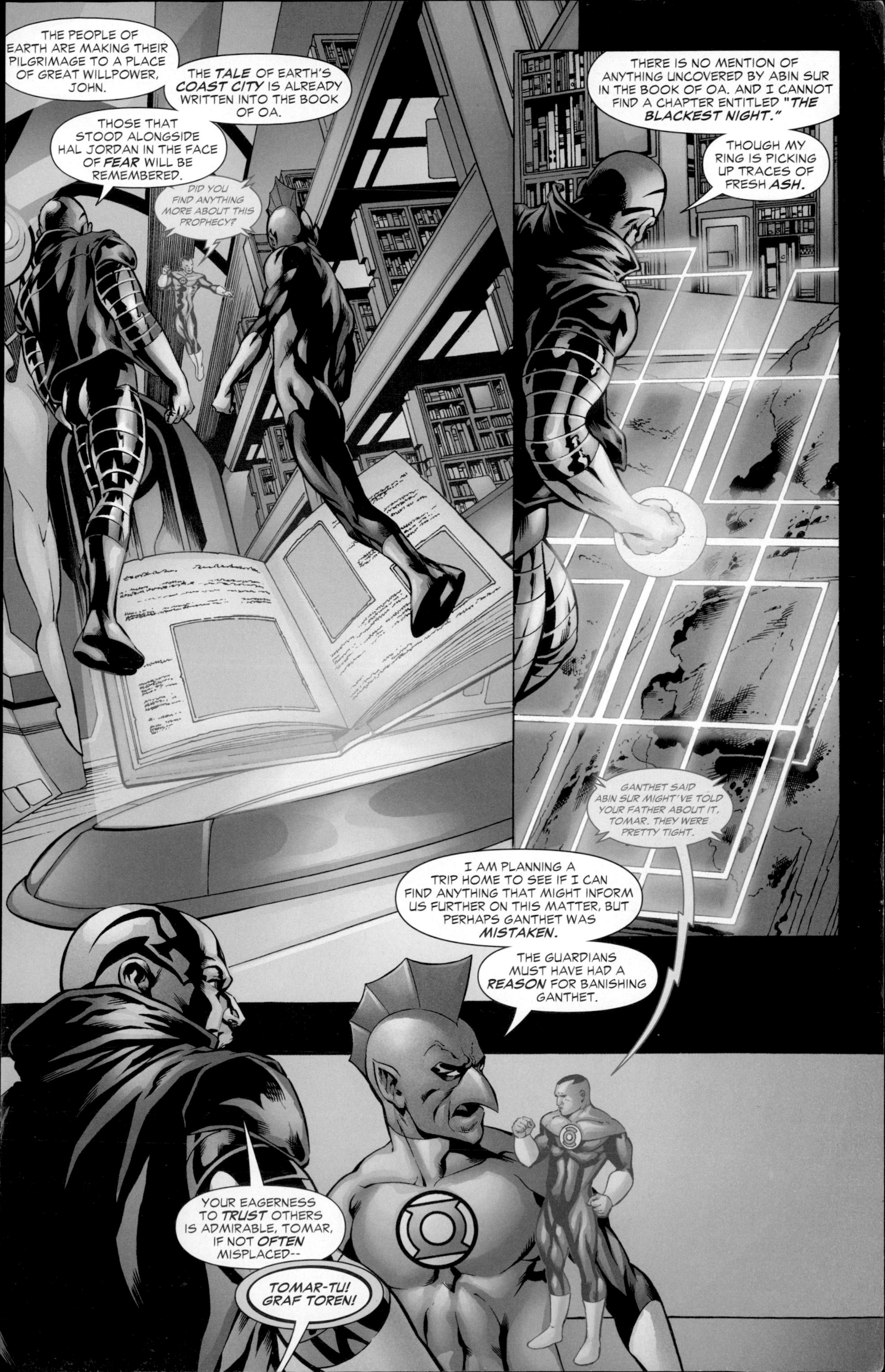
THE PEOPLE OF EARTH ARE MAKING THEIR PILGRIMAGE TO A PLACE OF GREAT WILLPOWER, JOHN.
THE TALE OF EARTH'S COAST CITY IS ALREADY WRITTEN INTO THE BOOK OF OA.
THOSE THAT STOOD ALONGSIDE HAL JORDAN IN THE FACE OF FEAR WILL BE REMEMBERED.
DID YOU FIND ANYTHING MORE ABOUT THIS PROPHECY?
THERE IS NO MENTION OF ANYTHING UNCOVERED BY ABIN SUR IN THE BOOK OF OA. AND I CANNOT FIND A CHAPTER ENTITLED "THE BLACKEST NIGHT."
THOUGH MY RING IS PICKING UP TRACES OF FRESH ASH.
GANTHET SAID ABIN SUR MIGHT'VE TOLD YOUR FATHER ABOUT IT, TOMAR. THEY WERE PRETTY TIGHT.
I AM PLANNING A TRIP HOME TO SEE IF I CAN FIND ANYTHING THAT MIGHT INFORM US FURTHER ON THIS MATTER, BUT PERHAPS GANTHET WAS MISTAKEN.
THE GUARDIANS MUST HAVE HAD A REASON FOR BANISHING GANTHET.
YOUR EAGERNESS TO TRUST OTHERS IS ADMIRABLE, TOMAR, IF NOT OFTEN MISPLACED--
TOMAR-TU! GRAF TOREN!

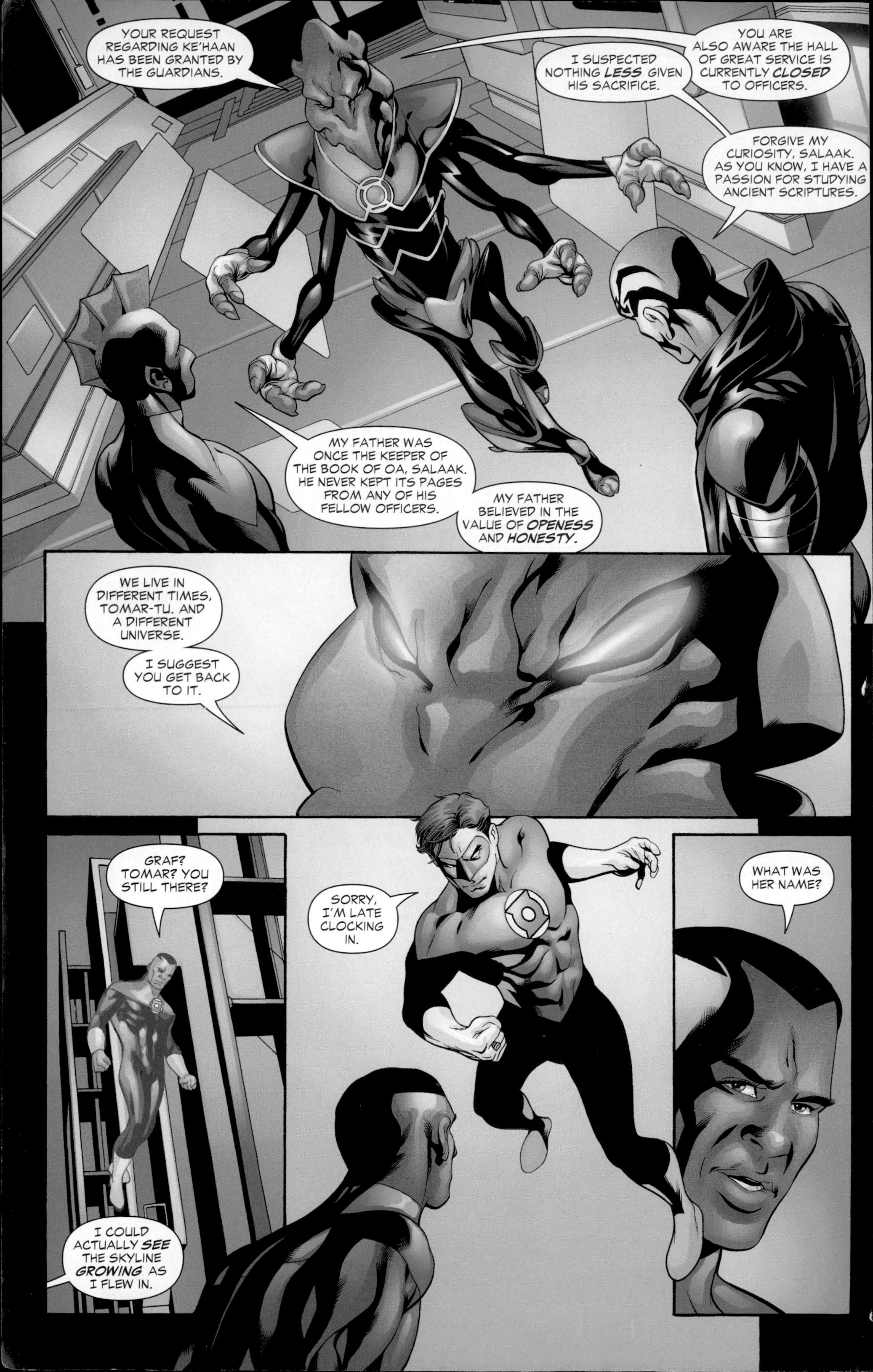
YOUR REQUEST REGARDING KE'HAAN HAS BEEN GRANTED BY THE GUARDIANS.
I SUSPECTED NOTHING LESS GIVEN HIS SACRIFICE.
YOU ARE ALSO AWARE THE HALL OF GREAT SERVICE IS CURRENTLY CLOSED TO OFFICERS.
FORGIVE MY CURIOSITY, SALAAK. AS YOU KNOW, I HAVE A PASSION FOR STUDYING ANCIENT SCRIPTURES.
MY FATHER WAS ONCE THE KEEPER OF THE BOOK OF OA, SALAAK. HE NEVER KEPT ITS PAGES FROM ANY OF HIS FELLOW OFFICERS.
MY FATHER BELIEVED IN THE VALUE OF OPENESS AND HONESTY.
WE LIVE IN DIFFERENT TIMES, TOMAR-TU. AND A DIFFERENT UNIVERSE.
I SUGGEST YOU GET BACK TO IT.
GRAF? TOMAR? YOU STILL THERE?
SORRY, I'M LATE CLOCKING IN.
WHAT WAS HER NAME?
I COULD ACTUALLY SEE THE SKYLINE GROWING AS I FLEW IN.

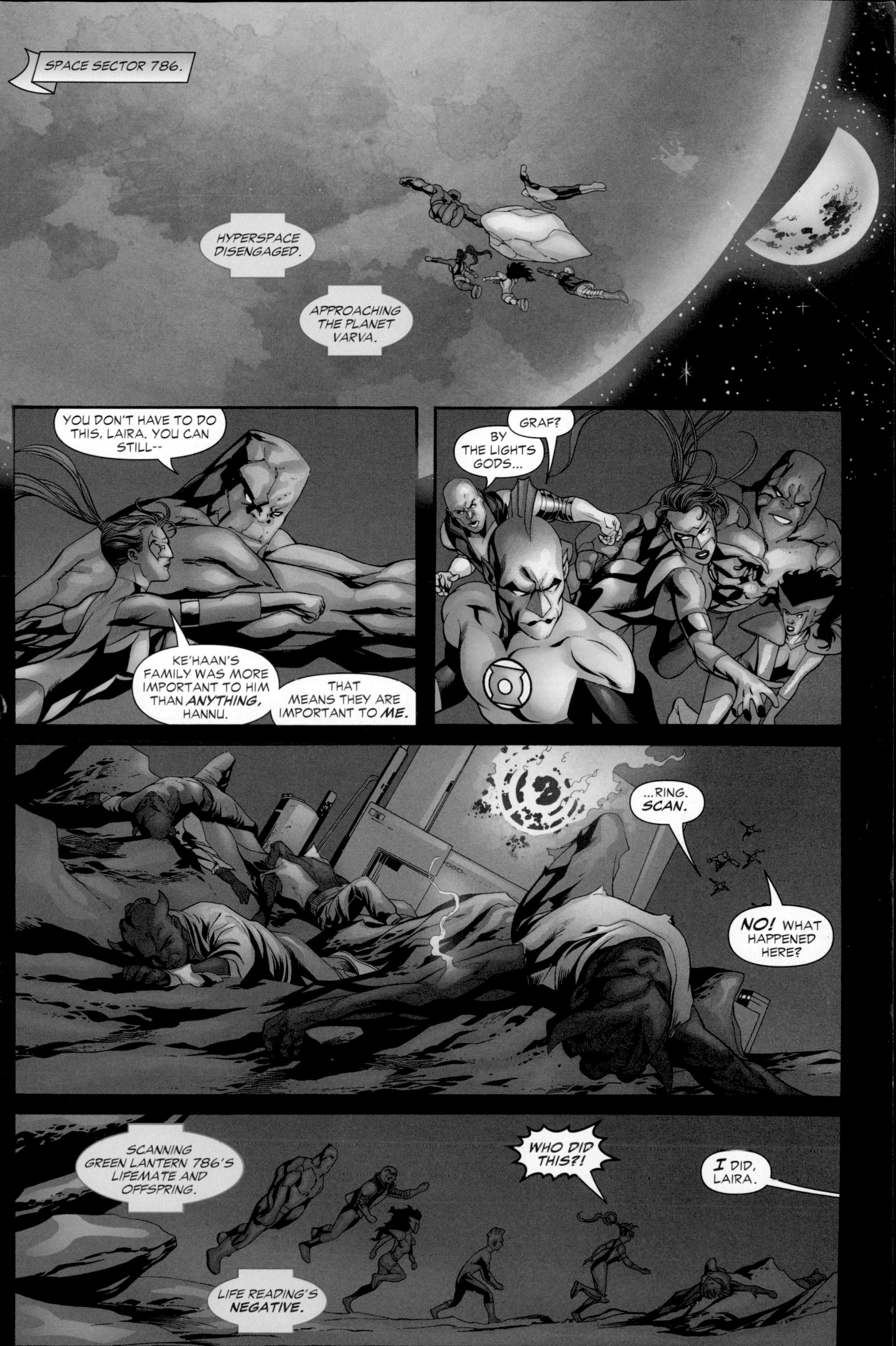
SPACE SECTOR 786.
HYPERSPACE DISENGAGED.
APPROACHING THE PLANET VARVA.
YOU DON'T HAVE TO DO THIS, LAIRA. YOU CAN STILL--
KE'HAAN'S FAMILY WAS MORE IMPORTANT TO HIM THAN ANYTHING, HANNU.
THAT MEANS THEY ARE IMPORTANT TO ME.
GRAF?
BY THE LIGHTS GODS...
...RING. SCAN.
NO! WHAT HAPPENED HERE?
SCANNING GREEN LANTERN 786'S LIFEMATE AND OFFSPRING.
LIFE READING'S NEGATIVE.
WHO DID THIS?!
I DID, LAIRA.

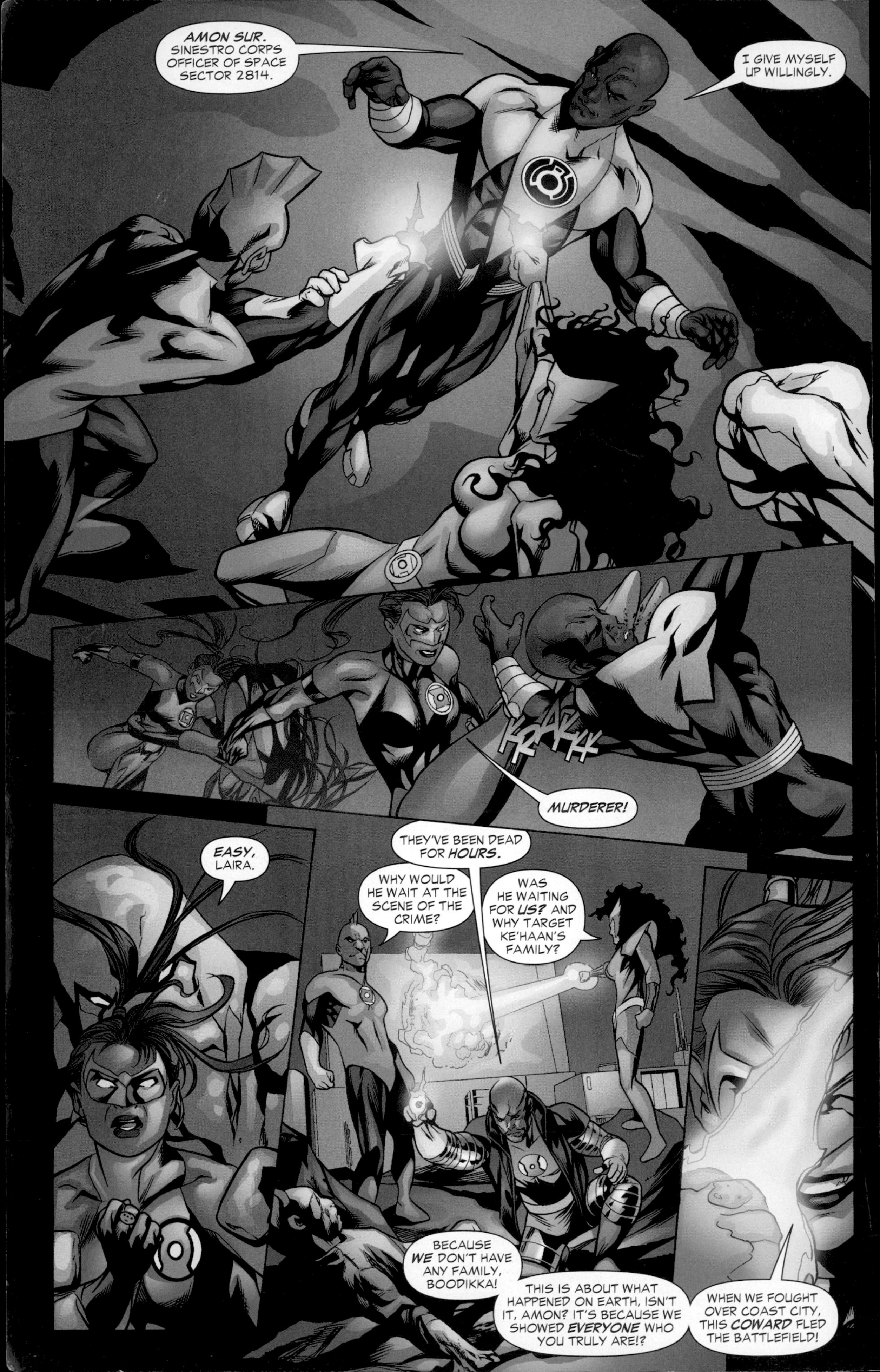
AMON SUR. SINESTRO CORPS OFFICER OF SPACE SECTOR 2814.
I GIVE MYSELF UP WILLINGLY.
KRAKKK
MURDERER!
EASY, LAIRA.
THEY'VE BEEN DEAD FOR HOURS.
WHY WOULD HE WAIT AT THE SCENE OF THE CRIME?
WAS HE WAITING FOR US? AND WHY TARGET KE'HAAN'S FAMILY?
BECAUSE WE DON'T HAVE ANY FAMILY, BOODIKKA!
THIS IS ABOUT WHAT HAPPENED ON EARTH, ISN'T IT, AMON? IT'S BECAUSE WE SHOWED EVERYONE WHO YOU TRULY ARE!?
WHEN WE FOUGHT OVER COAST CITY, THIS COWARD FLED THE BATTLEFIELD!

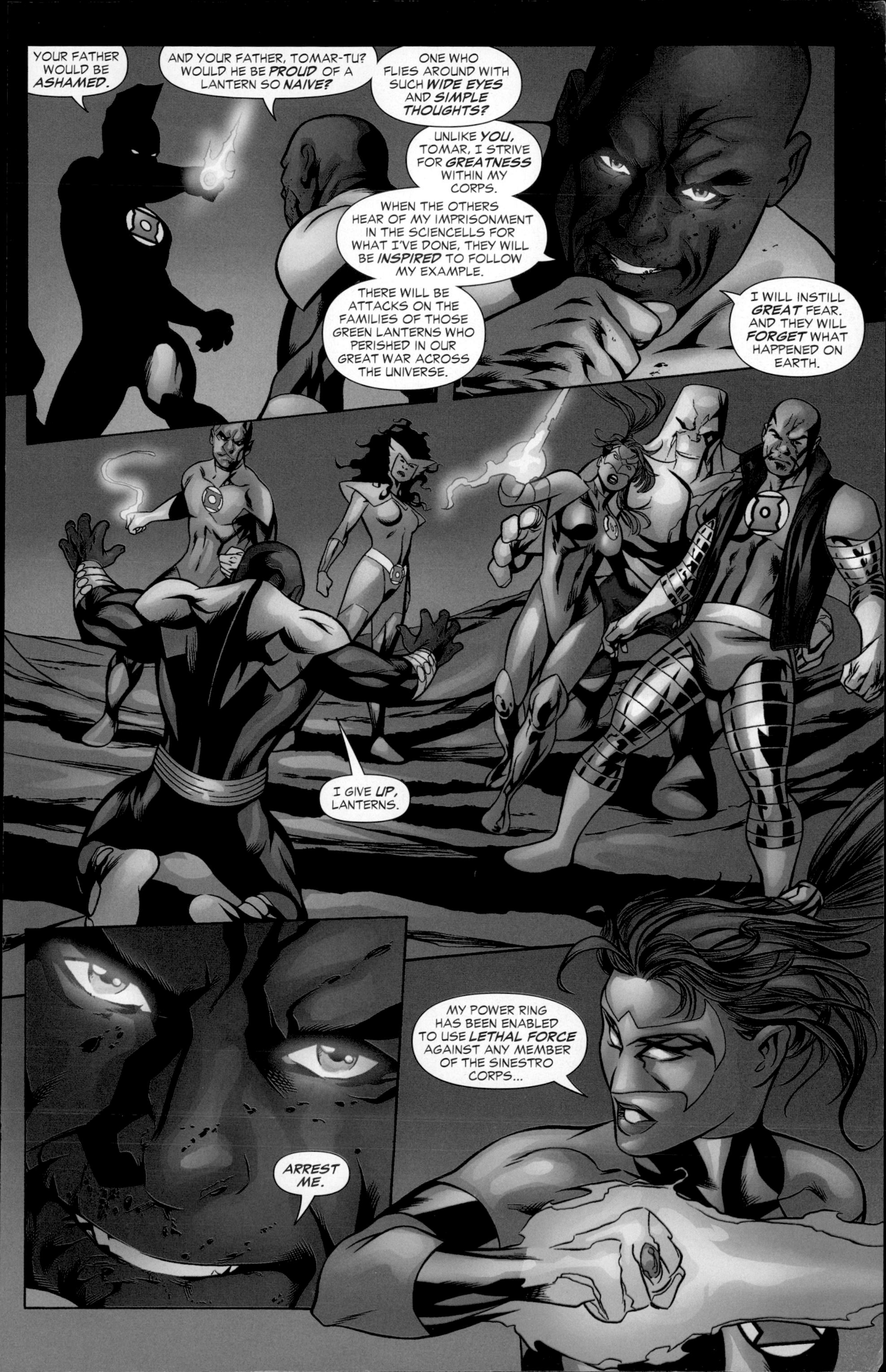
YOUR FATHER WOULD BE ASHAMED.
AND YOUR FATHER, TOMAR-TU? WOULD HE BE PROUD OF A LANTERN SO NAIVE?
ONE WHO FLIES AROUND WITH SUCH WIDE EYES AND SIMPLE THOUGHTS?
UNLIKE YOU, TOMAR, I STRIVE FOR GREATNESS WITHIN MY CORPS.
WHEN THE OTHERS HEAR OF MY IMPRISONMENT IN THE SCIENCELLS FOR WHAT I'VE DONE, THEY WILL BE INSPIRED TO FOLLOW MY EXAMPLE.
THERE WILL BE ATTACKS ON THE FAMILIES OF THOSE GREEN LANTERNS WHO PERISHED IN OUR GREAT WAR ACROSS THE UNIVERSE.
I WILL INSTILL GREAT FEAR. AND THEY WILL FORGET WHAT HAPPENED ON EARTH.
I GIVE UP, LANTERNS.
MY POWER RING HAS BEEN ENABLED TO USE LETHAL FORCE AGAINST ANY MEMBER OF THE SINESTRO CORPS...
ARREST ME.

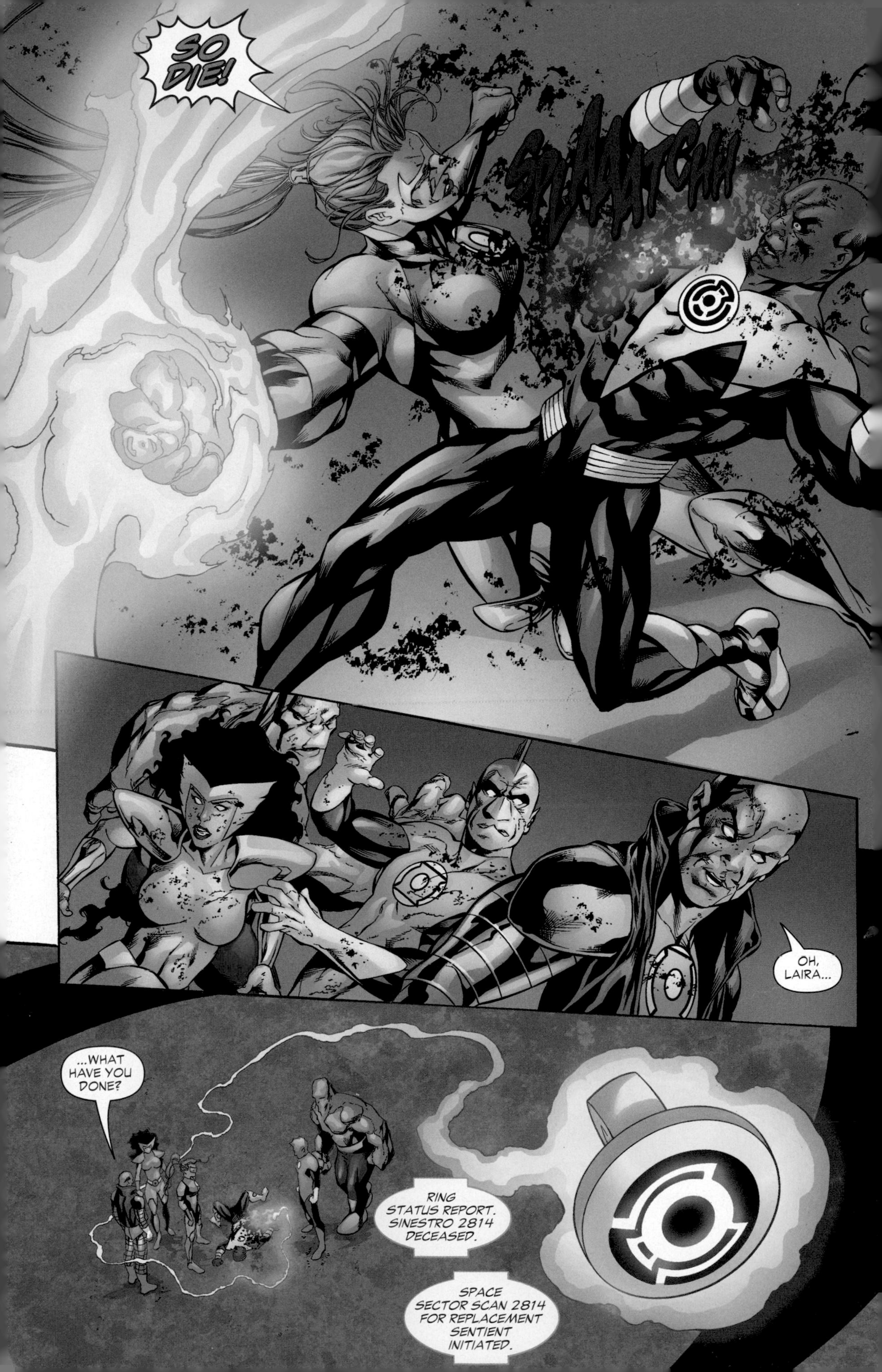
SO DIE!
SPLAAATCHH
OH, LAIRA...
...WHAT HAVE YOU DONE?
RING STATUS REPORT. SINESTRO 2814 DECEASED.
SPACE SECTOR SCAN 2814 FOR REPLACEMENT SENTIENT INITIATED.

GREEN LANTERN 27 Cover by Mike McKone, Andy Lanning and Moose Baumann

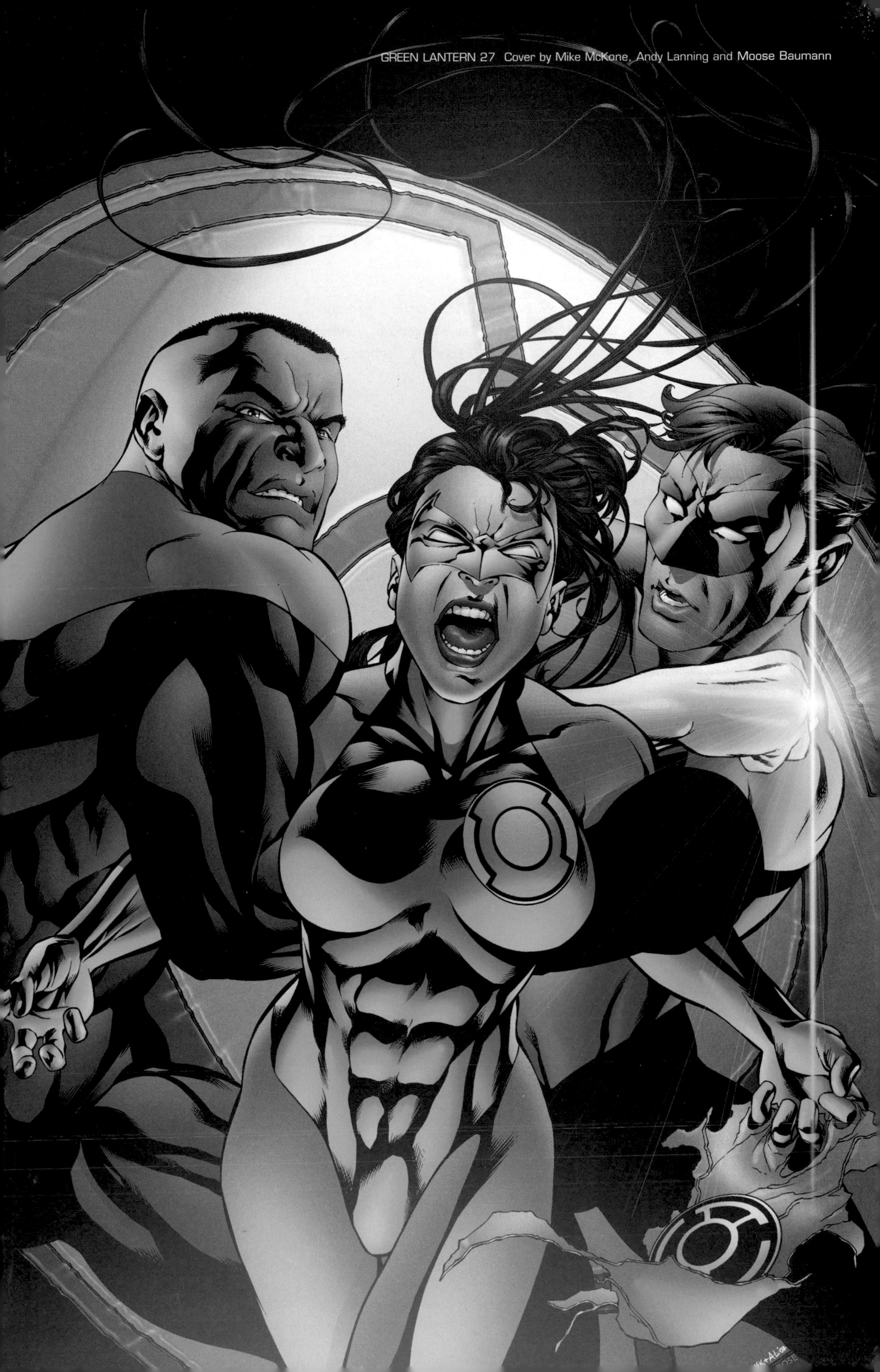

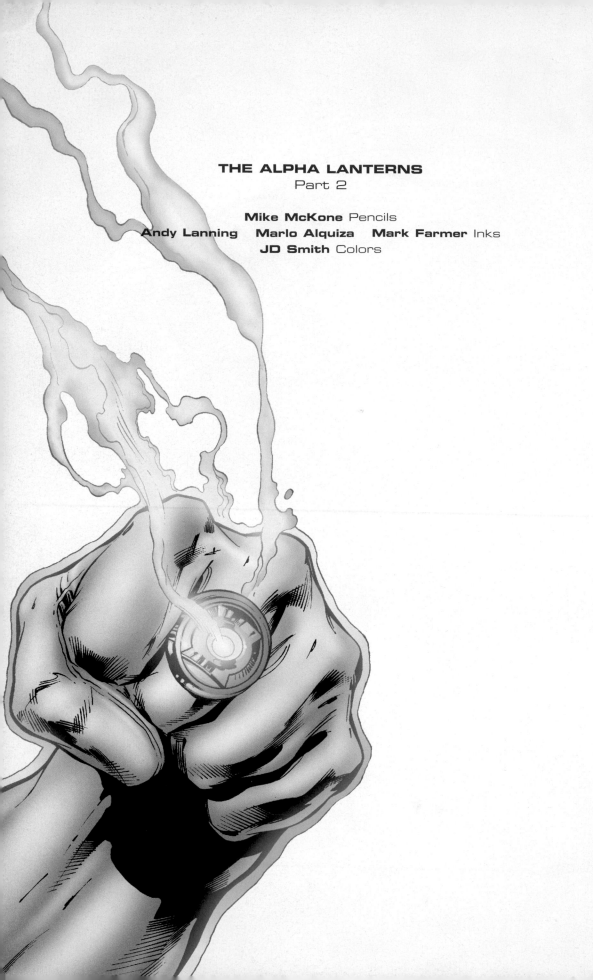

THE ALPHA LANTERNS
Part 2

Mike McKone Pencils
Andy Lanning   **Marlo Alquiza**   **Mark Farmer** Inks
JD Smith Colors

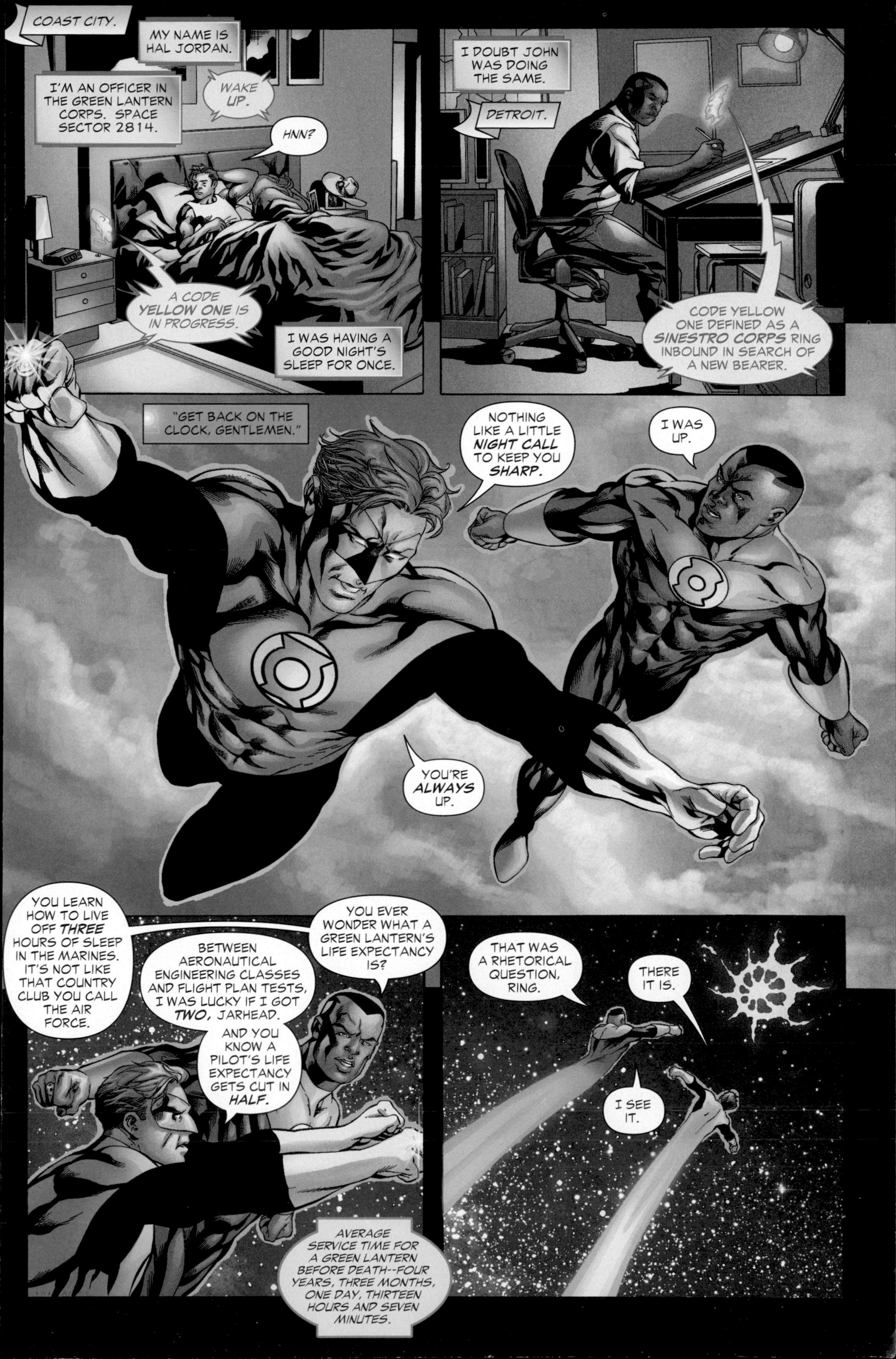
COAST CITY.
MY NAME IS HAL JORDAN.
I'M AN OFFICER IN THE GREEN LANTERN CORPS. SPACE SECTOR 2814.
WAKE UP.
HNN?
A CODE YELLOW ONE IS IN PROGRESS.
I WAS HAVING A GOOD NIGHT'S SLEEP FOR ONCE.
I DOUBT JOHN WAS DOING THE SAME.
DETROIT.
CODE YELLOW ONE DEFINED AS A SINESTRO CORPS RING INBOUND IN SEARCH OF A NEW BEARER.
"GET BACK ON THE CLOCK, GENTLEMEN."
NOTHING LIKE A LITTLE NIGHT CALL TO KEEP YOU SHARP.
I WAS UP.
YOU'RE ALWAYS UP.
YOU LEARN HOW TO LIVE OFF THREE HOURS OF SLEEP IN THE MARINES. IT'S NOT LIKE THAT COUNTRY CLUB YOU CALL THE AIR FORCE.
BETWEEN AERONAUTICAL ENGINEERING CLASSES AND FLIGHT PLAN TESTS, I WAS LUCKY IF I GOT TWO, JARHEAD.
AND YOU KNOW A PILOT'S LIFE EXPECTANCY GETS CUT IN HALF.
YOU EVER WONDER WHAT A GREEN LANTERN'S LIFE EXPECTANCY IS?
AVERAGE SERVICE TIME FOR A GREEN LANTERN BEFORE DEATH--FOUR YEARS, THREE MONTHS, ONE DAY, THIRTEEN HOURS AND SEVEN MINUTES.
THAT WAS A RHETORICAL QUESTION, RING.
THERE IT IS.
I SEE IT.

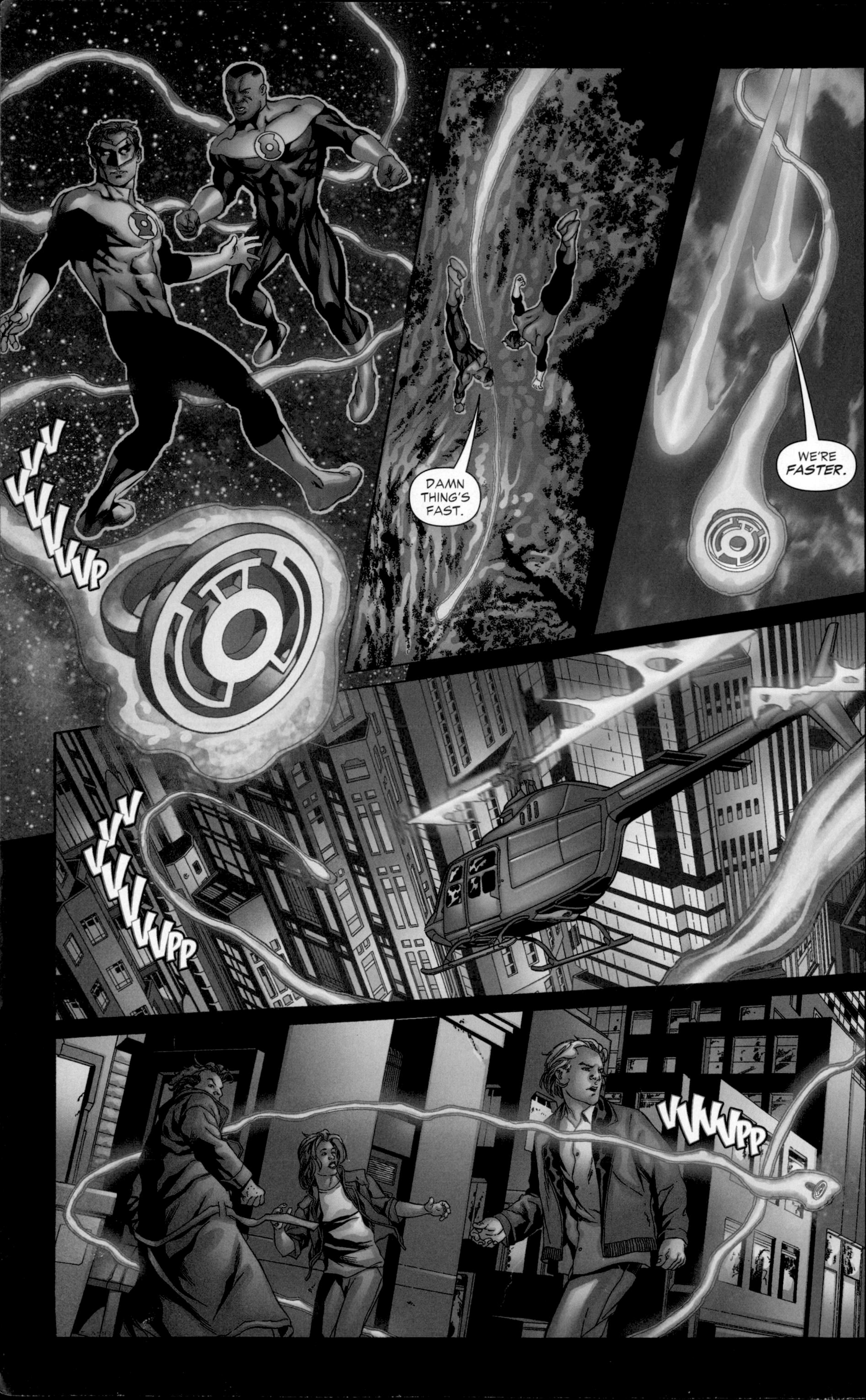
VVVVVVVVP
DAMN THING'S FAST.
WE'RE FASTER.
VVVVVVVVPP
VVVVPP

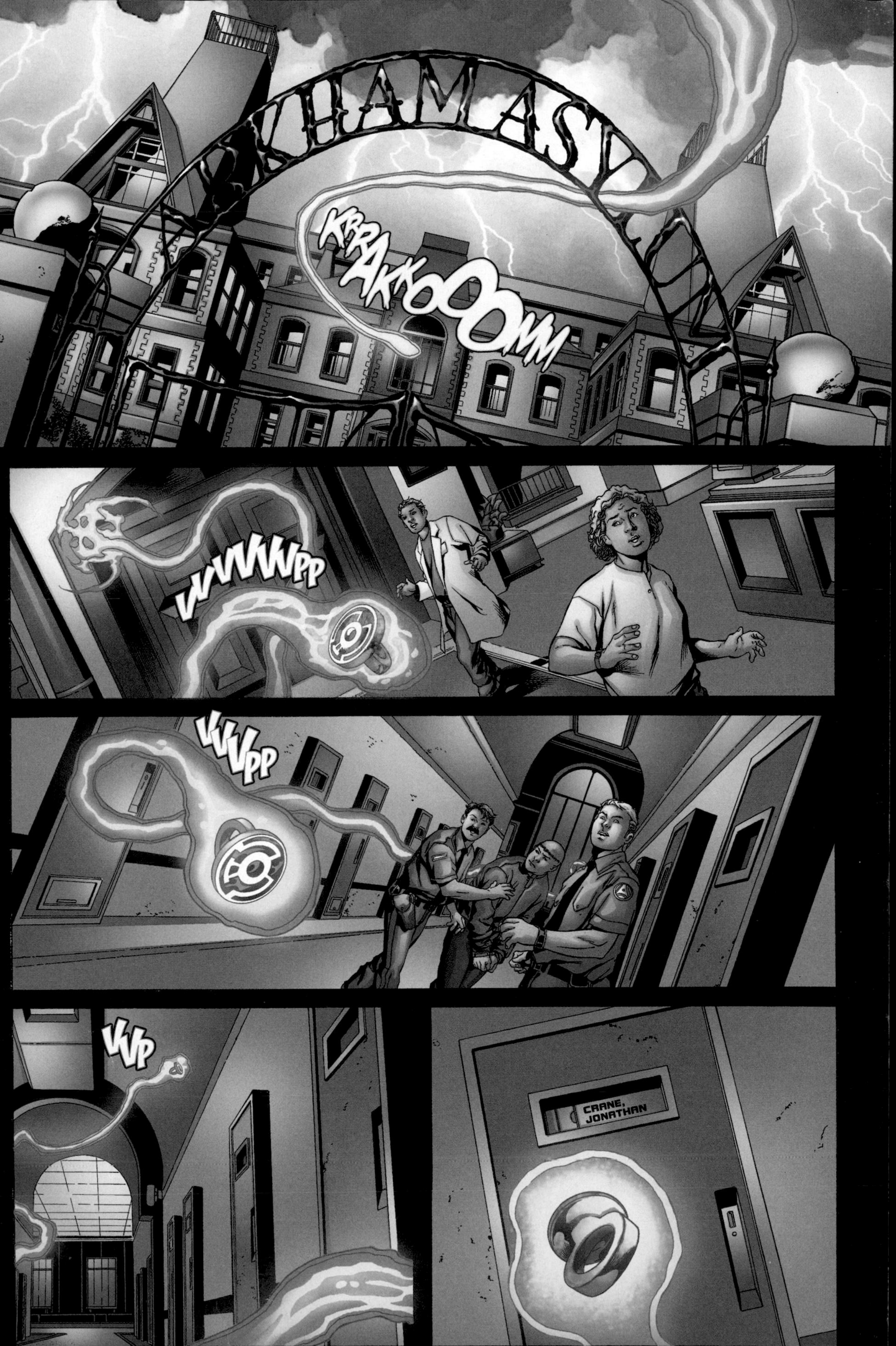
KRRAKKOOOMM
VVVVVVPP
VVVPP
VVP
CRANE, JONATHAN

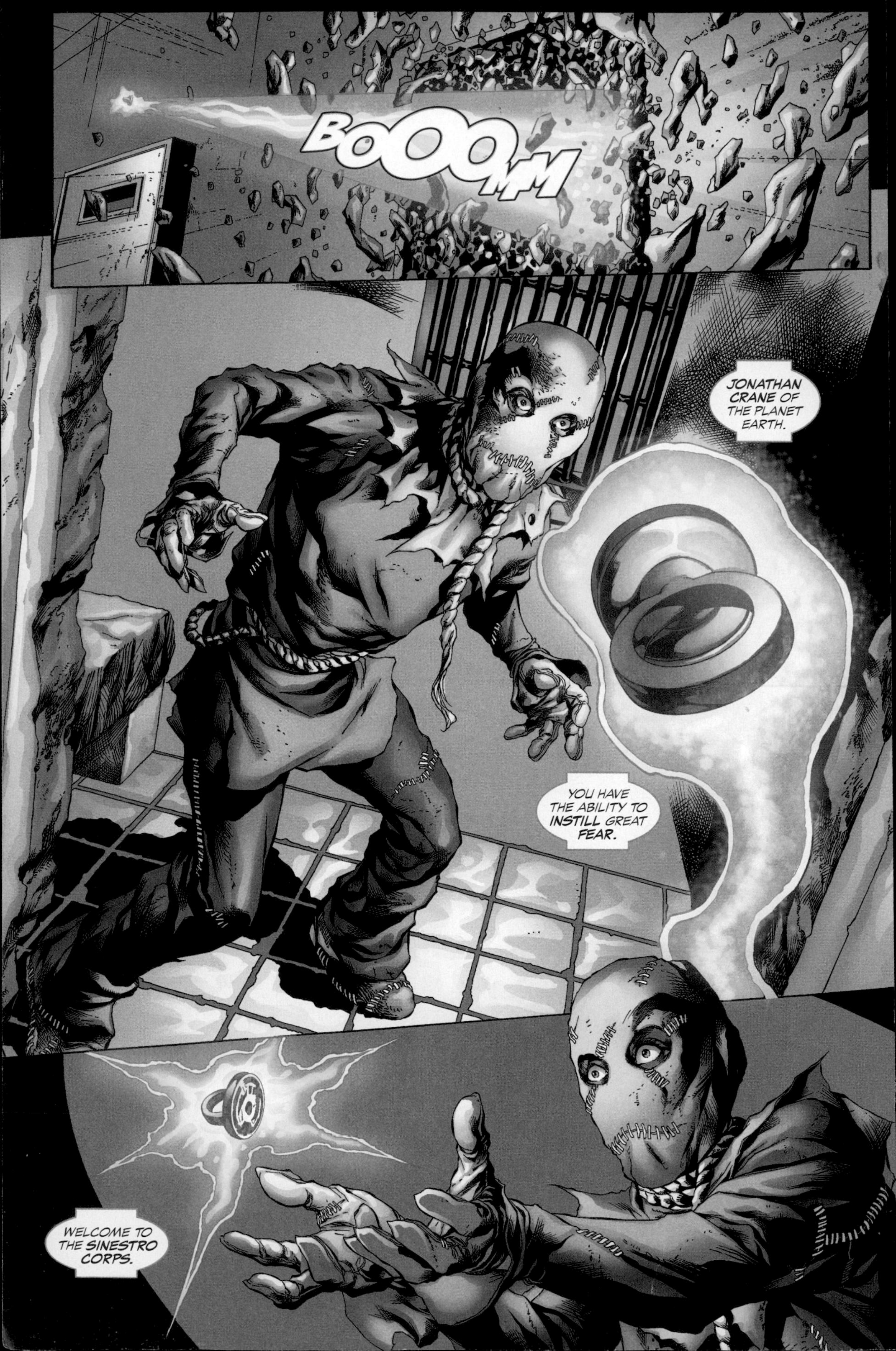
BOOOMM
JONATHAN CRANE OF THE PLANET EARTH.
YOU HAVE THE ABILITY TO INSTILL GREAT FEAR.
WELCOME TO THE SINESTRO CORPS.

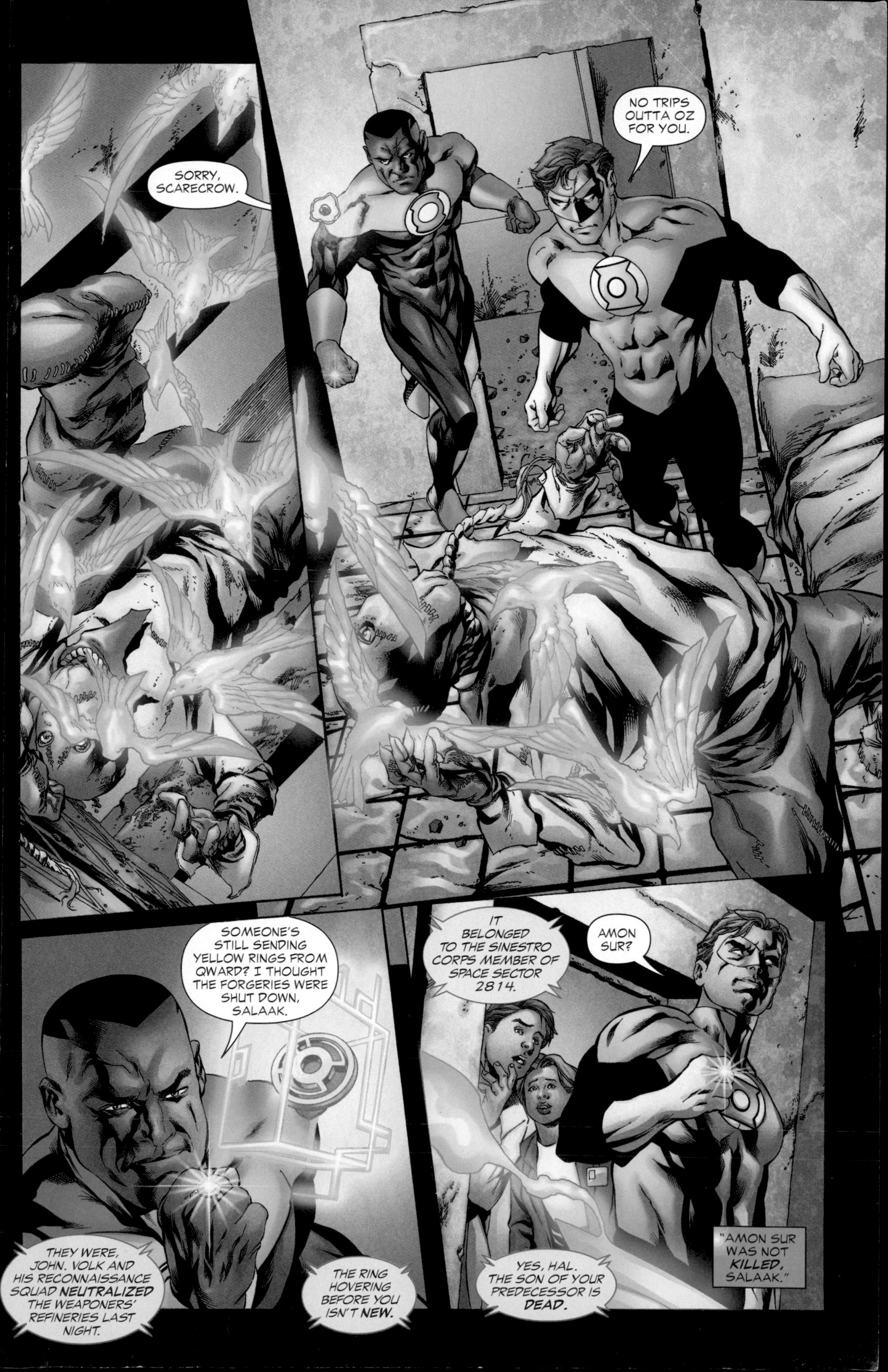
SORRY, SCARECROW.
NO TRIPS OUTTA OZ FOR YOU.
SOMEONE'S STILL SENDING YELLOW RINGS FROM QWARD? I THOUGHT THE FORGERIES WERE SHUT DOWN, SALAAK.
THEY WERE, JOHN. VOLK AND HIS RECONNAISSANCE SQUAD NEUTRALIZED THE WEAPONERS' REFINERIES LAST NIGHT.
THE RING HOVERING BEFORE YOU ISN'T NEW.
IT BELONGED TO THE SINESTRO CORPS MEMBER OF SPACE SECTOR 2814.
AMON SUR?
YES, HAL. THE SON OF YOUR PREDECESSOR IS DEAD.
"AMON SUR WAS NOT KILLED, SALAAK."

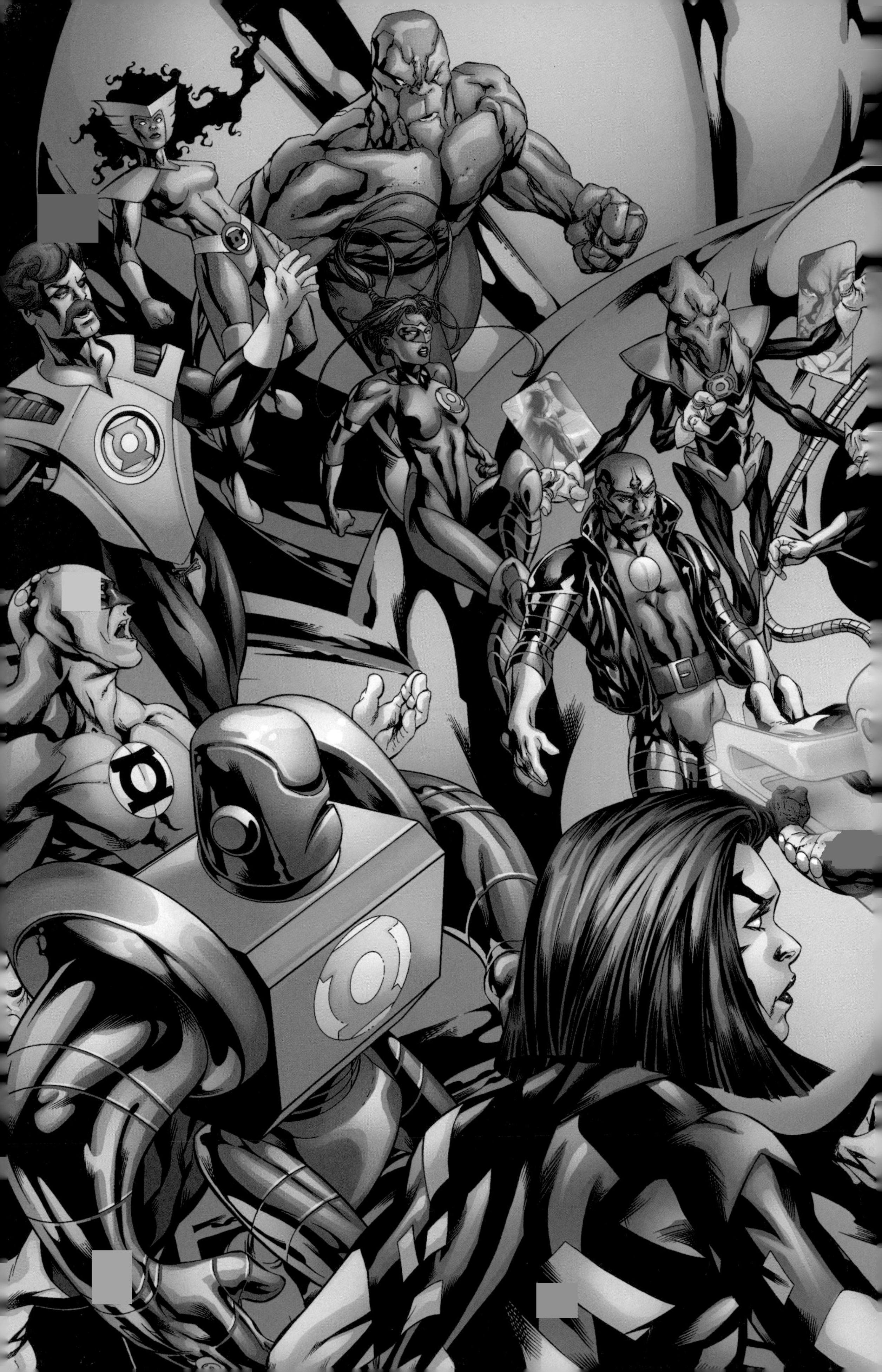

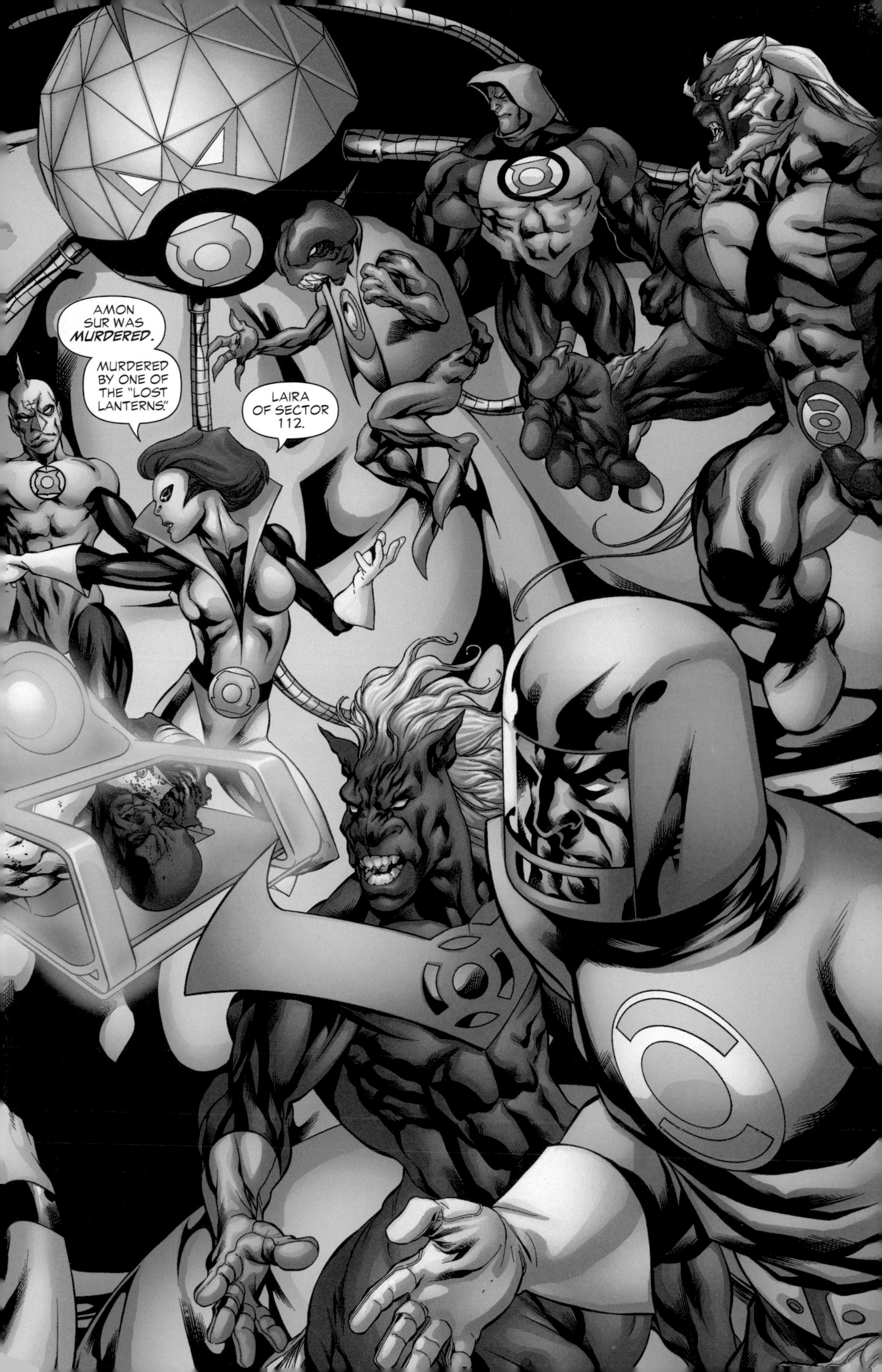

AMON SUR WAS ***MURDERED.***
MURDERED BY ONE OF THE "LOST LANTERNS."
LAIRA OF SECTOR 112.

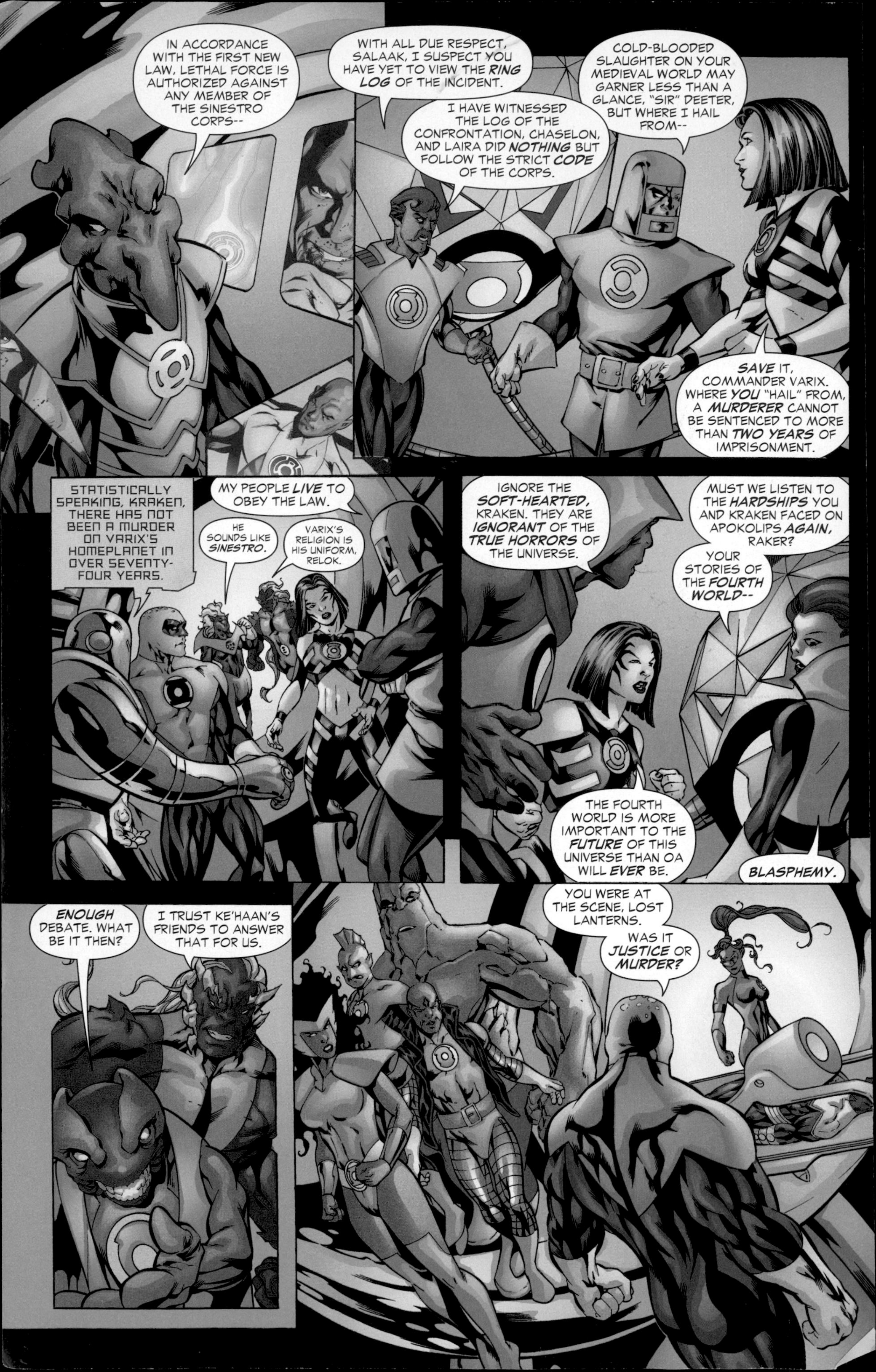

IN ACCORDANCE WITH THE FIRST NEW LAW, LETHAL FORCE IS AUTHORIZED AGAINST ANY MEMBER OF THE SINESTRO CORPS--
WITH ALL DUE RESPECT, SALAAK, I SUSPECT YOU HAVE YET TO VIEW THE *RING LOG* OF THE INCIDENT.
I HAVE WITNESSED THE LOG OF THE CONFRONTATION, CHASELON, AND LAIRA DID *NOTHING* BUT FOLLOW THE STRICT *CODE* OF THE CORPS.
COLD-BLOODED SLAUGHTER ON YOUR MEDIEVAL WORLD MAY GARNER LESS THAN A GLANCE, "SIR" DEETER, BUT WHERE I HAIL FROM--
SAVE IT, COMMANDER VARIX. WHERE *YOU* "HAIL" FROM, A *MURDERER* CANNOT BE SENTENCED TO MORE THAN *TWO YEARS* OF IMPRISONMENT.
STATISTICALLY SPEAKING, KRAKEN, THERE HAS NOT BEEN A MURDER ON VARIX'S HOMEPLANET IN OVER SEVENTY-FOUR YEARS.
MY PEOPLE *LIVE* TO OBEY THE LAW.
HE SOUNDS LIKE *SINESTRO*.
VARIX'S RELIGION IS HIS UNIFORM, RELOK.
IGNORE THE *SOFT-HEARTED*, KRAKEN. THEY ARE *IGNORANT* OF THE *TRUE HORRORS* OF THE UNIVERSE.
MUST WE LISTEN TO THE *HARDSHIPS* YOU AND KRAKEN FACED ON APOKOLIPS *AGAIN*, RAKER?
YOUR STORIES OF THE *FOURTH WORLD*--
THE FOURTH WORLD IS MORE IMPORTANT TO THE *FUTURE* OF THIS UNIVERSE THAN OA WILL *EVER* BE.
BLASPHEMY.
ENOUGH DEBATE. WHAT BE IT THEN?
I TRUST KE'HAAN'S FRIENDS TO ANSWER THAT FOR US.
YOU WERE AT THE SCENE, LOST LANTERNS.
WAS IT *JUSTICE* OR *MURDER?*

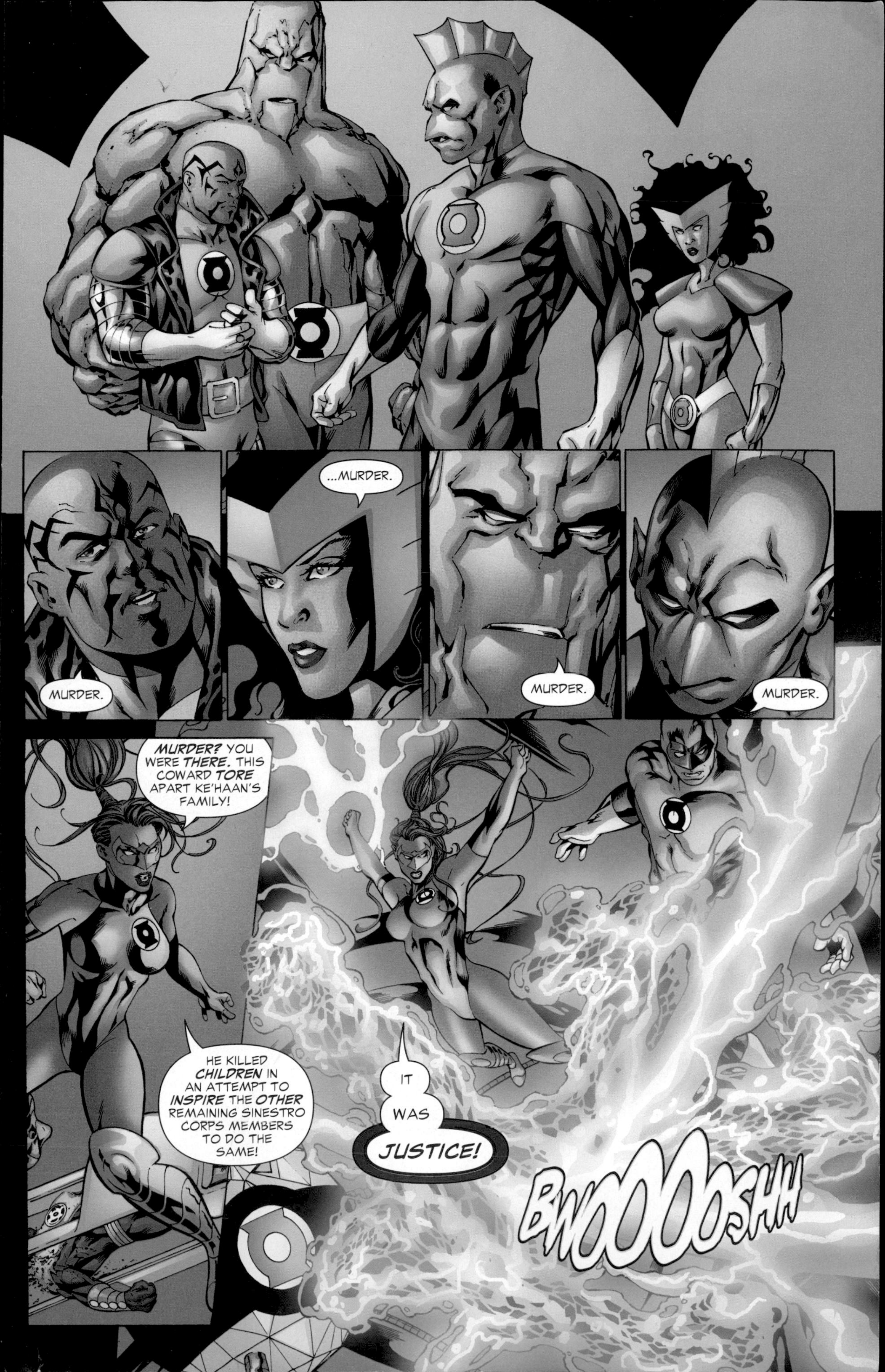

MURDER.
...MURDER.
MURDER.
MURDER.
MURDER? YOU WERE THERE. THIS COWARD TORE APART KE'HAAN'S FAMILY!
HE KILLED CHILDREN IN AN ATTEMPT TO INSPIRE THE OTHER REMAINING SINESTRO CORPS MEMBERS TO DO THE SAME!
IT WAS JUSTICE!
BWOOOOSHH

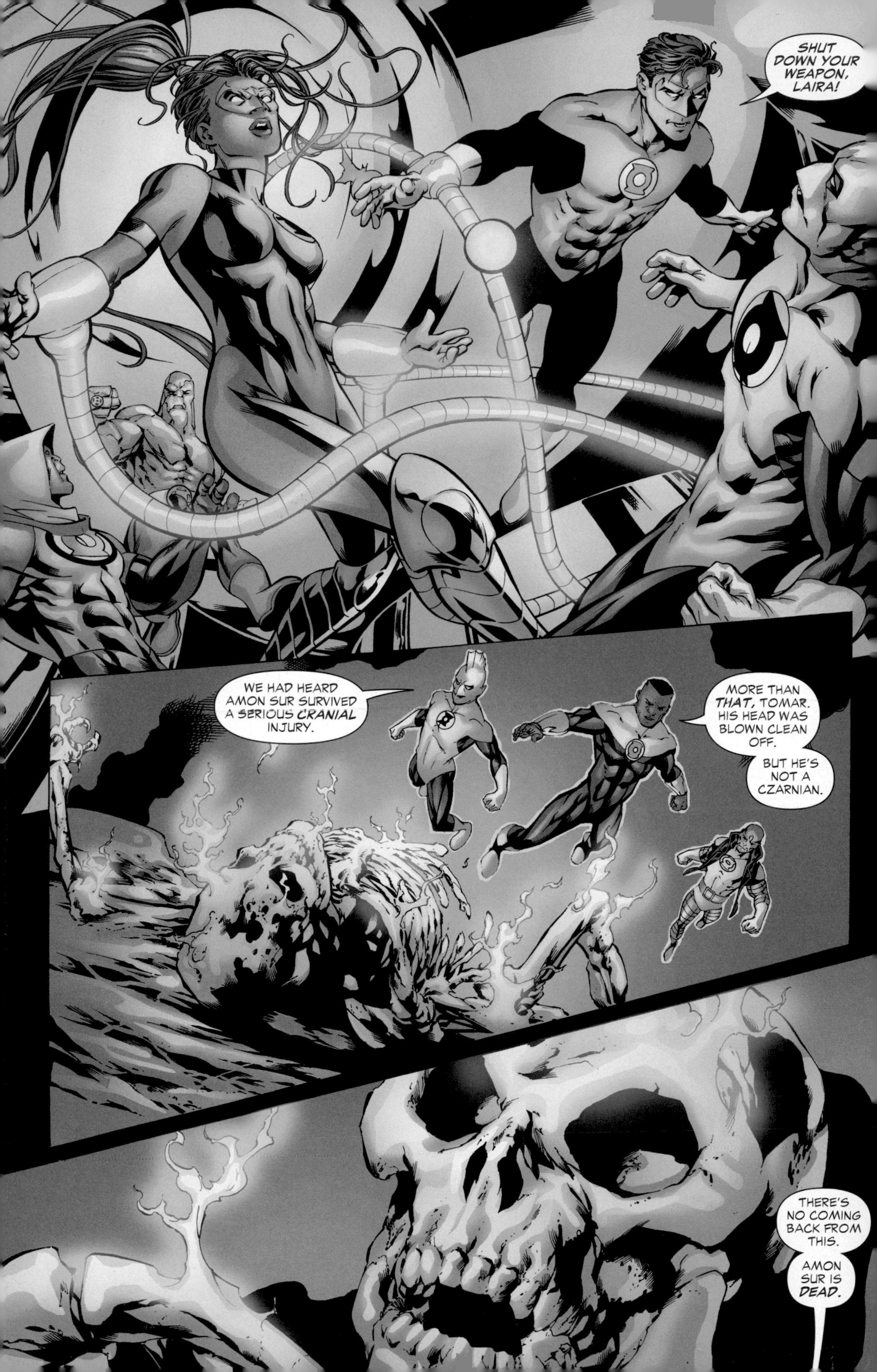
SHUT DOWN YOUR WEAPON, LAIRA!
WE HAD HEARD AMON SUR SURVIVED A SERIOUS CRANIAL INJURY.
MORE THAN THAT, TOMAR. HIS HEAD WAS BLOWN CLEAN OFF.
BUT HE'S NOT A CZARNIAN.
THERE'S NO COMING BACK FROM THIS.
AMON SUR IS DEAD.

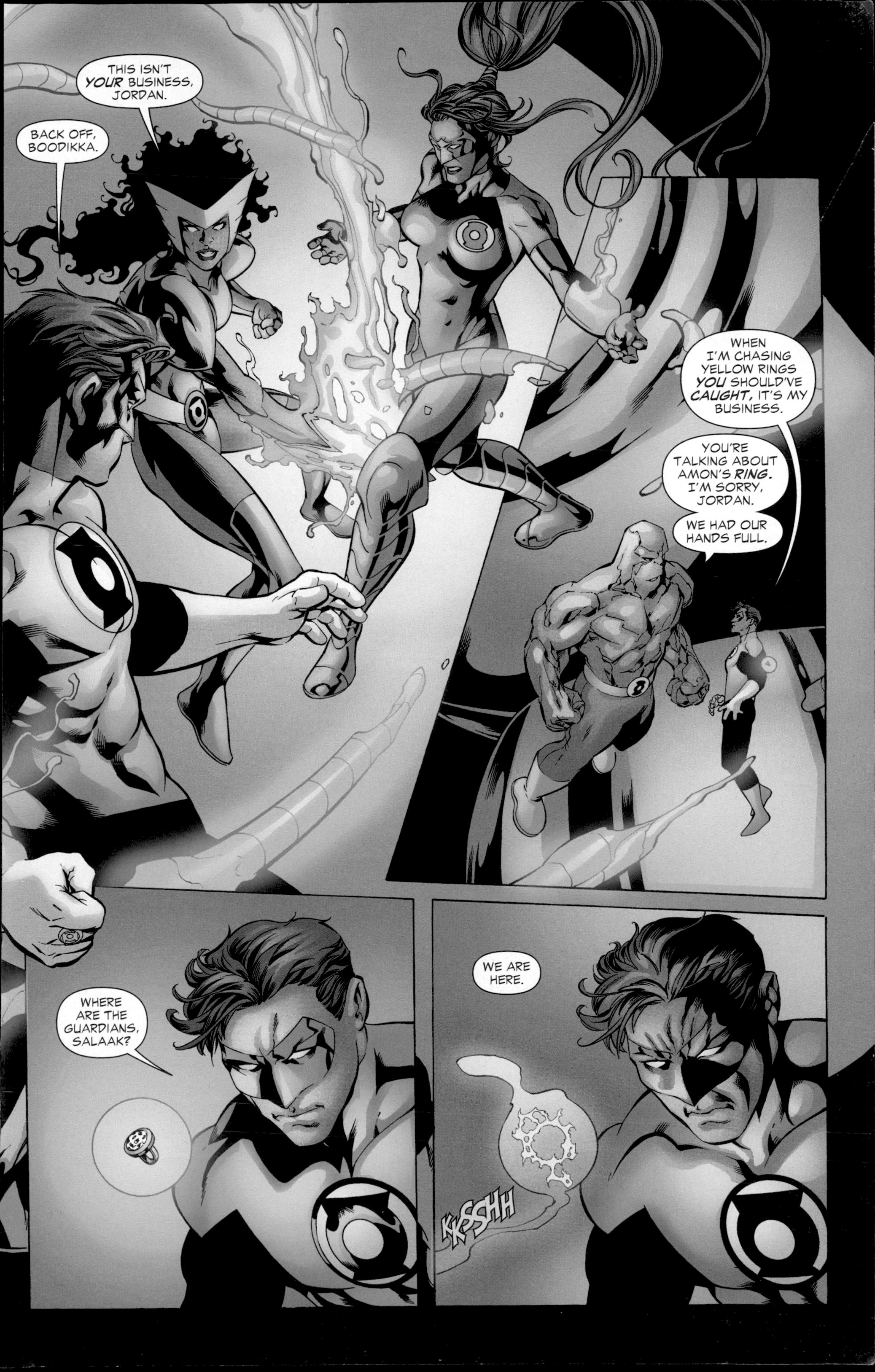
BACK OFF, BOODIKKA.
THIS ISN'T YOUR BUSINESS, JORDAN.
WHEN I'M CHASING YELLOW RINGS YOU SHOULD'VE CAUGHT, IT'S MY BUSINESS.
YOU'RE TALKING ABOUT AMON'S RING. I'M SORRY, JORDAN.
WE HAD OUR HANDS FULL.
WHERE ARE THE GUARDIANS, SALAAK?
WE ARE HERE.
KKSSHH

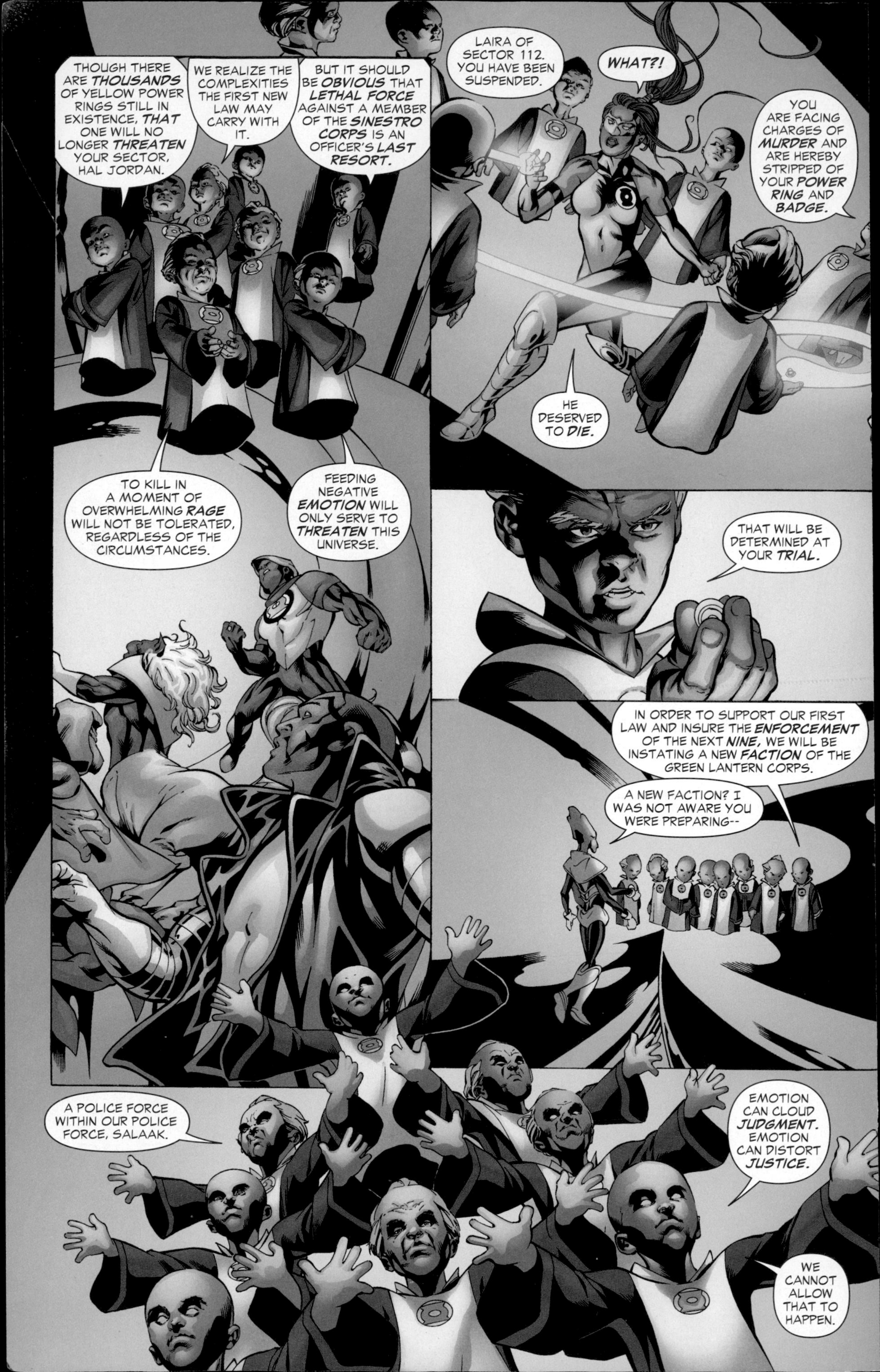
THOUGH THERE ARE THOUSANDS OF YELLOW POWER RINGS STILL IN EXISTENCE, THAT ONE WILL NO LONGER THREATEN YOUR SECTOR, HAL JORDAN.
WE REALIZE THE COMPLEXITIES THE FIRST NEW LAW MAY CARRY WITH IT.
BUT IT SHOULD BE OBVIOUS THAT LETHAL FORCE AGAINST A MEMBER OF THE SINESTRO CORPS IS AN OFFICER'S LAST RESORT.
LAIRA OF SECTOR 112. YOU HAVE BEEN SUSPENDED.
WHAT?!
YOU ARE FACING CHARGES OF MURDER AND ARE HEREBY STRIPPED OF YOUR POWER RING AND BADGE.
HE DESERVED TO DIE.
TO KILL IN A MOMENT OF OVERWHELMING RAGE WILL NOT BE TOLERATED, REGARDLESS OF THE CIRCUMSTANCES.
FEEDING NEGATIVE EMOTION WILL ONLY SERVE TO THREATEN THIS UNIVERSE.
THAT WILL BE DETERMINED AT YOUR TRIAL.
IN ORDER TO SUPPORT OUR FIRST LAW AND INSURE THE ENFORCEMENT OF THE NEXT NINE, WE WILL BE INSTATING A NEW FACTION OF THE GREEN LANTERN CORPS.
A NEW FACTION? I WAS NOT AWARE YOU WERE PREPARING--
A POLICE FORCE WITHIN OUR POLICE FORCE, SALAAK.
EMOTION CAN CLOUD JUDGMENT. EMOTION CAN DISTORT JUSTICE.
WE CANNOT ALLOW THAT TO HAPPEN.

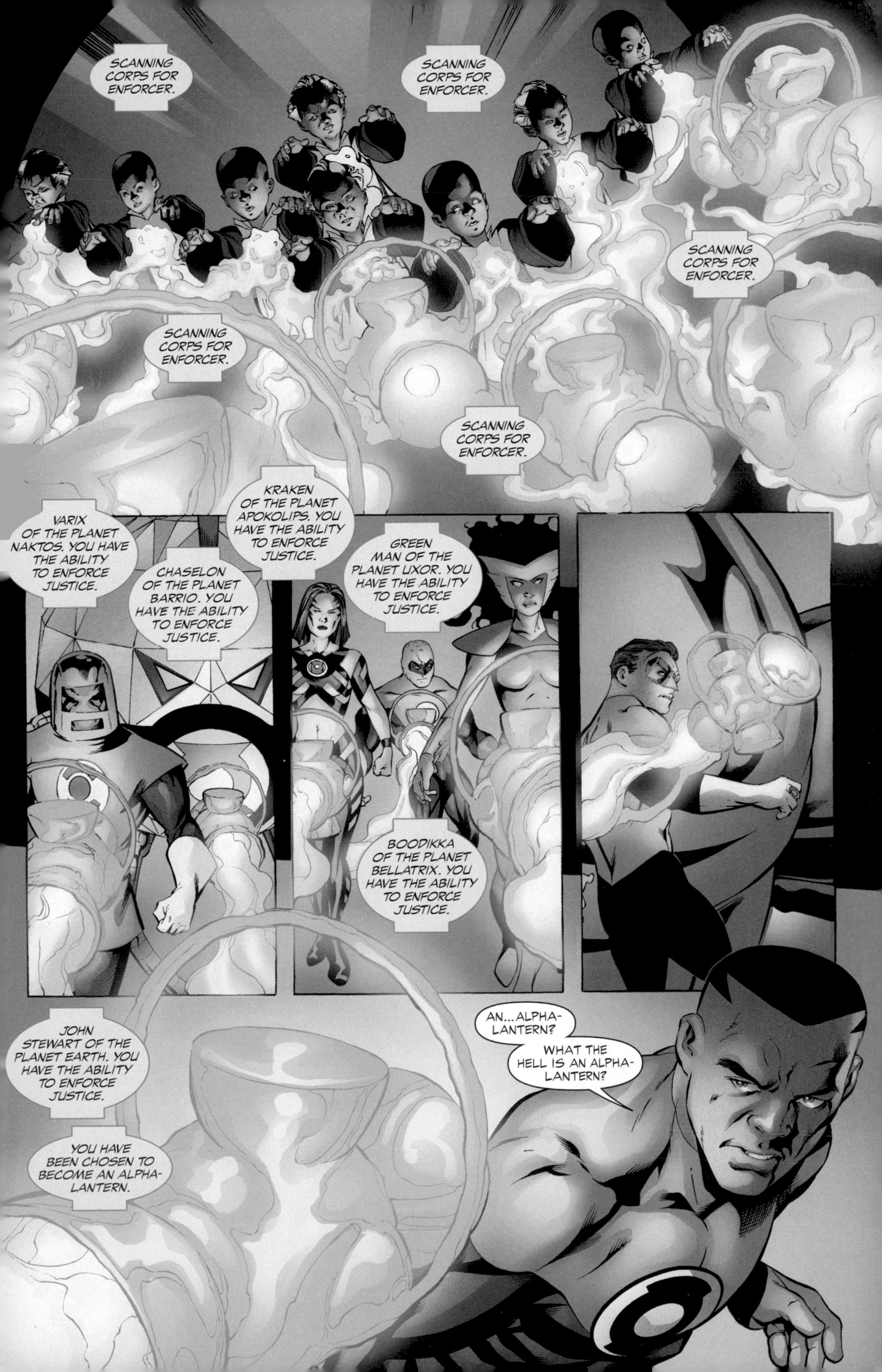
SCANNING CORPS FOR ENFORCER.
SCANNING CORPS FOR ENFORCER.
SCANNING CORPS FOR ENFORCER.
SCANNING CORPS FOR ENFORCER.
SCANNING CORPS FOR ENFORCER.
VARIX OF THE PLANET NAKTOS. YOU HAVE THE ABILITY TO ENFORCE JUSTICE.
KRAKEN OF THE PLANET APOKOLIPS. YOU HAVE THE ABILITY TO ENFORCE JUSTICE.
CHASELON OF THE PLANET BARRIO. YOU HAVE THE ABILITY TO ENFORCE JUSTICE.
GREEN MAN OF THE PLANET UXOR. YOU HAVE THE ABILITY TO ENFORCE JUSTICE.
BOODIKKA OF THE PLANET BELLATRIX. YOU HAVE THE ABILITY TO ENFORCE JUSTICE.
JOHN STEWART OF THE PLANET EARTH. YOU HAVE THE ABILITY TO ENFORCE JUSTICE.
YOU HAVE BEEN CHOSEN TO BECOME AN ALPHA-LANTERN.
AN...ALPHA-LANTERN?
WHAT THE HELL IS AN ALPHA-LANTERN?

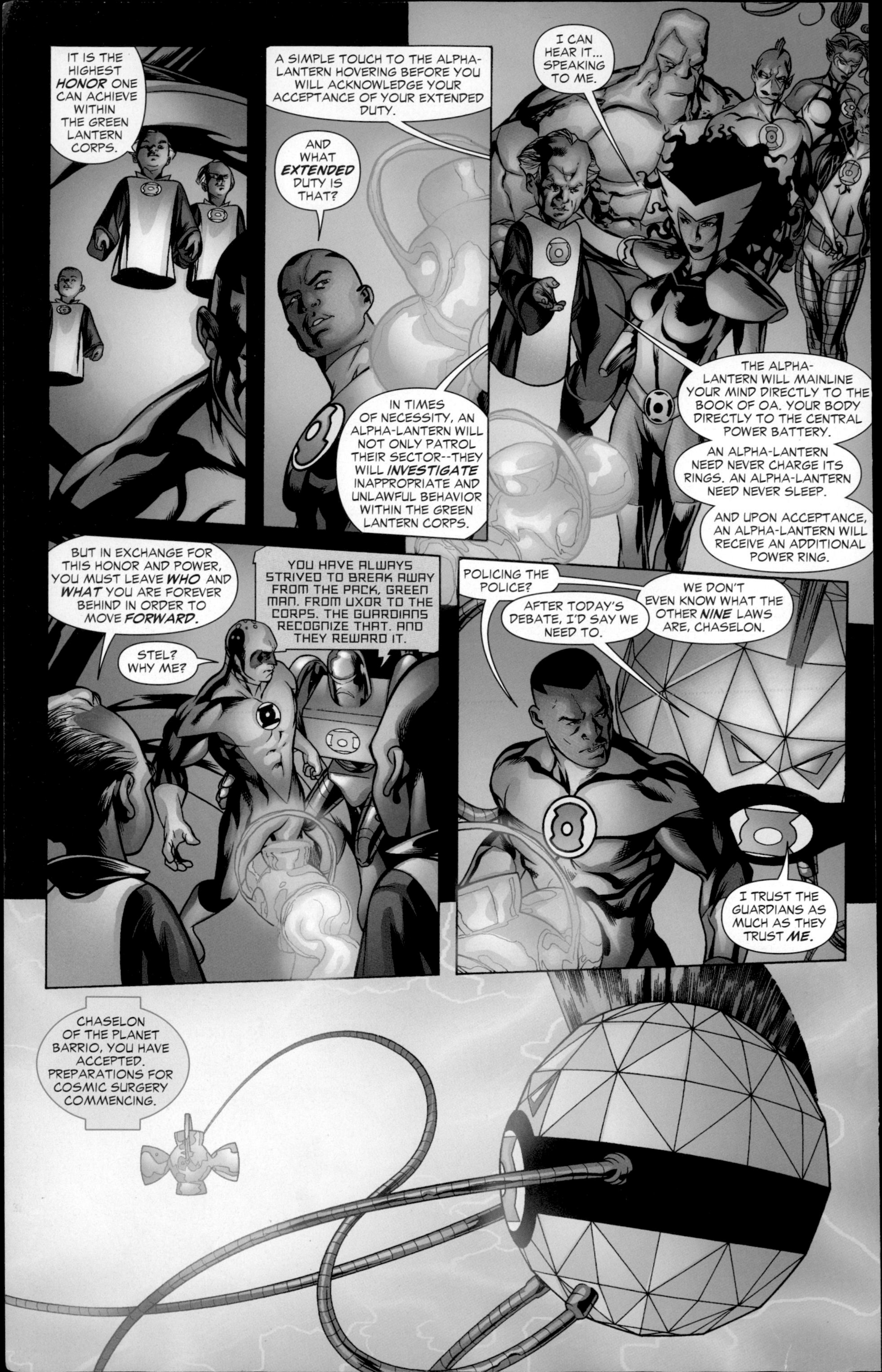
IT IS THE HIGHEST HONOR ONE CAN ACHIEVE WITHIN THE GREEN LANTERN CORPS.
A SIMPLE TOUCH TO THE ALPHA-LANTERN HOVERING BEFORE YOU WILL ACKNOWLEDGE YOUR ACCEPTANCE OF YOUR EXTENDED DUTY.
AND WHAT EXTENDED DUTY IS THAT?
IN TIMES OF NECESSITY, AN ALPHA-LANTERN WILL NOT ONLY PATROL THEIR SECTOR--THEY WILL INVESTIGATE INAPPROPRIATE AND UNLAWFUL BEHAVIOR WITHIN THE GREEN LANTERN CORPS.
I CAN HEAR IT... SPEAKING TO ME.
THE ALPHA-LANTERN WILL MAINLINE YOUR MIND DIRECTLY TO THE BOOK OF OA. YOUR BODY DIRECTLY TO THE CENTRAL POWER BATTERY.
AN ALPHA-LANTERN NEED NEVER CHARGE ITS RINGS. AN ALPHA-LANTERN NEED NEVER SLEEP.
AND UPON ACCEPTANCE, AN ALPHA-LANTERN WILL RECEIVE AN ADDITIONAL POWER RING.
BUT IN EXCHANGE FOR THIS HONOR AND POWER, YOU MUST LEAVE WHO AND WHAT YOU ARE FOREVER BEHIND IN ORDER TO MOVE FORWARD.
YOU HAVE ALWAYS STRIVED TO BREAK AWAY FROM THE PACK, GREEN MAN. FROM UXOR TO THE CORPS. THE GUARDIANS RECOGNIZE THAT. AND THEY REWARD IT.
STEL? WHY ME?
POLICING THE POLICE?
AFTER TODAY'S DEBATE, I'D SAY WE NEED TO.
WE DON'T EVEN KNOW WHAT THE OTHER NINE LAWS ARE, CHASELON.
I TRUST THE GUARDIANS AS MUCH AS THEY TRUST ME.
CHASELON OF THE PLANET BARRIO, YOU HAVE ACCEPTED. PREPARATIONS FOR COSMIC SURGERY COMMENCING.

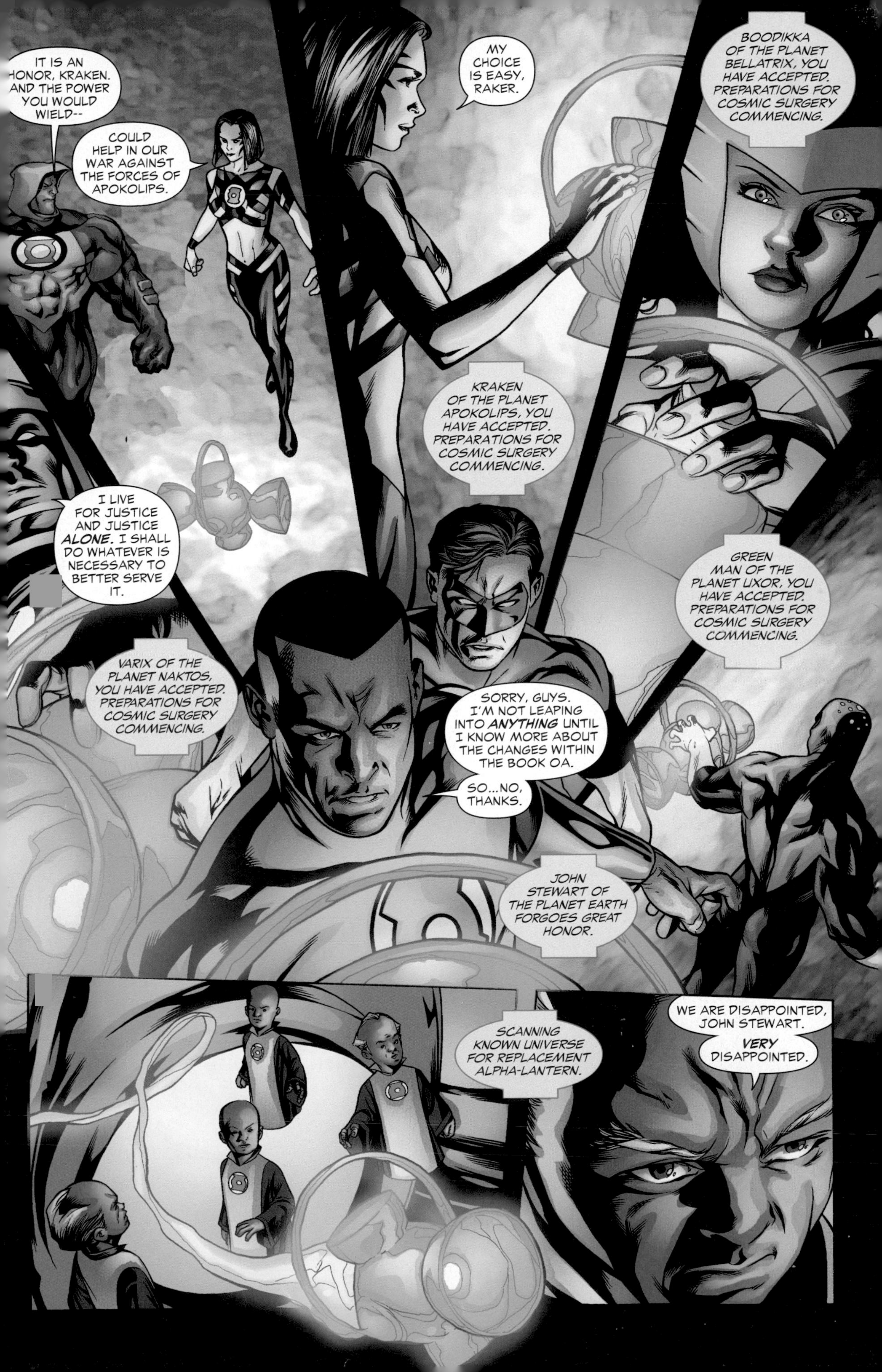
IT IS AN HONOR, KRAKEN. AND THE POWER YOU WOULD WIELD--
COULD HELP IN OUR WAR AGAINST THE FORCES OF APOKOLIPS.
MY CHOICE IS EASY, RAKER.
BOODIKKA OF THE PLANET BELLATRIX, YOU HAVE ACCEPTED. PREPARATIONS FOR COSMIC SURGERY COMMENCING.
KRAKEN OF THE PLANET APOKOLIPS, YOU HAVE ACCEPTED. PREPARATIONS FOR COSMIC SURGERY COMMENCING.
I LIVE FOR JUSTICE AND JUSTICE ALONE. I SHALL DO WHATEVER IS NECESSARY TO BETTER SERVE IT.
GREEN MAN OF THE PLANET UXOR, YOU HAVE ACCEPTED. PREPARATIONS FOR COSMIC SURGERY COMMENCING.
VARIX OF THE PLANET NAKTOS, YOU HAVE ACCEPTED. PREPARATIONS FOR COSMIC SURGERY COMMENCING.
SORRY, GUYS. I'M NOT LEAPING INTO ANYTHING UNTIL I KNOW MORE ABOUT THE CHANGES WITHIN THE BOOK OA.
SO...NO, THANKS.
JOHN STEWART OF THE PLANET EARTH FORGOES GREAT HONOR.
SCANNING KNOWN UNIVERSE FOR REPLACEMENT ALPHA-LANTERN.
WE ARE DISAPPOINTED, JOHN STEWART. VERY DISAPPOINTED.

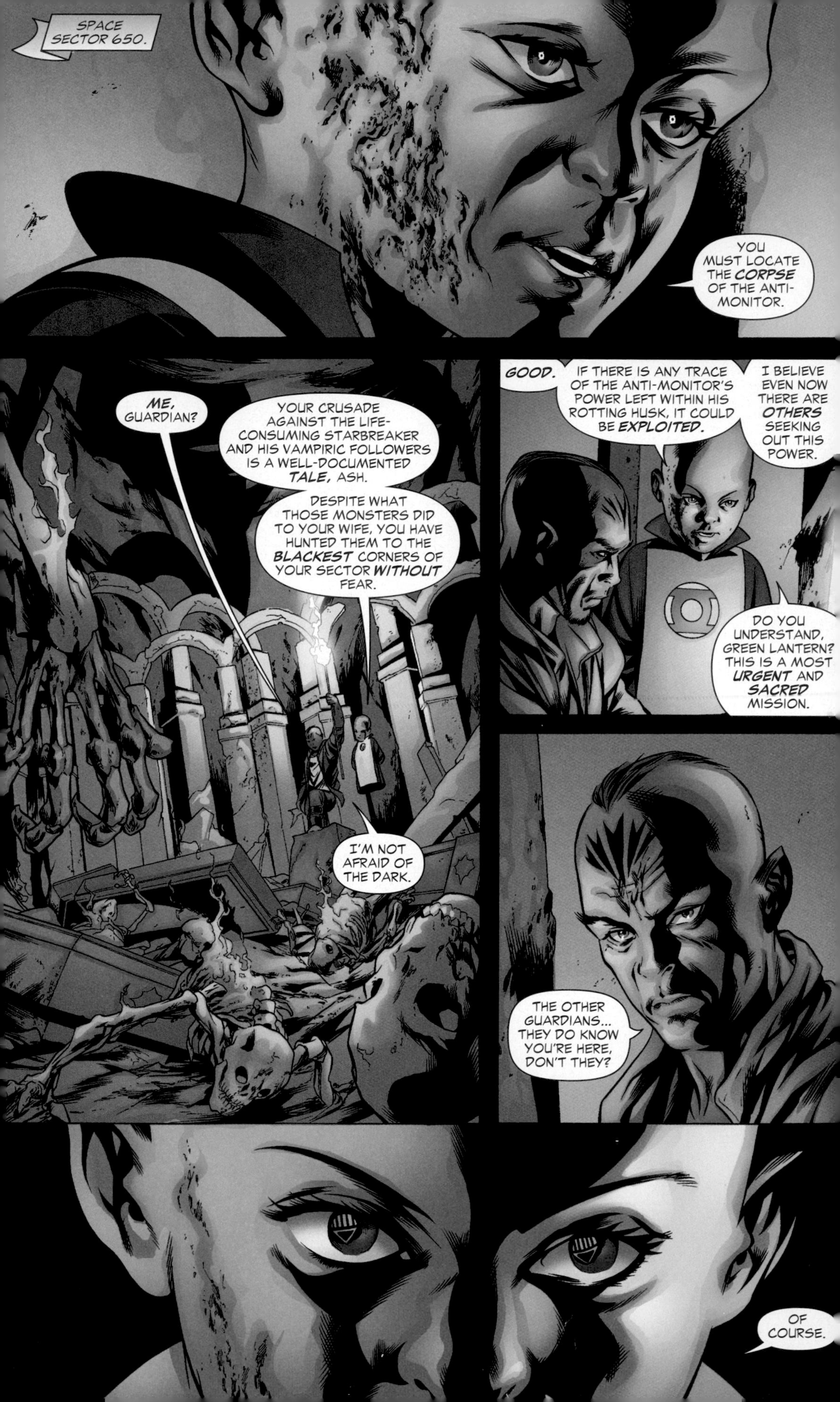

SPACE SECTOR 650.
YOU MUST LOCATE THE CORPSE OF THE ANTI-MONITOR.
ME, GUARDIAN?
YOUR CRUSADE AGAINST THE LIFE-CONSUMING STARBREAKER AND HIS VAMPIRIC FOLLOWERS IS A WELL-DOCUMENTED TALE, ASH.
DESPITE WHAT THOSE MONSTERS DID TO YOUR WIFE, YOU HAVE HUNTED THEM TO THE BLACKEST CORNERS OF YOUR SECTOR WITHOUT FEAR.
I'M NOT AFRAID OF THE DARK.
GOOD.
IF THERE IS ANY TRACE OF THE ANTI-MONITOR'S POWER LEFT WITHIN HIS ROTTING HUSK, IT COULD BE EXPLOITED.
I BELIEVE EVEN NOW THERE ARE OTHERS SEEKING OUT THIS POWER.
DO YOU UNDERSTAND, GREEN LANTERN? THIS IS A MOST URGENT AND SACRED MISSION.
THE OTHER GUARDIANS... THEY DO KNOW YOU'RE HERE, DON'T THEY?
OF COURSE.

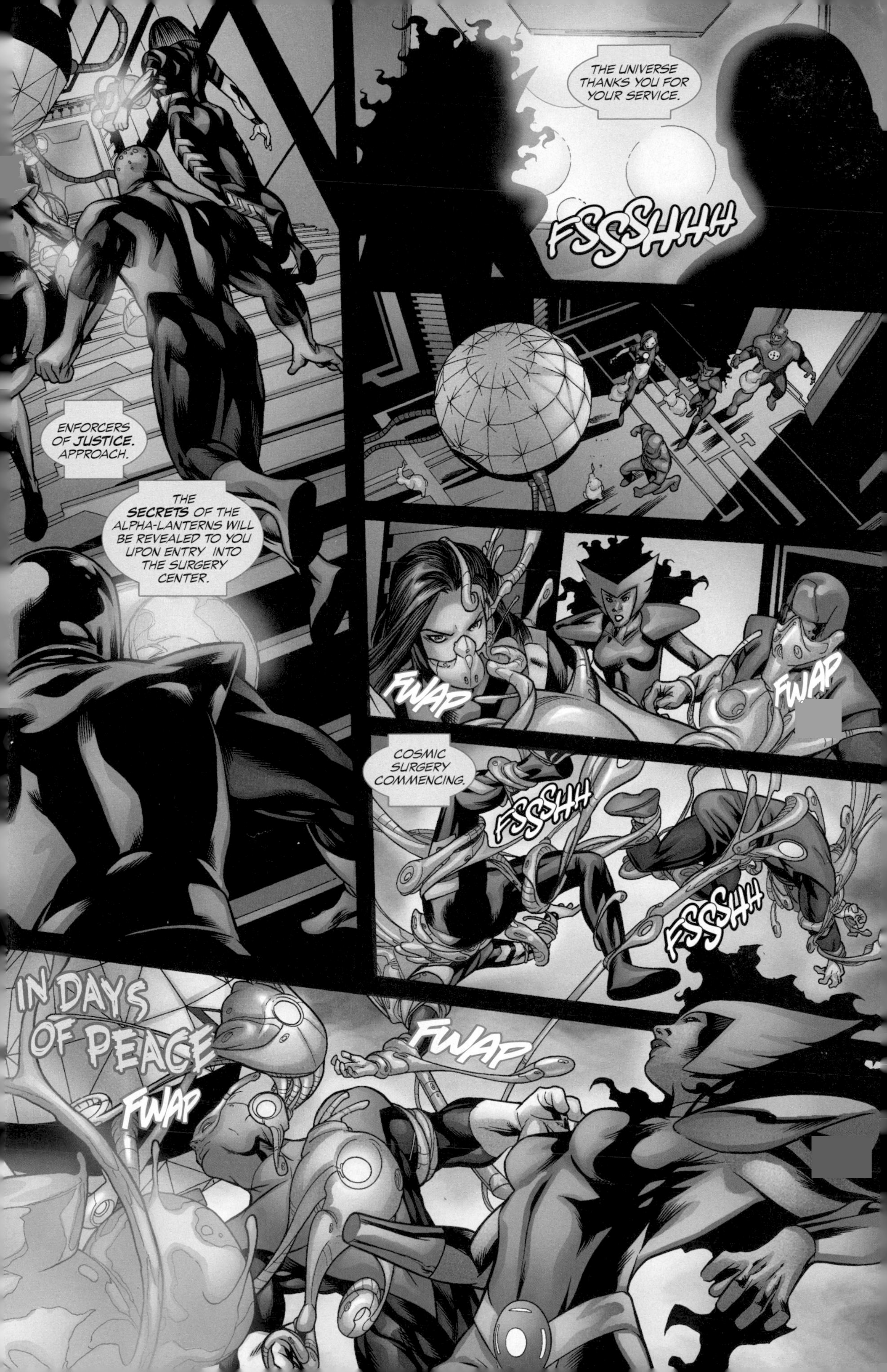
ENFORCERS OF JUSTICE. APPROACH.
THE SECRETS OF THE ALPHA-LANTERNS WILL BE REVEALED TO YOU UPON ENTRY INTO THE SURGERY CENTER.
THE UNIVERSE THANKS YOU FOR YOUR SERVICE.
FSSHHH
FWAP
FWAP
COSMIC SURGERY COMMENCING.
FSSHH
FSSHH
IN DAYS OF PEACE
FWAP
FWAP

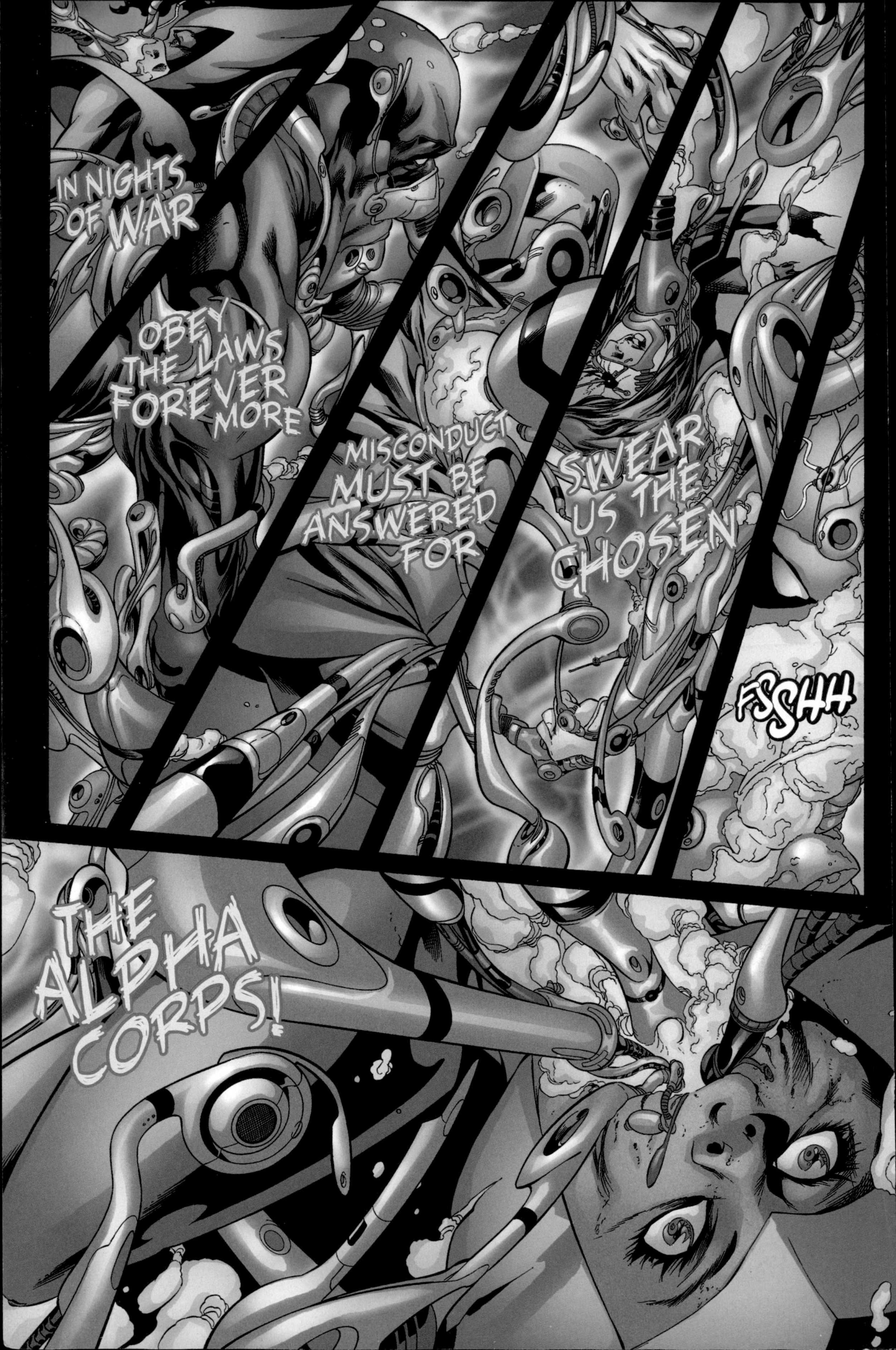
IN NIGHTS OF WAR
OBEY THE LAWS FOREVER MORE
MISCONDUCT MUST BE ANSWERED FOR
SWEAR US THE CHOSEN
FSSHH
THE ALPHA CORPS!

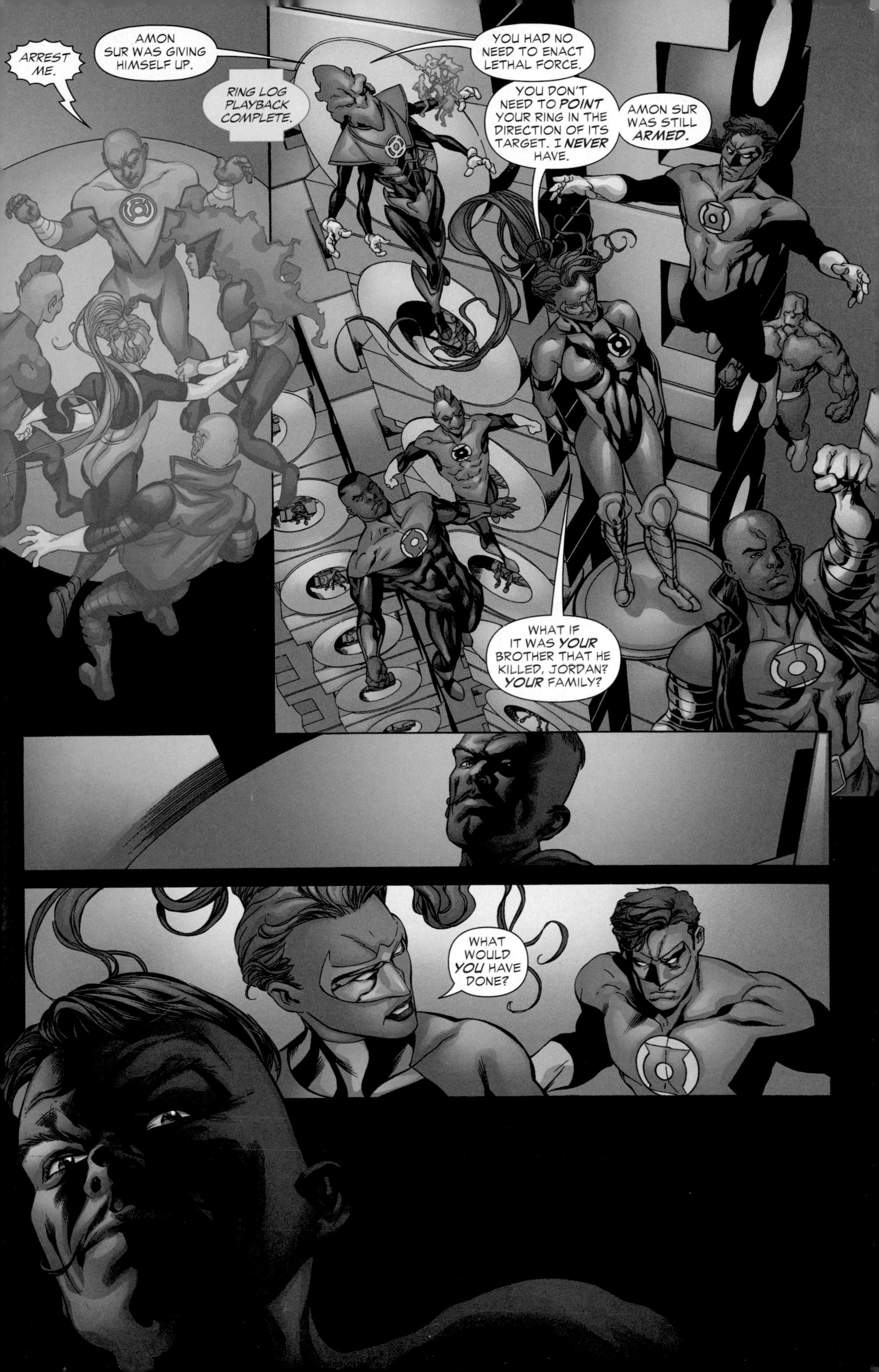
ARREST ME.
AMON SUR WAS GIVING HIMSELF UP.
RING LOG PLAYBACK COMPLETE.
YOU HAD NO NEED TO ENACT LETHAL FORCE.
YOU DON'T NEED TO POINT YOUR RING IN THE DIRECTION OF ITS TARGET. I NEVER HAVE.
AMON SUR WAS STILL ARMED.
WHAT IF IT WAS YOUR BROTHER THAT HE KILLED, JORDAN? YOUR FAMILY?
WHAT WOULD YOU HAVE DONE?

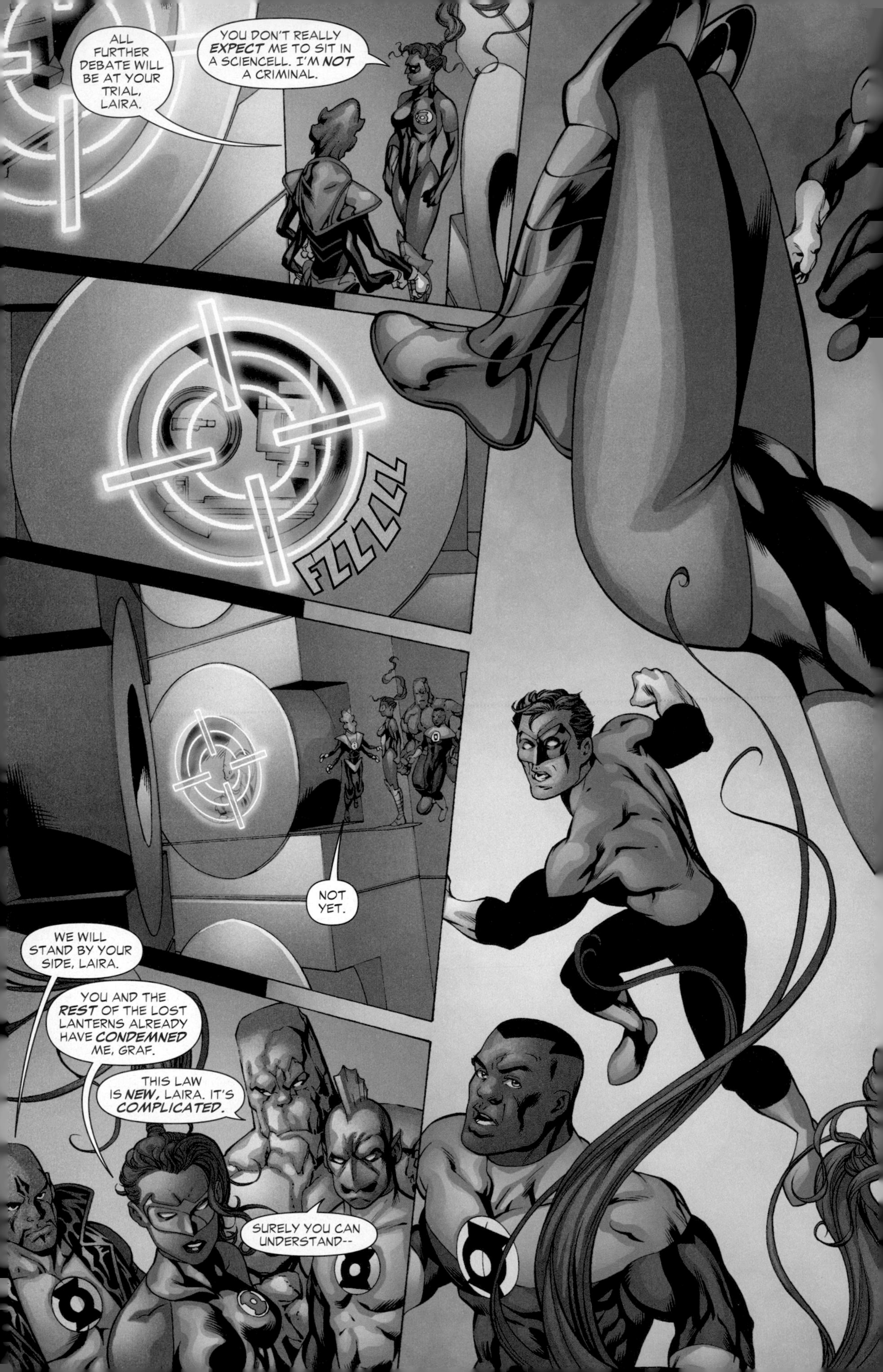
ALL FURTHER DEBATE WILL BE AT YOUR TRIAL, LAIRA.
YOU DON'T REALLY EXPECT ME TO SIT IN A SCIENCELL. I'M NOT A CRIMINAL.
FZZZZZL
NOT YET.
WE WILL STAND BY YOUR SIDE, LAIRA.
YOU AND THE REST OF THE LOST LANTERNS ALREADY HAVE CONDEMNED ME, GRAF.
THIS LAW IS NEW, LAIRA. IT'S COMPLICATED.
SURELY YOU CAN UNDERSTAND--

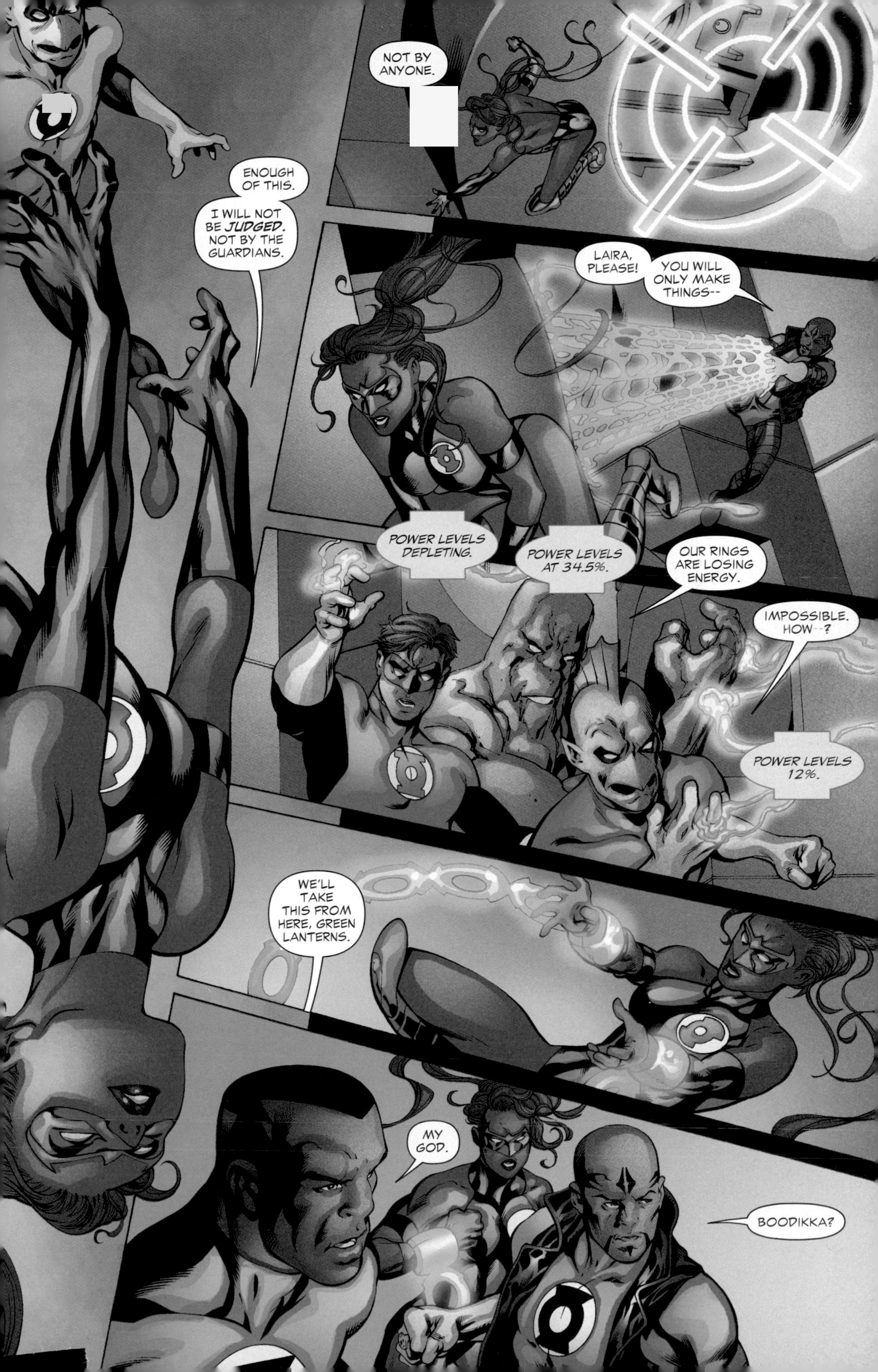
ENOUGH OF THIS.
I WILL NOT BE *JUDGED*. NOT BY THE GUARDIANS.
NOT BY ANYONE.
LAIRA, PLEASE!
YOU WILL ONLY MAKE THINGS--
POWER LEVELS DEPLETING.
POWER LEVELS AT 34.5%.
OUR RINGS ARE LOSING ENERGY.
IMPOSSIBLE. HOW--?
POWER LEVELS 12%.
WE'LL TAKE THIS FROM HERE, GREEN LANTERNS.
MY GOD.
BOODIKKA?

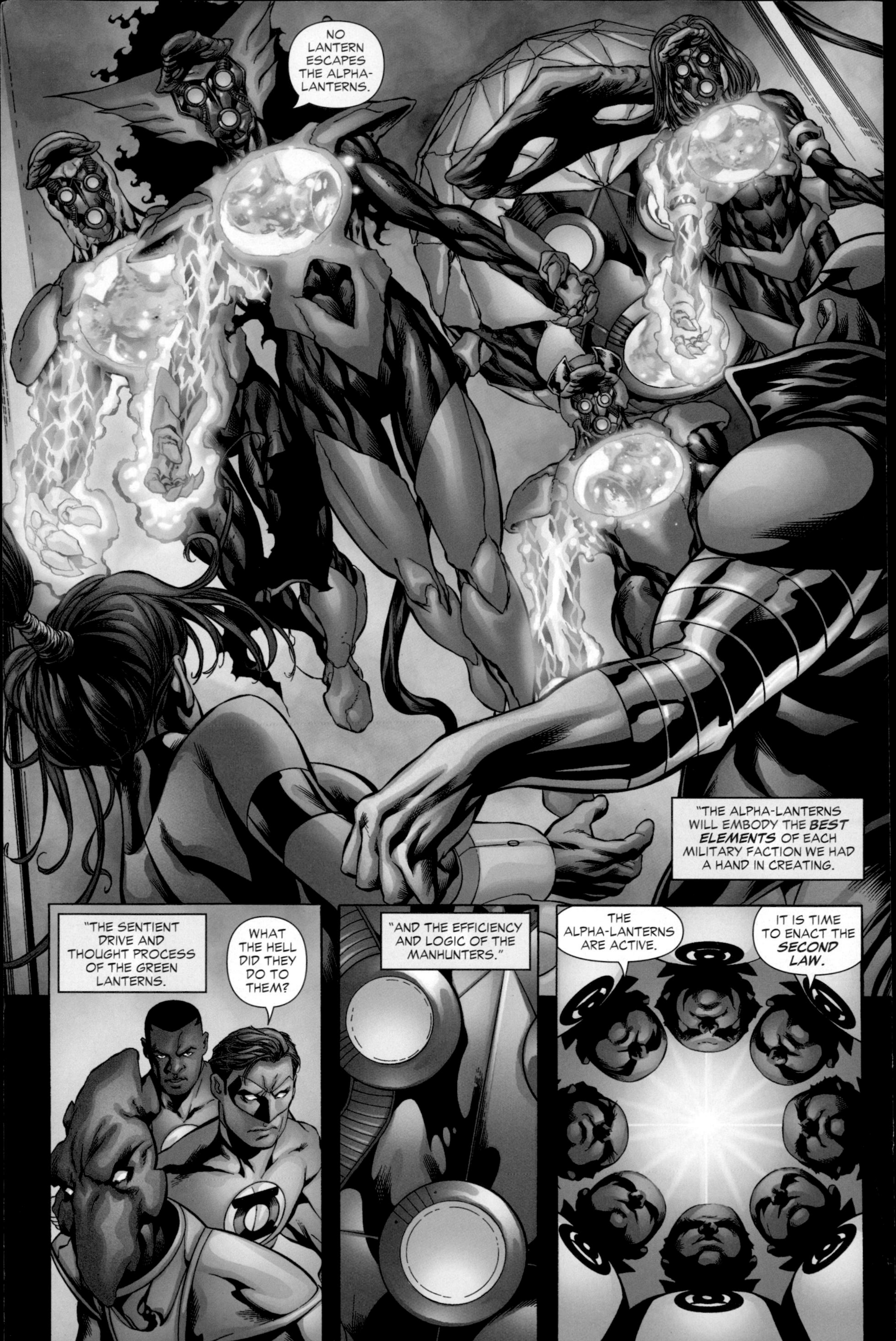
NO LANTERN ESCAPES THE ALPHA-LANTERNS.
"THE ALPHA-LANTERNS WILL EMBODY THE BEST ELEMENTS OF EACH MILITARY FACTION WE HAD A HAND IN CREATING.
"THE SENTIENT DRIVE AND THOUGHT PROCESS OF THE GREEN LANTERNS.
WHAT THE HELL DID THEY DO TO THEM?
"AND THE EFFICIENCY AND LOGIC OF THE MANHUNTERS."
THE ALPHA-LANTERNS ARE ACTIVE.
IT IS TIME TO ENACT THE SECOND LAW.

GREEN LANTERN 28 Cover by Mike McKone, Andy Lanning and Moose Baumann

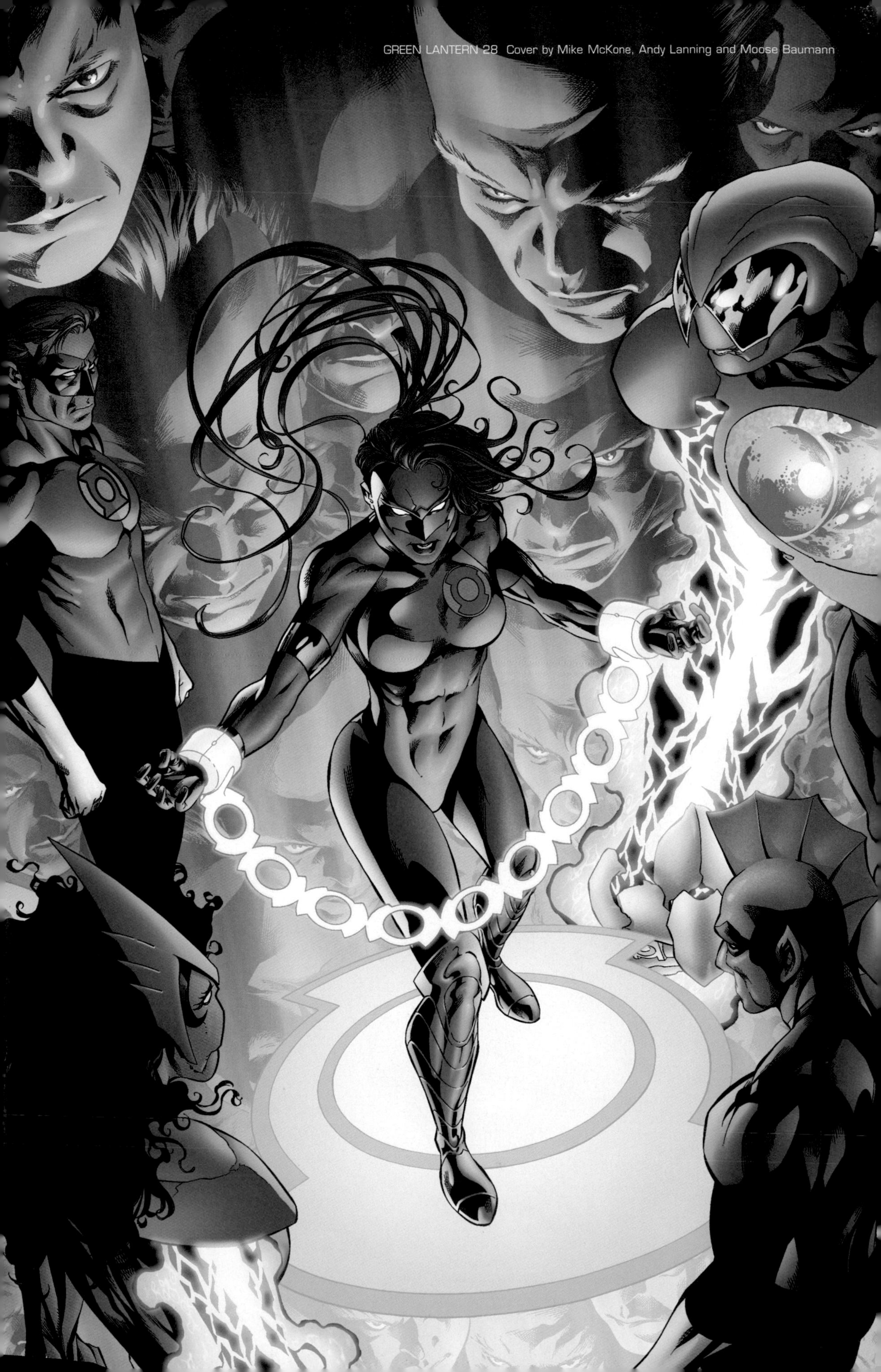

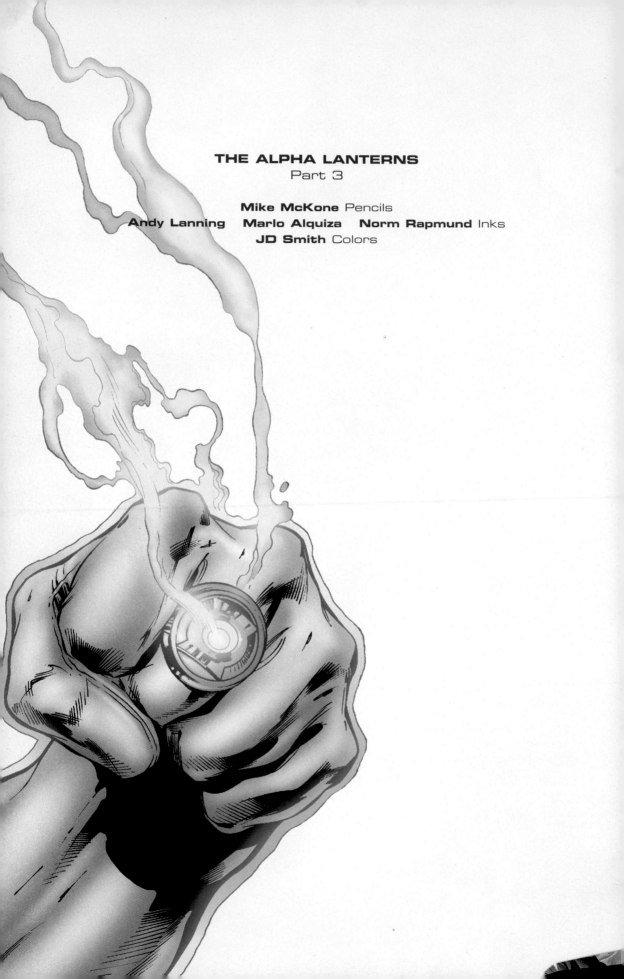

THE ALPHA LANTERNS
Part 3

Mike McKone Pencils
Andy Lanning   **Marlo Alquiza**   **Norm Rapmund** Inks
JD Smith Colors

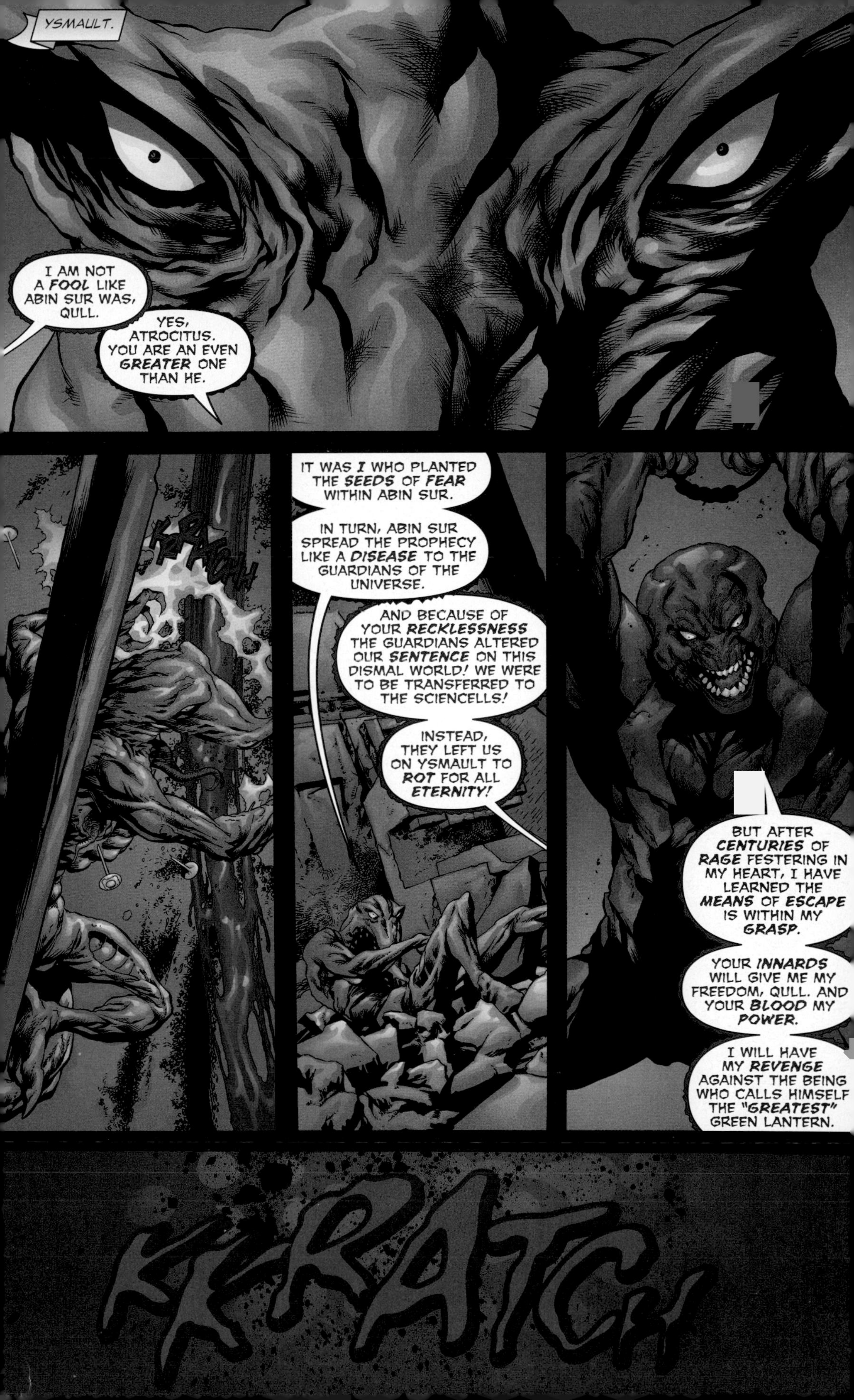
YSMAULT.
I AM NOT A FOOL LIKE ABIN SUR WAS, QULL.
YES, ATROCITUS. YOU ARE AN EVEN GREATER ONE THAN HE.
KKRATCH
IT WAS I WHO PLANTED THE SEEDS OF FEAR WITHIN ABIN SUR.
IN TURN, ABIN SUR SPREAD THE PROPHECY LIKE A DISEASE TO THE GUARDIANS OF THE UNIVERSE.
AND BECAUSE OF YOUR RECKLESSNESS THE GUARDIANS ALTERED OUR SENTENCE ON THIS DISMAL WORLD! WE WERE TO BE TRANSFERRED TO THE SCIENCELLS!
INSTEAD, THEY LEFT US ON YSMAULT TO ROT FOR ALL ETERNITY!
BUT AFTER CENTURIES OF RAGE FESTERING IN MY HEART, I HAVE LEARNED THE MEANS OF ESCAPE IS WITHIN MY GRASP.
YOUR INNARDS WILL GIVE ME MY FREEDOM, QULL. AND YOUR BLOOD MY POWER.
I WILL HAVE MY REVENGE AGAINST THE BEING WHO CALLS HIMSELF THE "GREATEST" GREEN LANTERN.
KKRATCH

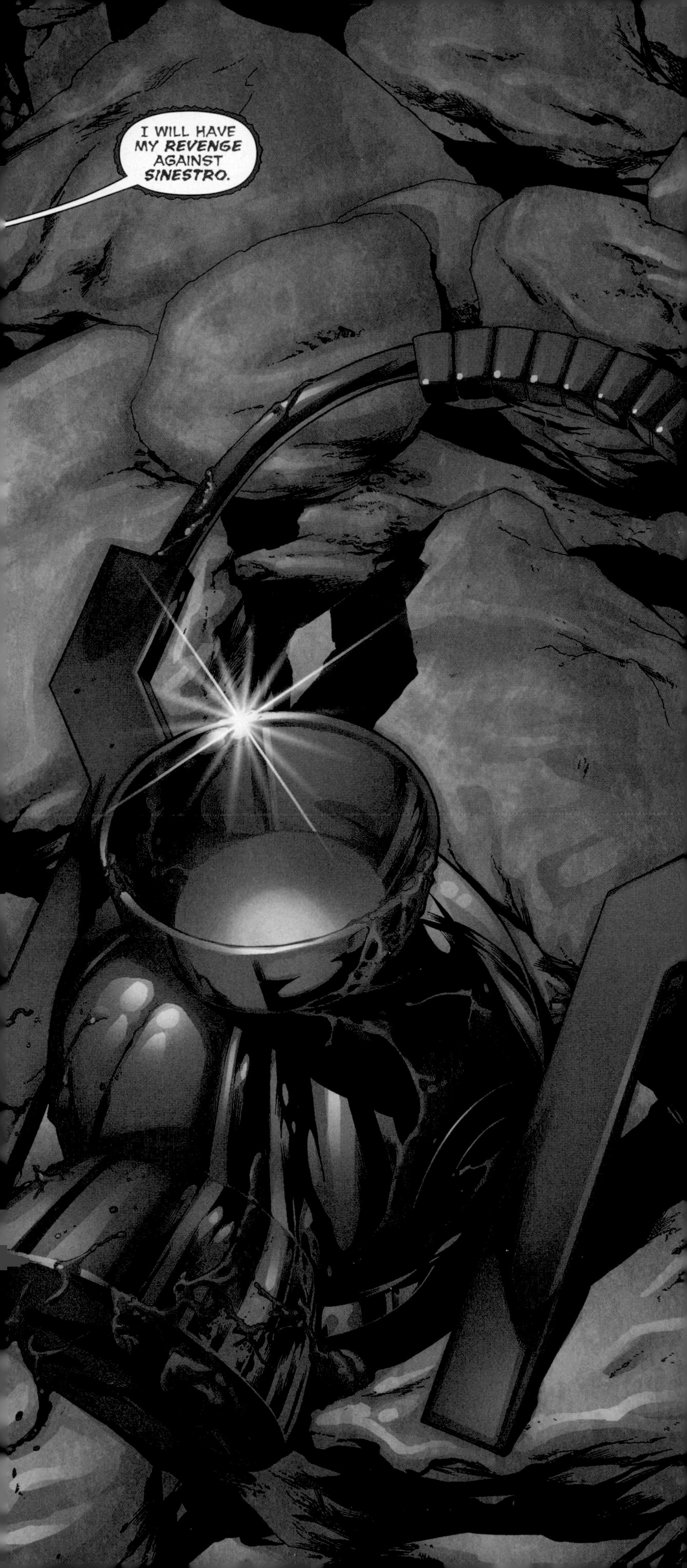
I WILL HAVE MY REVENGE AGAINST SINESTRO.

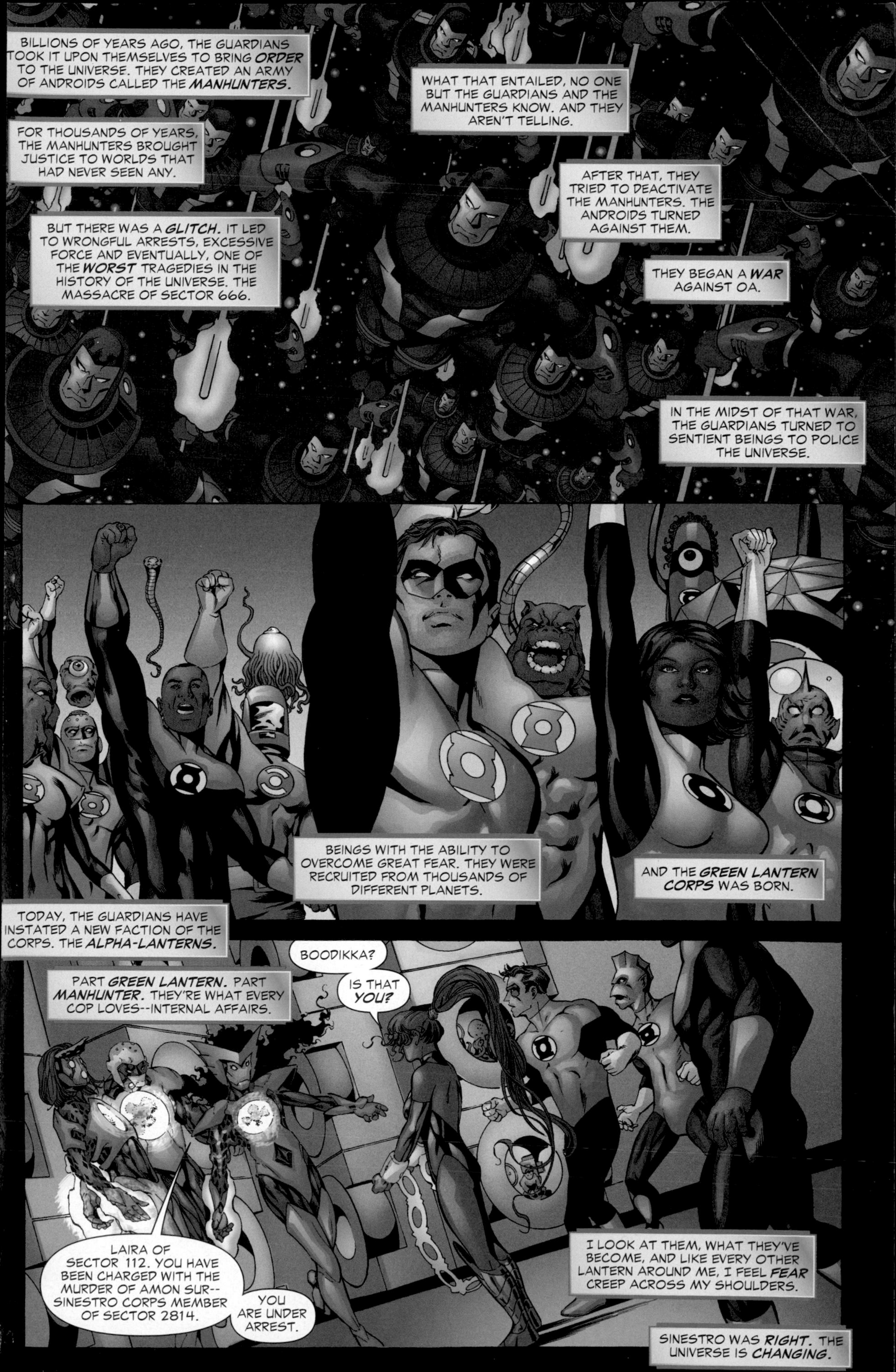

BILLIONS OF YEARS AGO, THE GUARDIANS TOOK IT UPON THEMSELVES TO BRING ORDER TO THE UNIVERSE. THEY CREATED AN ARMY OF ANDROIDS CALLED THE MANHUNTERS.
FOR THOUSANDS OF YEARS, THE MANHUNTERS BROUGHT JUSTICE TO WORLDS THAT HAD NEVER SEEN ANY.
BUT THERE WAS A GLITCH. IT LED TO WRONGFUL ARRESTS, EXCESSIVE FORCE AND EVENTUALLY, ONE OF THE WORST TRAGEDIES IN THE HISTORY OF THE UNIVERSE. THE MASSACRE OF SECTOR 666.
WHAT THAT ENTAILED, NO ONE BUT THE GUARDIANS AND THE MANHUNTERS KNOW. AND THEY AREN'T TELLING.
AFTER THAT, THEY TRIED TO DEACTIVATE THE MANHUNTERS. THE ANDROIDS TURNED AGAINST THEM.
THEY BEGAN A WAR AGAINST OA.
IN THE MIDST OF THAT WAR, THE GUARDIANS TURNED TO SENTIENT BEINGS TO POLICE THE UNIVERSE.
BEINGS WITH THE ABILITY TO OVERCOME GREAT FEAR. THEY WERE RECRUITED FROM THOUSANDS OF DIFFERENT PLANETS.
AND THE GREEN LANTERN CORPS WAS BORN.
TODAY, THE GUARDIANS HAVE INSTATED A NEW FACTION OF THE CORPS. THE ALPHA-LANTERNS.
PART GREEN LANTERN. PART MANHUNTER. THEY'RE WHAT EVERY COP LOVES--INTERNAL AFFAIRS.
BOODIKKA?
IS THAT YOU?
LAIRA OF SECTOR 112. YOU HAVE BEEN CHARGED WITH THE MURDER OF AMON SUR-- SINESTRO CORPS MEMBER OF SECTOR 2814.
YOU ARE UNDER ARREST.
I LOOK AT THEM, WHAT THEY'VE BECOME, AND LIKE EVERY OTHER LANTERN AROUND ME, I FEEL FEAR CREEP ACROSS MY SHOULDERS.
SINESTRO WAS RIGHT. THE UNIVERSE IS CHANGING.

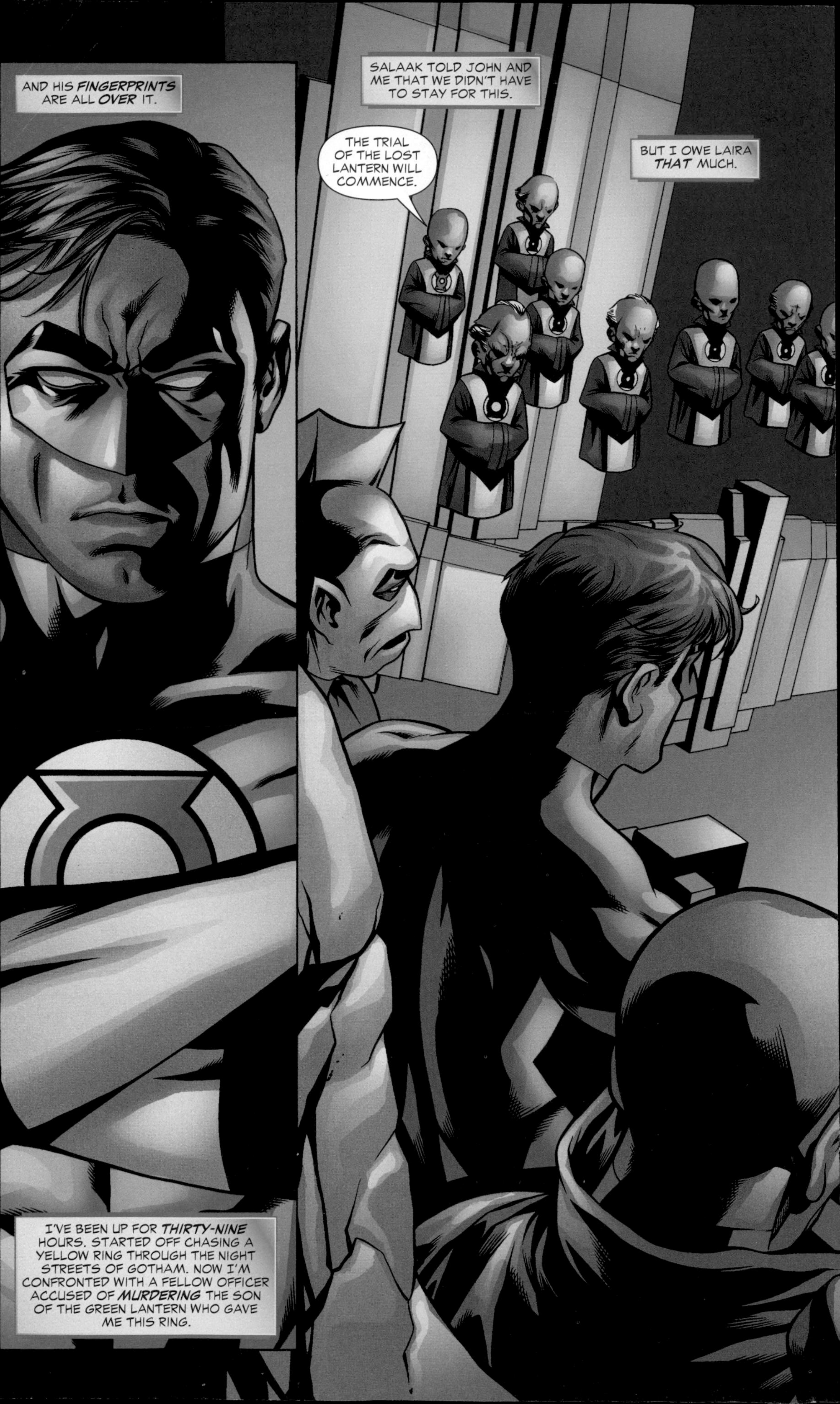
AND HIS FINGERPRINTS ARE ALL OVER IT.
SALAAK TOLD JOHN AND ME THAT WE DIDN'T HAVE TO STAY FOR THIS.
THE TRIAL OF THE LOST LANTERN WILL COMMENCE.
BUT I OWE LAIRA THAT MUCH.
I'VE BEEN UP FOR THIRTY-NINE HOURS. STARTED OFF CHASING A YELLOW RING THROUGH THE NIGHT STREETS OF GOTHAM. NOW I'M CONFRONTED WITH A FELLOW OFFICER ACCUSED OF MURDERING THE SON OF THE GREEN LANTERN WHO GAVE ME THIS RING.

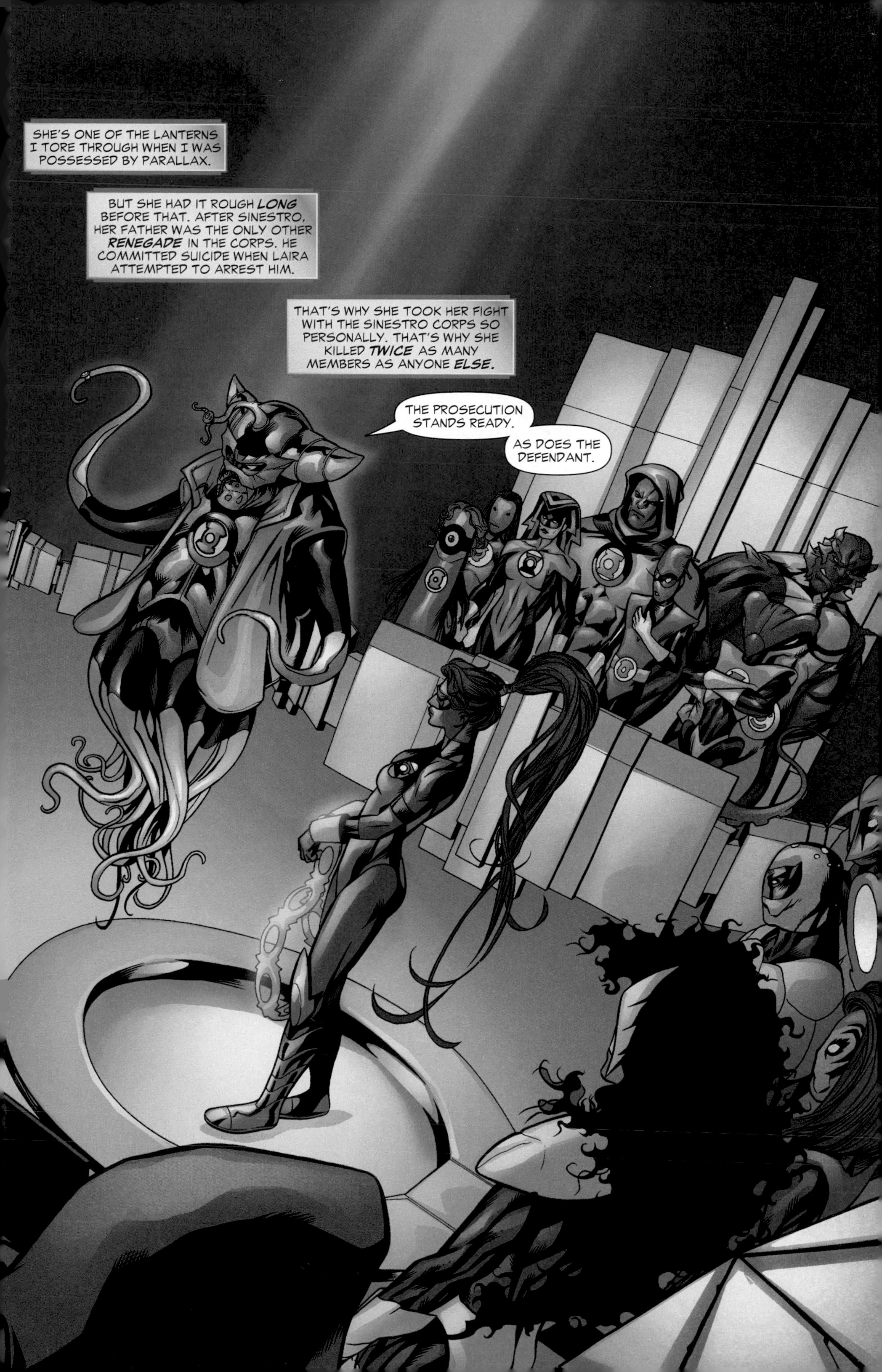
SHE'S ONE OF THE LANTERNS I TORE THROUGH WHEN I WAS POSSESSED BY PARALLAX.
BUT SHE HAD IT ROUGH LONG BEFORE THAT. AFTER SINESTRO, HER FATHER WAS THE ONLY OTHER RENEGADE IN THE CORPS. HE COMMITTED SUICIDE WHEN LAIRA ATTEMPTED TO ARREST HIM.
THAT'S WHY SHE TOOK HER FIGHT WITH THE SINESTRO CORPS SO PERSONALLY. THAT'S WHY SHE KILLED TWICE AS MANY MEMBERS AS ANYONE ELSE.
THE PROSECUTION STANDS READY.
AS DOES THE DEFENDANT.

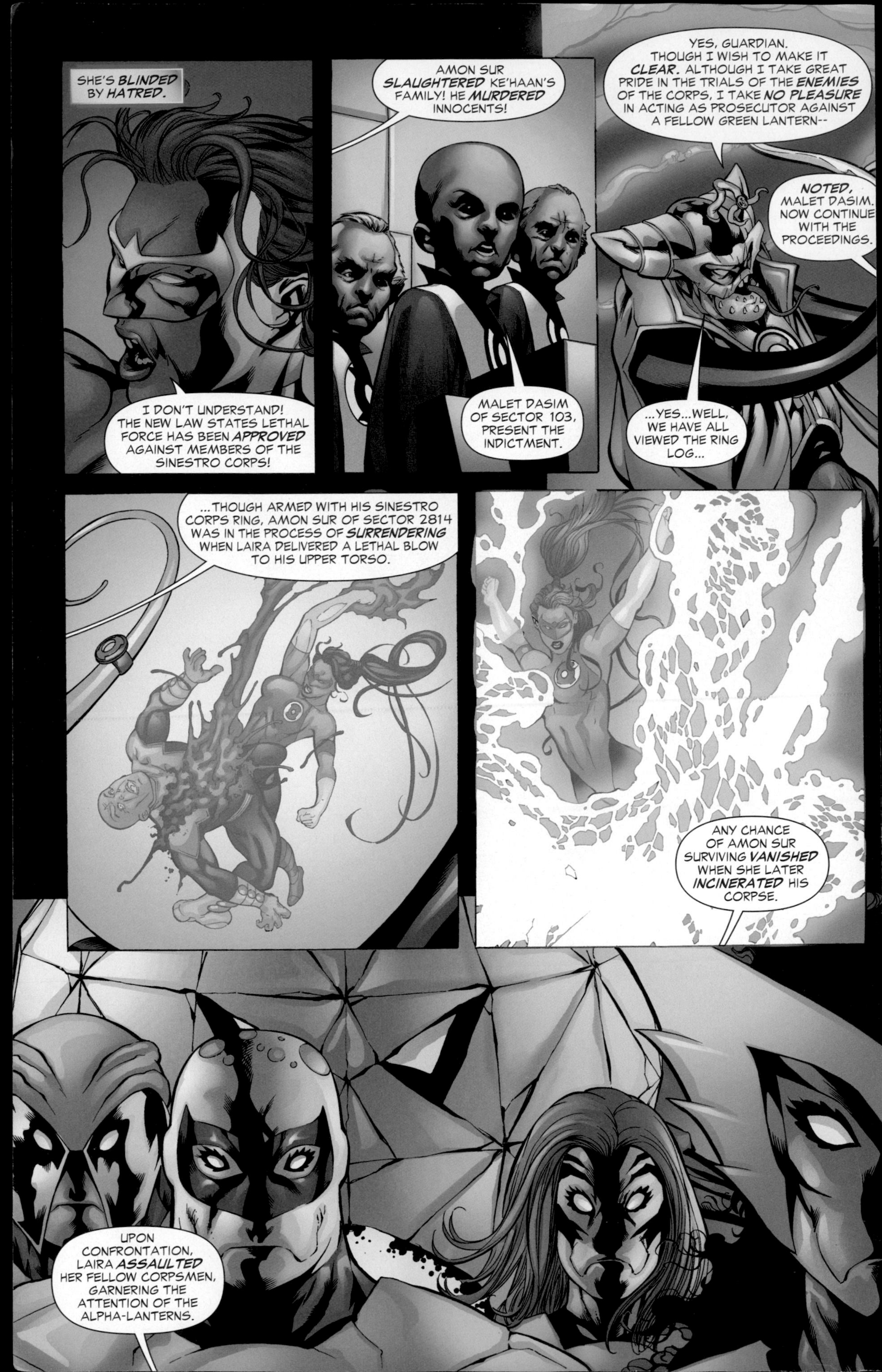
SHE'S BLINDED BY HATRED.
I DON'T UNDERSTAND! THE NEW LAW STATES LETHAL FORCE HAS BEEN APPROVED AGAINST MEMBERS OF THE SINESTRO CORPS!
AMON SUR SLAUGHTERED KE'HAAN'S FAMILY! HE MURDERED INNOCENTS!
MALET DASIM OF SECTOR 103, PRESENT THE INDICTMENT.
YES, GUARDIAN. THOUGH I WISH TO MAKE IT CLEAR. ALTHOUGH I TAKE GREAT PRIDE IN THE TRIALS OF THE ENEMIES OF THE CORPS, I TAKE NO PLEASURE IN ACTING AS PROSECUTOR AGAINST A FELLOW GREEN LANTERN--
NOTED, MALET DASIM. NOW CONTINUE WITH THE PROCEEDINGS.
...YES...WELL, WE HAVE ALL VIEWED THE RING LOG...
...THOUGH ARMED WITH HIS SINESTRO CORPS RING, AMON SUR OF SECTOR 2814 WAS IN THE PROCESS OF SURRENDERING WHEN LAIRA DELIVERED A LETHAL BLOW TO HIS UPPER TORSO.
ANY CHANCE OF AMON SUR SURVIVING VANISHED WHEN SHE LATER INCINERATED HIS CORPSE.
UPON CONFRONTATION, LAIRA ASSAULTED HER FELLOW CORPSMEN, GARNERING THE ATTENTION OF THE ALPHA-LANTERNS.

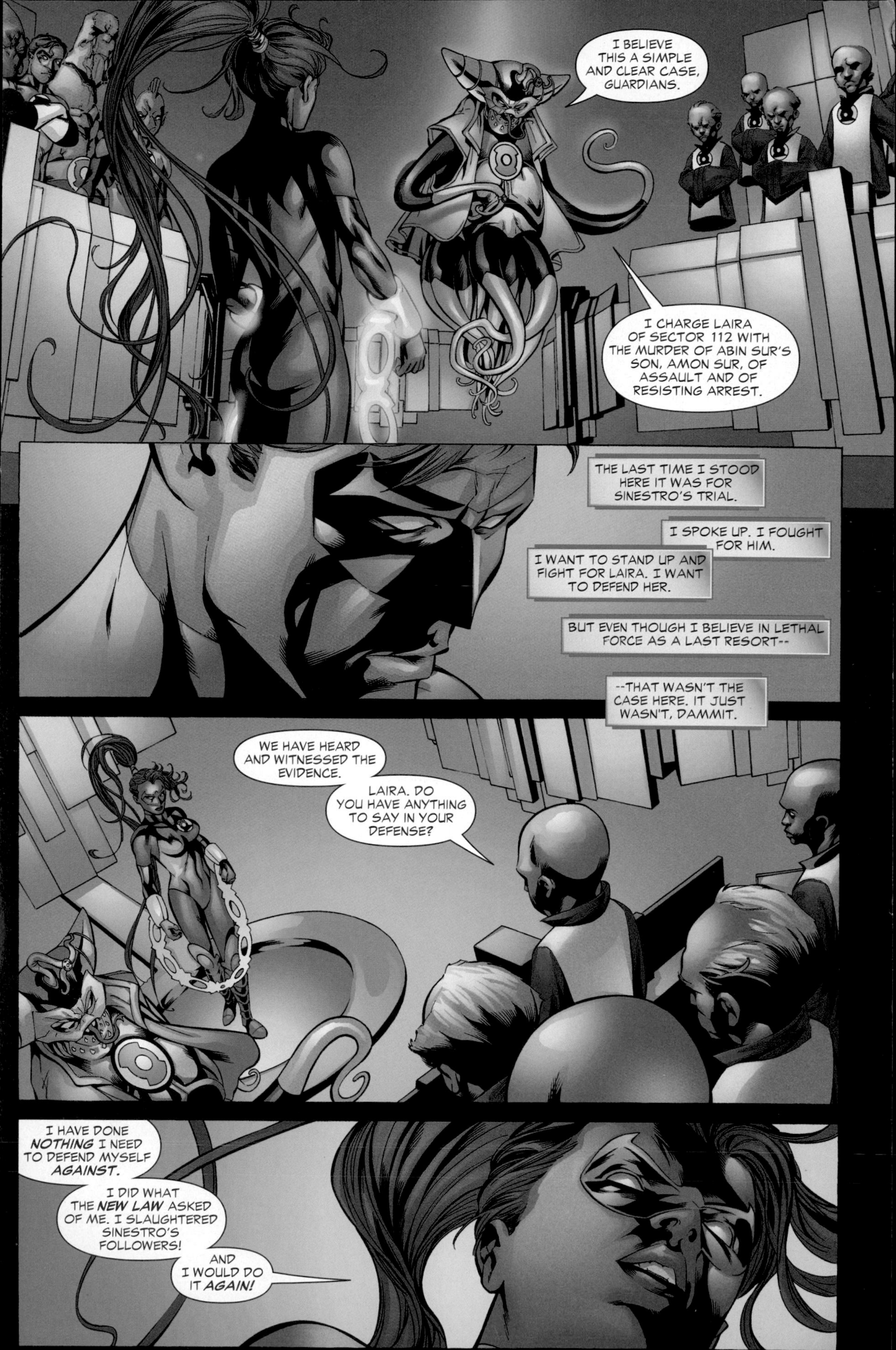

I BELIEVE THIS A SIMPLE AND CLEAR CASE, GUARDIANS.
I CHARGE LAIRA OF SECTOR 112 WITH THE MURDER OF ABIN SUR'S SON, AMON SUR, OF ASSAULT AND OF RESISTING ARREST.
THE LAST TIME I STOOD HERE IT WAS FOR SINESTRO'S TRIAL.
I SPOKE UP. I FOUGHT FOR HIM.
I WANT TO STAND UP AND FIGHT FOR LAIRA. I WANT TO DEFEND HER.
BUT EVEN THOUGH I BELIEVE IN LETHAL FORCE AS A LAST RESORT--
--THAT WASN'T THE CASE HERE. IT JUST WASN'T, DAMMIT.
WE HAVE HEARD AND WITNESSED THE EVIDENCE.
LAIRA. DO YOU HAVE ANYTHING TO SAY IN YOUR DEFENSE?
I HAVE DONE ***NOTHING*** I NEED TO DEFEND MYSELF ***AGAINST.***
I DID WHAT THE ***NEW LAW*** ASKED OF ME. I SLAUGHTERED SINESTRO'S FOLLOWERS!
AND I WOULD DO IT ***AGAIN!***

YOU ABUSED THE POWER OF THE RING, LAIRA.

YOU LASHED OUT WITH THE *ANGER* THAT LURKS IN YOUR HEART. YOU ARE ON THE ROAD TO BECOMING A *RENEGADE* OF THE GREEN LANTERN CORPS.

ALPHA-LANTERN BOODIKKA.

WHAT IS YOUR JUDGMENT?

AFTER ALL WE'VE BEEN THROUGH...ON THE MANHUNTER HOMEWORLD, ON QWARD, YOU TURN YOUR BACK ON ME *NOW?*

I HAVE REDEDICATED MYSELF TO *JUSTICE,* LAIRA. THAT IS ALL.

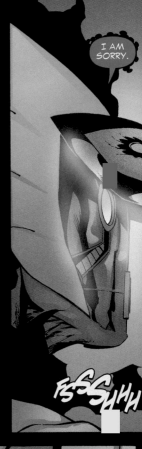

I AM SORRY.

FSSSHHH

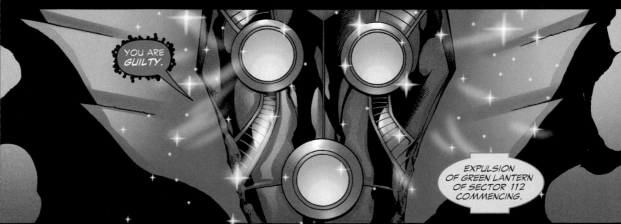

YOU ARE *GUILTY.*

EXPULSION OF GREEN LANTERN OF SECTOR 112 COMMENCING.

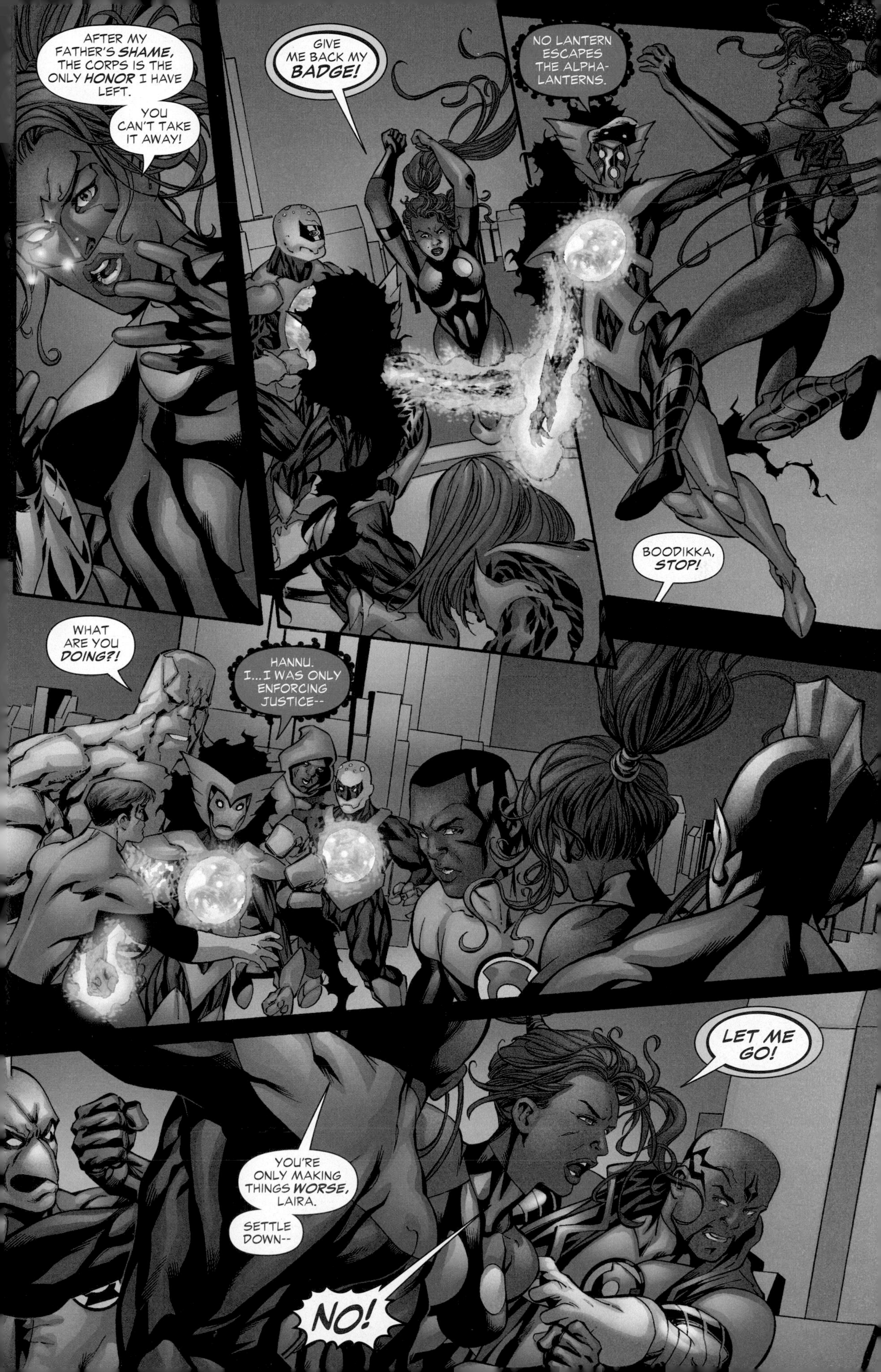
AFTER MY FATHER'S SHAME, THE CORPS IS THE ONLY HONOR I HAVE LEFT.
YOU CAN'T TAKE IT AWAY!
GIVE ME BACK MY BADGE!
NO LANTERN ESCAPES THE ALPHA-LANTERNS.
BOODIKKA, STOP!
WHAT ARE YOU DOING?!
HANNU. I...I WAS ONLY ENFORCING JUSTICE--
LET ME GO!
YOU'RE ONLY MAKING THINGS WORSE, LAIRA.
SETTLE DOWN--
NO!

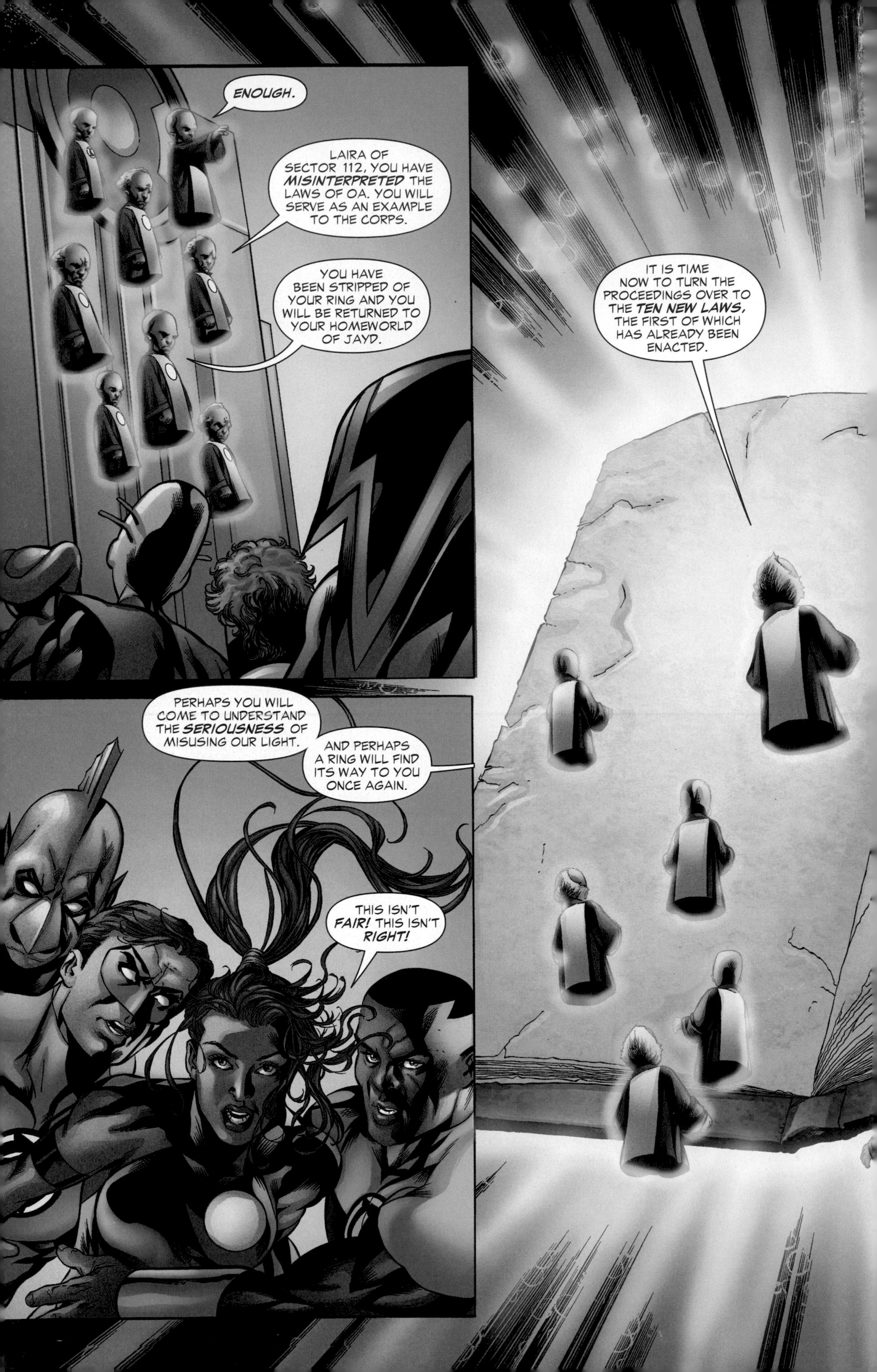
ENOUGH.
LAIRA OF SECTOR 112, YOU HAVE MISINTERPRETED THE LAWS OF OA. YOU WILL SERVE AS AN EXAMPLE TO THE CORPS.
YOU HAVE BEEN STRIPPED OF YOUR RING AND YOU WILL BE RETURNED TO YOUR HOMEWORLD OF JAYD.
PERHAPS YOU WILL COME TO UNDERSTAND THE SERIOUSNESS OF MISUSING OUR LIGHT.
AND PERHAPS A RING WILL FIND ITS WAY TO YOU ONCE AGAIN.
THIS ISN'T FAIR! THIS ISN'T RIGHT!
IT IS TIME NOW TO TURN THE PROCEEDINGS OVER TO THE TEN NEW LAWS, THE FIRST OF WHICH HAS ALREADY BEEN ENACTED.

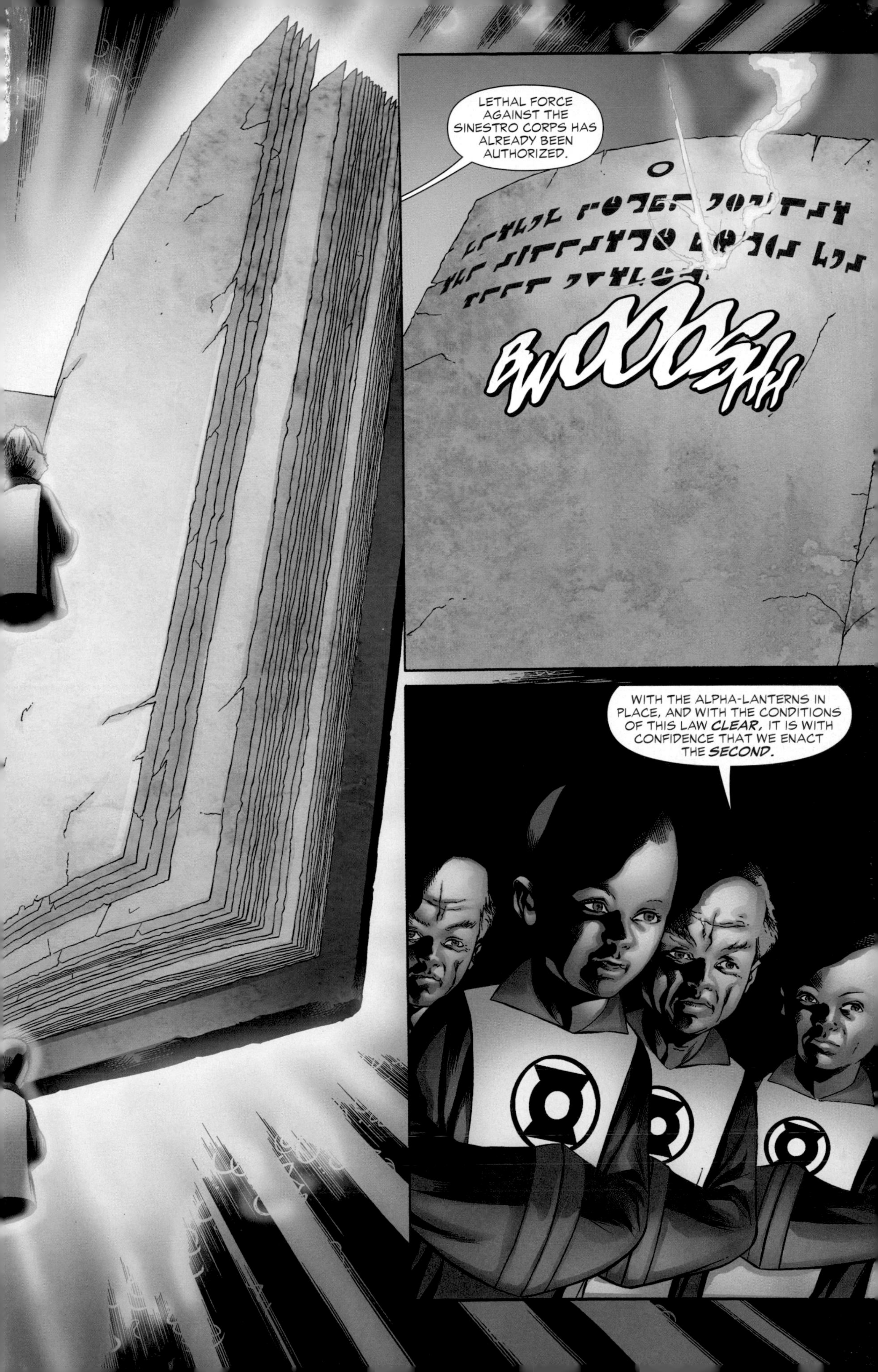
LETHAL FORCE AGAINST THE SINESTRO CORPS HAS ALREADY BEEN AUTHORIZED.
BWOOOSHH
WITH THE ALPHA-LANTERNS IN PLACE, AND WITH THE CONDITIONS OF THIS LAW CLEAR, IT IS WITH CONFIDENCE THAT WE ENACT THE SECOND.

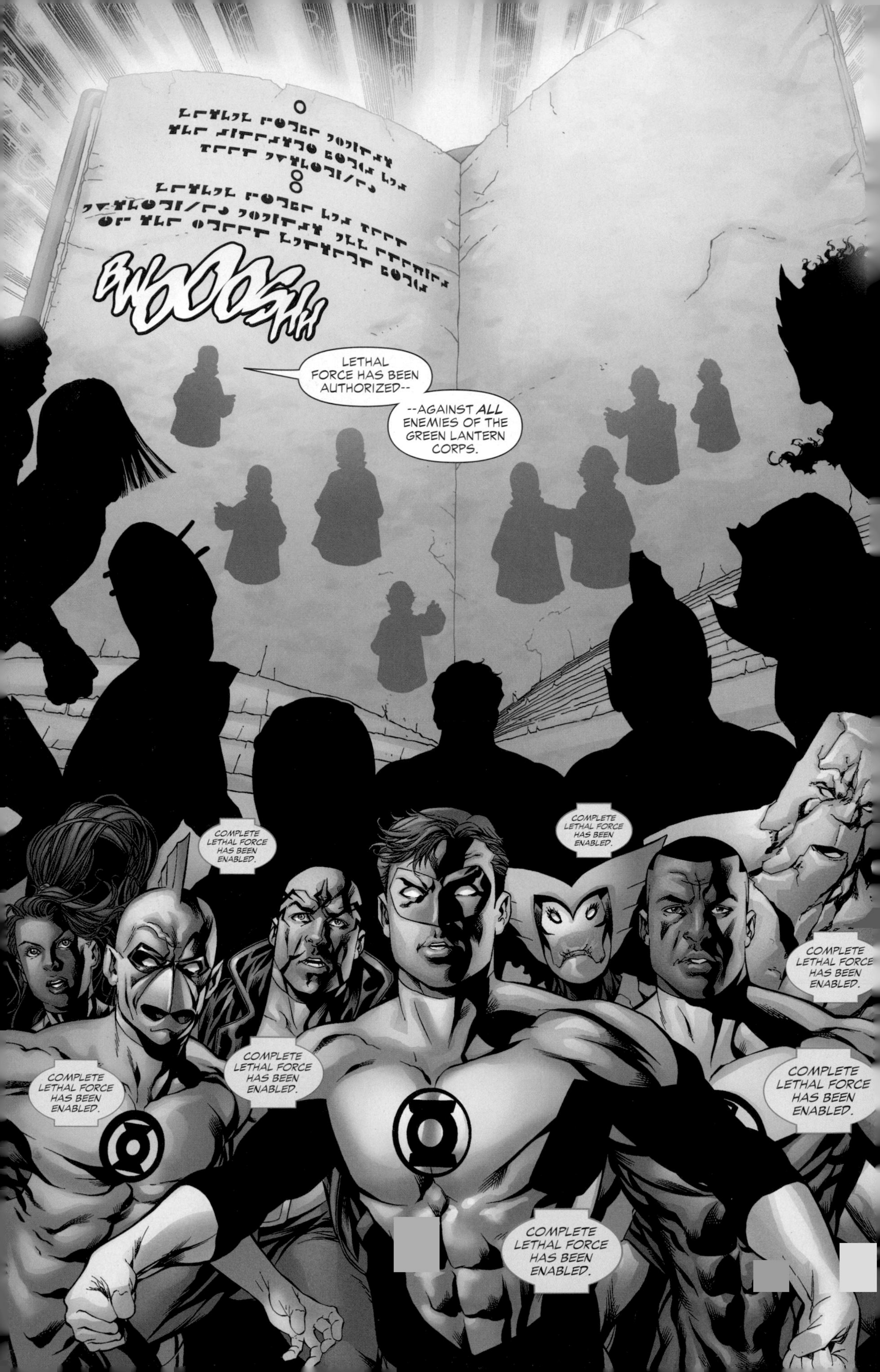
BWOOOSHH
LETHAL FORCE HAS BEEN AUTHORIZED--
--AGAINST ALL ENEMIES OF THE GREEN LANTERN CORPS.
COMPLETE LETHAL FORCE HAS BEEN ENABLED.
COMPLETE LETHAL FORCE HAS BEEN ENABLED.
COMPLETE LETHAL FORCE HAS BEEN ENABLED.
COMPLETE LETHAL FORCE HAS BEEN ENABLED.
COMPLETE LETHAL FORCE HAS BEEN ENABLED.
COMPLETE LETHAL FORCE HAS BEEN ENABLED.
COMPLETE LETHAL FORCE HAS BEEN ENABLED.

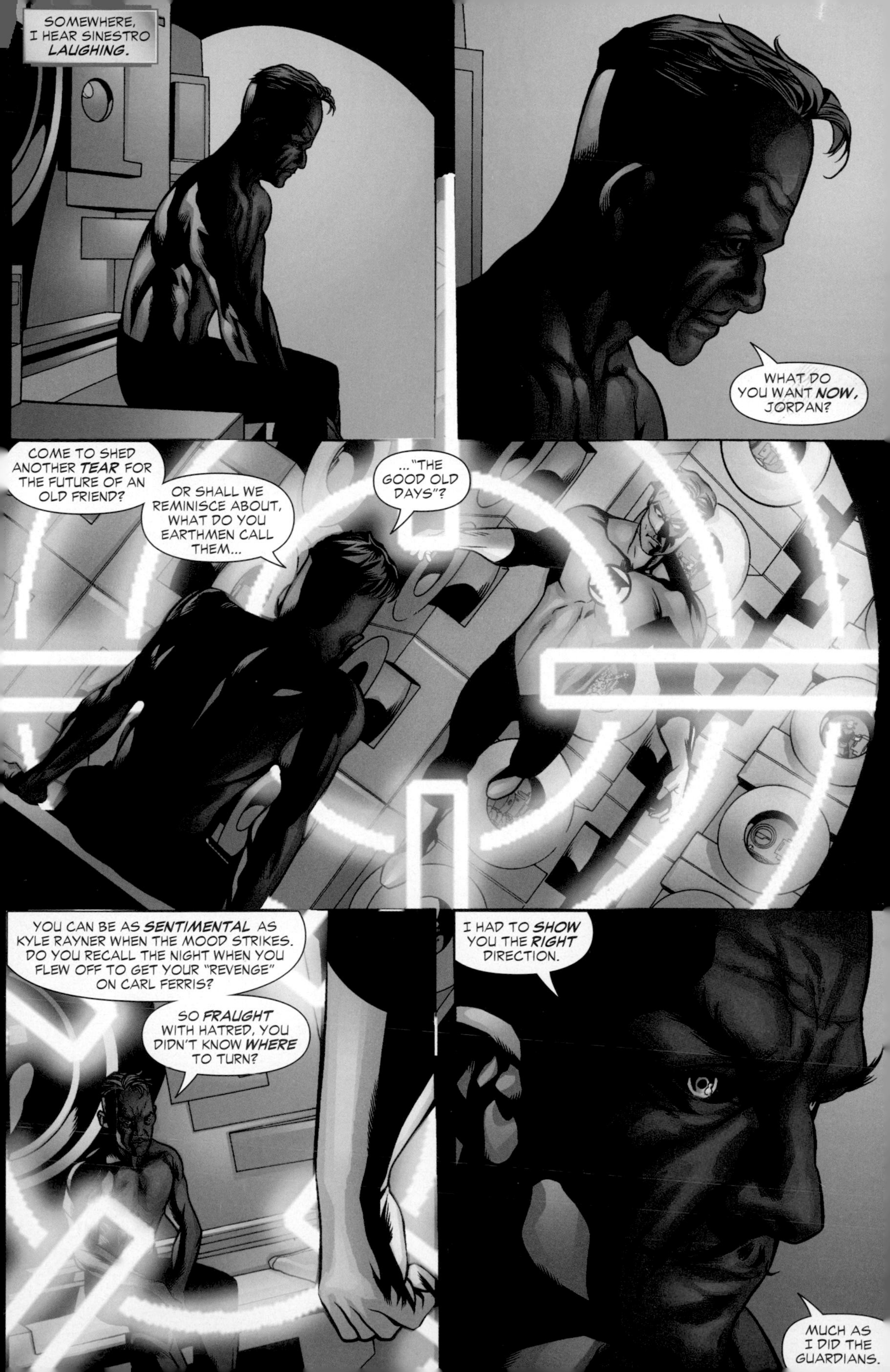
SOMEWHERE, I HEAR SINESTRO LAUGHING.
WHAT DO YOU WANT NOW, JORDAN?
COME TO SHED ANOTHER TEAR FOR THE FUTURE OF AN OLD FRIEND?
OR SHALL WE REMINISCE ABOUT, WHAT DO YOU EARTHMEN CALL THEM...
..."THE GOOD OLD DAYS"?
YOU CAN BE AS SENTIMENTAL AS KYLE RAYNER WHEN THE MOOD STRIKES. DO YOU RECALL THE NIGHT WHEN YOU FLEW OFF TO GET YOUR "REVENGE" ON CARL FERRIS?
SO FRAUGHT WITH HATRED, YOU DIDN'T KNOW WHERE TO TURN?
I HAD TO SHOW YOU THE RIGHT DIRECTION.
MUCH AS I DID THE GUARDIANS.

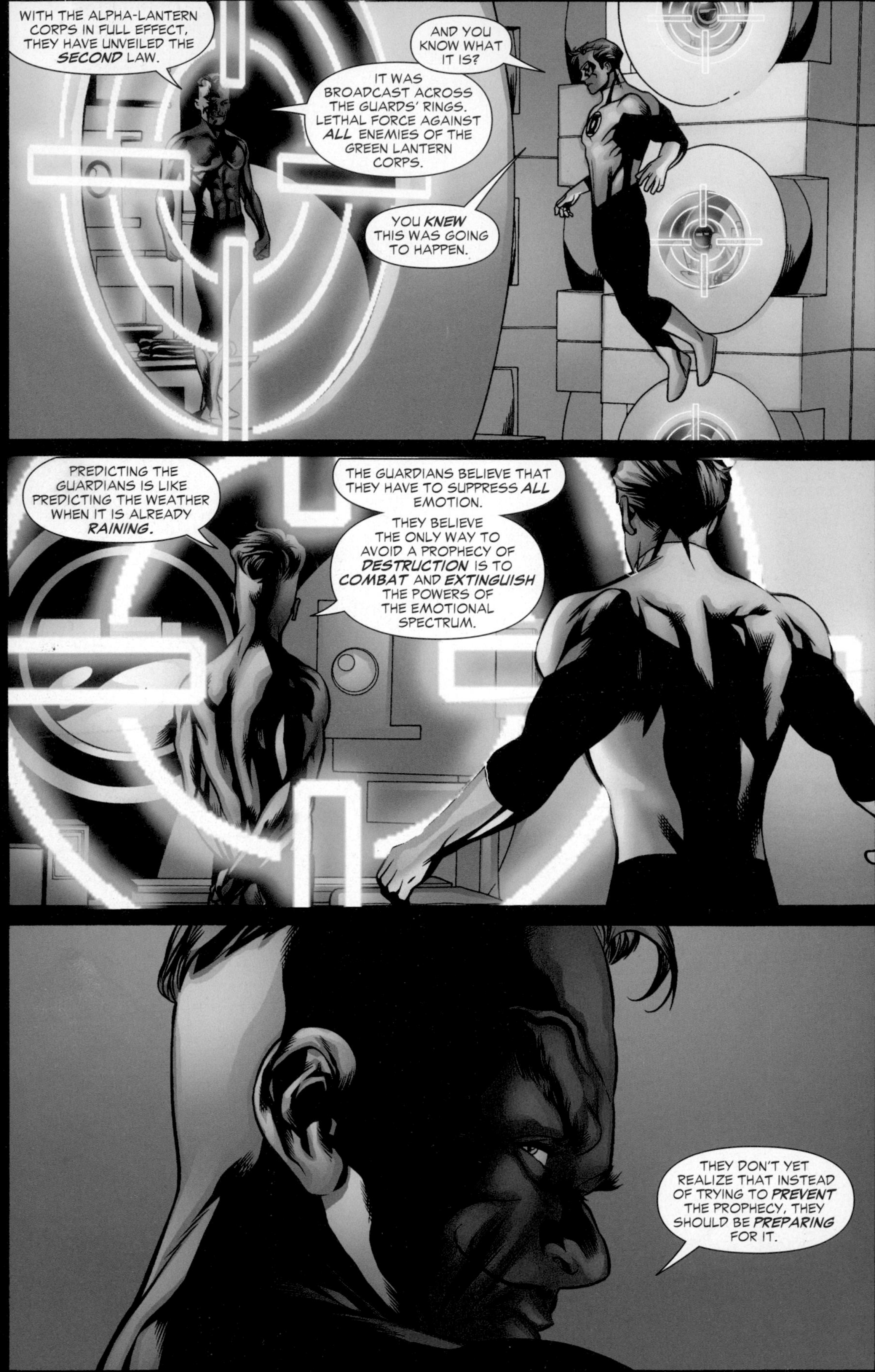
WITH THE ALPHA-LANTERN CORPS IN FULL EFFECT, THEY HAVE UNVEILED THE SECOND LAW.
AND YOU KNOW WHAT IT IS?
IT WAS BROADCAST ACROSS THE GUARDS' RINGS. LETHAL FORCE AGAINST ALL ENEMIES OF THE GREEN LANTERN CORPS.
YOU KNEW THIS WAS GOING TO HAPPEN.
PREDICTING THE GUARDIANS IS LIKE PREDICTING THE WEATHER WHEN IT IS ALREADY RAINING.
THE GUARDIANS BELIEVE THAT THEY HAVE TO SUPPRESS ALL EMOTION.
THEY BELIEVE THE ONLY WAY TO AVOID A PROPHECY OF DESTRUCTION IS TO COMBAT AND EXTINGUISH THE POWERS OF THE EMOTIONAL SPECTRUM.
THEY DON'T YET REALIZE THAT INSTEAD OF TRYING TO PREVENT THE PROPHECY, THEY SHOULD BE PREPARING FOR IT.

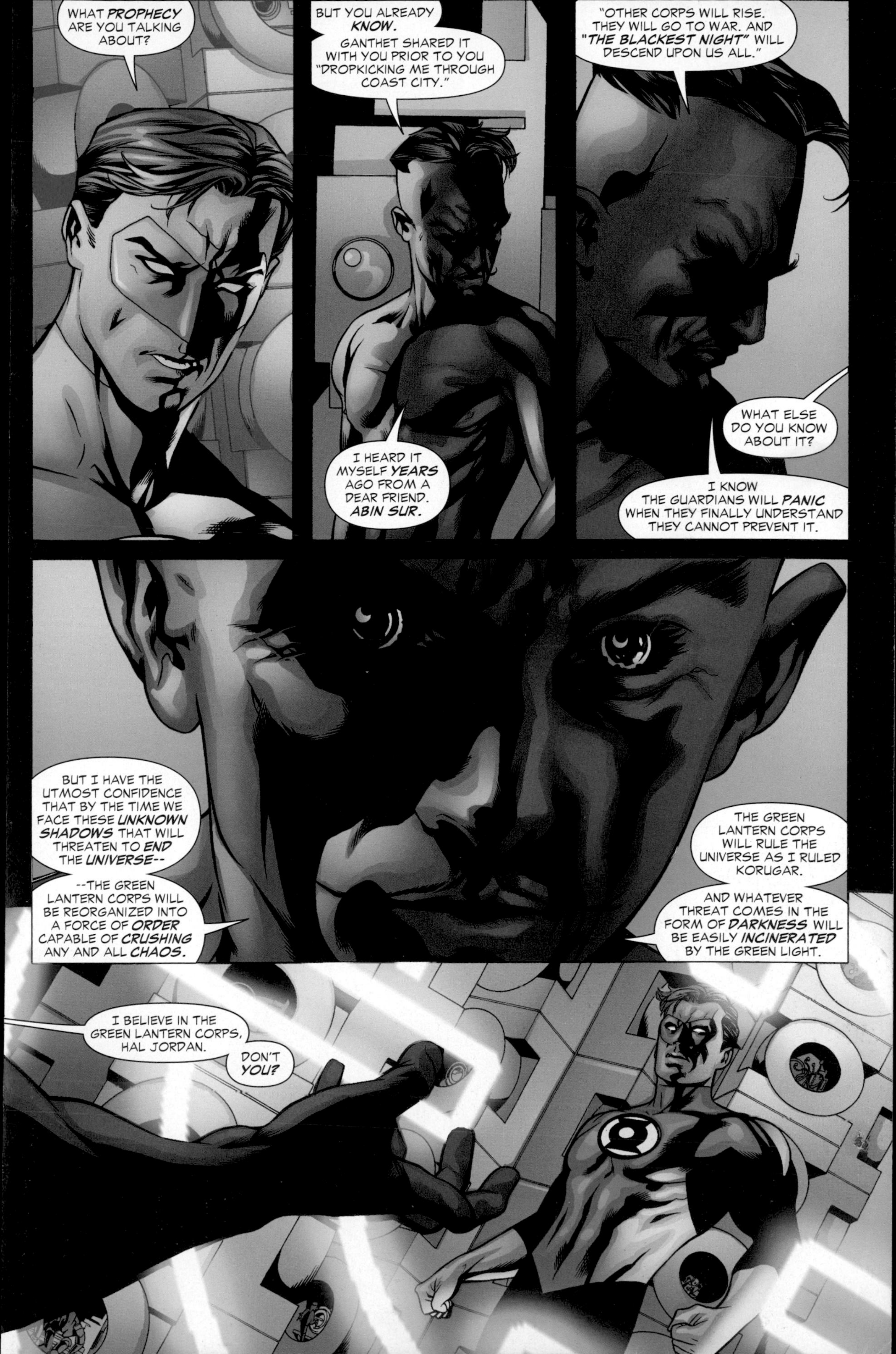

WHAT PROPHECY ARE YOU TALKING ABOUT?
BUT YOU ALREADY KNOW.
GANTHET SHARED IT WITH YOU PRIOR TO YOU "DROPKICKING ME THROUGH COAST CITY."
I HEARD IT MYSELF YEARS AGO FROM A DEAR FRIEND. ABIN SUR.
"OTHER CORPS WILL RISE. THEY WILL GO TO WAR. AND "THE BLACKEST NIGHT" WILL DESCEND UPON US ALL."
WHAT ELSE DO YOU KNOW ABOUT IT?
I KNOW THE GUARDIANS WILL PANIC WHEN THEY FINALLY UNDERSTAND THEY CANNOT PREVENT IT.
BUT I HAVE THE UTMOST CONFIDENCE THAT BY THE TIME WE FACE THESE UNKNOWN SHADOWS THAT WILL THREATEN TO END THE UNIVERSE--
--THE GREEN LANTERN CORPS WILL BE REORGANIZED INTO A FORCE OF ORDER CAPABLE OF CRUSHING ANY AND ALL CHAOS.
THE GREEN LANTERN CORPS WILL RULE THE UNIVERSE AS I RULED KORUGAR.
AND WHATEVER THREAT COMES IN THE FORM OF DARKNESS WILL BE EASILY INCINERATED BY THE GREEN LIGHT.
I BELIEVE IN THE GREEN LANTERN CORPS, HAL JORDAN.
DON'T YOU?

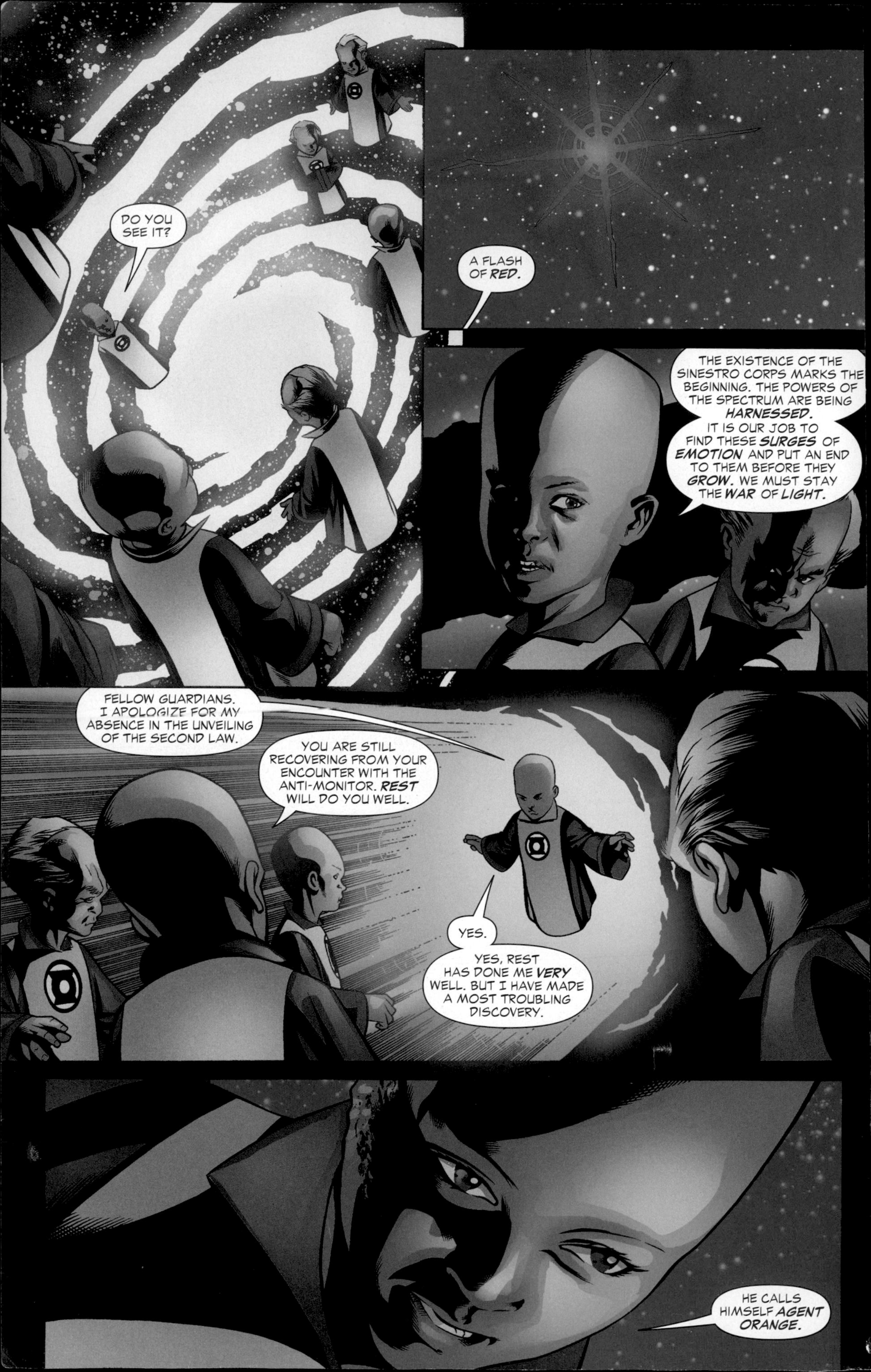
DO YOU SEE IT?
A FLASH OF RED.
THE EXISTENCE OF THE SINESTRO CORPS MARKS THE BEGINNING. THE POWERS OF THE SPECTRUM ARE BEING HARNESSED. IT IS OUR JOB TO FIND THESE SURGES OF EMOTION AND PUT AN END TO THEM BEFORE THEY GROW. WE MUST STAY THE WAR OF LIGHT.
FELLOW GUARDIANS. I APOLOGIZE FOR MY ABSENCE IN THE UNVEILING OF THE SECOND LAW.
YOU ARE STILL RECOVERING FROM YOUR ENCOUNTER WITH THE ANTI-MONITOR. REST WILL DO YOU WELL.
YES.
YES, REST HAS DONE ME VERY WELL. BUT I HAVE MADE A MOST TROUBLING DISCOVERY.
HE CALLS HIMSELF AGENT ORANGE.

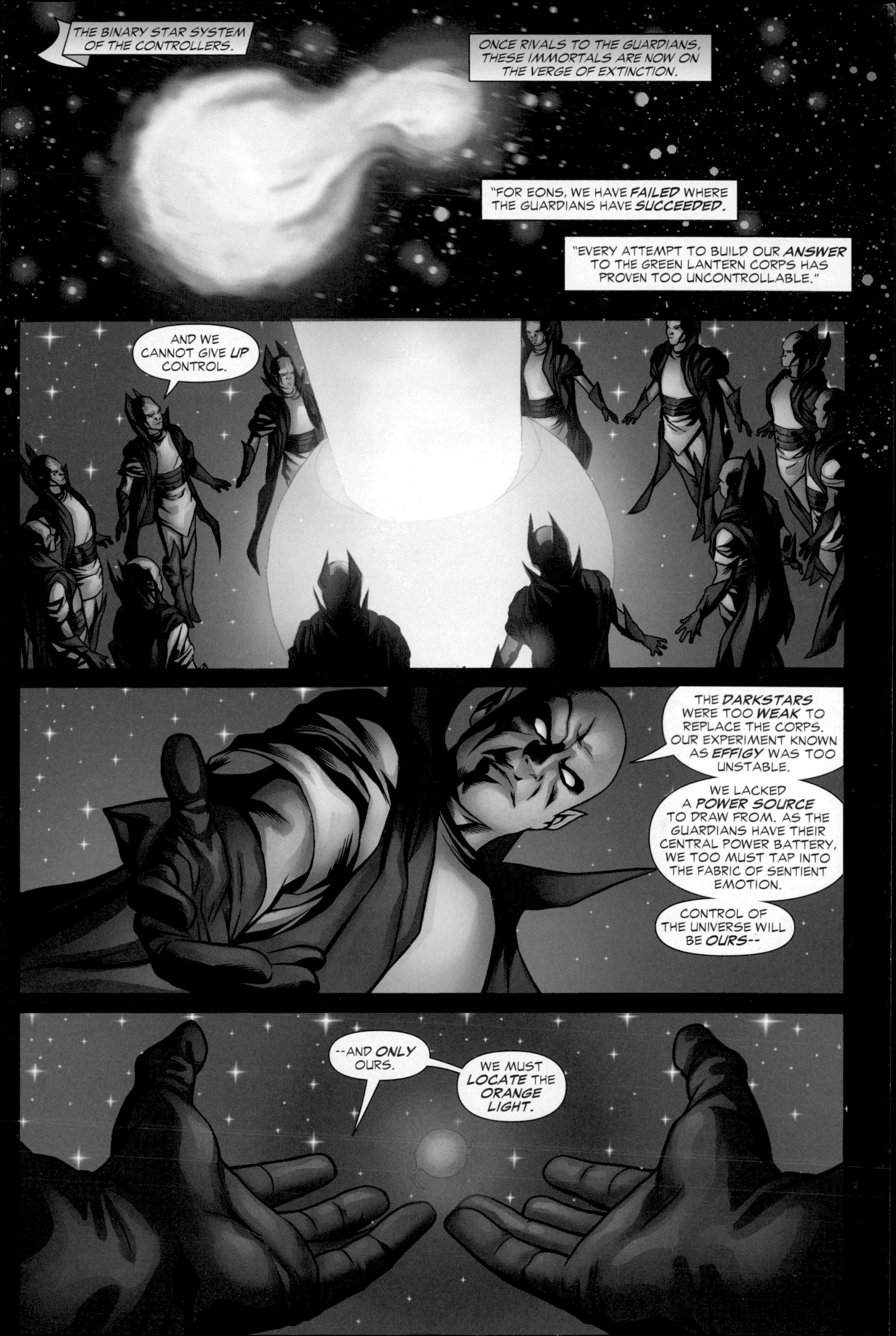

THE BINARY STAR SYSTEM OF THE CONTROLLERS.
ONCE RIVALS TO THE GUARDIANS, THESE IMMORTALS ARE NOW ON THE VERGE OF EXTINCTION.
"FOR EONS, WE HAVE FAILED WHERE THE GUARDIANS HAVE SUCCEEDED.
"EVERY ATTEMPT TO BUILD OUR ANSWER TO THE GREEN LANTERN CORPS HAS PROVEN TOO UNCONTROLLABLE."
AND WE CANNOT GIVE UP CONTROL.
THE DARKSTARS WERE TOO WEAK TO REPLACE THE CORPS. OUR EXPERIMENT KNOWN AS EFFIGY WAS TOO UNSTABLE.
WE LACKED A POWER SOURCE TO DRAW FROM. AS THE GUARDIANS HAVE THEIR CENTRAL POWER BATTERY, WE TOO MUST TAP INTO THE FABRIC OF SENTIENT EMOTION.
CONTROL OF THE UNIVERSE WILL BE OURS--
--AND ONLY OURS.
WE MUST LOCATE THE ORANGE LIGHT.

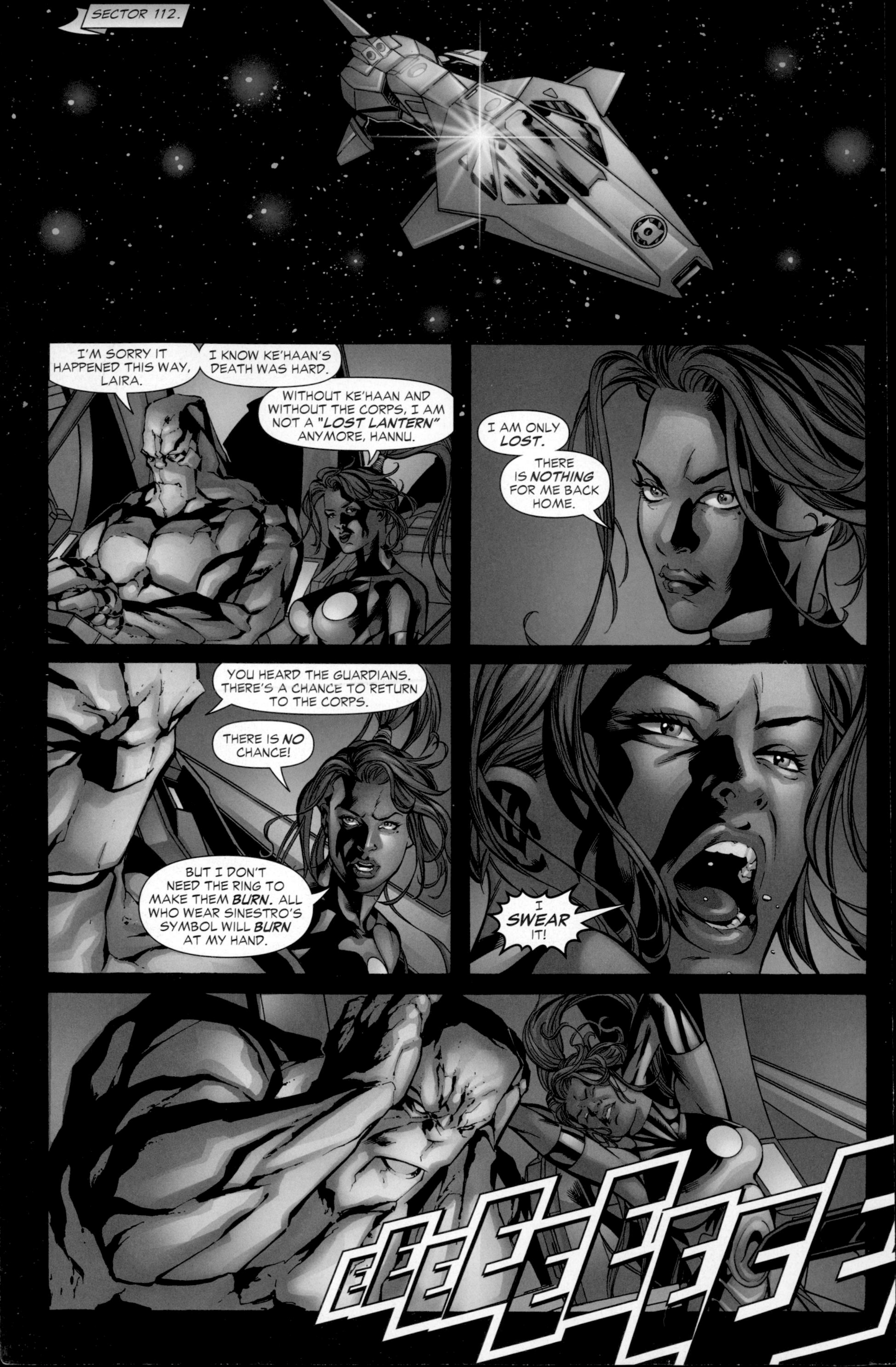
SECTOR 112.
I'M SORRY IT HAPPENED THIS WAY, LAIRA.
I KNOW KE'HAAN'S DEATH WAS HARD.
WITHOUT KE'HAAN AND WITHOUT THE CORPS, I AM NOT A "LOST LANTERN" ANYMORE, HANNU.
I AM ONLY LOST.
THERE IS NOTHING FOR ME BACK HOME.
YOU HEARD THE GUARDIANS. THERE'S A CHANCE TO RETURN TO THE CORPS.
THERE IS NO CHANCE!
BUT I DON'T NEED THE RING TO MAKE THEM BURN. ALL WHO WEAR SINESTRO'S SYMBOL WILL BURN AT MY HAND.
I SWEAR IT!
EEEEEEEEE

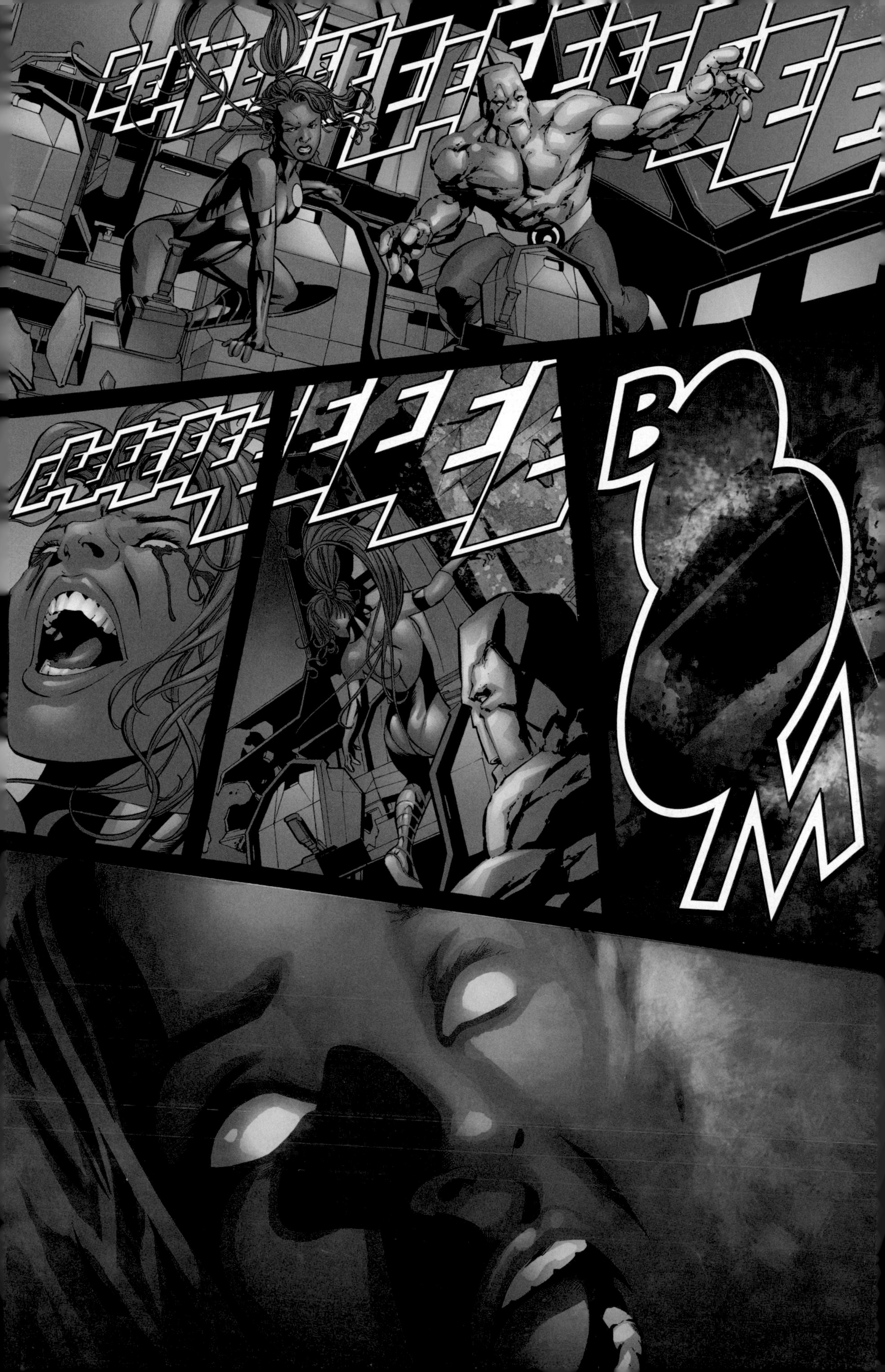
EEEEEEEEEEEEEEEE
EEEEEEEEEE
BOOM

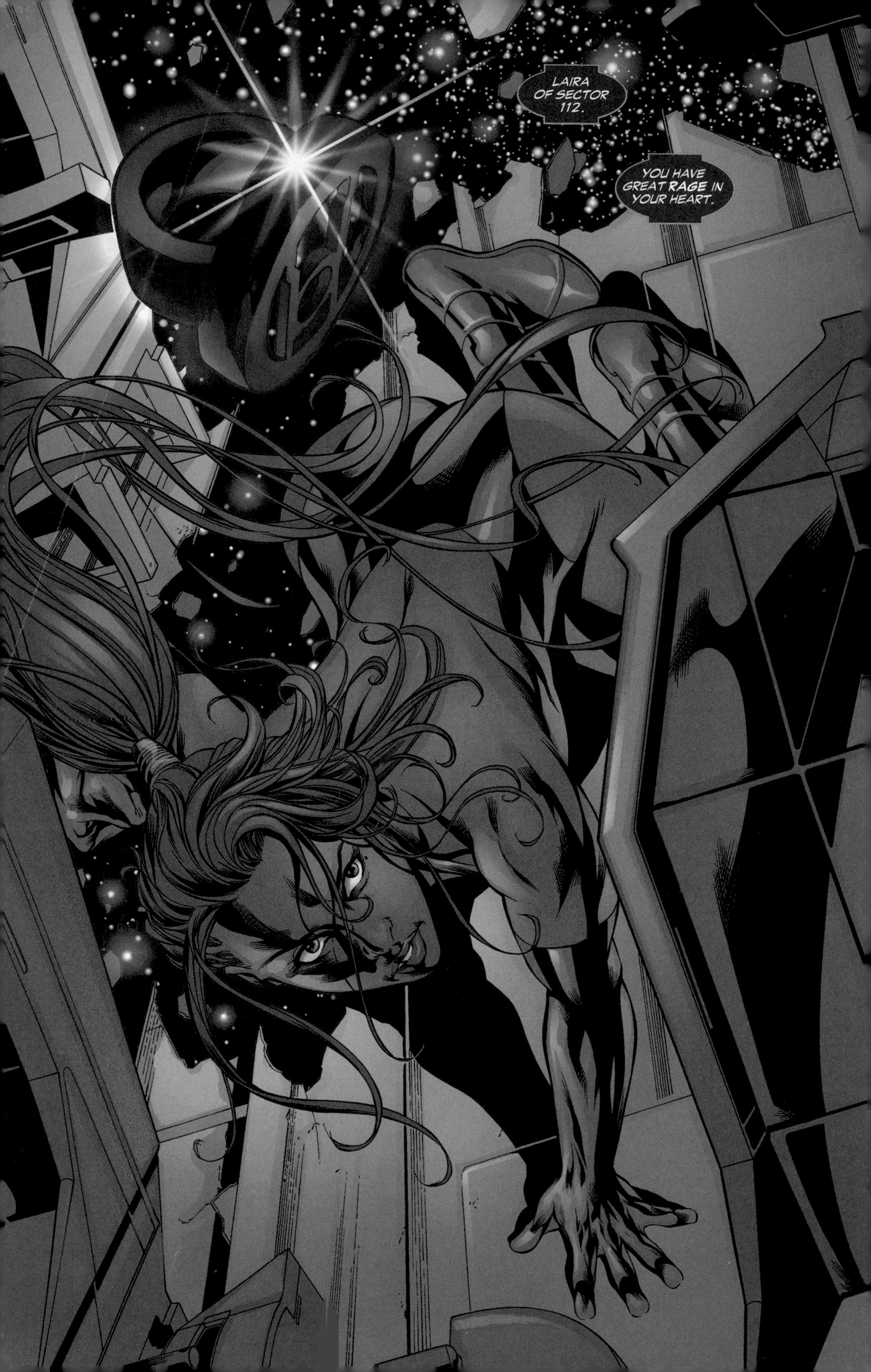
LAIRA OF SECTOR 112.
YOU HAVE GREAT RAGE IN YOUR HEART.

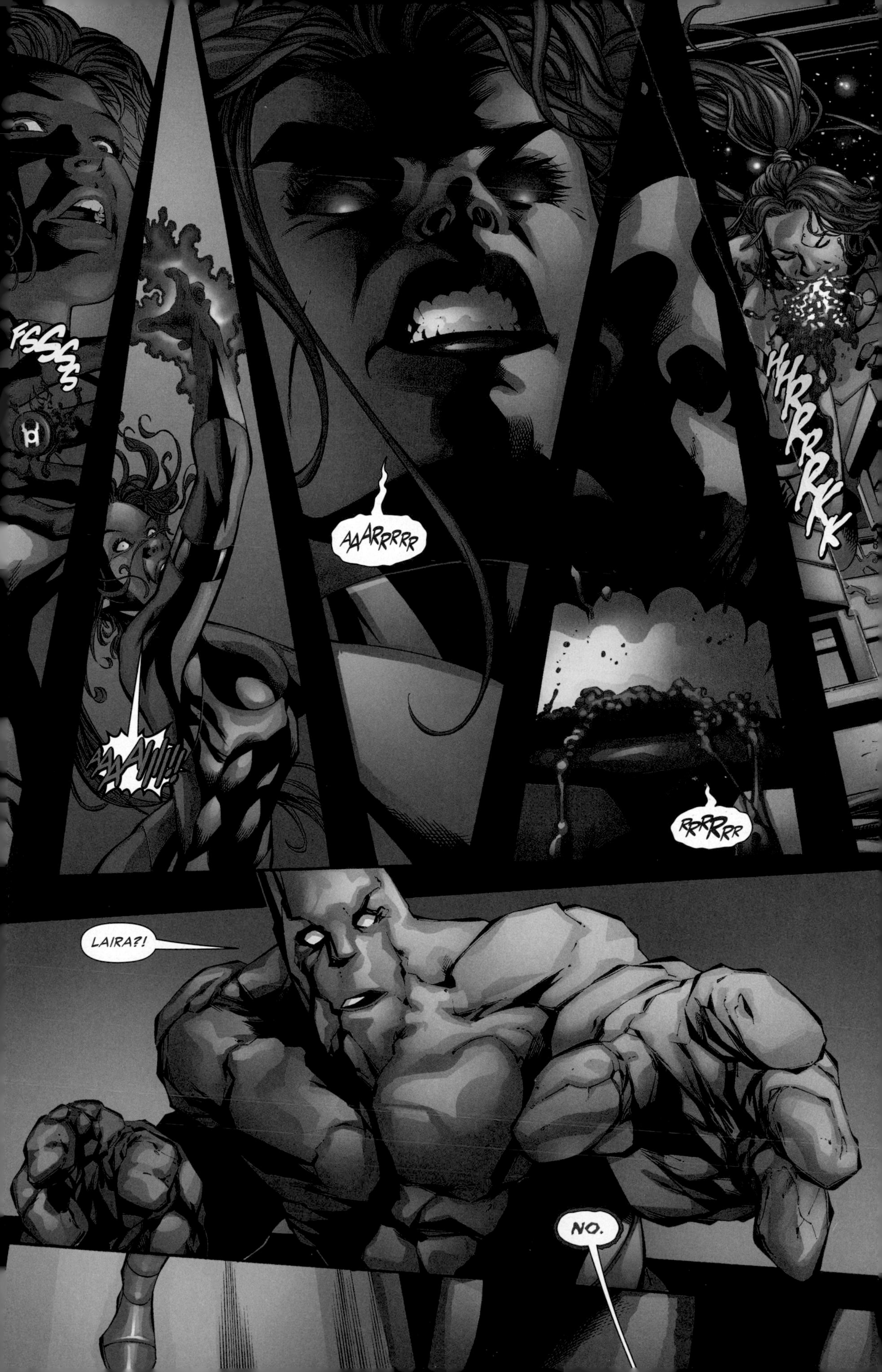

FSSSSS
AAAAIIII!
AAARRRRR
HHRRRRKKK
RRRRRR
LAIRA?!
NO.

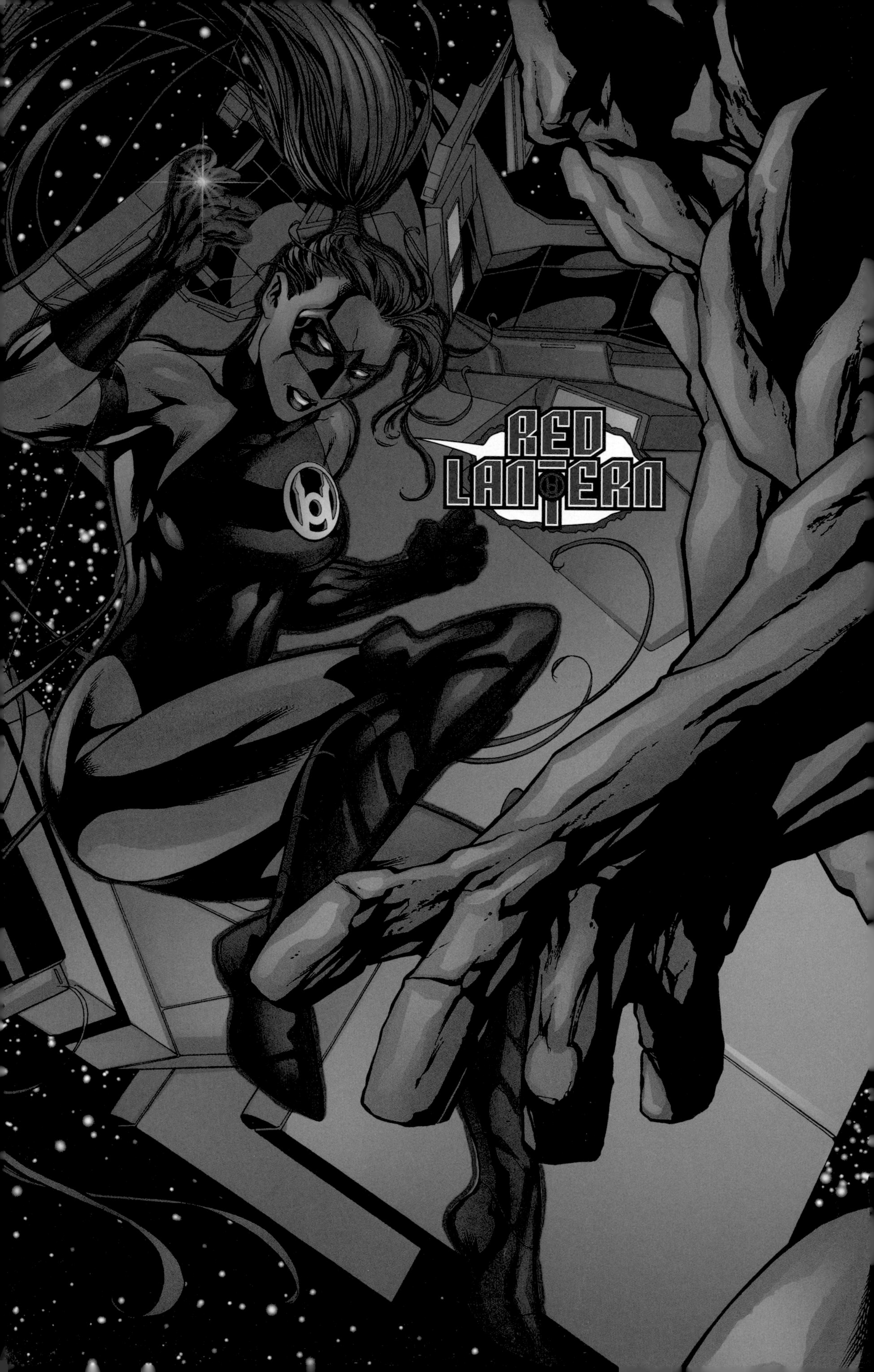
RED
LANTERN

FINAL CRISIS: RAGE OF THE RED LANTERNS
Cover by Shane Davis, Sandra Hope and Nei Ruffino

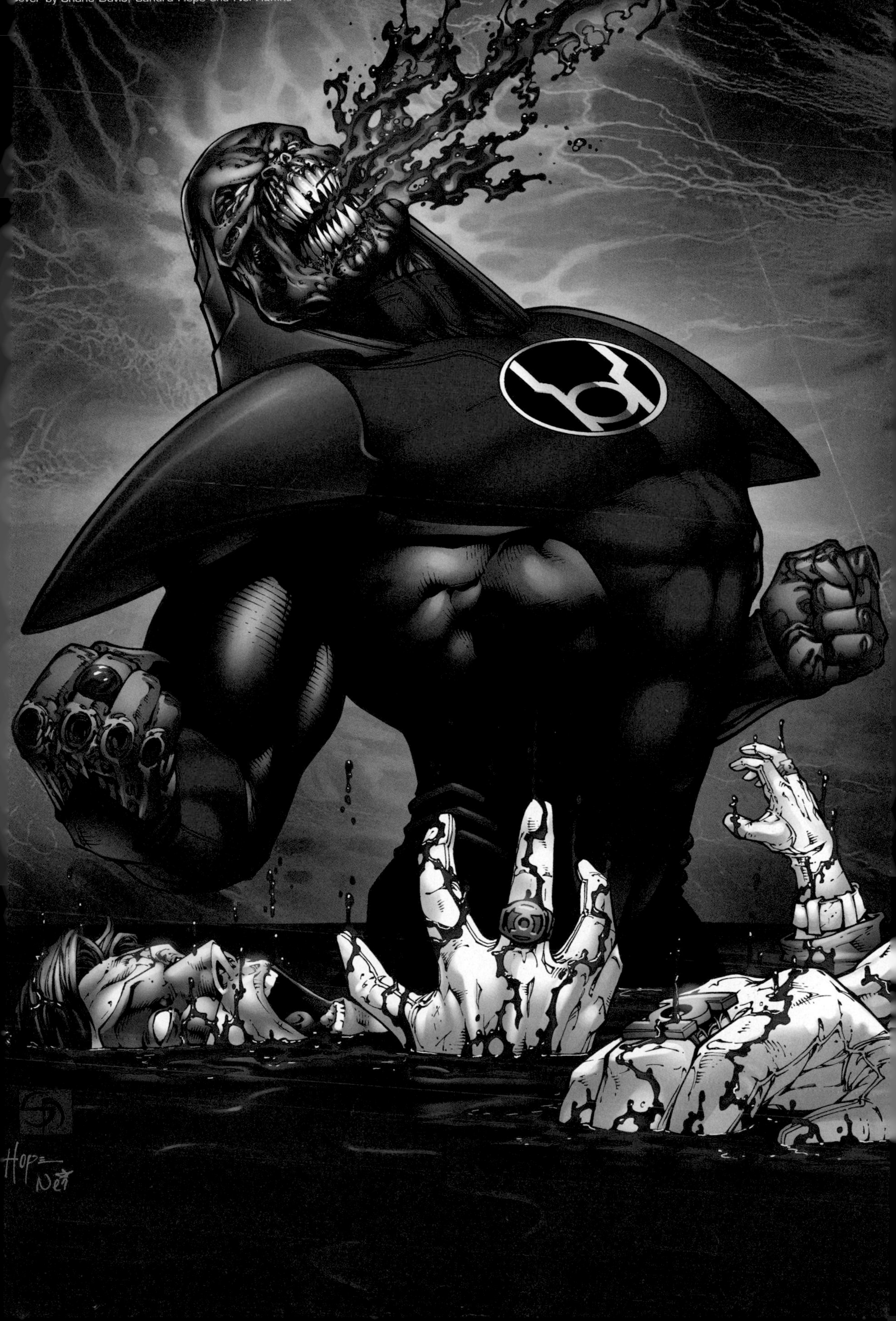
Hope
Nei

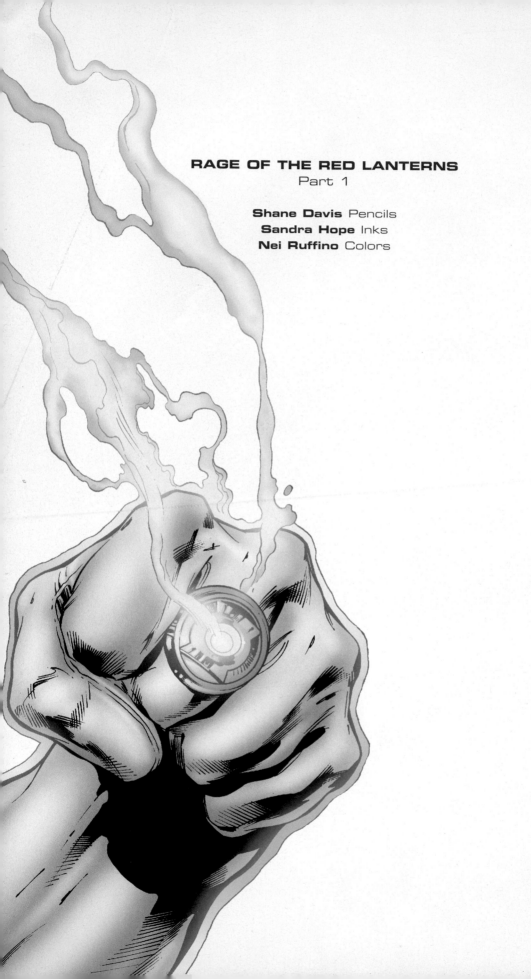

RAGE OF THE RED LANTERNS
Part 1

Shane Davis Pencils
Sandra Hope Inks
Nei Ruffino Colors

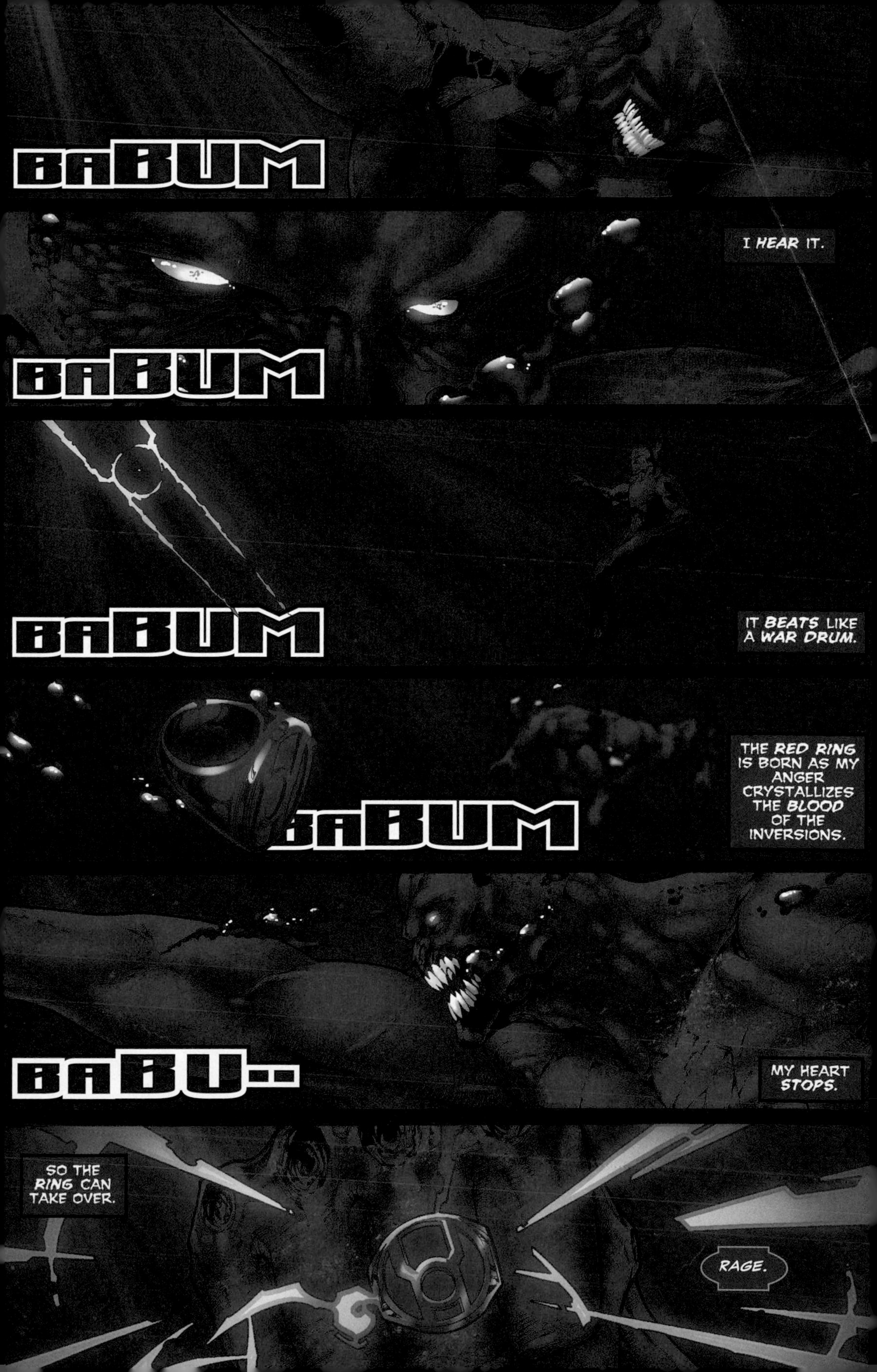

BABUM
I HEAR IT.
BABUM
BABUM
IT BEATS LIKE A WAR DRUM.
THE RED RING IS BORN AS MY ANGER CRYSTALLIZES THE BLOOD OF THE INVERSIONS.
BABUM
MY HEART STOPS.
BABU--
SO THE RING CAN TAKE OVER.
RAGE.

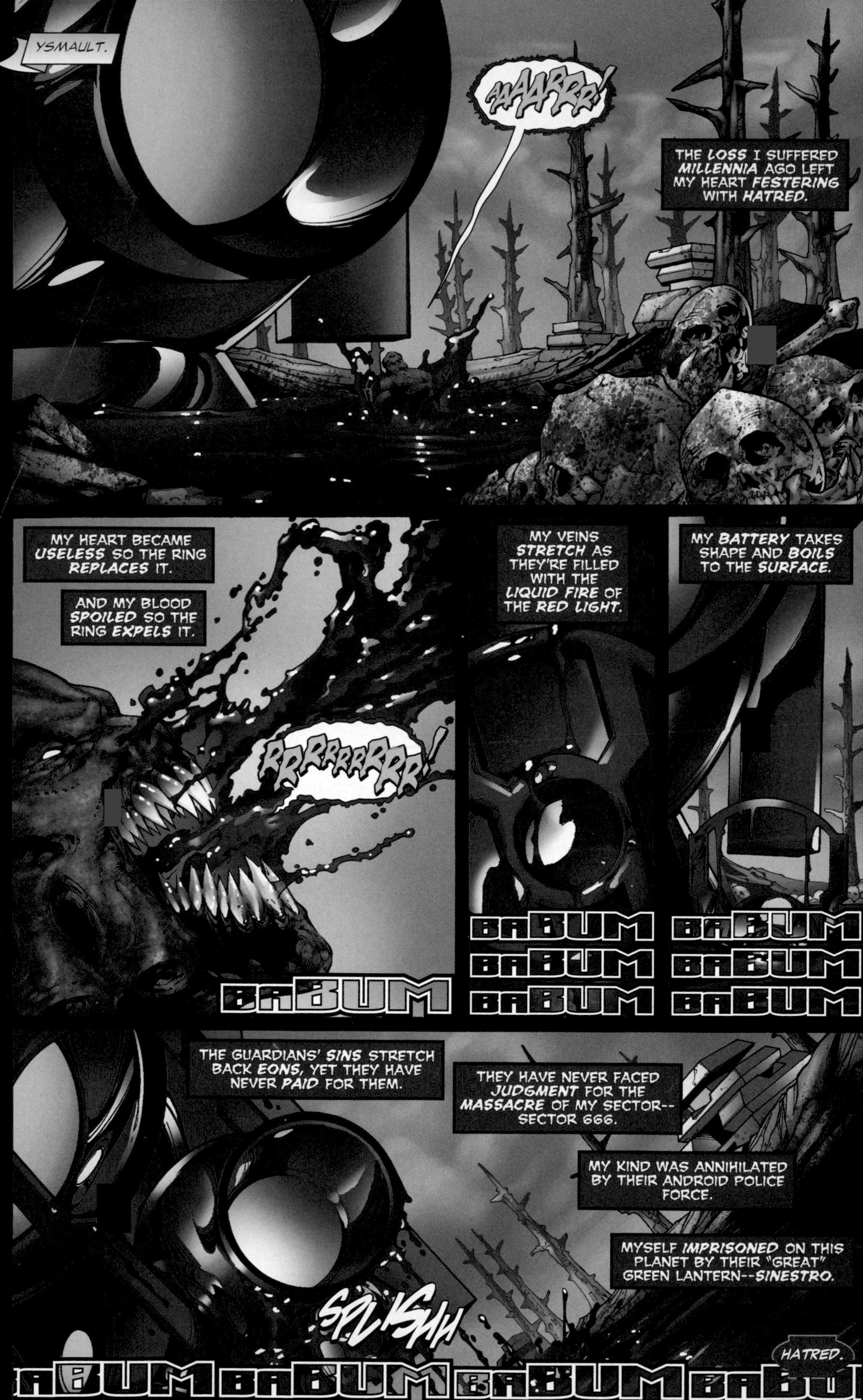

YSMAULT.
AAAARRR!
THE LOSS I SUFFERED MILLENNIA AGO LEFT MY HEART FESTERING WITH HATRED.
MY HEART BECAME USELESS SO THE RING REPLACES IT.
AND MY BLOOD SPOILED SO THE RING EXPELS IT.
RRRRRRRRR!
BABUM
MY VEINS STRETCH AS THEY'RE FILLED WITH THE LIQUID FIRE OF THE RED LIGHT.
BABUM
BABUM
BABUM
MY BATTERY TAKES SHAPE AND BOILS TO THE SURFACE.
BABUM
BABUM
BABUM
THE GUARDIANS' SINS STRETCH BACK EONS, YET THEY HAVE NEVER PAID FOR THEM.
THEY HAVE NEVER FACED JUDGMENT FOR THE MASSACRE OF MY SECTOR-- SECTOR 666.
MY KIND WAS ANNIHILATED BY THEIR ANDROID POLICE FORCE.
MYSELF IMPRISONED ON THIS PLANET BY THEIR "GREAT" GREEN LANTERN--SINESTRO.
SPLISHH
HATRED.
BUM BABUM BABUM

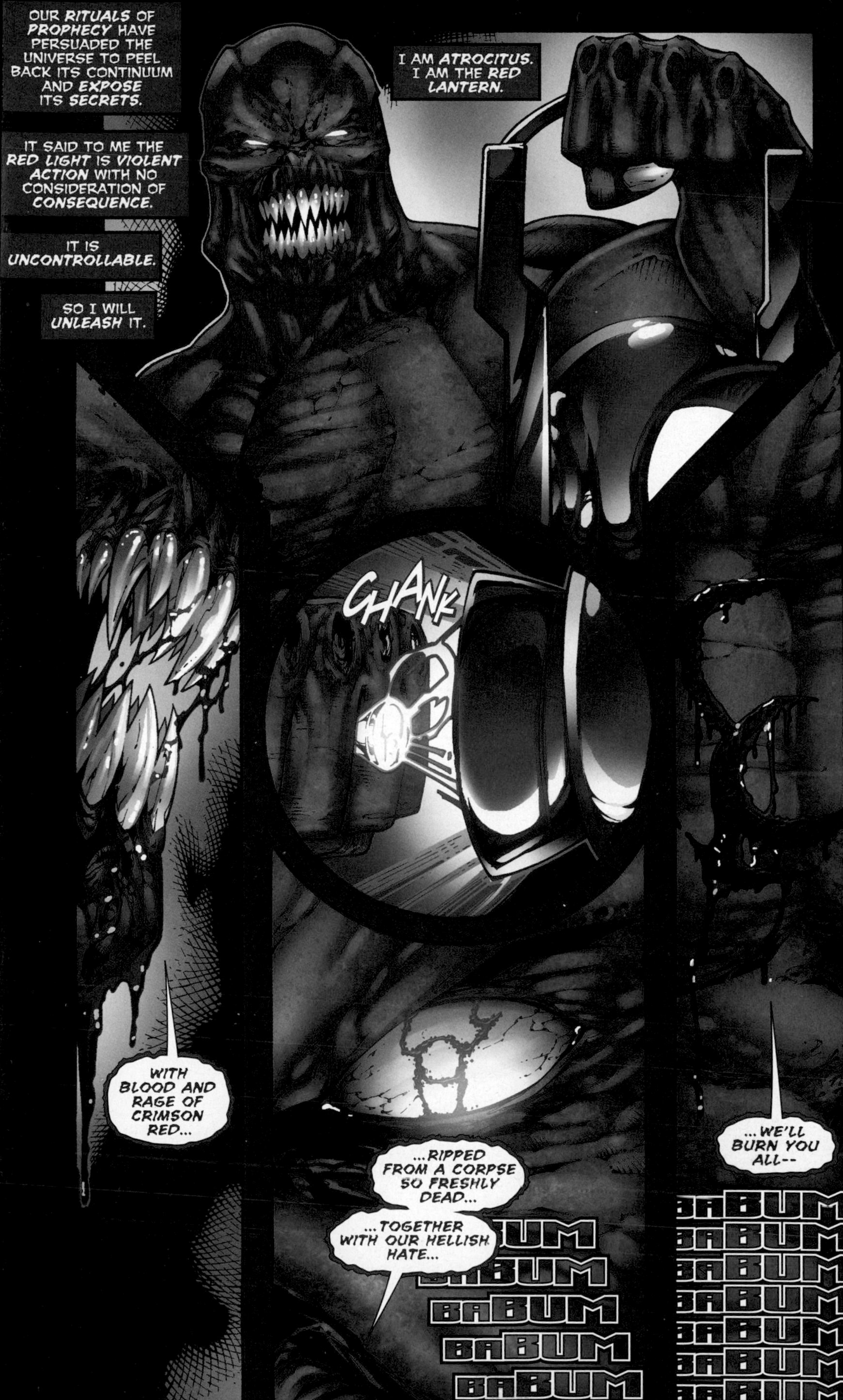

OUR RITUALS OF PROPHECY HAVE PERSUADED THE UNIVERSE TO PEEL BACK ITS CONTINUUM AND EXPOSE ITS SECRETS.
I AM ATROCITUS. I AM THE RED LANTERN.
IT SAID TO ME THE RED LIGHT IS VIOLENT ACTION WITH NO CONSIDERATION OF CONSEQUENCE.
IT IS UNCONTROLLABLE.
SO I WILL UNLEASH IT.
CHANK
WITH BLOOD AND RAGE OF CRIMSON RED...
...RIPPED FROM A CORPSE SO FRESHLY DEAD...
...TOGETHER WITH OUR HELLISH HATE...
...WE'LL BURN YOU ALL--
BABUM BABUM BABUM BABUM BABUM
BABUM BABUM BABUM BABUM BABUM BABUM BABUM

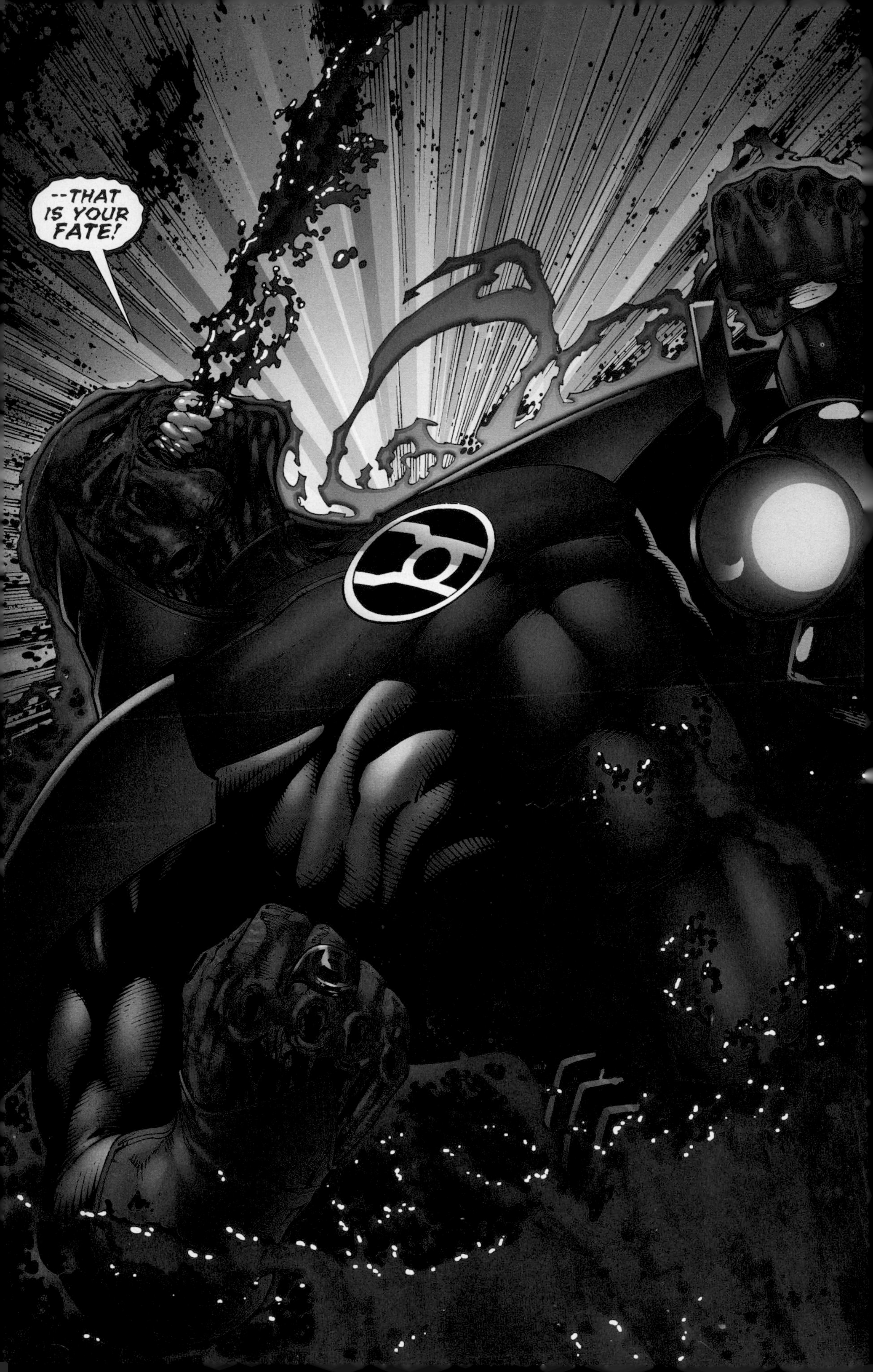
--THAT IS YOUR FATE!

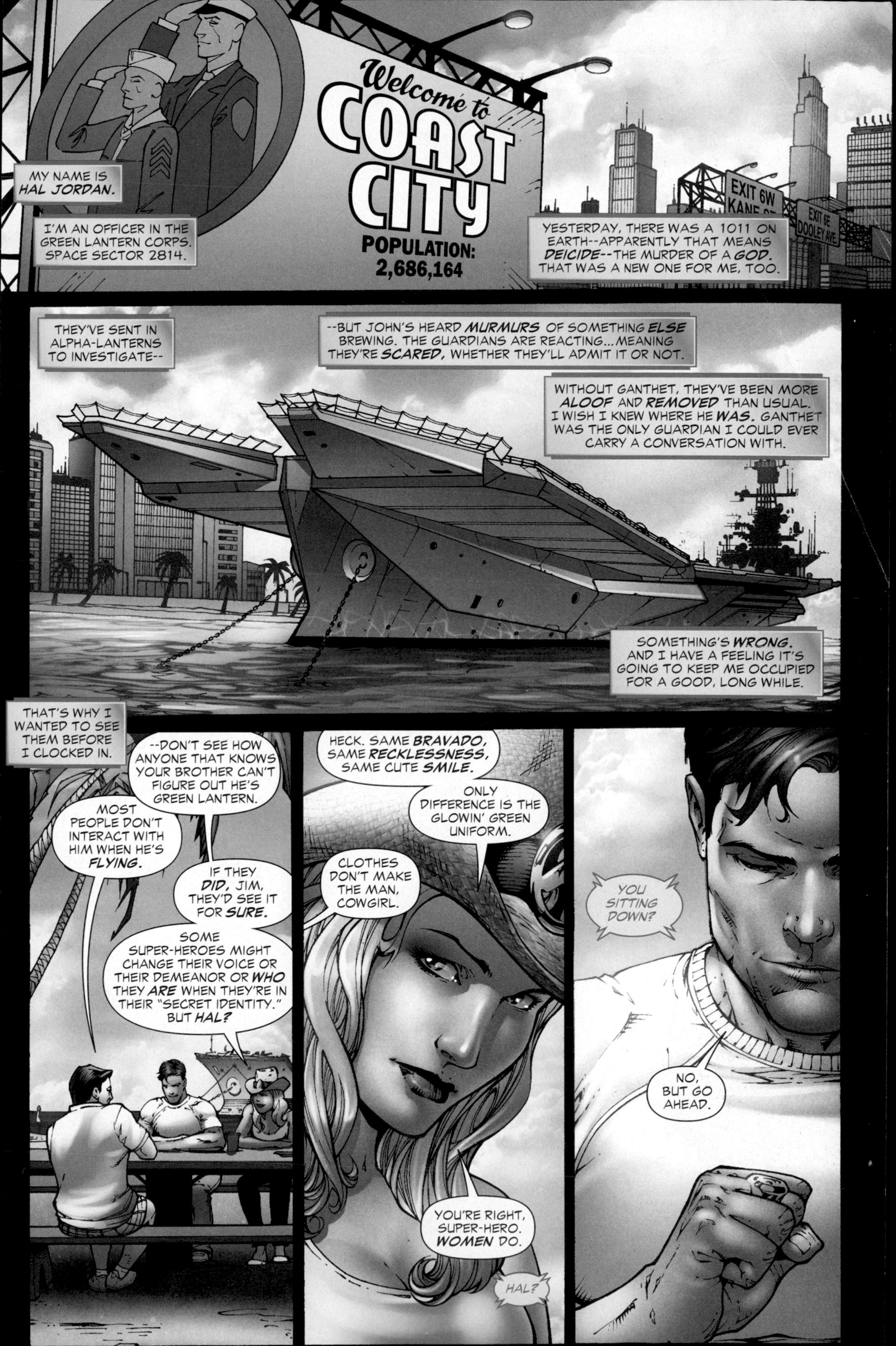
Welcome to COAST CITY
POPULATION: 2,686,164
MY NAME IS HAL JORDAN.
I'M AN OFFICER IN THE GREEN LANTERN CORPS. SPACE SECTOR 2814.
EXIT 6W KANE
EXIT 6E DOOLEY AVE
YESTERDAY, THERE WAS A 1011 ON EARTH--APPARENTLY THAT MEANS DEICIDE--THE MURDER OF A GOD. THAT WAS A NEW ONE FOR ME, TOO.
THEY'VE SENT IN ALPHA-LANTERNS TO INVESTIGATE--
--BUT JOHN'S HEARD MURMURS OF SOMETHING ELSE BREWING. THE GUARDIANS ARE REACTING... MEANING THEY'RE SCARED, WHETHER THEY'LL ADMIT IT OR NOT.
WITHOUT GANTHET, THEY'VE BEEN MORE ALOOF AND REMOVED THAN USUAL. I WISH I KNEW WHERE HE WAS. GANTHET WAS THE ONLY GUARDIAN I COULD EVER CARRY A CONVERSATION WITH.
SOMETHING'S WRONG. AND I HAVE A FEELING IT'S GOING TO KEEP ME OCCUPIED FOR A GOOD, LONG WHILE.
THAT'S WHY I WANTED TO SEE THEM BEFORE I CLOCKED IN.
--DON'T SEE HOW ANYONE THAT KNOWS YOUR BROTHER CAN'T FIGURE OUT HE'S GREEN LANTERN.
MOST PEOPLE DON'T INTERACT WITH HIM WHEN HE'S FLYING.
IF THEY DID, JIM, THEY'D SEE IT FOR SURE.
SOME SUPER-HEROES MIGHT CHANGE THEIR VOICE OR THEIR DEMEANOR OR WHO THEY ARE WHEN THEY'RE IN THEIR "SECRET IDENTITY." BUT HAL?
HECK. SAME BRAVADO, SAME RECKLESSNESS, SAME CUTE SMILE.
ONLY DIFFERENCE IS THE GLOWIN' GREEN UNIFORM.
CLOTHES DON'T MAKE THE MAN, COWGIRL.
YOU'RE RIGHT, SUPER-HERO. WOMEN DO.
HAL?
YOU SITTING DOWN?
NO, BUT GO AHEAD.

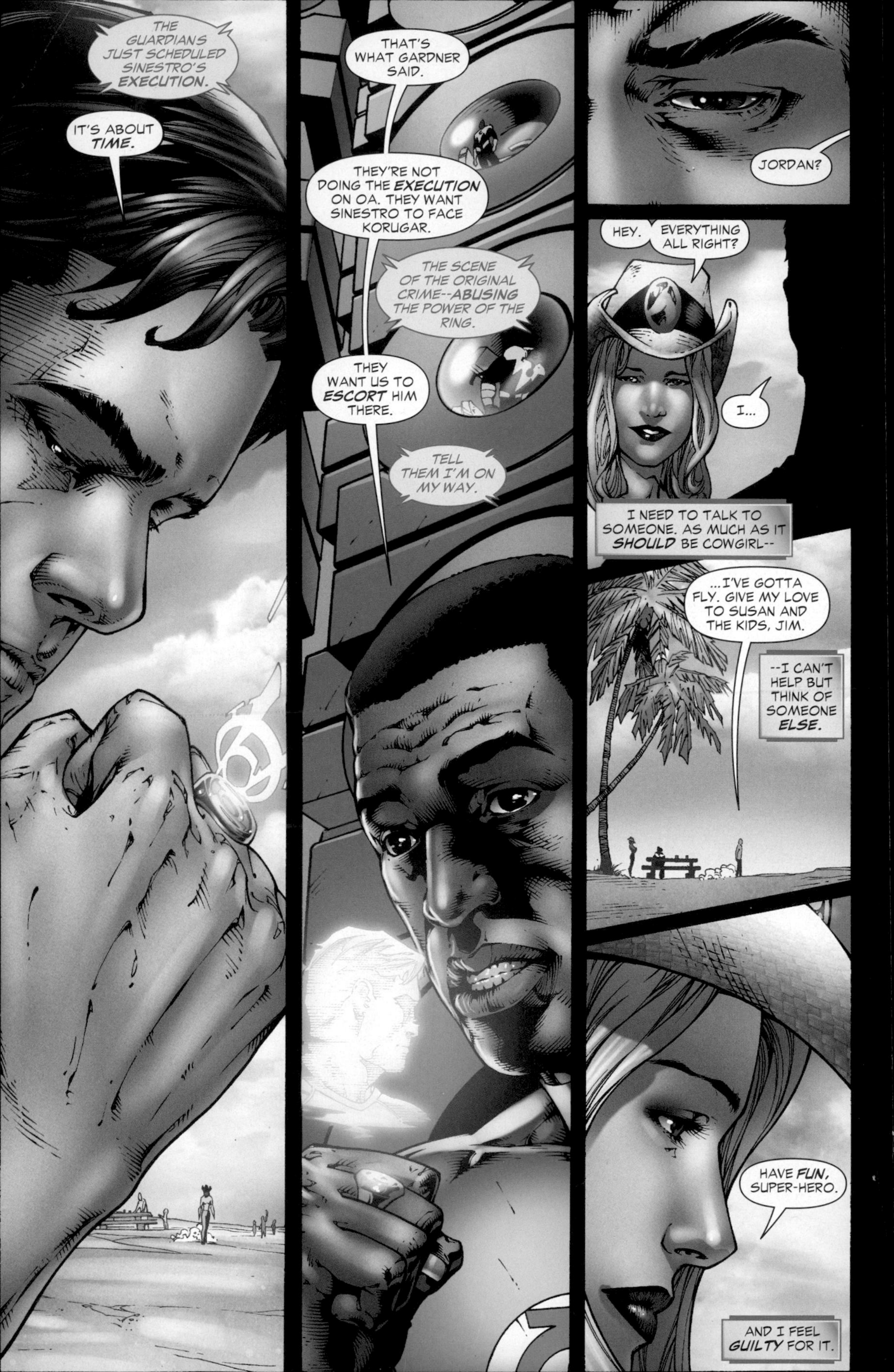
THE GUARDIANS JUST SCHEDULED SINESTRO'S EXECUTION.
IT'S ABOUT TIME.
THAT'S WHAT GARDNER SAID.
THEY'RE NOT DOING THE EXECUTION ON OA. THEY WANT SINESTRO TO FACE KORUGAR.
THE SCENE OF THE ORIGINAL CRIME--ABUSING THE POWER OF THE RING.
THEY WANT US TO ESCORT HIM THERE.
TELL THEM I'M ON MY WAY.
JORDAN?
HEY.
EVERYTHING ALL RIGHT?
I...
I NEED TO TALK TO SOMEONE. AS MUCH AS IT SHOULD BE COWGIRL--
...I'VE GOTTA FLY. GIVE MY LOVE TO SUSAN AND THE KIDS, JIM.
--I CAN'T HELP BUT THINK OF SOMEONE ELSE.
HAVE FUN, SUPER-HERO.
AND I FEEL GUILTY FOR IT.

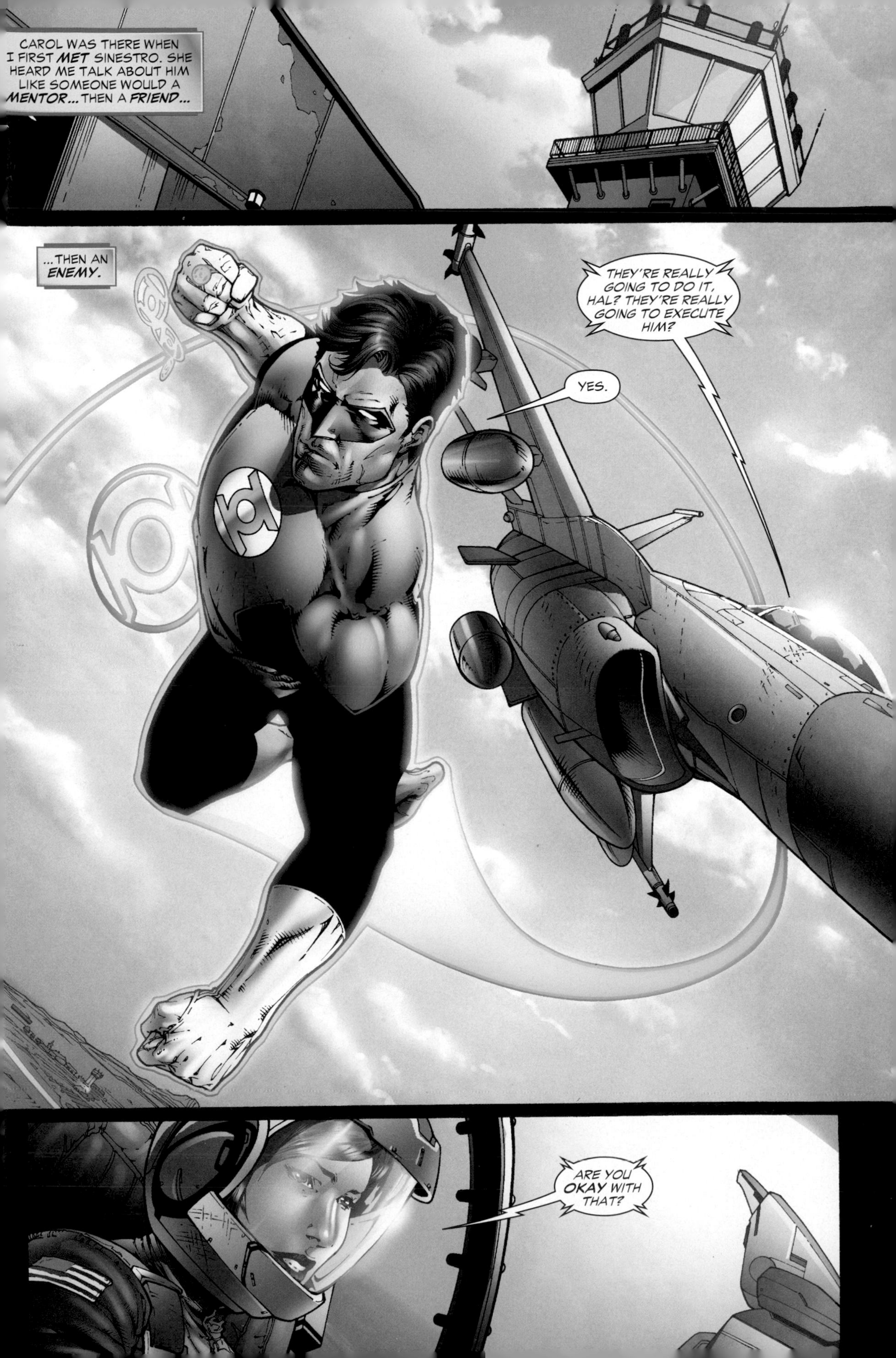
CAROL WAS THERE WHEN I FIRST MET SINESTRO. SHE HEARD ME TALK ABOUT HIM LIKE SOMEONE WOULD A MENTOR... THEN A FRIEND...
...THEN AN ENEMY.
THEY'RE REALLY GOING TO DO IT, HAL? THEY'RE REALLY GOING TO EXECUTE HIM?
YES.
ARE YOU OKAY WITH THAT?

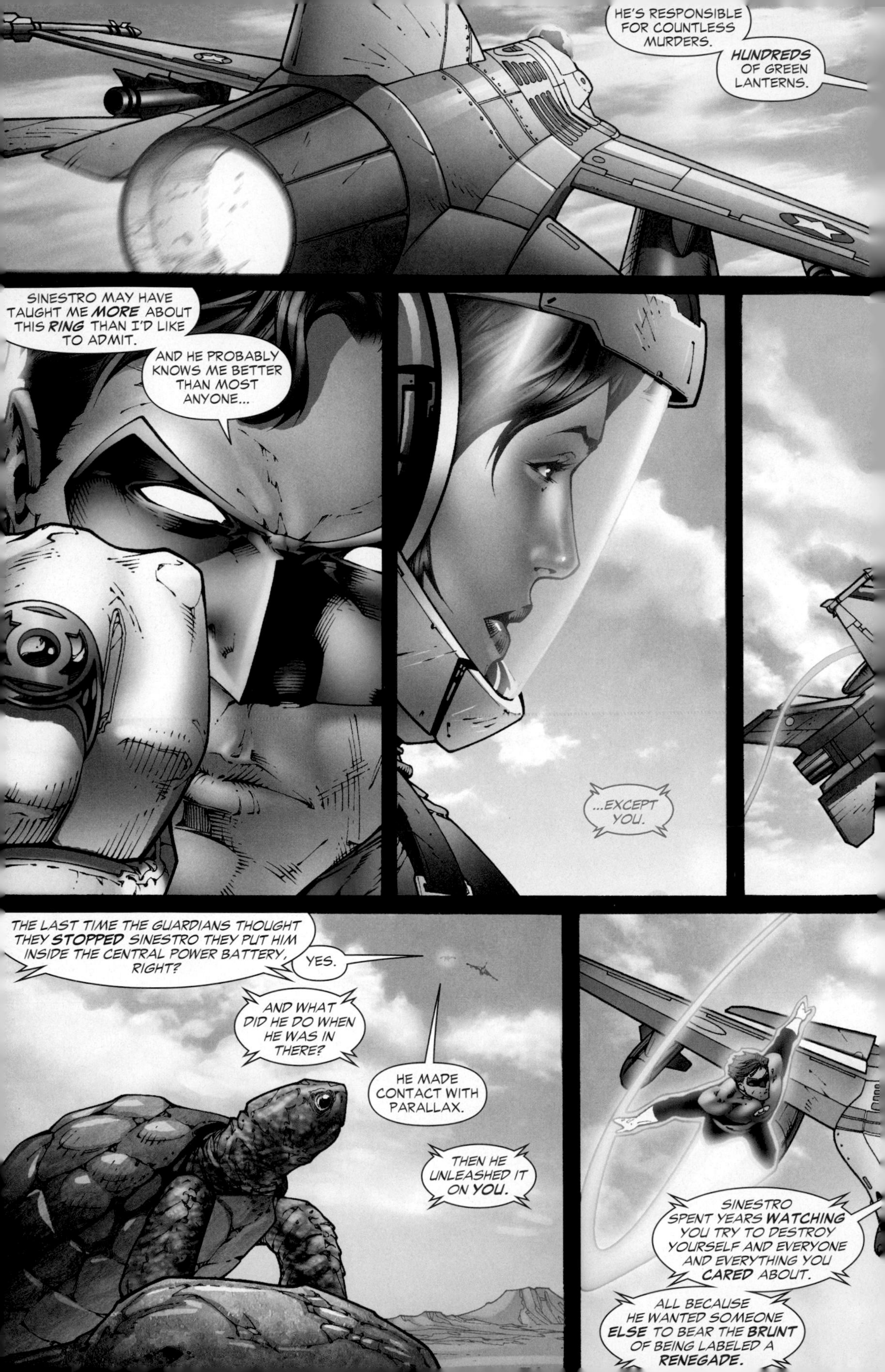
HE'S RESPONSIBLE FOR COUNTLESS MURDERS.
HUNDREDS OF GREEN LANTERNS.
SINESTRO MAY HAVE TAUGHT ME MORE ABOUT THIS RING THAN I'D LIKE TO ADMIT.
AND HE PROBABLY KNOWS ME BETTER THAN MOST ANYONE...
...EXCEPT YOU.
THE LAST TIME THE GUARDIANS THOUGHT THEY STOPPED SINESTRO THEY PUT HIM INSIDE THE CENTRAL POWER BATTERY, RIGHT?
YES.
AND WHAT DID HE DO WHEN HE WAS IN THERE?
HE MADE CONTACT WITH PARALLAX.
THEN HE UNLEASHED IT ON YOU.
SINESTRO SPENT YEARS WATCHING YOU TRY TO DESTROY YOURSELF AND EVERYONE AND EVERYTHING YOU CARED ABOUT.
ALL BECAUSE HE WANTED SOMEONE ELSE TO BEAR THE BRUNT OF BEING LABELED A RENEGADE.

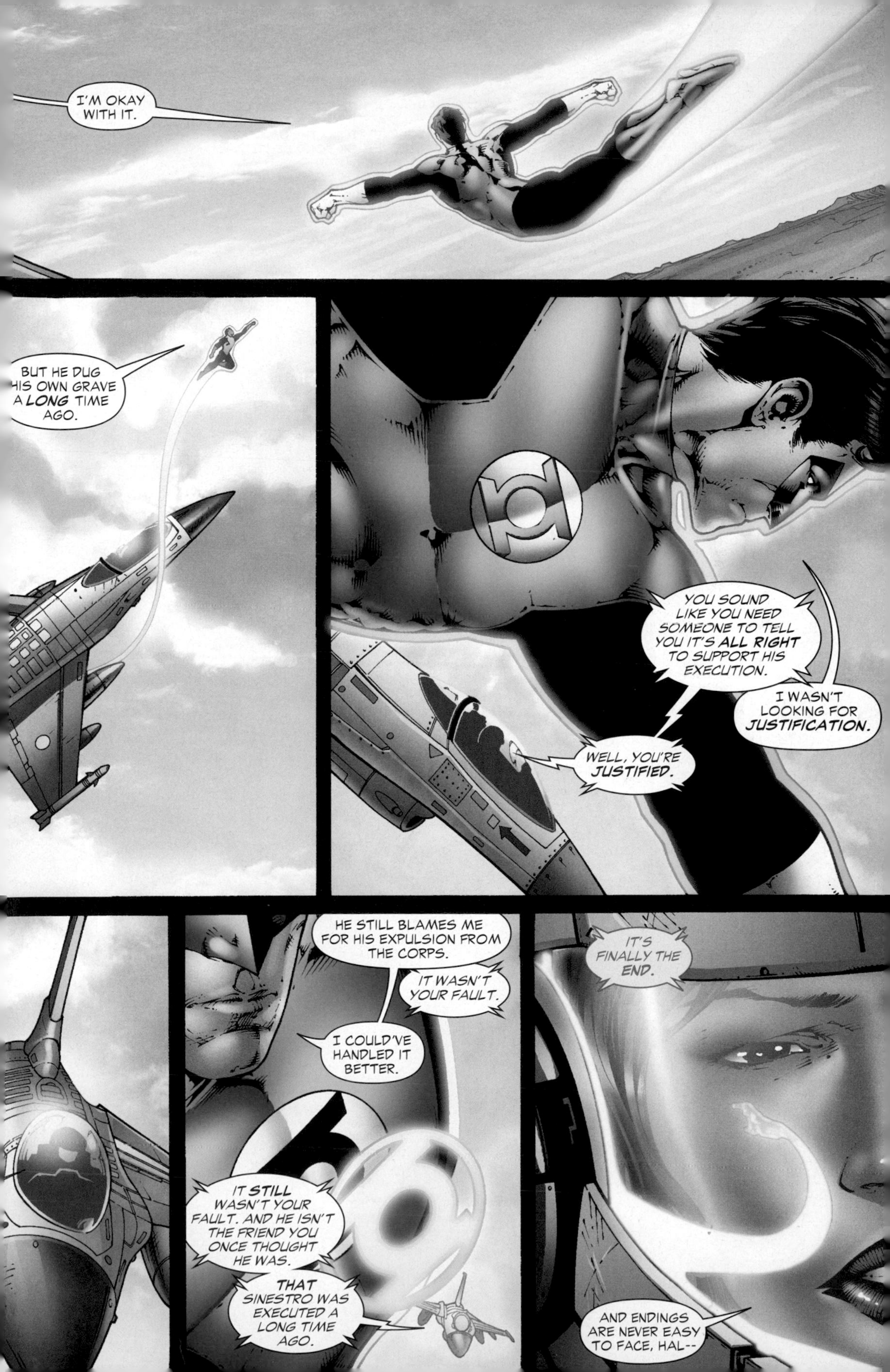
I'M OKAY WITH IT.
BUT HE DUG HIS OWN GRAVE A LONG TIME AGO.
YOU SOUND LIKE YOU NEED SOMEONE TO TELL YOU IT'S ALL RIGHT TO SUPPORT HIS EXECUTION.
I WASN'T LOOKING FOR JUSTIFICATION.
WELL, YOU'RE JUSTIFIED.
HE STILL BLAMES ME FOR HIS EXPULSION FROM THE CORPS.
IT WASN'T YOUR FAULT.
I COULD'VE HANDLED IT BETTER.
IT STILL WASN'T YOUR FAULT. AND HE ISN'T THE FRIEND YOU ONCE THOUGHT HE WAS.
THAT SINESTRO WAS EXECUTED A LONG TIME AGO.
IT'S FINALLY THE END.
AND ENDINGS ARE NEVER EASY TO FACE, HAL--

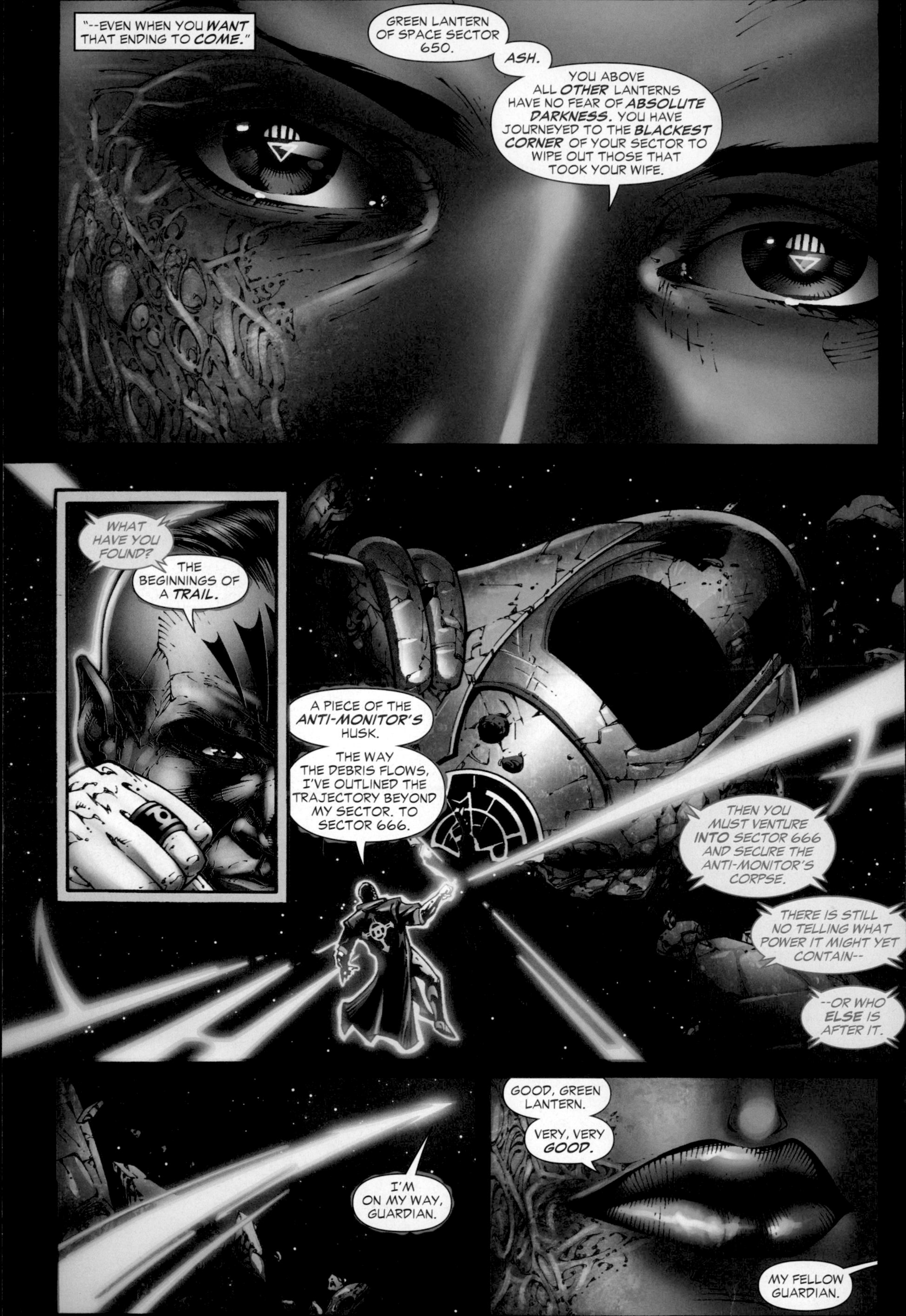
"--EVEN WHEN YOU WANT THAT ENDING TO COME."
GREEN LANTERN OF SPACE SECTOR 650.
ASH.
YOU ABOVE ALL OTHER LANTERNS HAVE NO FEAR OF ABSOLUTE DARKNESS. YOU HAVE JOURNEYED TO THE BLACKEST CORNER OF YOUR SECTOR TO WIPE OUT THOSE THAT TOOK YOUR WIFE.
WHAT HAVE YOU FOUND?
THE BEGINNINGS OF A TRAIL.
A PIECE OF THE ANTI-MONITOR'S HUSK.
THE WAY THE DEBRIS FLOWS, I'VE OUTLINED THE TRAJECTORY BEYOND MY SECTOR. TO SECTOR 666.
THEN YOU MUST VENTURE INTO SECTOR 666 AND SECURE THE ANTI-MONITOR'S CORPSE.
THERE IS STILL NO TELLING WHAT POWER IT MIGHT YET CONTAIN--
--OR WHO ELSE IS AFTER IT.
I'M ON MY WAY, GUARDIAN.
GOOD, GREEN LANTERN.
VERY, VERY GOOD.
MY FELLOW GUARDIAN.

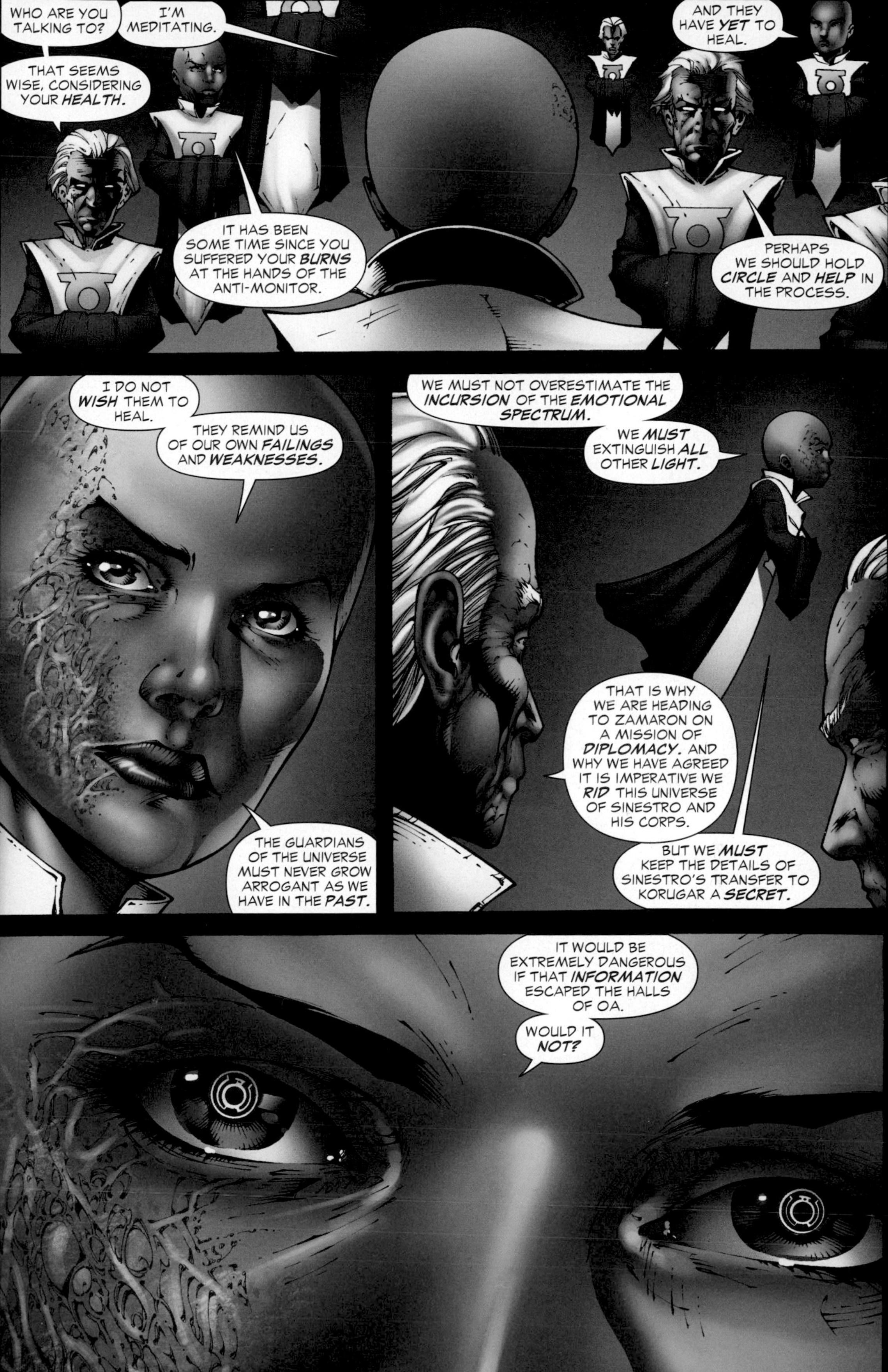
WHO ARE YOU TALKING TO?
I'M MEDITATING.
THAT SEEMS WISE, CONSIDERING YOUR HEALTH.
IT HAS BEEN SOME TIME SINCE YOU SUFFERED YOUR BURNS AT THE HANDS OF THE ANTI-MONITOR.
AND THEY HAVE YET TO HEAL.
PERHAPS WE SHOULD HOLD CIRCLE AND HELP IN THE PROCESS.
I DO NOT WISH THEM TO HEAL.
THEY REMIND US OF OUR OWN FAILINGS AND WEAKNESSES.
THE GUARDIANS OF THE UNIVERSE MUST NEVER GROW ARROGANT AS WE HAVE IN THE PAST.
WE MUST NOT OVERESTIMATE THE INCURSION OF THE EMOTIONAL SPECTRUM.
WE MUST EXTINGUISH ALL OTHER LIGHT.
THAT IS WHY WE ARE HEADING TO ZAMARON ON A MISSION OF DIPLOMACY. AND WHY WE HAVE AGREED IT IS IMPERATIVE WE RID THIS UNIVERSE OF SINESTRO AND HIS CORPS.
BUT WE MUST KEEP THE DETAILS OF SINESTRO'S TRANSFER TO KORUGAR A SECRET.
IT WOULD BE EXTREMELY DANGEROUS IF THAT INFORMATION ESCAPED THE HALLS OF OA.
WOULD IT NOT?

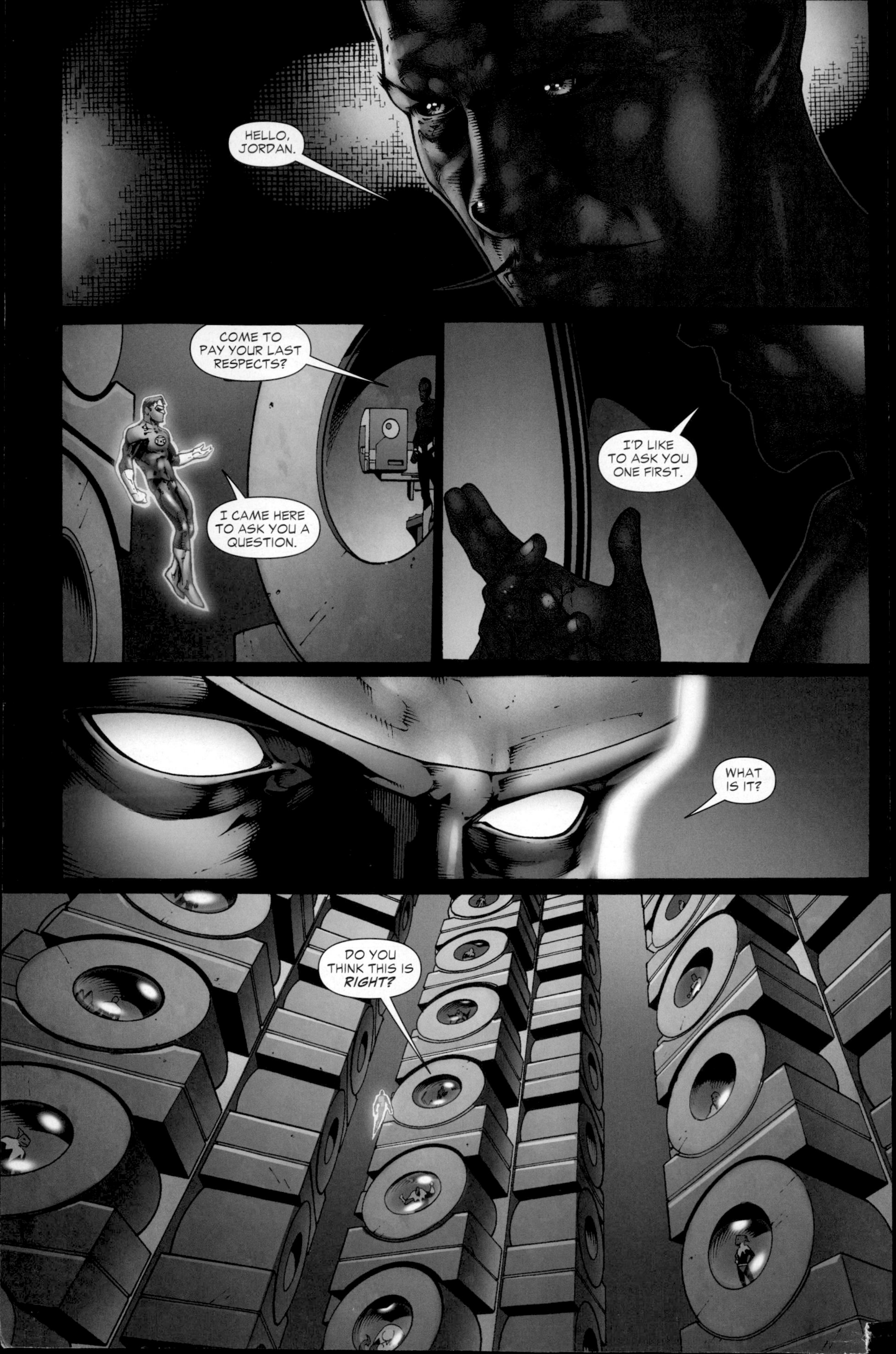
HELLO, JORDAN.
COME TO PAY YOUR LAST RESPECTS?
I CAME HERE TO ASK YOU A QUESTION.
I'D LIKE TO ASK YOU ONE FIRST.
WHAT IS IT?
DO YOU THINK THIS IS *RIGHT?*

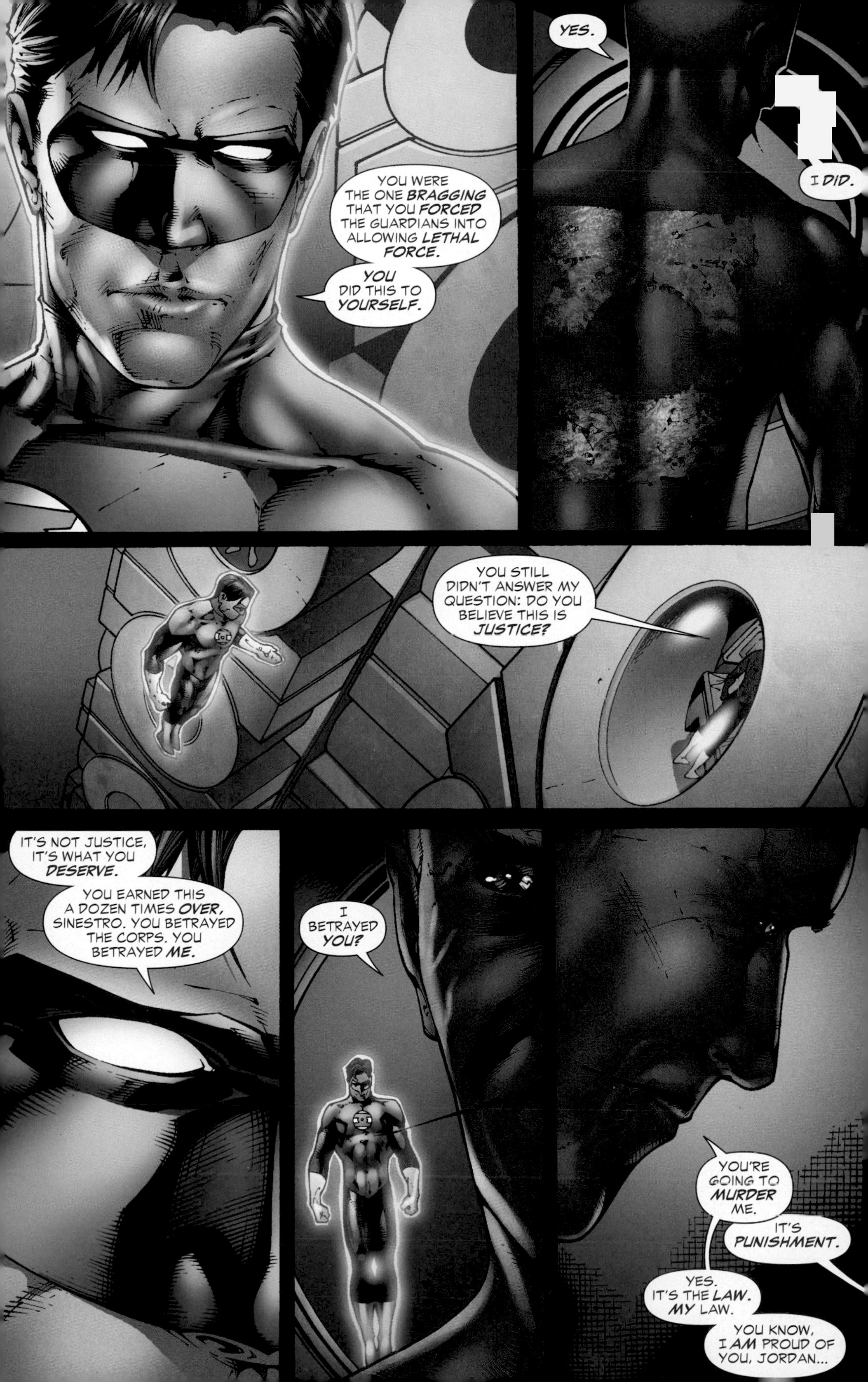
YOU WERE THE ONE BRAGGING THAT YOU FORCED THE GUARDIANS INTO ALLOWING LETHAL FORCE.
YOU DID THIS TO YOURSELF.
YES.
I DID.
YOU STILL DIDN'T ANSWER MY QUESTION: DO YOU BELIEVE THIS IS JUSTICE?
IT'S NOT JUSTICE, IT'S WHAT YOU DESERVE.
YOU EARNED THIS A DOZEN TIMES OVER, SINESTRO. YOU BETRAYED THE CORPS. YOU BETRAYED ME.
I BETRAYED YOU?
YOU'RE GOING TO MURDER ME.
IT'S PUNISHMENT.
YES. IT'S THE LAW. MY LAW.
YOU KNOW, I AM PROUD OF YOU, JORDAN...

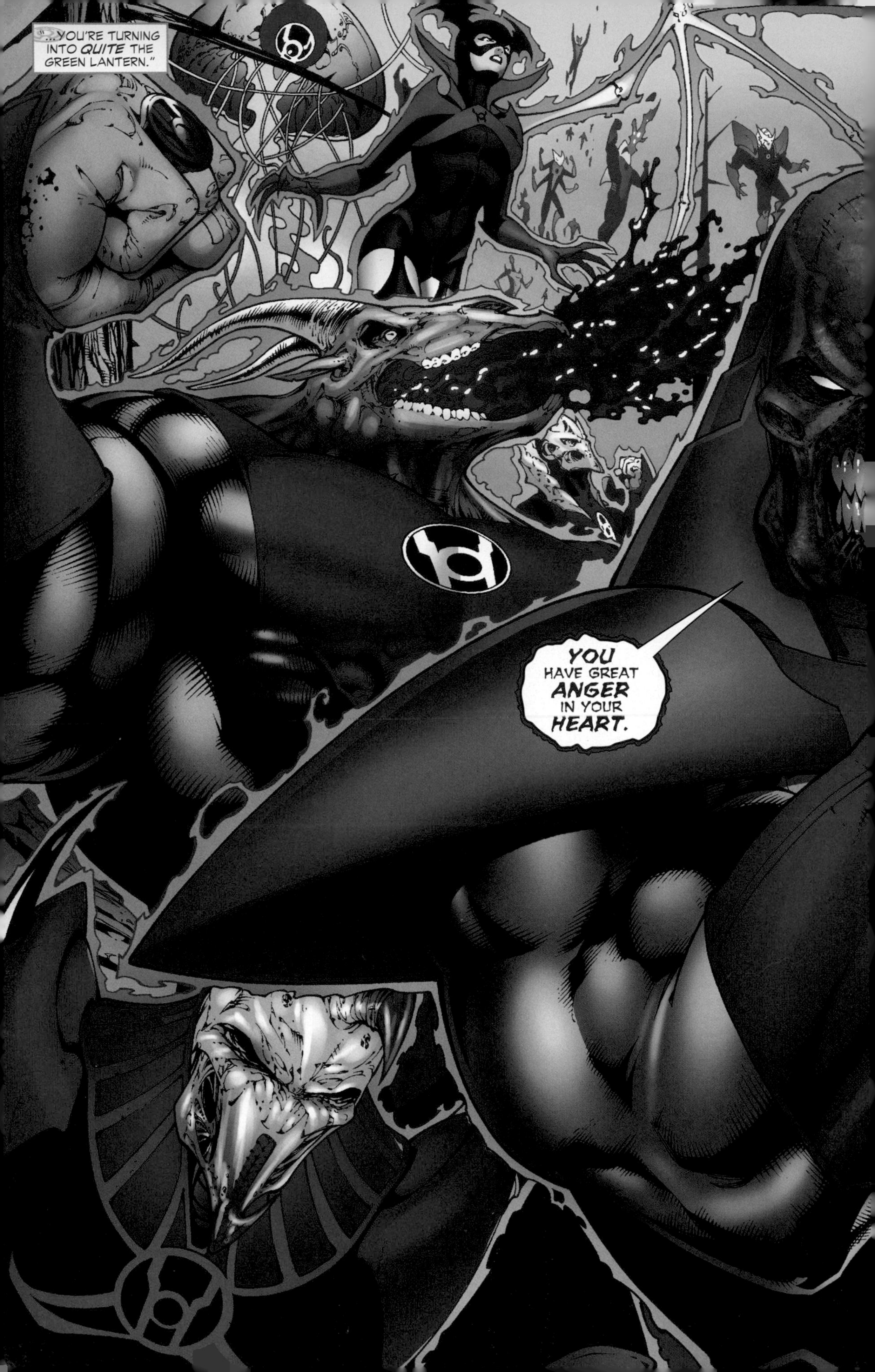
"...YOU'RE TURNING INTO QUITE THE GREEN LANTERN."
YOU HAVE GREAT ANGER IN YOUR HEART.

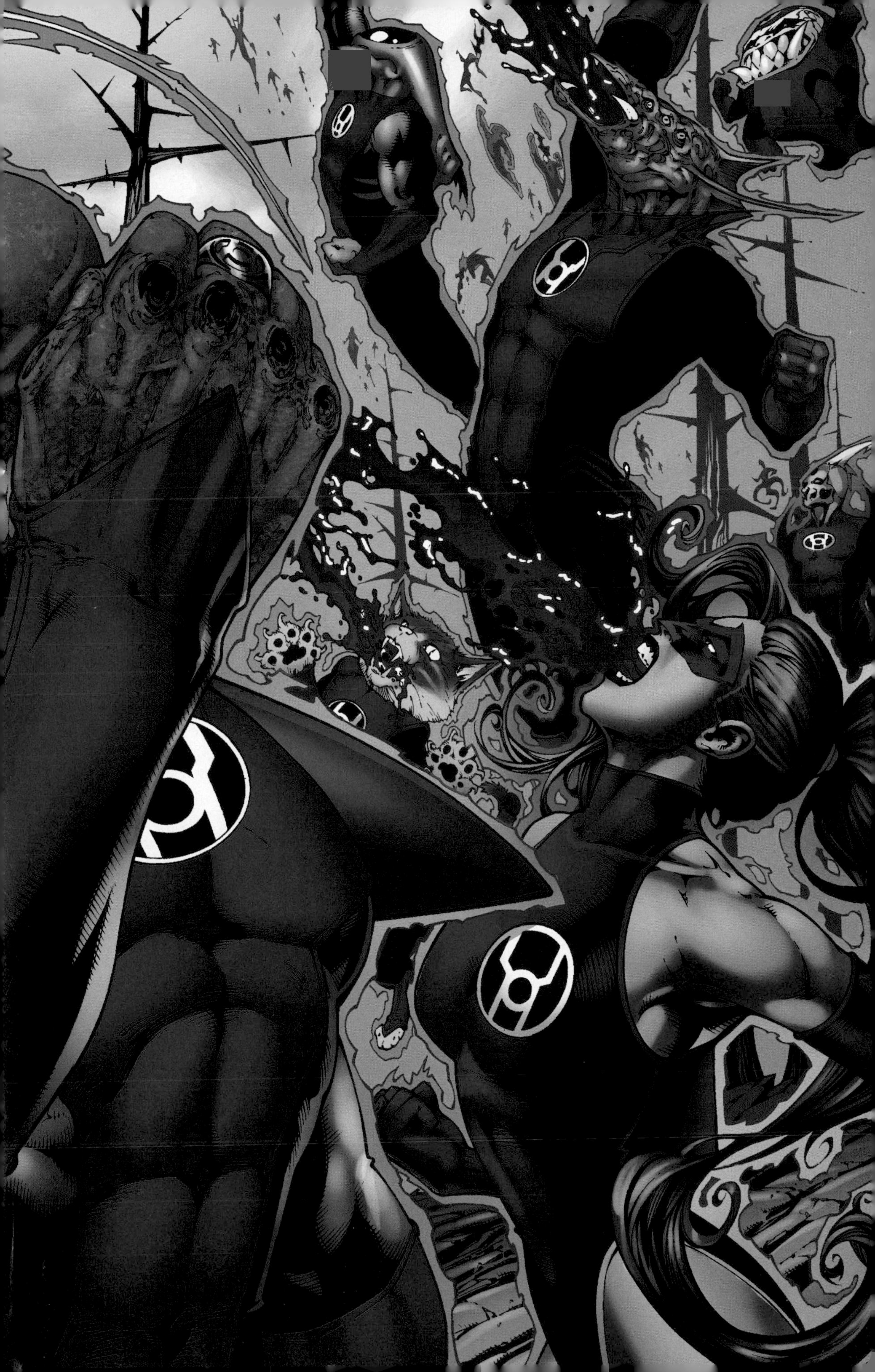

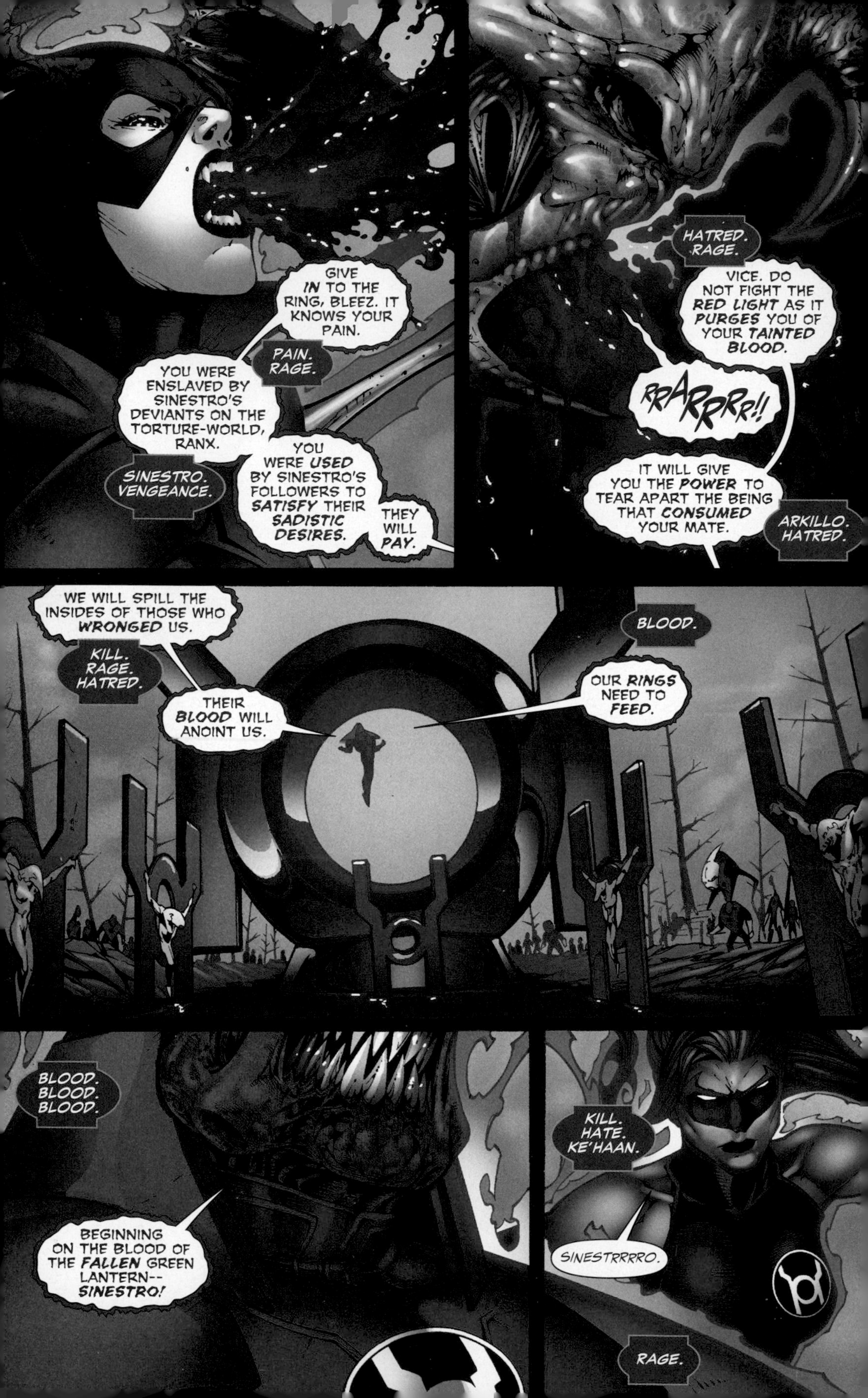
GIVE IN TO THE RING, BLEEZ. IT KNOWS YOUR PAIN.
PAIN. RAGE.
YOU WERE ENSLAVED BY SINESTRO'S DEVIANTS ON THE TORTURE-WORLD, RANX.
SINESTRO. VENGEANCE.
YOU WERE USED BY SINESTRO'S FOLLOWERS TO SATISFY THEIR SADISTIC DESIRES.
THEY WILL PAY.
HATRED. RAGE.
VICE. DO NOT FIGHT THE RED LIGHT AS IT PURGES YOU OF YOUR TAINTED BLOOD.
RRAARRRR!!
IT WILL GIVE YOU THE POWER TO TEAR APART THE BEING THAT CONSUMED YOUR MATE.
ARKILLO. HATRED.
WE WILL SPILL THE INSIDES OF THOSE WHO WRONGED US.
KILL. RAGE. HATRED.
THEIR BLOOD WILL ANOINT US.
BLOOD.
OUR RINGS NEED TO FEED.
BLOOD. BLOOD. BLOOD.
BEGINNING ON THE BLOOD OF THE FALLEN GREEN LANTERN-- SINESTRO!
KILL. HATE. KE'HAAN.
SINESTRRRRO.
RAGE.

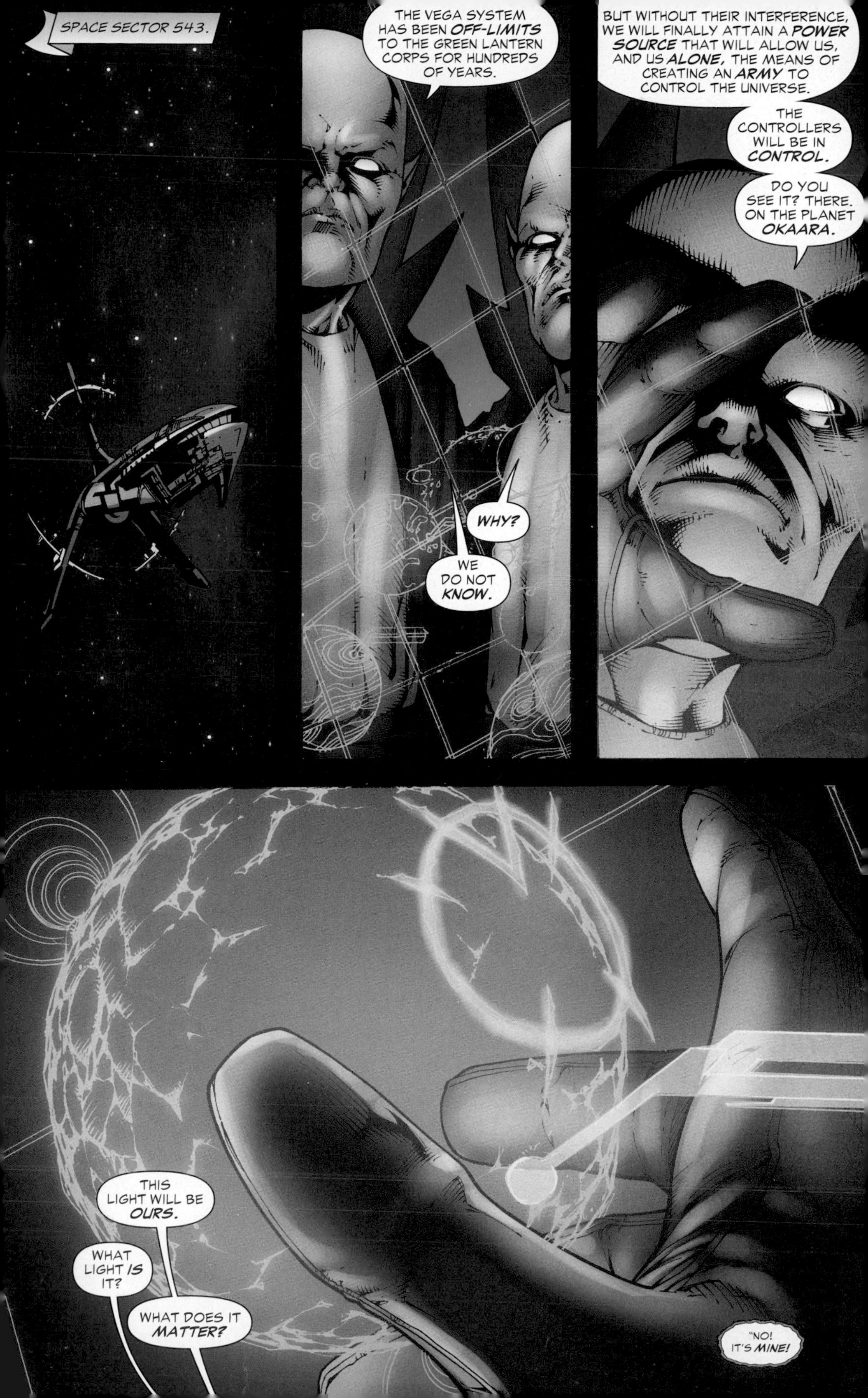
SPACE SECTOR 543.
THE VEGA SYSTEM HAS BEEN OFF-LIMITS TO THE GREEN LANTERN CORPS FOR HUNDREDS OF YEARS.
WHY?
WE DO NOT KNOW.
BUT WITHOUT THEIR INTERFERENCE, WE WILL FINALLY ATTAIN A POWER SOURCE THAT WILL ALLOW US, AND US ALONE, THE MEANS OF CREATING AN ARMY TO CONTROL THE UNIVERSE.
THE CONTROLLERS WILL BE IN CONTROL.
DO YOU SEE IT? THERE. ON THE PLANET OKAARA.
THIS LIGHT WILL BE OURS.
WHAT LIGHT IS IT?
WHAT DOES IT MATTER?
"NO! IT'S MINE!

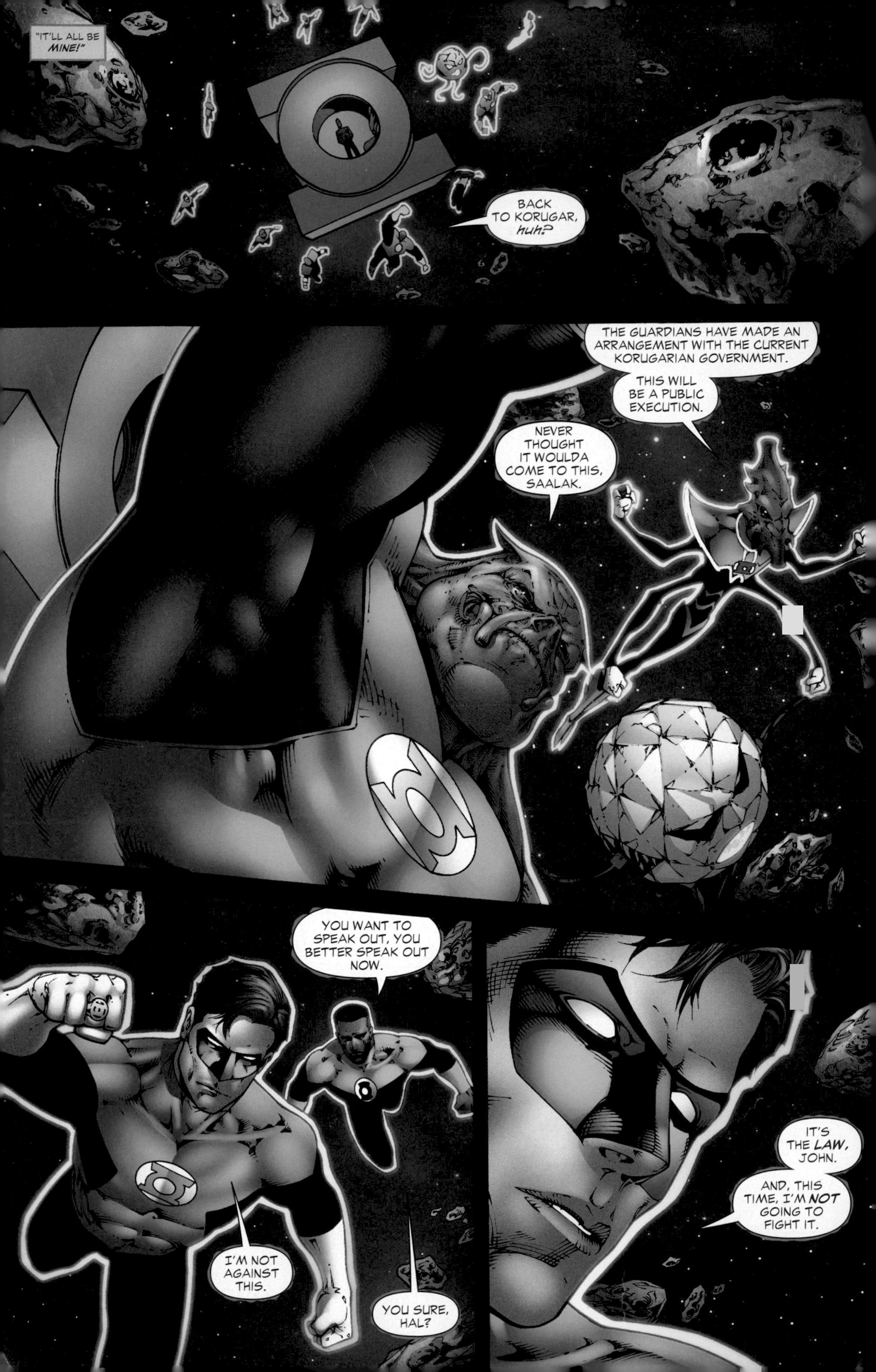
"IT'LL ALL BE MINE!"
BACK TO KORUGAR, huh?
THE GUARDIANS HAVE MADE AN ARRANGEMENT WITH THE CURRENT KORUGARIAN GOVERNMENT.
THIS WILL BE A PUBLIC EXECUTION.
NEVER THOUGHT IT WOULDA COME TO THIS, SAALAK.
YOU WANT TO SPEAK OUT, YOU BETTER SPEAK OUT NOW.
I'M NOT AGAINST THIS.
YOU SURE, HAL?
IT'S THE LAW, JOHN.
AND, THIS TIME, I'M NOT GOING TO FIGHT IT.

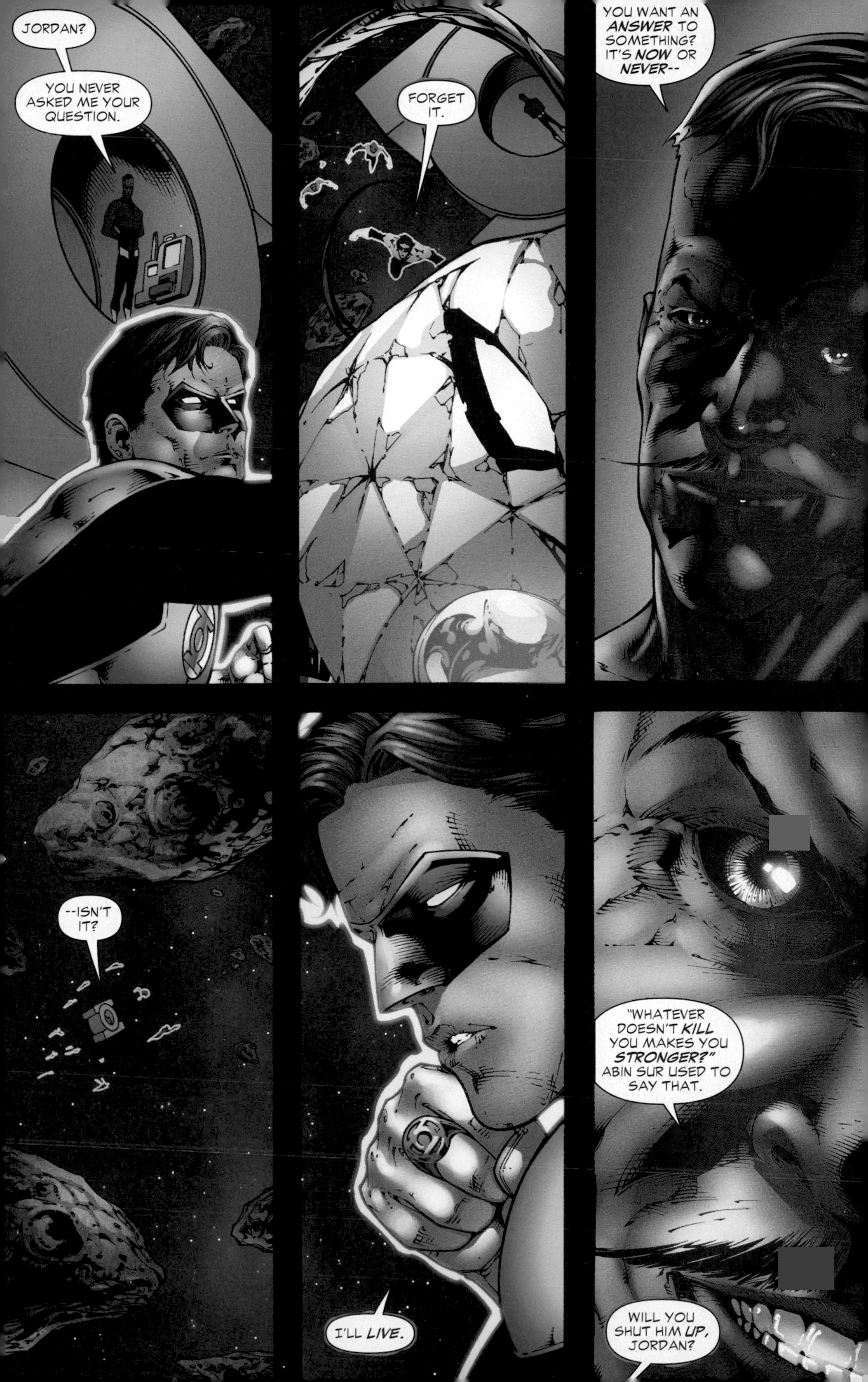
JORDAN?
YOU NEVER ASKED ME YOUR QUESTION.
FORGET IT.
YOU WANT AN **ANSWER** TO SOMETHING? IT'S **NOW** OR **NEVER**--
--ISN'T IT?
I'LL **LIVE.**
"WHATEVER DOESN'T **KILL** YOU MAKES YOU **STRONGER?**" ABIN SUR USED TO SAY THAT.
WILL YOU SHUT HIM **UP,** JORDAN?

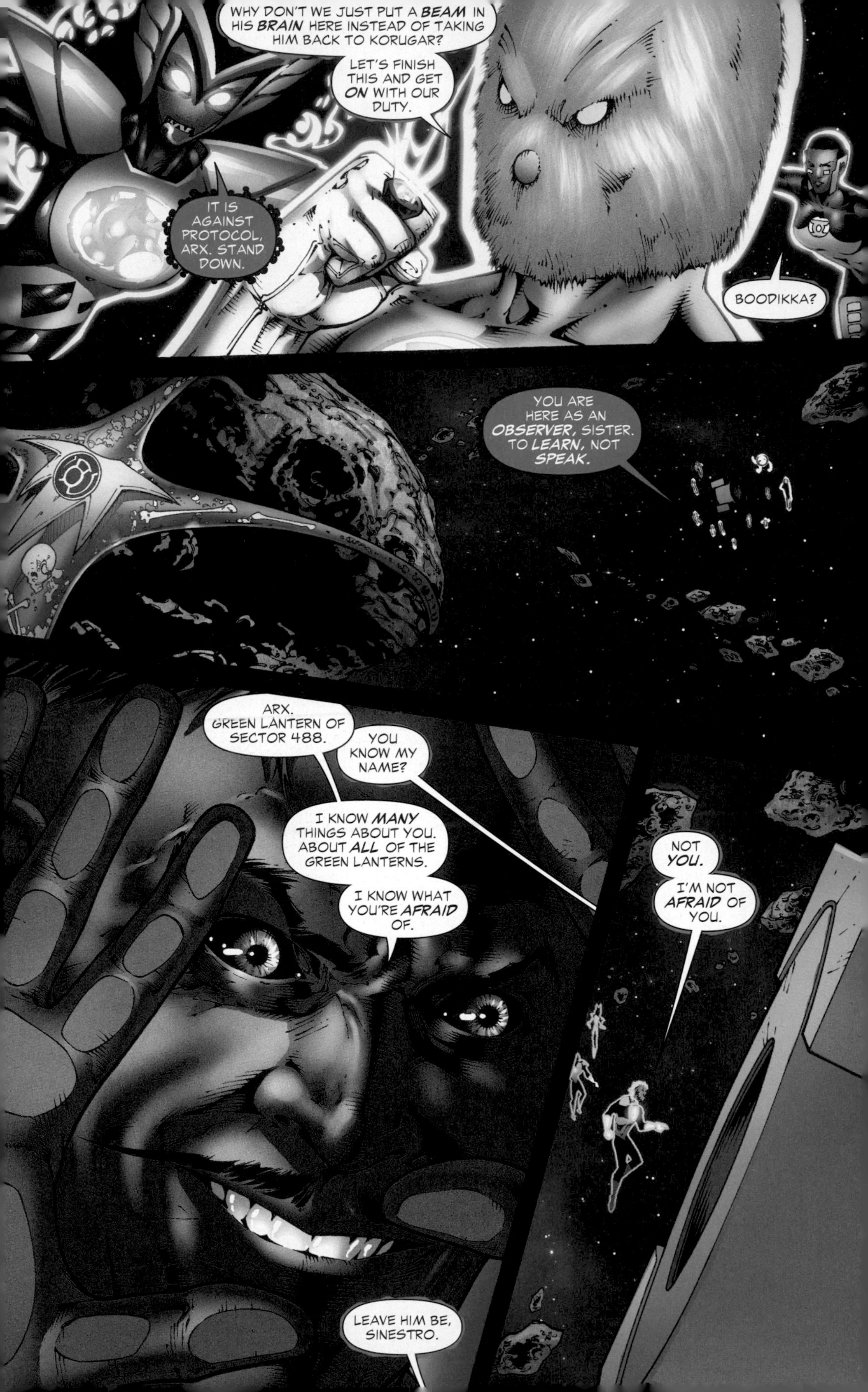
WHY DON'T WE JUST PUT A BEAM IN HIS BRAIN HERE INSTEAD OF TAKING HIM BACK TO KORUGAR?
LET'S FINISH THIS AND GET ON WITH OUR DUTY.
IT IS AGAINST PROTOCOL, ARX. STAND DOWN.
BOODIKKA?
YOU ARE HERE AS AN OBSERVER, SISTER. TO LEARN, NOT SPEAK.
ARX. GREEN LANTERN OF SECTOR 488.
YOU KNOW MY NAME?
I KNOW MANY THINGS ABOUT YOU. ABOUT ALL OF THE GREEN LANTERNS.
I KNOW WHAT YOU'RE AFRAID OF.
NOT YOU.
I'M NOT AFRAID OF YOU.
LEAVE HIM BE, SINESTRO.

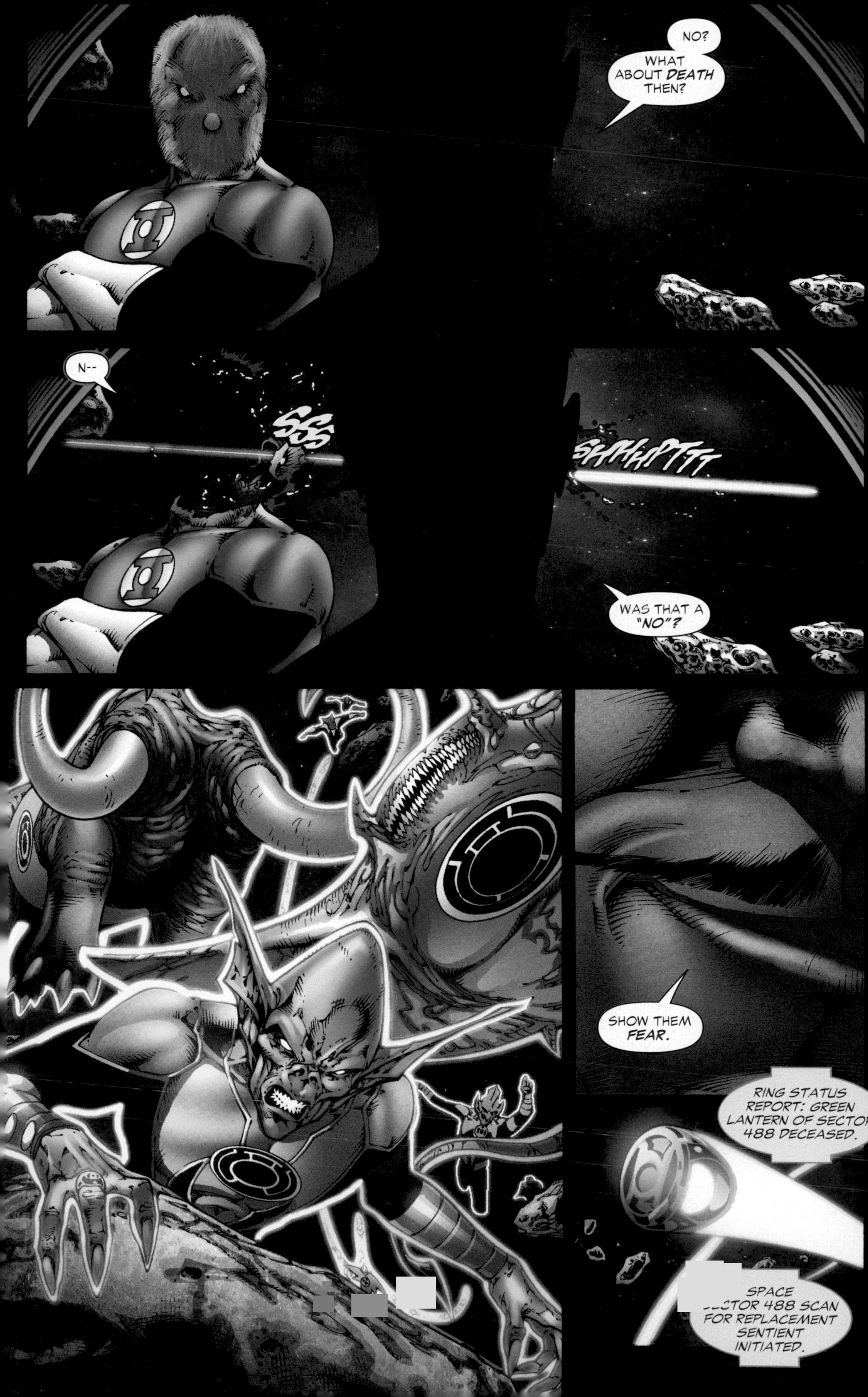
NO?
WHAT ABOUT DEATH THEN?
N--
SSS
SHHHPTTT
WAS THAT A "NO"?
SHOW THEM FEAR.
RING STATUS REPORT: GREEN LANTERN OF SECTOR 488 DECEASED.
FOR REPLACEMENT SENTIENT INITIATED.

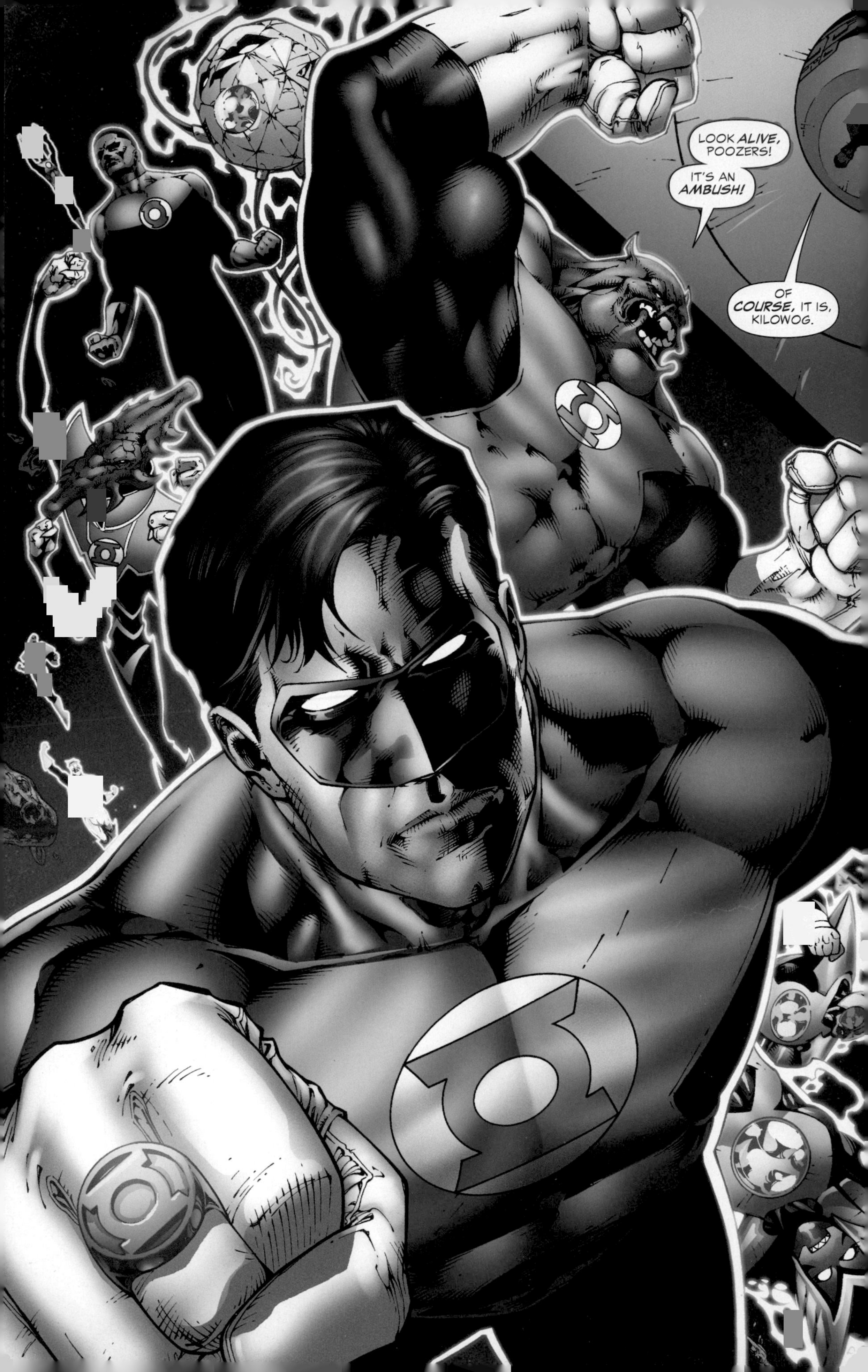
LOOK ALIVE, POOZERS!
IT'S AN AMBUSH!
OF COURSE, IT IS, KILOWOG.

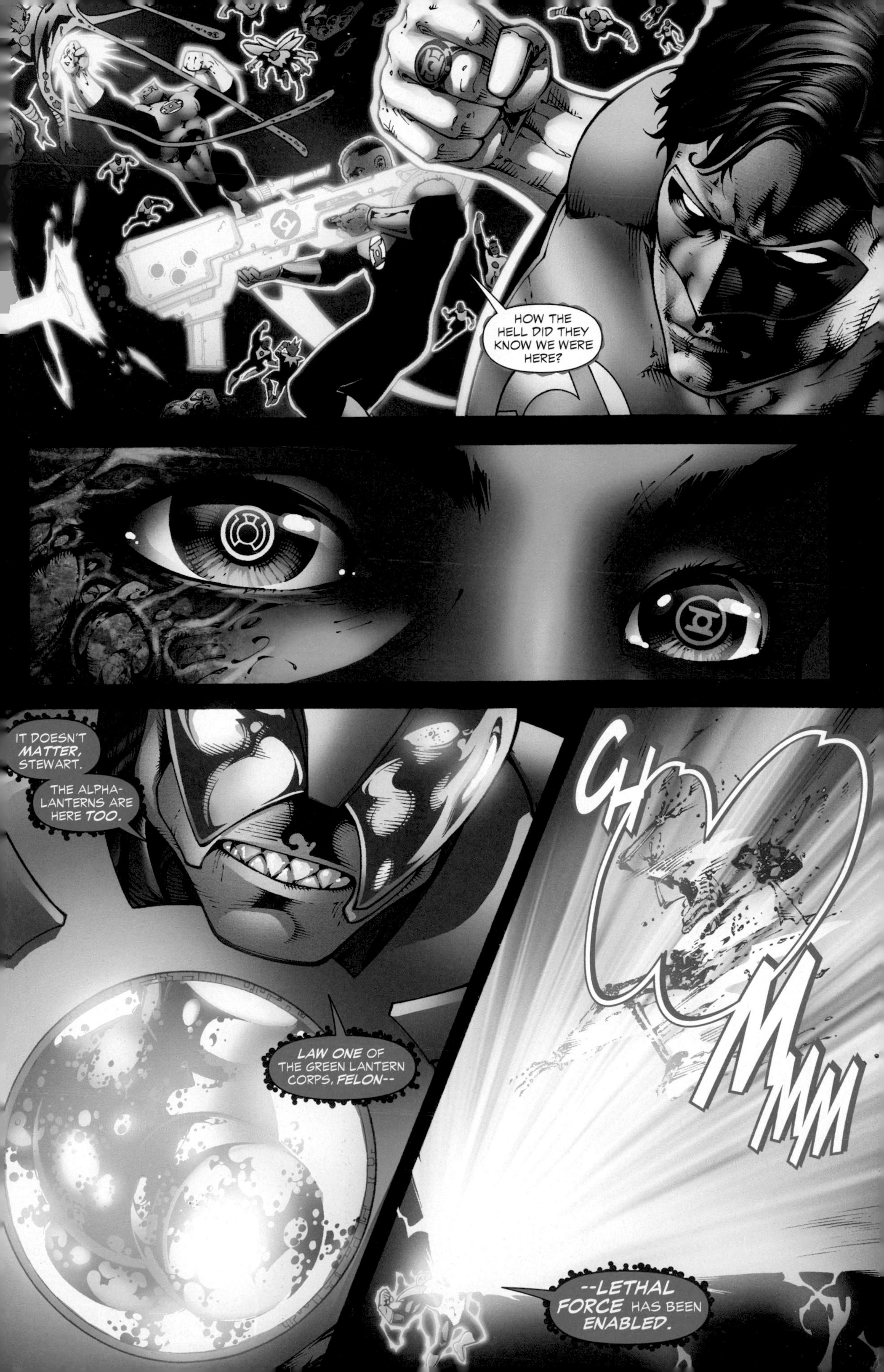
HOW THE HELL DID THEY KNOW WE WERE HERE?
IT DOESN'T *MATTER*, STEWART.
THE ALPHA-LANTERNS ARE HERE *TOO*.
LAW ONE OF THE GREEN LANTERN CORPS, *FELON*--
CHMMM
--*LETHAL FORCE* HAS BEEN *ENABLED*.

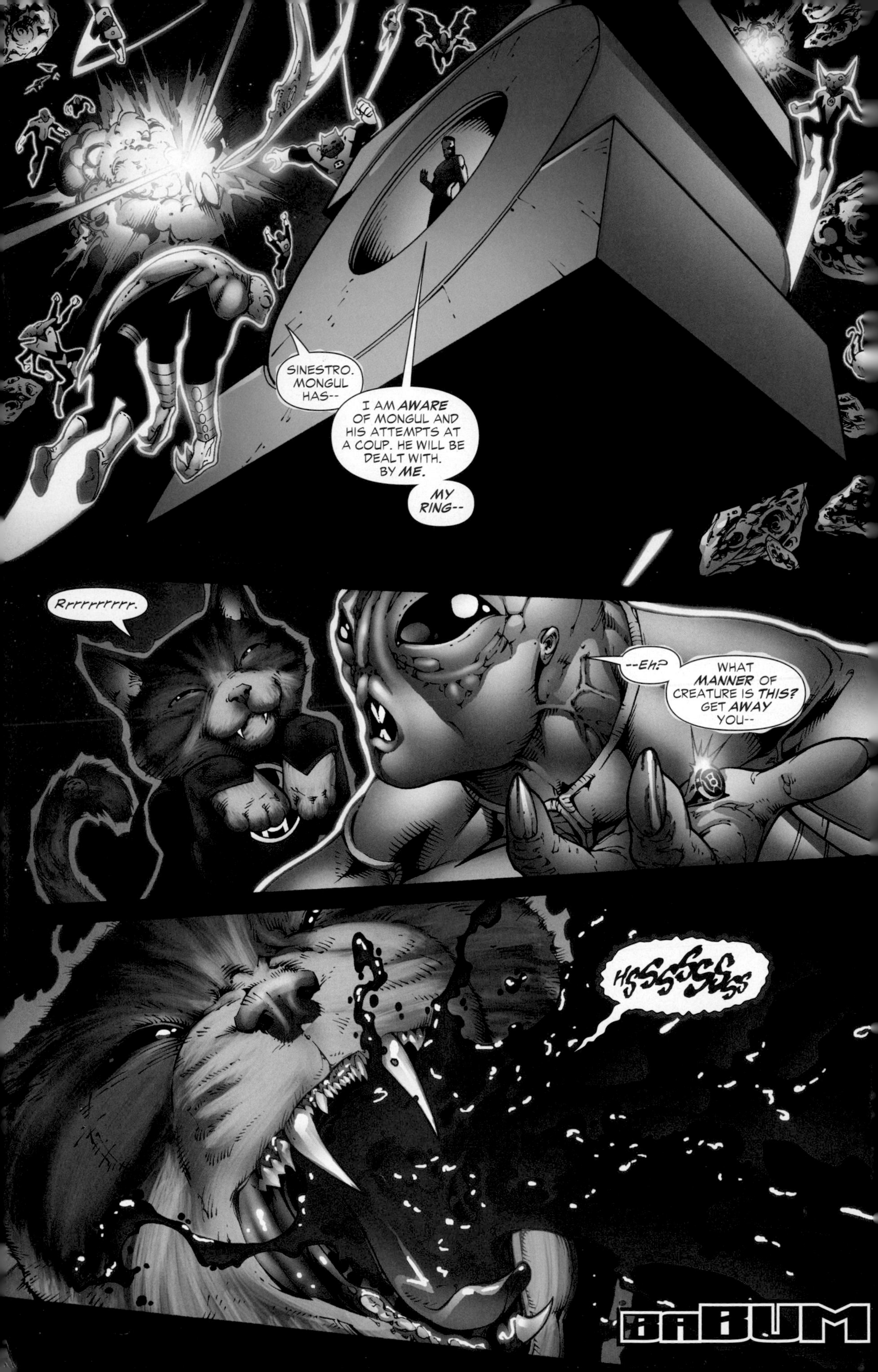
SINESTRO. MONGUL HAS--
I AM AWARE OF MONGUL AND HIS ATTEMPTS AT A COUP. HE WILL BE DEALT WITH. BY ME.
MY RING--
Rrrrrrrrrr.
--Eh?
WHAT MANNER OF CREATURE IS THIS? GET AWAY YOU--
HSSSSSSSss
BABUM

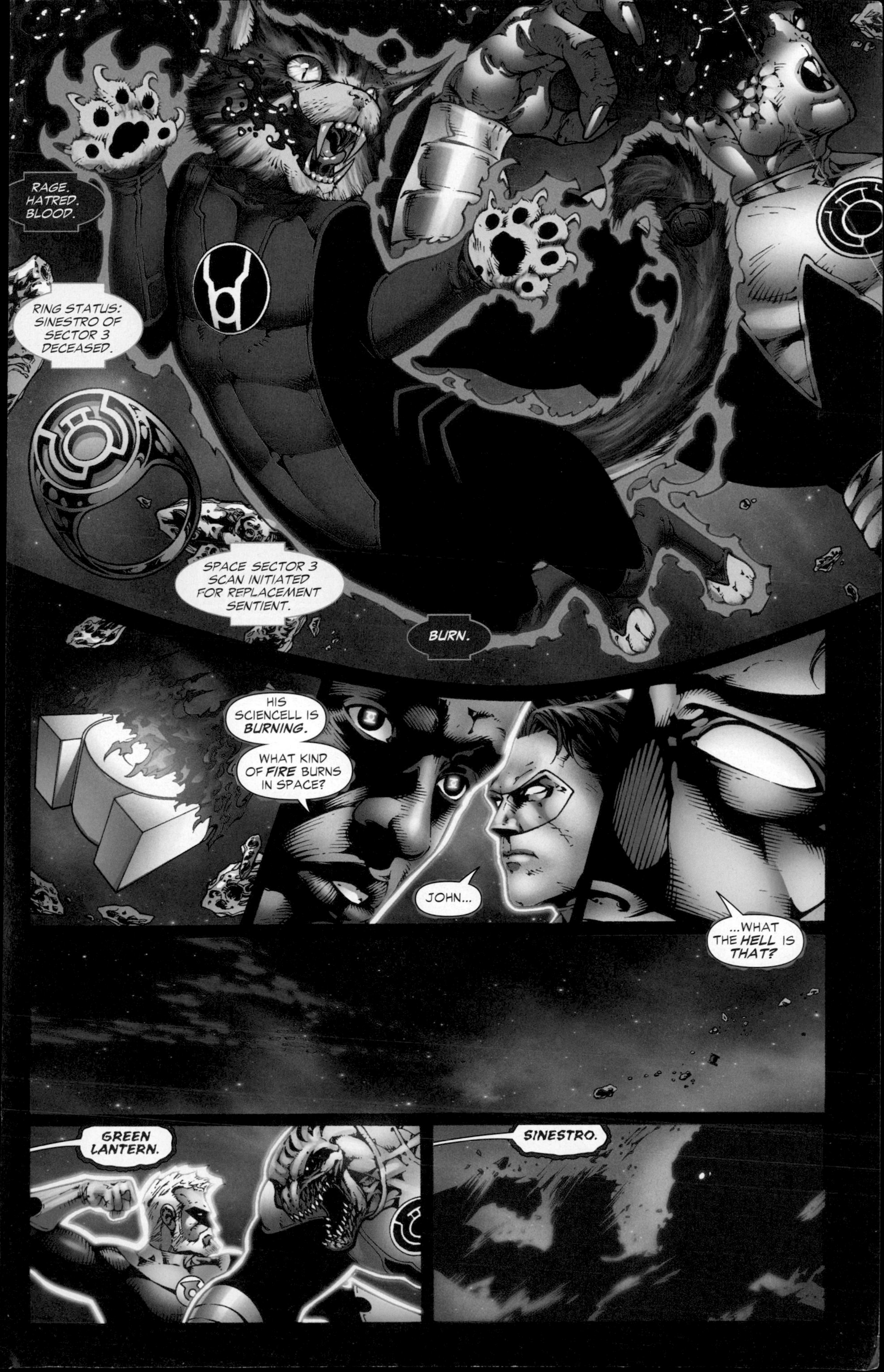

RAGE. HATRED. BLOOD.
RING STATUS: SINESTRO OF SECTOR 3 DECEASED.
SPACE SECTOR 3 SCAN INITIATED FOR REPLACEMENT SENTIENT.
BURN.
HIS SCIENCELL IS BURNING.
WHAT KIND OF FIRE BURNS IN SPACE?
JOHN...
...WHAT THE HELL IS THAT?
GREEN LANTERN.
SINESTRO.

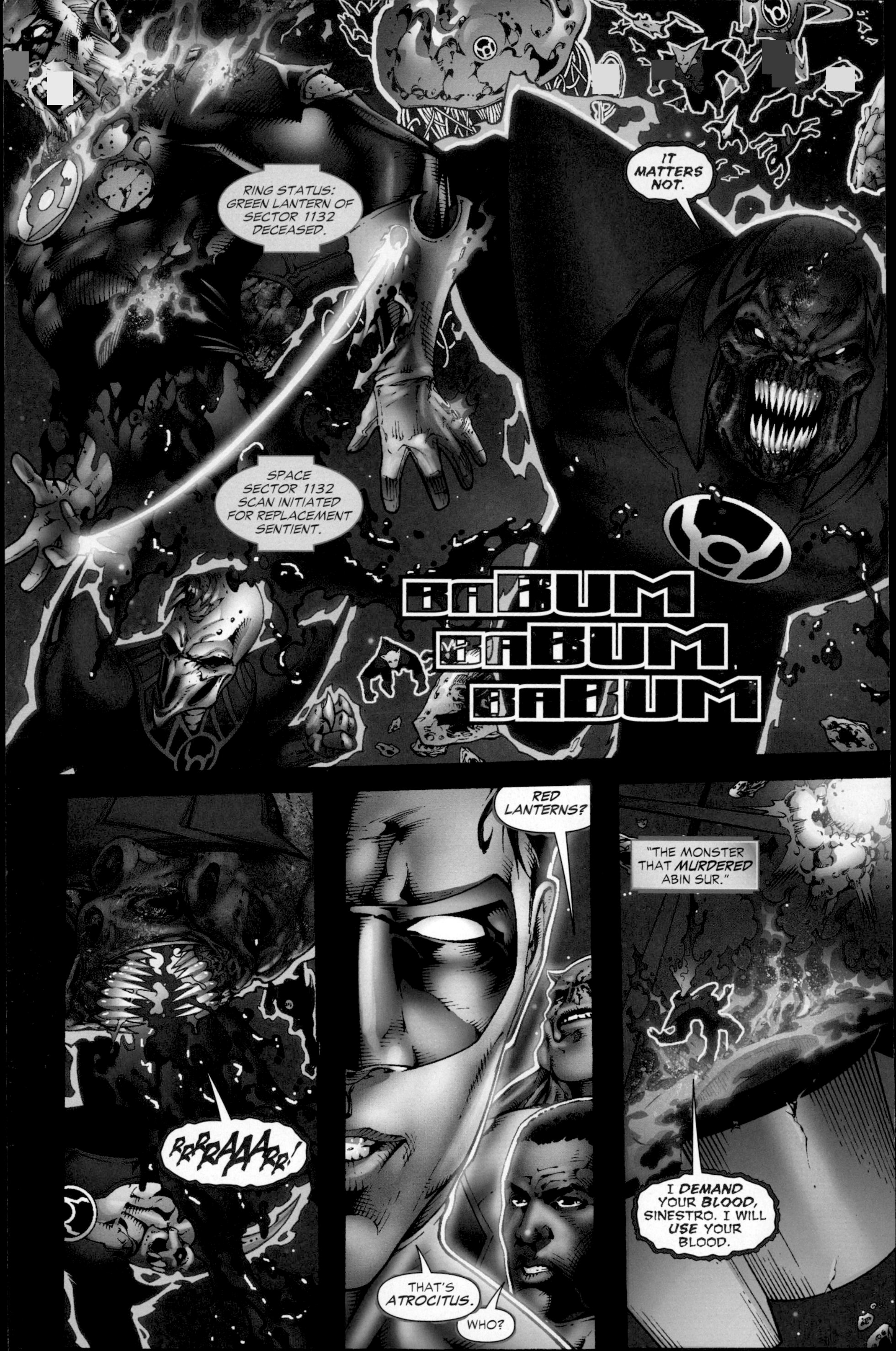
RING STATUS: GREEN LANTERN OF SECTOR 1132 DECEASED.
IT MATTERS NOT.
SPACE SECTOR 1132 SCAN INITIATED FOR REPLACEMENT SENTIENT.
BABUM BABUM BABUM
RRRRAAARR!
RED LANTERNS?
THAT'S ATROCITUS.
WHO?
"THE MONSTER THAT MURDERED ABIN SUR."
I DEMAND YOUR BLOOD, SINESTRO. I WILL USE YOUR BLOOD.

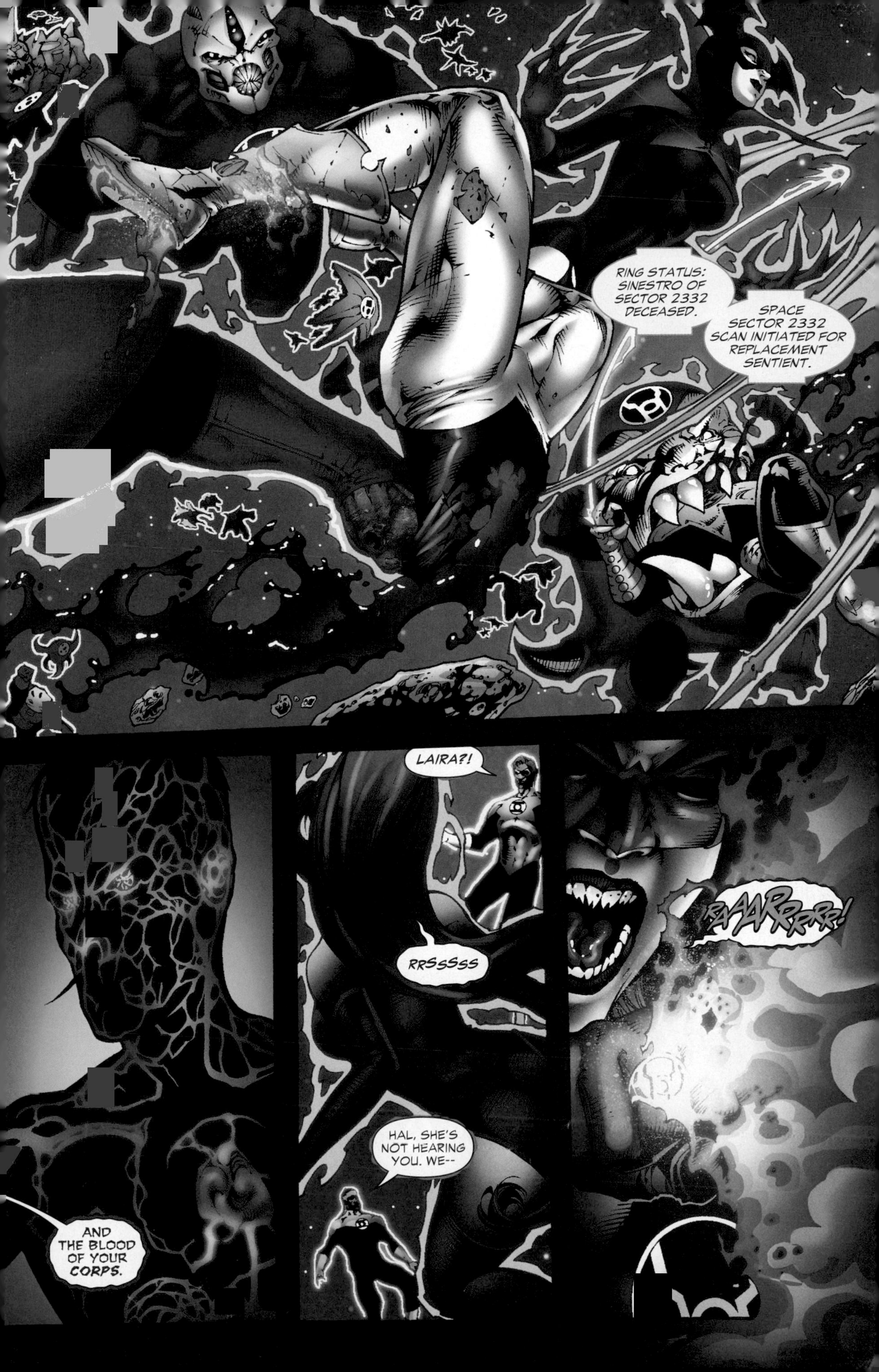
RING STATUS: SINESTRO OF SECTOR 2332 DECEASED.
SPACE SECTOR 2332 SCAN INITIATED FOR REPLACEMENT SENTIENT.
AND THE BLOOD OF YOUR CORPS.
LAIRA?!
RRSSSSS
HAL, SHE'S NOT HEARING YOU. WE--
RAAARRRRR!

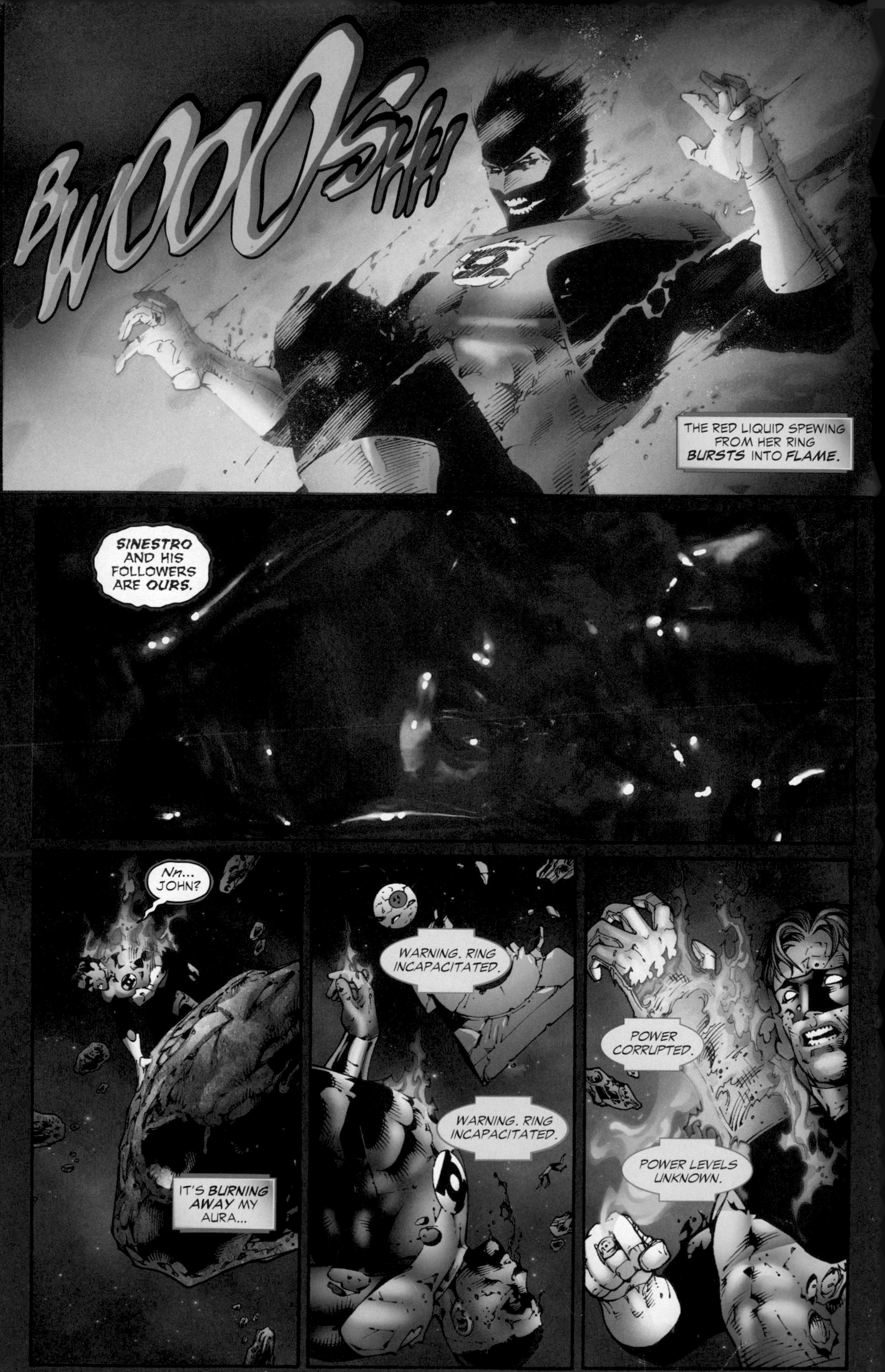

BWOOOSHH
THE RED LIQUID SPEWING FROM HER RING BURSTS INTO FLAME.
SINESTRO AND HIS FOLLOWERS ARE OURS.
Nn... JOHN?
IT'S BURNING AWAY MY AURA...
WARNING. RING INCAPACITATED.
WARNING. RING INCAPACITATED.
POWER CORRUPTED.
POWER LEVELS UNKNOWN.

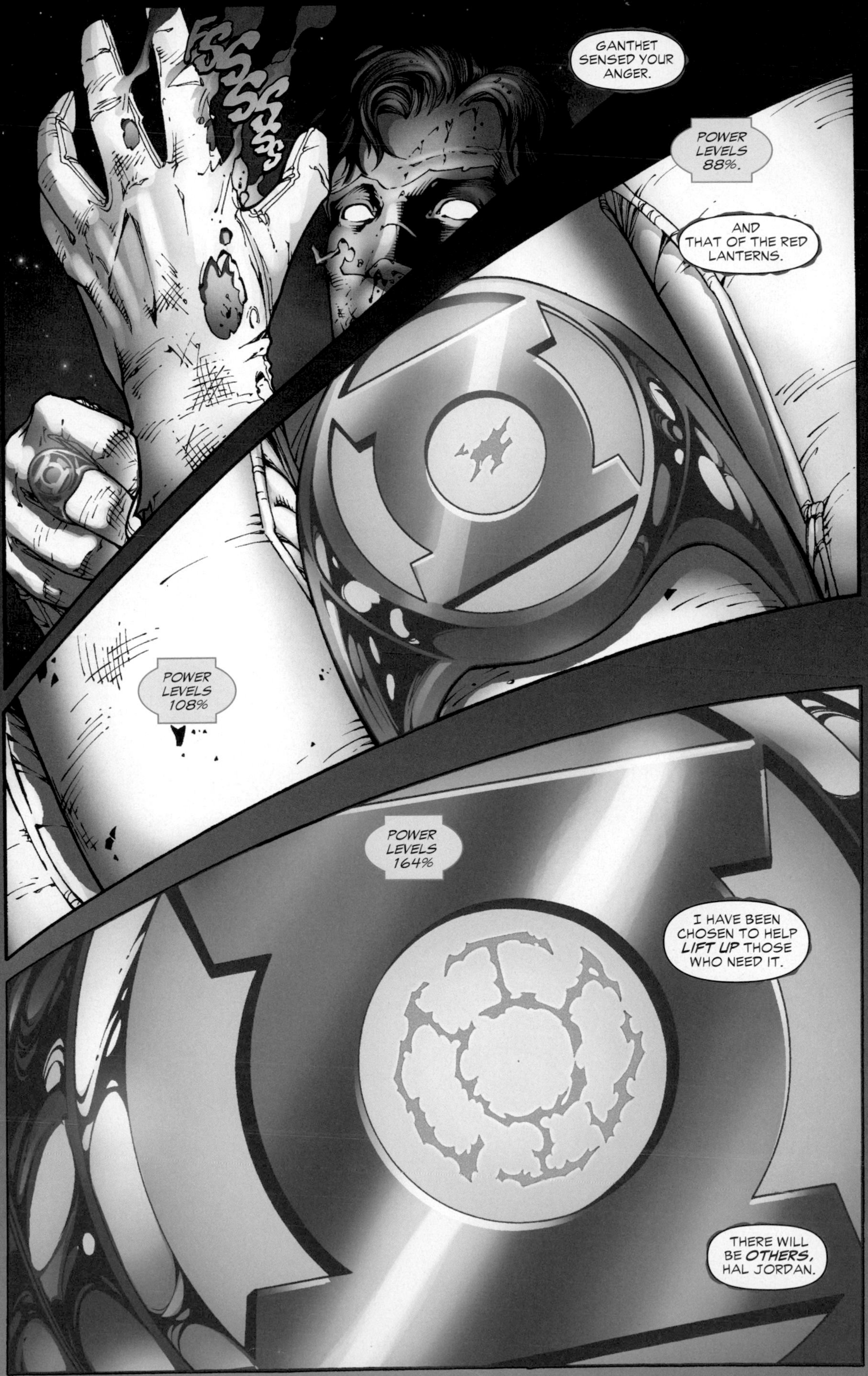
FSSSSSS
GANTHET SENSED YOUR ANGER.
POWER LEVELS 88%.
AND THAT OF THE RED LANTERNS.
POWER LEVELS 108%
POWER LEVELS 164%
I HAVE BEEN CHOSEN TO HELP *LIFT UP* THOSE WHO NEED IT.
THERE WILL BE *OTHERS,* HAL JORDAN.

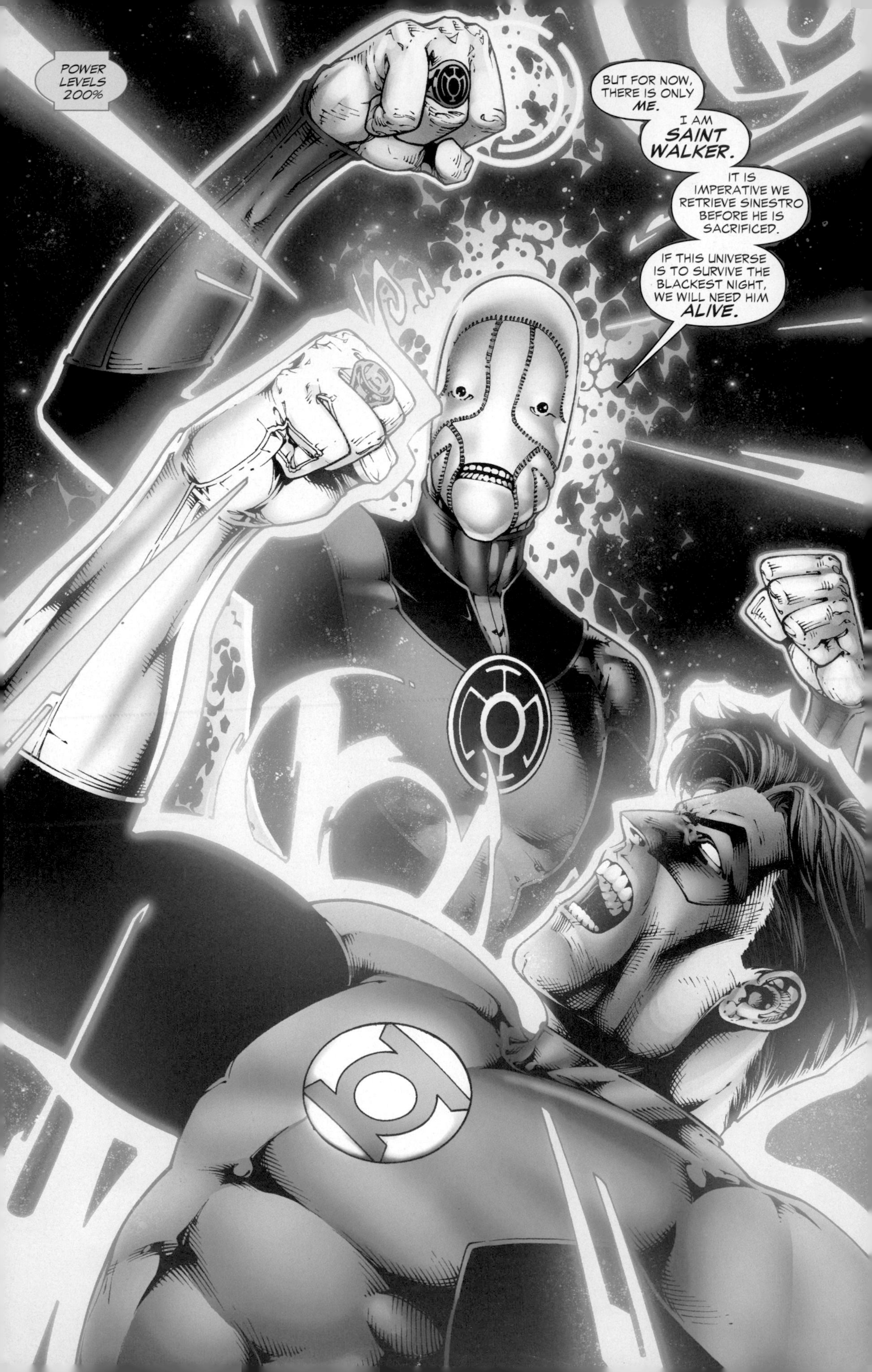
POWER LEVELS 200%
BUT FOR NOW, THERE IS ONLY *ME.*
I AM *SAINT WALKER.*
IT IS IMPERATIVE WE RETRIEVE SINESTRO BEFORE HE IS SACRIFICED.
IF THIS UNIVERSE IS TO SURVIVE THE BLACKEST NIGHT, WE WILL NEED HIM *ALIVE.*

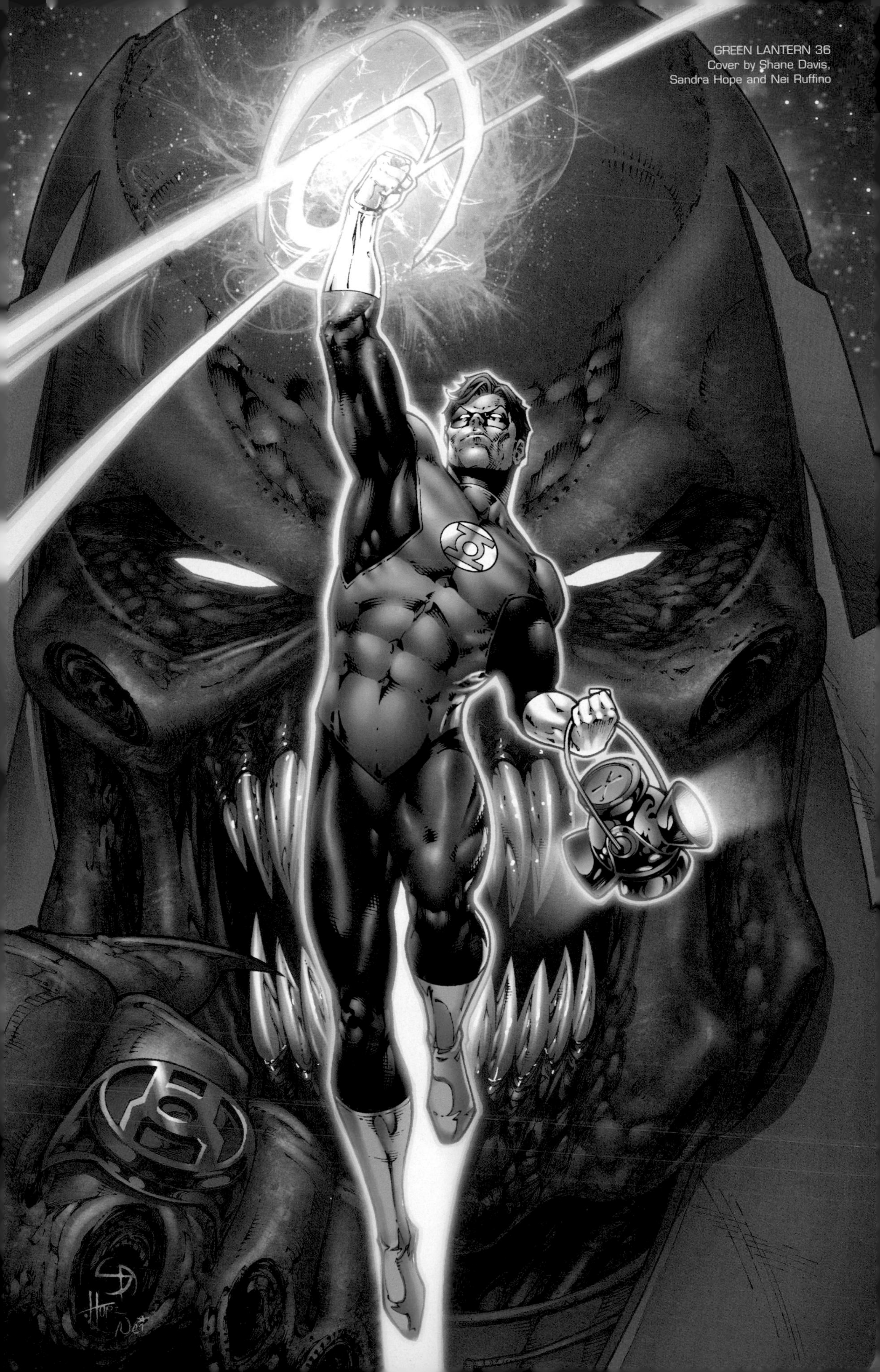

GREEN LANTERN 36
Cover by Shane Davis,
Sandra Hope and Nei Ruffino

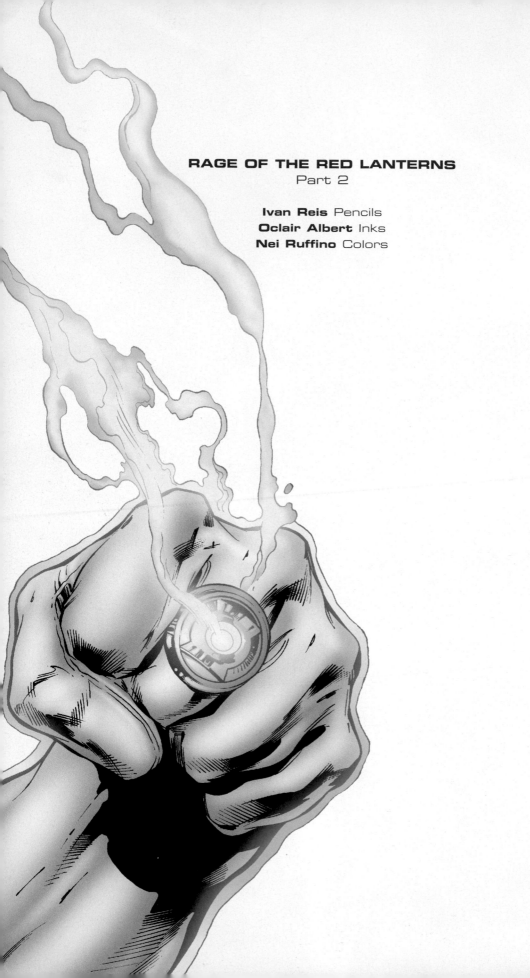

RAGE OF THE RED LANTERNS
Part 2

Ivan Reis Pencils
Oclair Albert Inks
Nei Ruffino Colors

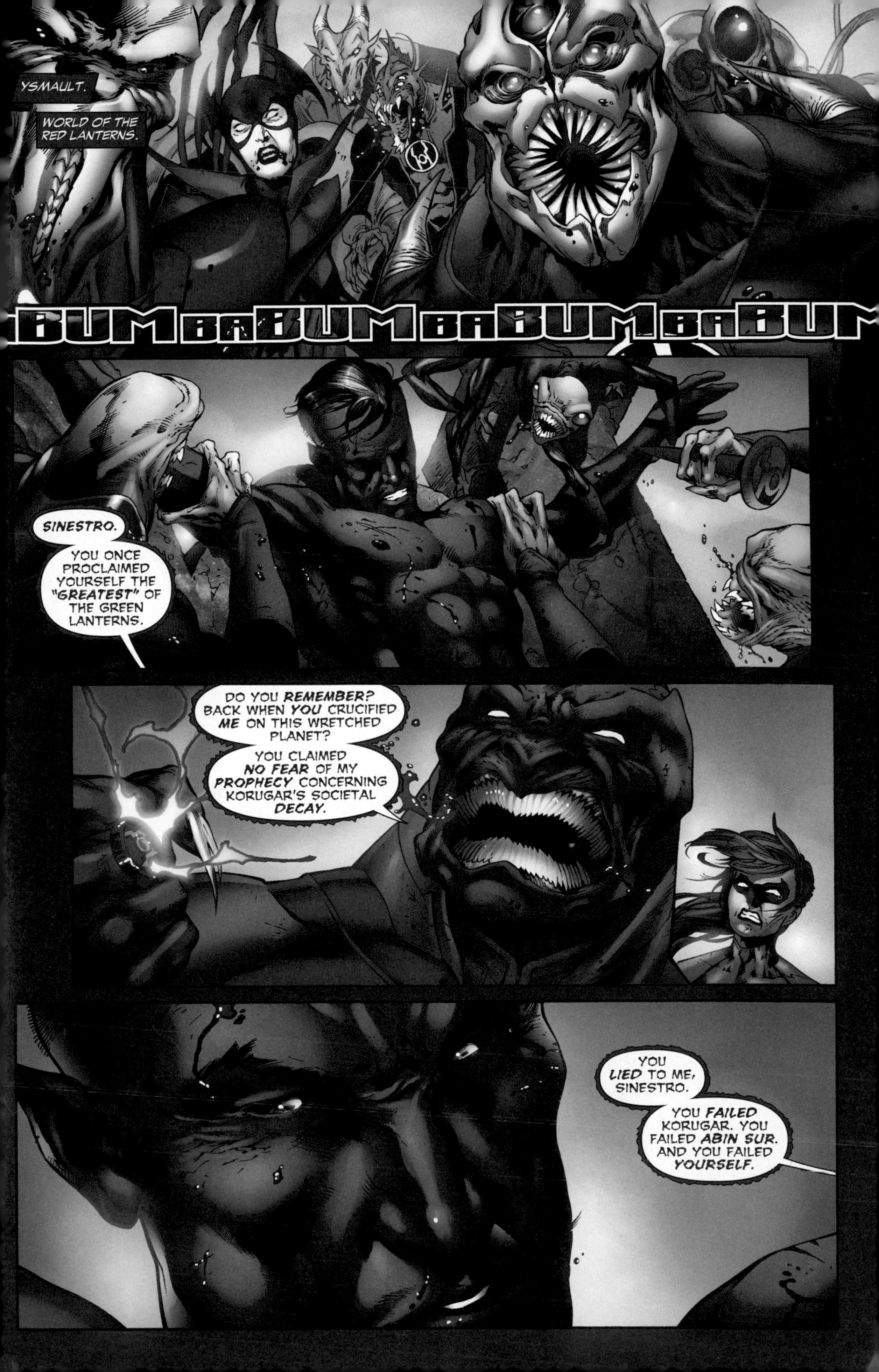
YSMAULT.
WORLD OF THE RED LANTERNS.
BUM BA BUM BA BUM BA BUM
SINESTRO.
YOU ONCE PROCLAIMED YOURSELF THE "GREATEST" OF THE GREEN LANTERNS.
DO YOU REMEMBER? BACK WHEN YOU CRUCIFIED ME ON THIS WRETCHED PLANET?
YOU CLAIMED NO FEAR OF MY PROPHECY CONCERNING KORUGAR'S SOCIETAL DECAY.
YOU LIED TO ME, SINESTRO.
YOU FAILED KORUGAR. YOU FAILED ABIN SUR. AND YOU FAILED YOURSELF.

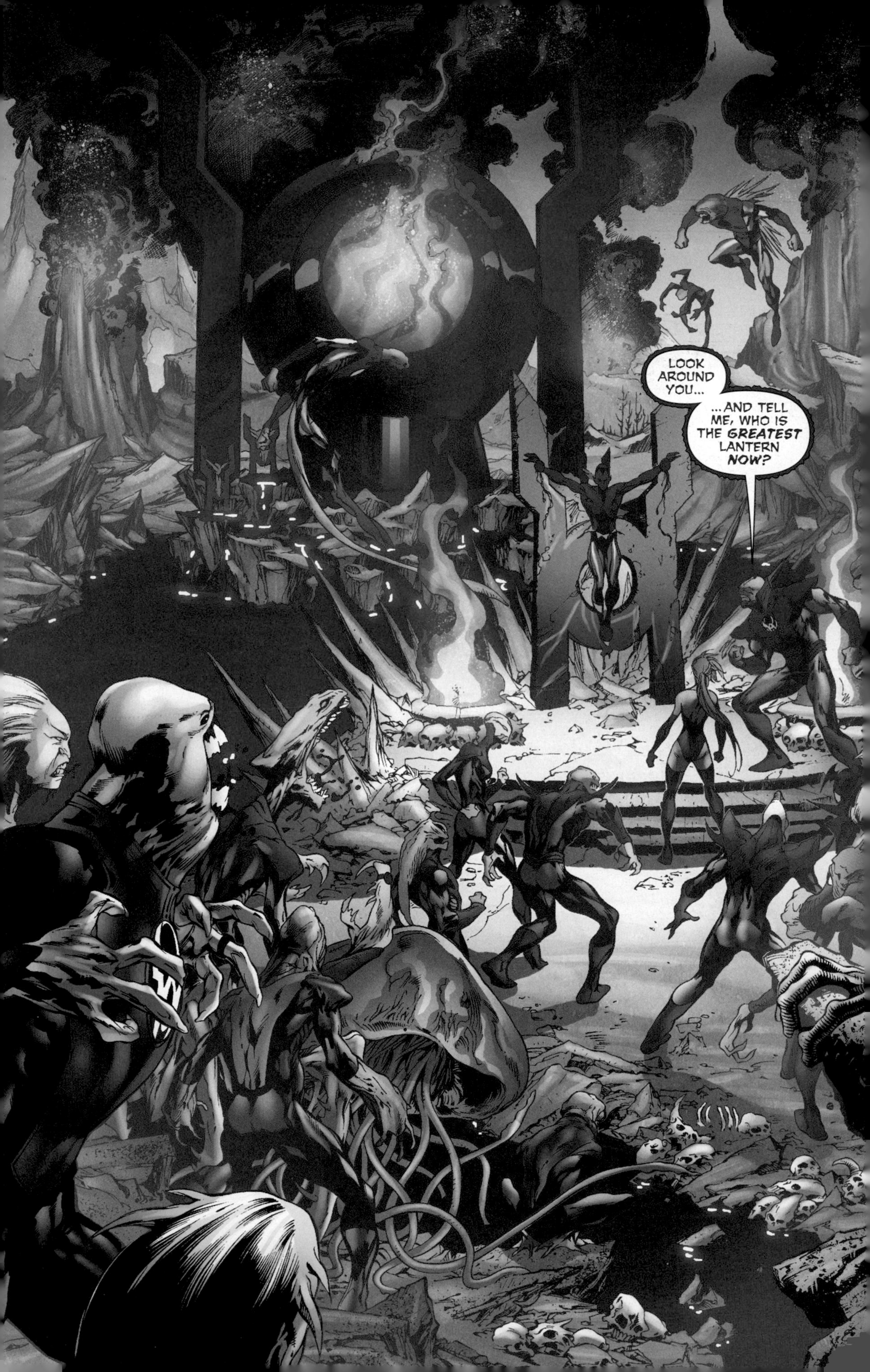
LOOK AROUND YOU...
...AND TELL ME, WHO IS THE GREATEST LANTERN NOW?

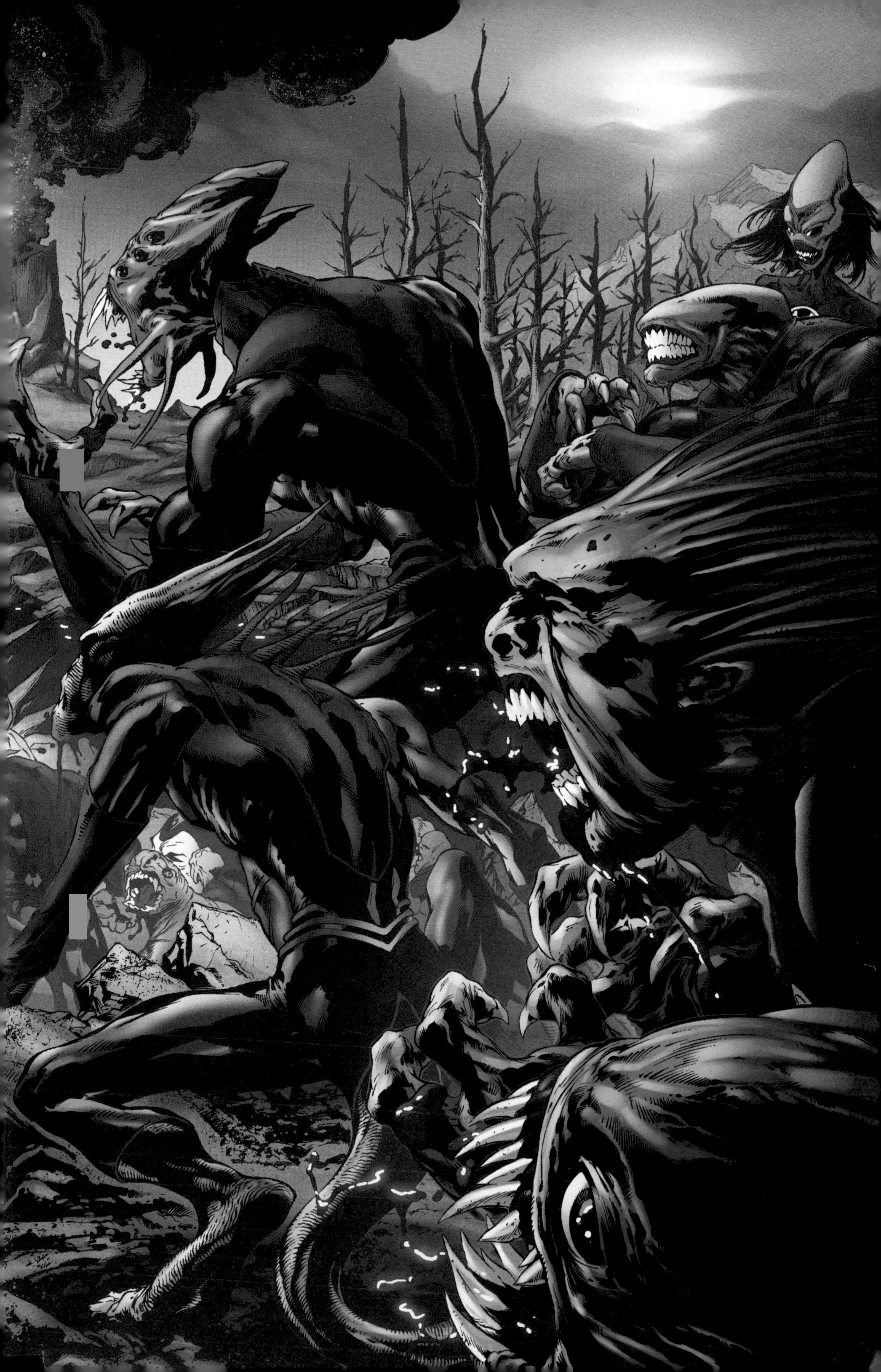

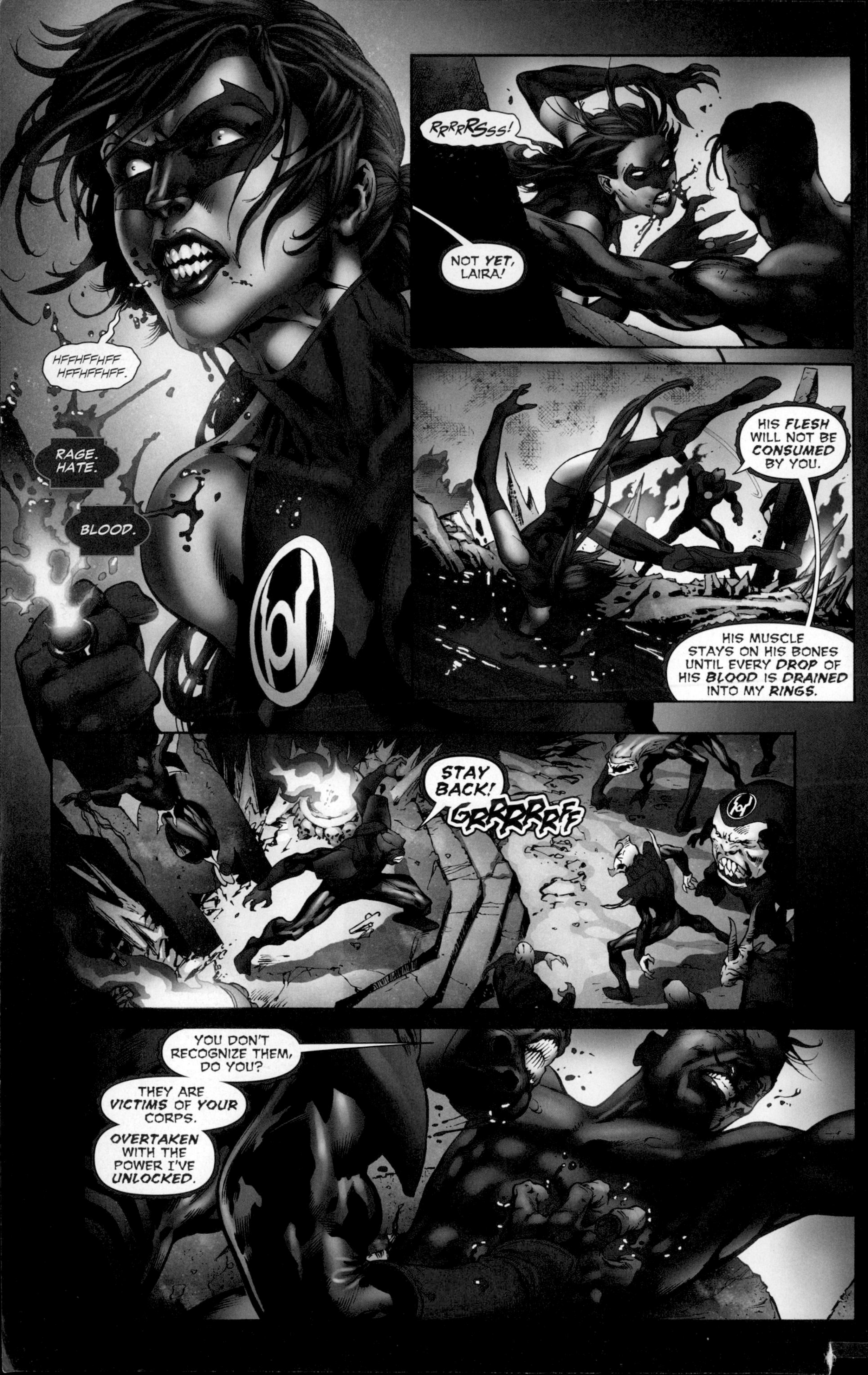
RRRRRSSS!
NOT YET, LAIRA!
HFFHFFHFF HFFHFFHFF.
RAGE. HATE.
BLOOD.
HIS FLESH WILL NOT BE CONSUMED BY YOU.
HIS MUSCLE STAYS ON HIS BONES UNTIL EVERY DROP OF HIS BLOOD IS DRAINED INTO MY RINGS.
STAY BACK!
GRRRRRFF
YOU DON'T RECOGNIZE THEM, DO YOU?
THEY ARE VICTIMS OF YOUR CORPS.
OVERTAKEN WITH THE POWER I'VE UNLOCKED.

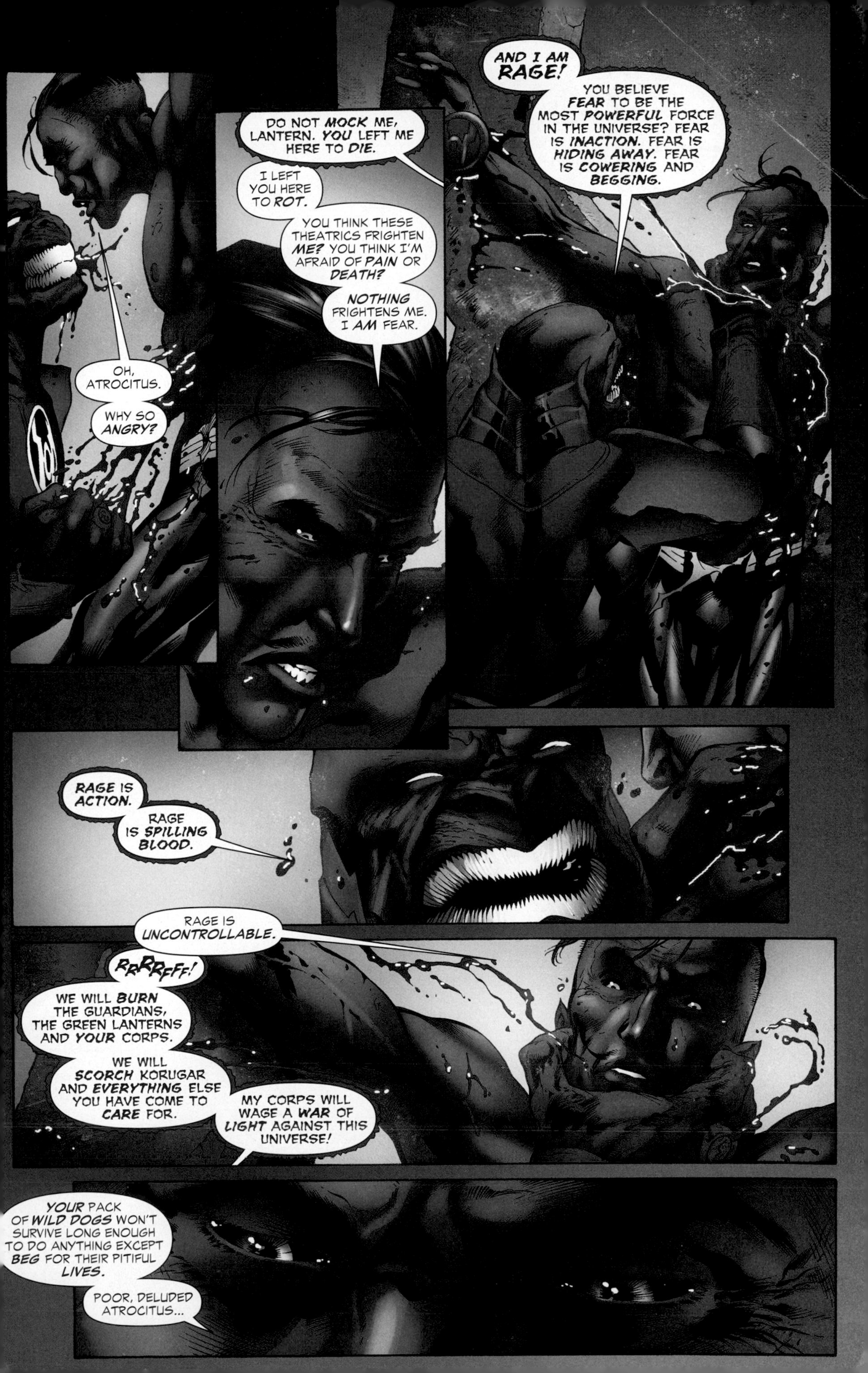

OH, ATROCITUS.
WHY SO ANGRY?
DO NOT MOCK ME, LANTERN. YOU LEFT ME HERE TO DIE.
I LEFT YOU HERE TO ROT.
YOU THINK THESE THEATRICS FRIGHTEN ME? YOU THINK I'M AFRAID OF PAIN OR DEATH?
NOTHING FRIGHTENS ME. I AM FEAR.
AND I AM RAGE!
YOU BELIEVE FEAR TO BE THE MOST POWERFUL FORCE IN THE UNIVERSE? FEAR IS INACTION. FEAR IS HIDING AWAY. FEAR IS COWERING AND BEGGING.
RAGE IS ACTION.
RAGE IS SPILLING BLOOD.
RAGE IS UNCONTROLLABLE.
RRRRFFF!
WE WILL BURN THE GUARDIANS, THE GREEN LANTERNS AND YOUR CORPS.
WE WILL SCORCH KORUGAR AND EVERYTHING ELSE YOU HAVE COME TO CARE FOR.
MY CORPS WILL WAGE A WAR OF LIGHT AGAINST THIS UNIVERSE!
YOUR PACK OF WILD DOGS WON'T SURVIVE LONG ENOUGH TO DO ANYTHING EXCEPT BEG FOR THEIR PITIFUL LIVES.
POOR, DELUDED ATROCITUS...

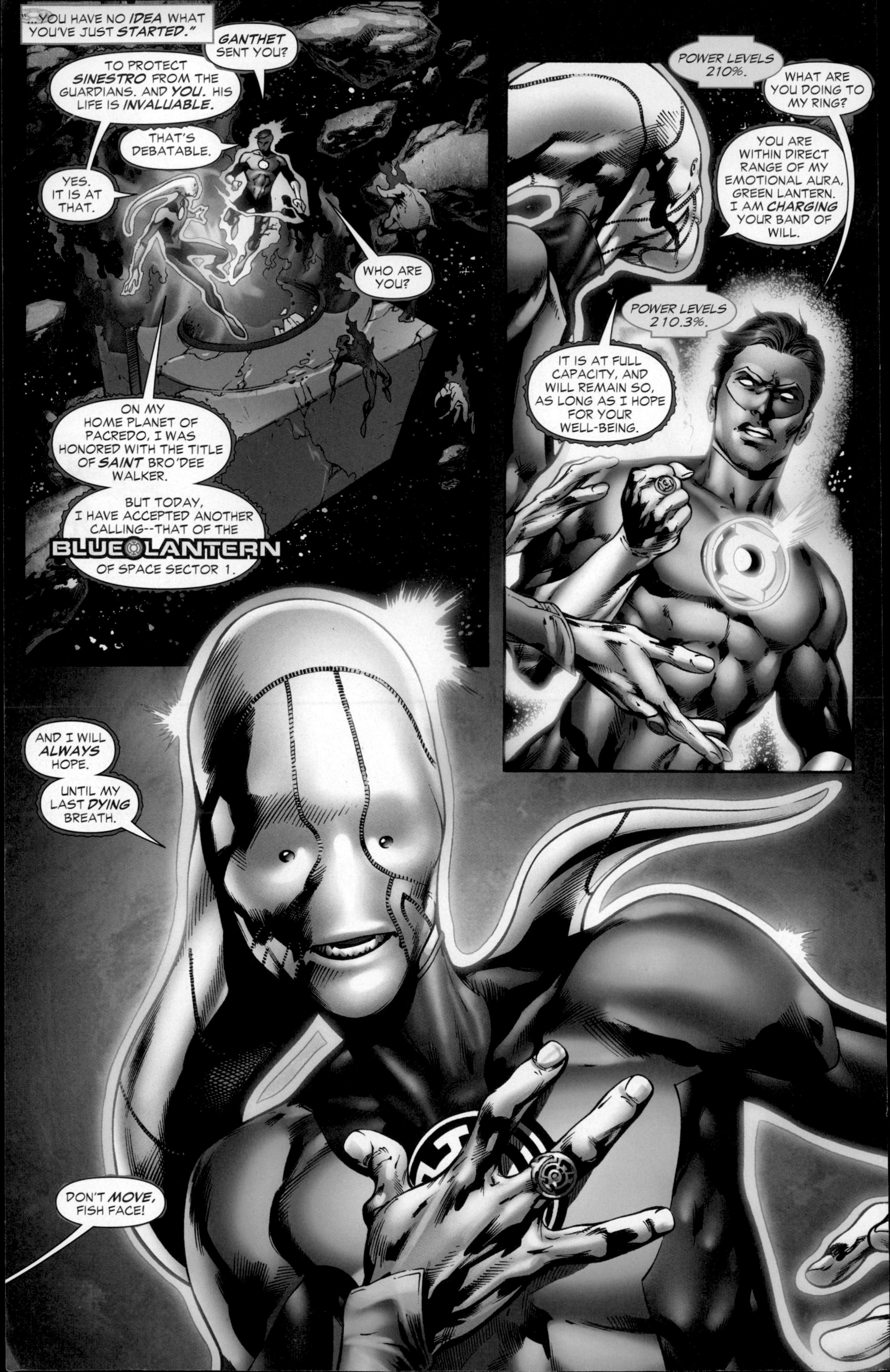
"...YOU HAVE NO IDEA WHAT YOU'VE JUST STARTED."
GANTHET SENT YOU?
TO PROTECT SINESTRO FROM THE GUARDIANS. AND YOU. HIS LIFE IS INVALUABLE.
THAT'S DEBATABLE.
YES. IT IS AT THAT.
WHO ARE YOU?
ON MY HOME PLANET OF PACREDO, I WAS HONORED WITH THE TITLE OF SAINT BRO'DEE WALKER.
BUT TODAY, I HAVE ACCEPTED ANOTHER CALLING--THAT OF THE BLUE LANTERN OF SPACE SECTOR 1.
POWER LEVELS 210%.
WHAT ARE YOU DOING TO MY RING?
YOU ARE WITHIN DIRECT RANGE OF MY EMOTIONAL AURA, GREEN LANTERN. I AM CHARGING YOUR BAND OF WILL.
POWER LEVELS 210.3%.
IT IS AT FULL CAPACITY, AND WILL REMAIN SO, AS LONG AS I HOPE FOR YOUR WELL-BEING.
AND I WILL ALWAYS HOPE.
UNTIL MY LAST DYING BREATH.
DON'T MOVE, FISH FACE!

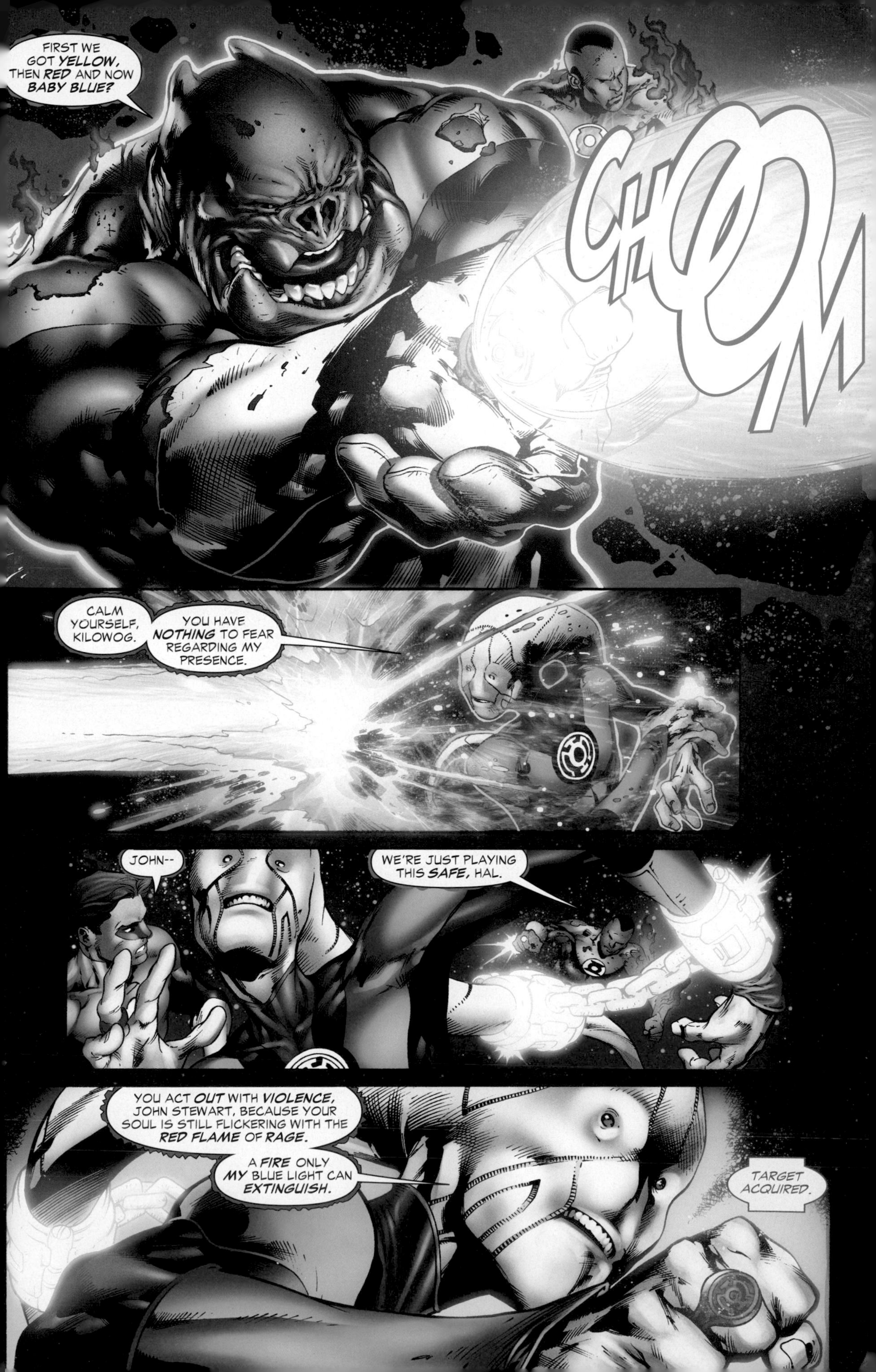
FIRST WE GOT YELLOW, THEN RED AND NOW BABY BLUE?
CHOOM
CALM YOURSELF, KILOWOG.
YOU HAVE NOTHING TO FEAR REGARDING MY PRESENCE.
JOHN--
WE'RE JUST PLAYING THIS SAFE, HAL.
YOU ACT OUT WITH VIOLENCE, JOHN STEWART, BECAUSE YOUR SOUL IS STILL FLICKERING WITH THE RED FLAME OF RAGE.
A FIRE ONLY MY BLUE LIGHT CAN EXTINGUISH.
TARGET ACQUIRED.

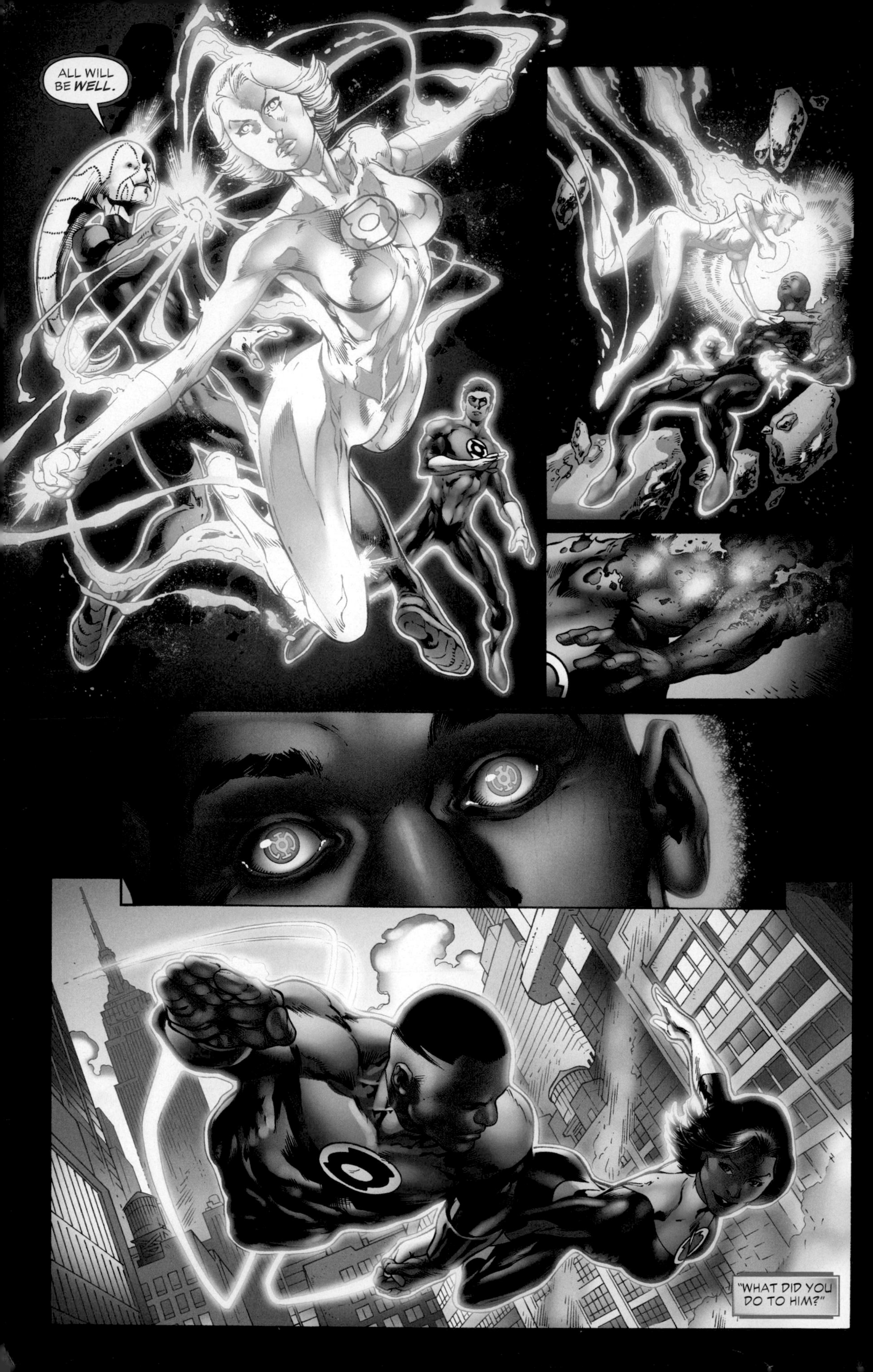
ALL WILL BE WELL.
"WHAT DID YOU DO TO HIM?"

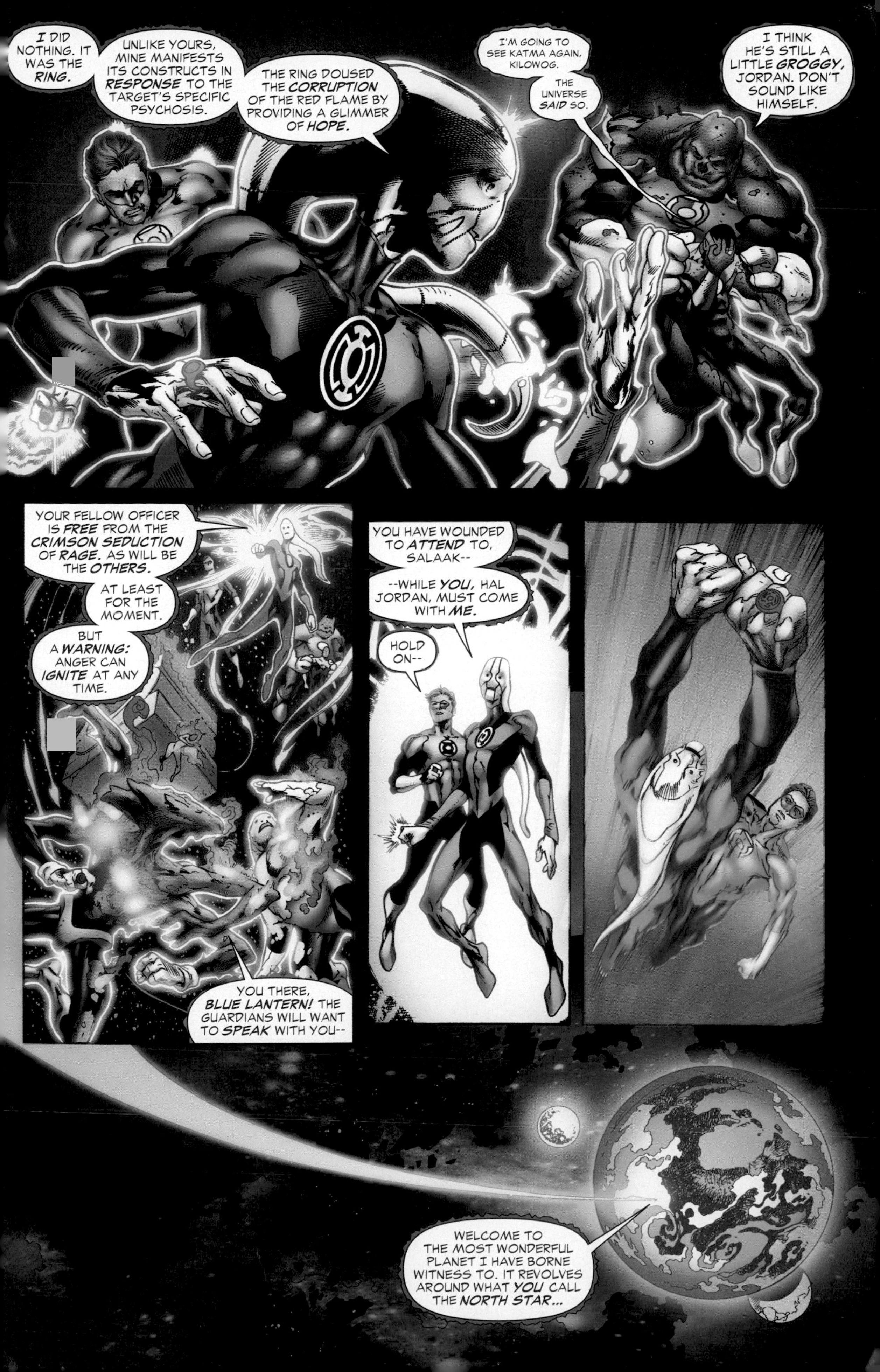
I DID NOTHING. IT WAS THE RING.
UNLIKE YOURS, MINE MANIFESTS ITS CONSTRUCTS IN RESPONSE TO THE TARGET'S SPECIFIC PSYCHOSIS.
THE RING DOUSED THE CORRUPTION OF THE RED FLAME BY PROVIDING A GLIMMER OF HOPE.
I'M GOING TO SEE KATMA AGAIN, KILOWOG.
THE UNIVERSE SAID SO.
I THINK HE'S STILL A LITTLE GROGGY, JORDAN. DON'T SOUND LIKE HIMSELF.
YOUR FELLOW OFFICER IS FREE FROM THE CRIMSON SEDUCTION OF RAGE. AS WILL BE THE OTHERS.
AT LEAST FOR THE MOMENT.
BUT A WARNING: ANGER CAN IGNITE AT ANY TIME.
YOU THERE, BLUE LANTERN! THE GUARDIANS WILL WANT TO SPEAK WITH YOU--
YOU HAVE WOUNDED TO ATTEND TO, SALAAK--
--WHILE YOU, HAL JORDAN, MUST COME WITH ME.
HOLD ON--
WELCOME TO THE MOST WONDERFUL PLANET I HAVE BORNE WITNESS TO. IT REVOLVES AROUND WHAT YOU CALL THE NORTH STAR...

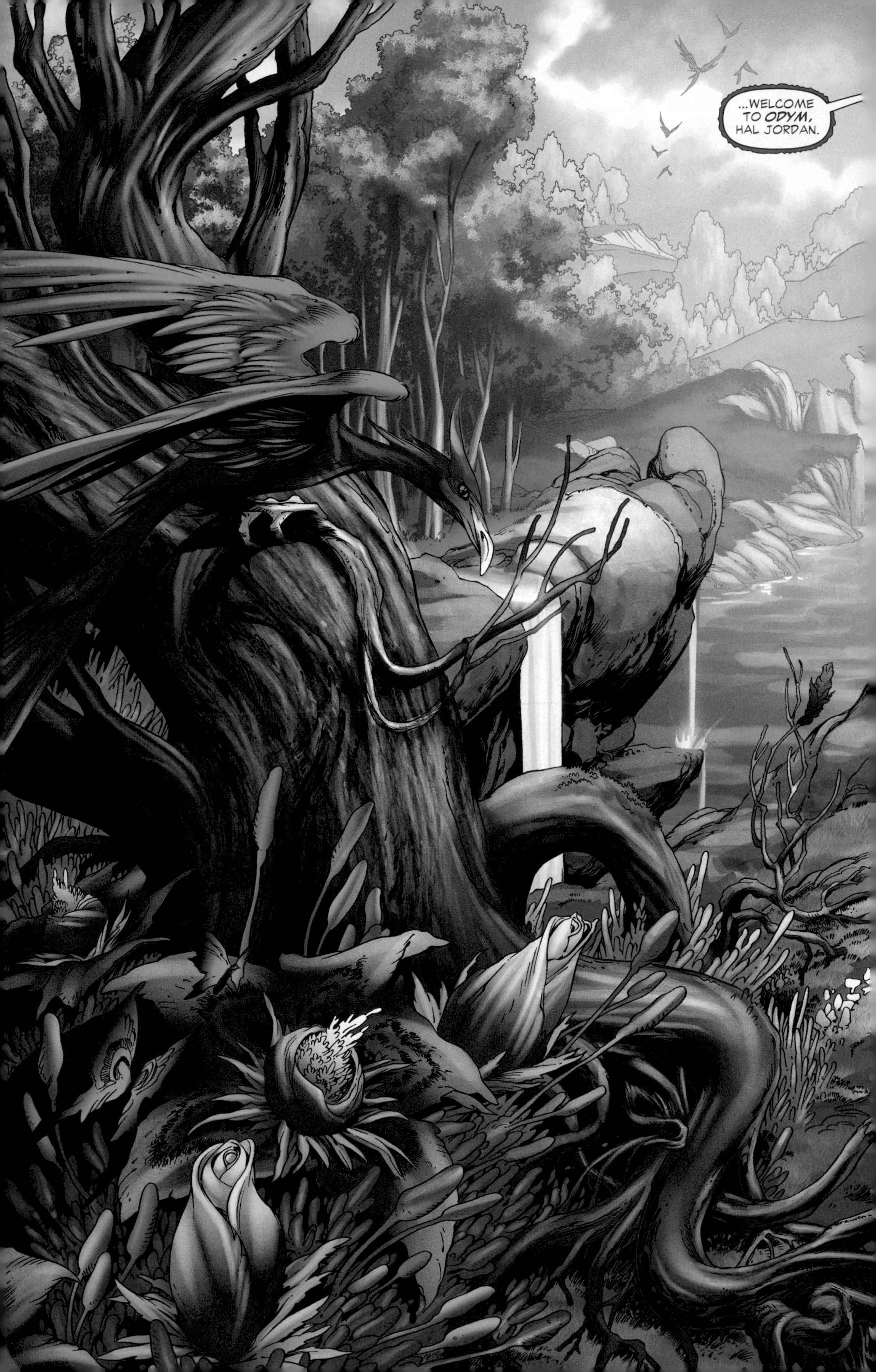
...WELCOME TO ODYM, HAL JORDAN.

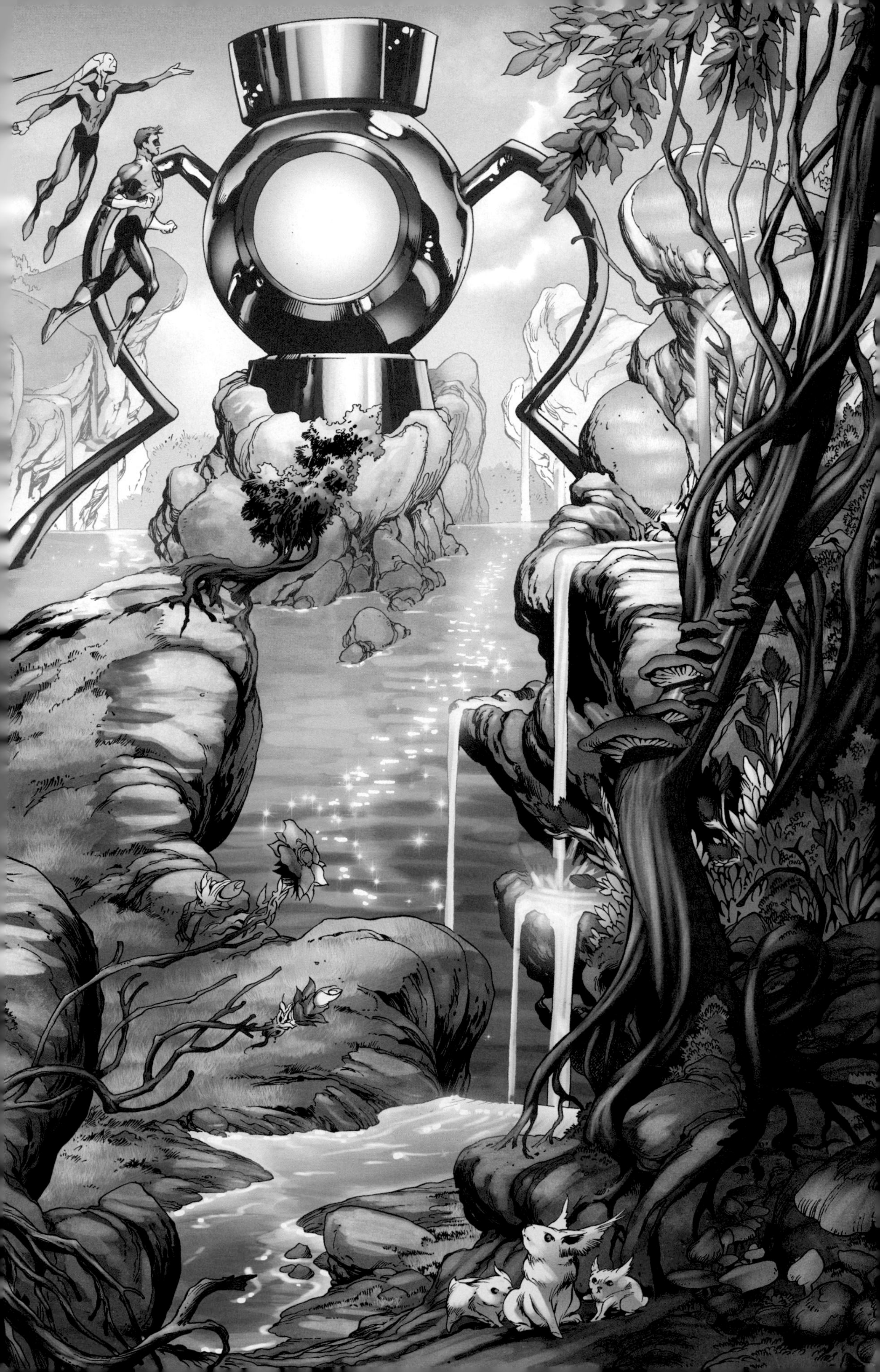

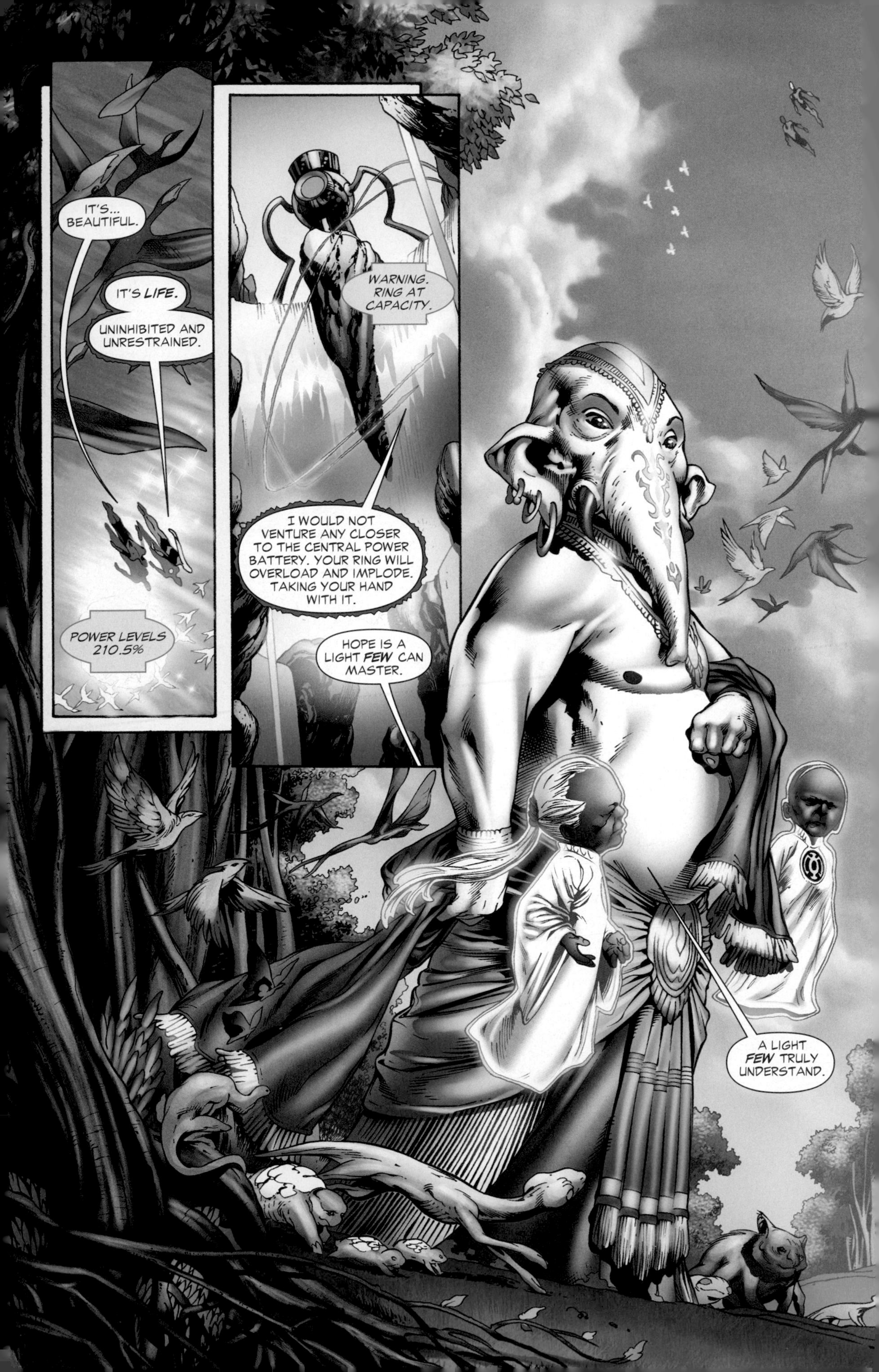
IT'S... BEAUTIFUL.
IT'S *LIFE.*
UNINHIBITED AND UNRESTRAINED.
POWER LEVELS 210.5%
WARNING. RING AT CAPACITY.
I WOULD NOT VENTURE ANY CLOSER TO THE CENTRAL POWER BATTERY. YOUR RING WILL OVERLOAD AND IMPLODE. TAKING YOUR HAND WITH IT.
HOPE IS A LIGHT *FEW* CAN MASTER.
A LIGHT *FEW* TRULY UNDERSTAND.

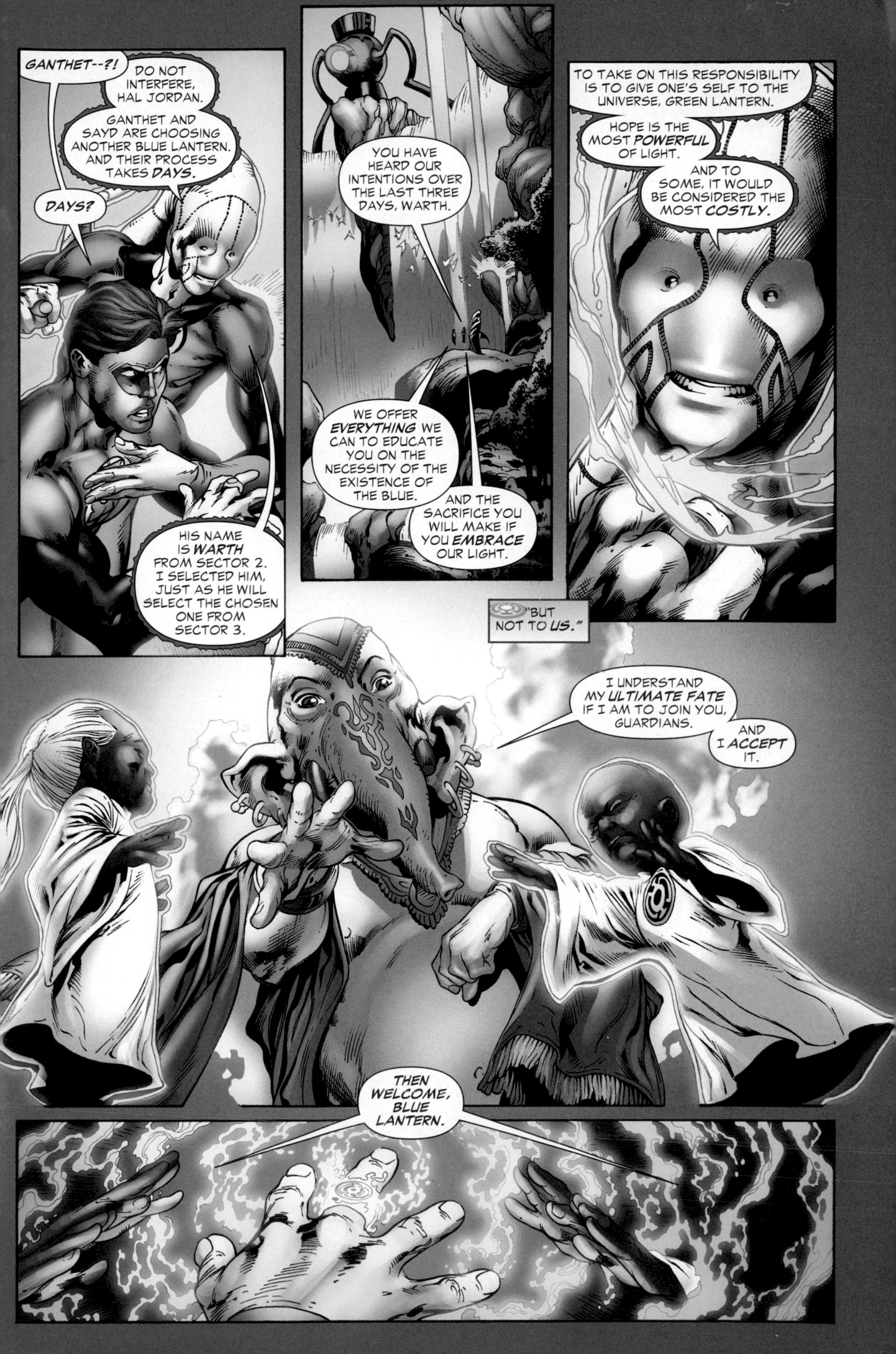
GANTHET--?!
DO NOT INTERFERE, HAL JORDAN.
GANTHET AND SAYD ARE CHOOSING ANOTHER BLUE LANTERN. AND THEIR PROCESS TAKES DAYS.
DAYS?
HIS NAME IS WARTH FROM SECTOR 2. I SELECTED HIM, JUST AS HE WILL SELECT THE CHOSEN ONE FROM SECTOR 3.
YOU HAVE HEARD OUR INTENTIONS OVER THE LAST THREE DAYS, WARTH.
WE OFFER EVERYTHING WE CAN TO EDUCATE YOU ON THE NECESSITY OF THE EXISTENCE OF THE BLUE.
AND THE SACRIFICE YOU WILL MAKE IF YOU EMBRACE OUR LIGHT.
TO TAKE ON THIS RESPONSIBILITY IS TO GIVE ONE'S SELF TO THE UNIVERSE, GREEN LANTERN.
HOPE IS THE MOST POWERFUL OF LIGHT.
AND TO SOME, IT WOULD BE CONSIDERED THE MOST COSTLY.
"BUT NOT TO US."
I UNDERSTAND MY ULTIMATE FATE IF I AM TO JOIN YOU, GUARDIANS.
AND I ACCEPT IT.
THEN WELCOME, BLUE LANTERN.

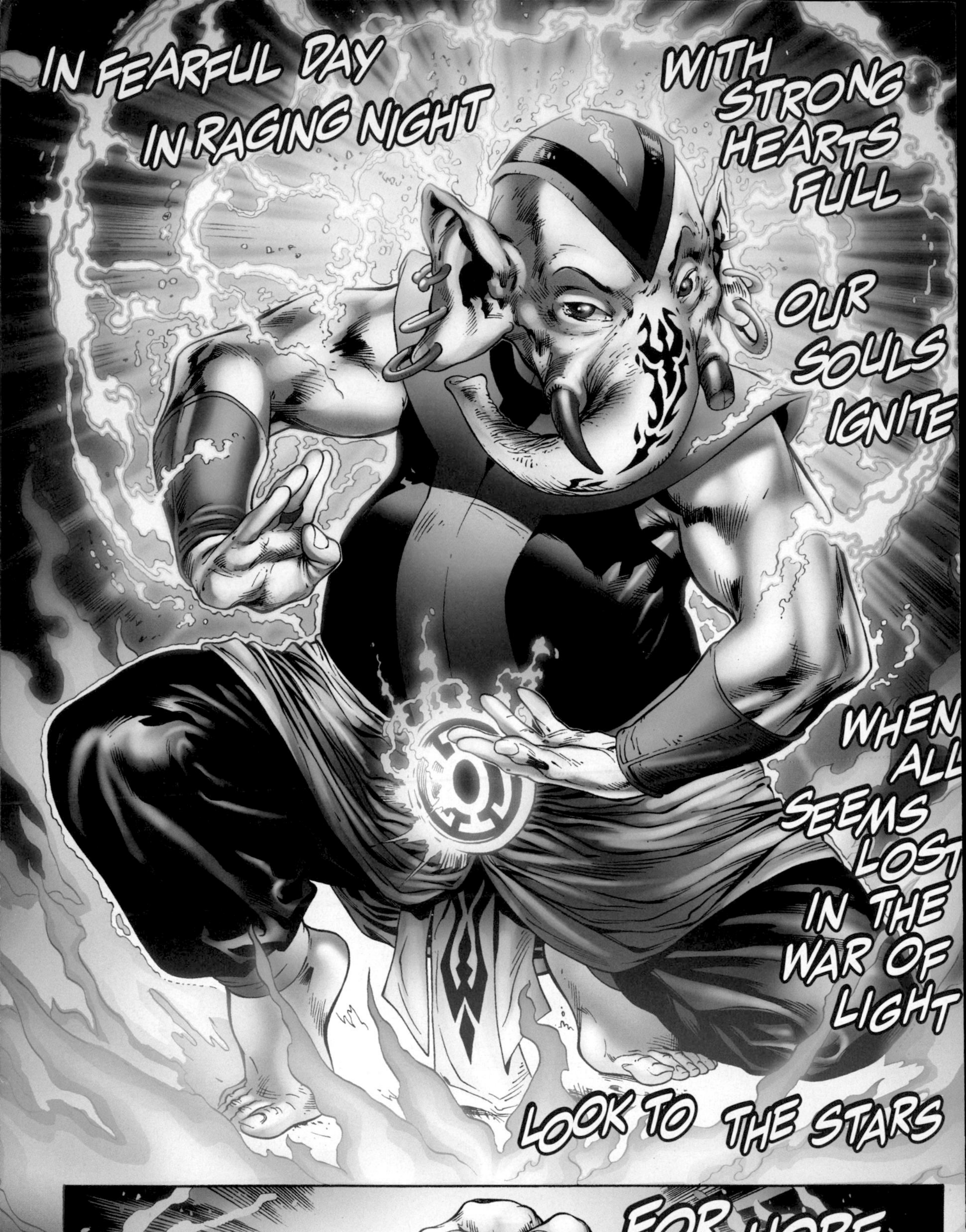
IN FEARFUL DAY
IN RAGING NIGHT
WITH STRONG HEARTS FULL
OUR SOULS IGNITE
WHEN ALL SEEMS LOST IN THE WAR OF LIGHT
LOOK TO THE STARS
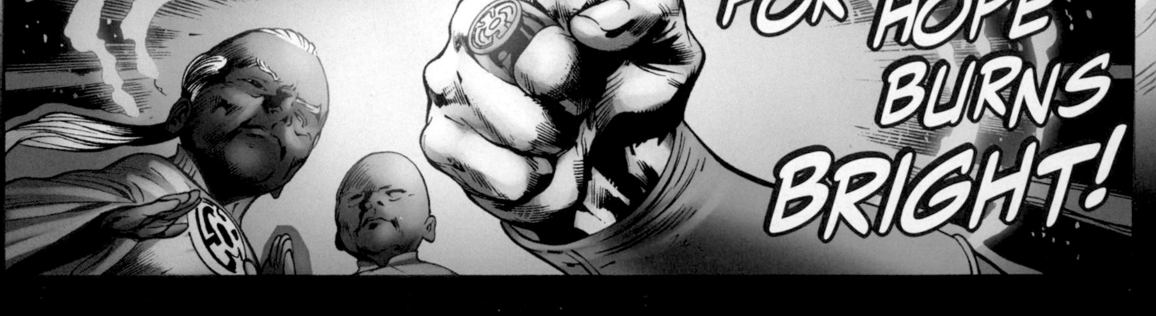
FOR HOPE BURNS BRIGHT!

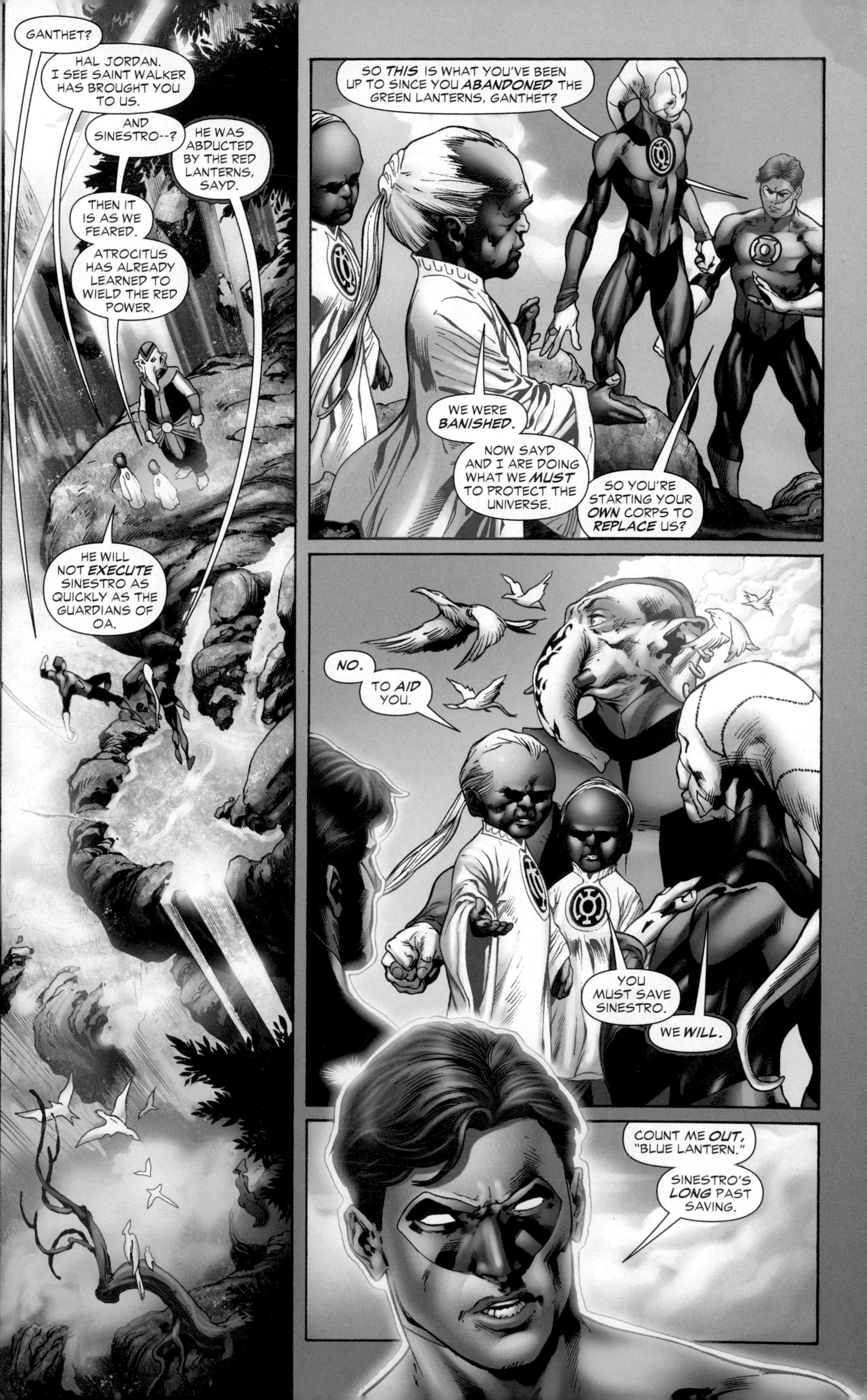
GANTHET?
HAL JORDAN. I SEE SAINT WALKER HAS BROUGHT YOU TO US.
AND SINESTRO--?
HE WAS ABDUCTED BY THE RED LANTERNS, SAYD.
THEN IT IS AS WE FEARED.
ATROCITUS HAS ALREADY LEARNED TO WIELD THE RED POWER.
HE WILL NOT EXECUTE SINESTRO AS QUICKLY AS THE GUARDIANS OF OA.
SO THIS IS WHAT YOU'VE BEEN UP TO SINCE YOU ABANDONED THE GREEN LANTERNS, GANTHET?
WE WERE BANISHED.
NOW SAYD AND I ARE DOING WHAT WE MUST TO PROTECT THE UNIVERSE.
SO YOU'RE STARTING YOUR OWN CORPS TO REPLACE US?
NO.
TO AID YOU.
YOU MUST SAVE SINESTRO.
WE WILL.
COUNT ME OUT, "BLUE LANTERN."
SINESTRO'S LONG PAST SAVING.

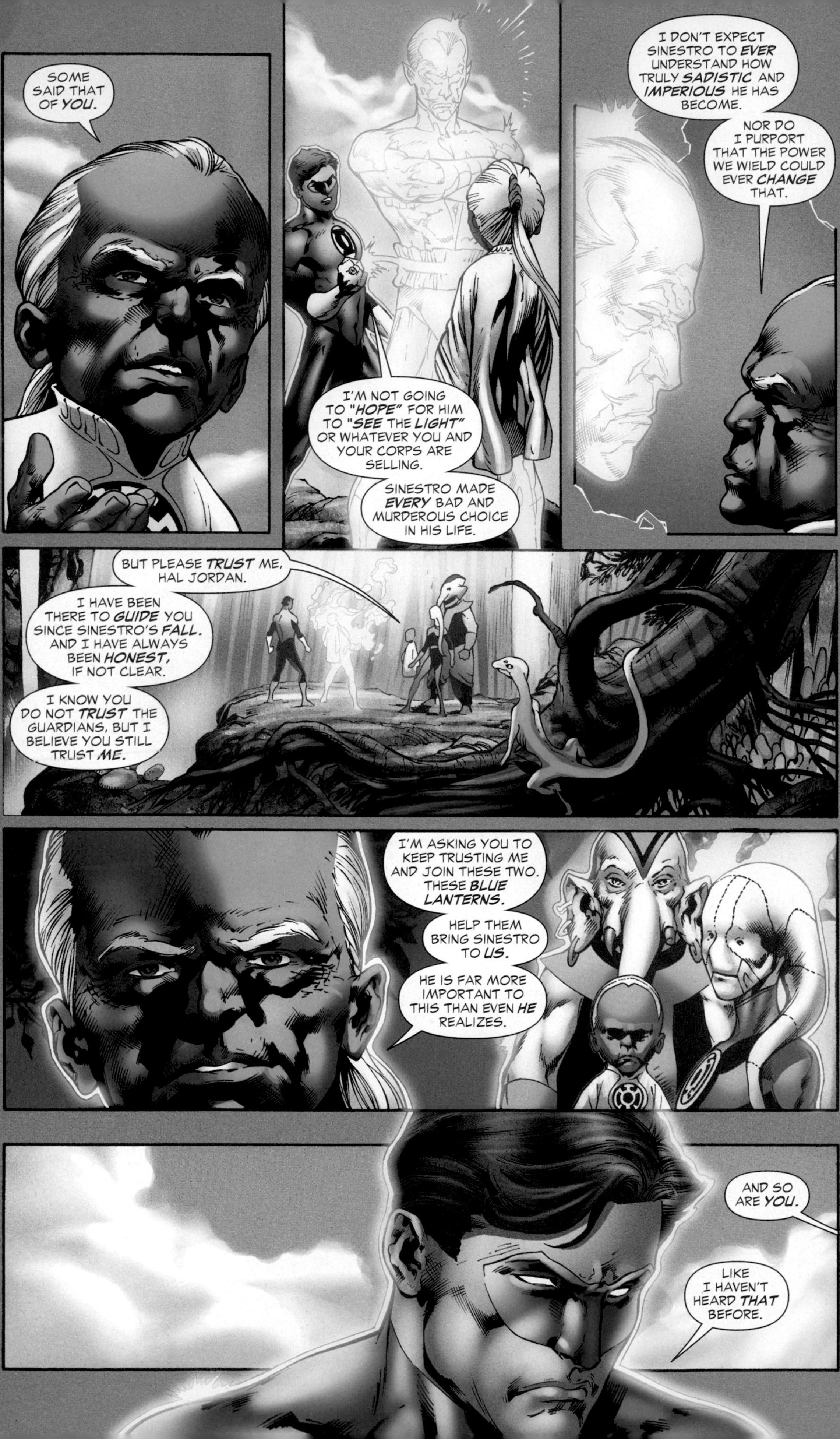
SOME SAID THAT OF YOU.
I'M NOT GOING TO "HOPE" FOR HIM TO "SEE THE LIGHT" OR WHATEVER YOU AND YOUR CORPS ARE SELLING.
SINESTRO MADE EVERY BAD AND MURDEROUS CHOICE IN HIS LIFE.
I DON'T EXPECT SINESTRO TO EVER UNDERSTAND HOW TRULY SADISTIC AND IMPERIOUS HE HAS BECOME.
NOR DO I PURPORT THAT THE POWER WE WIELD COULD EVER CHANGE THAT.
BUT PLEASE TRUST ME, HAL JORDAN.
I HAVE BEEN THERE TO GUIDE YOU SINCE SINESTRO'S FALL. AND I HAVE ALWAYS BEEN HONEST, IF NOT CLEAR.
I KNOW YOU DO NOT TRUST THE GUARDIANS, BUT I BELIEVE YOU STILL TRUST ME.
I'M ASKING YOU TO KEEP TRUSTING ME AND JOIN THESE TWO. THESE BLUE LANTERNS.
HELP THEM BRING SINESTRO TO US.
HE IS FAR MORE IMPORTANT TO THIS THAN EVEN HE REALIZES.
AND SO ARE YOU.
LIKE I HAVEN'T HEARD THAT BEFORE.

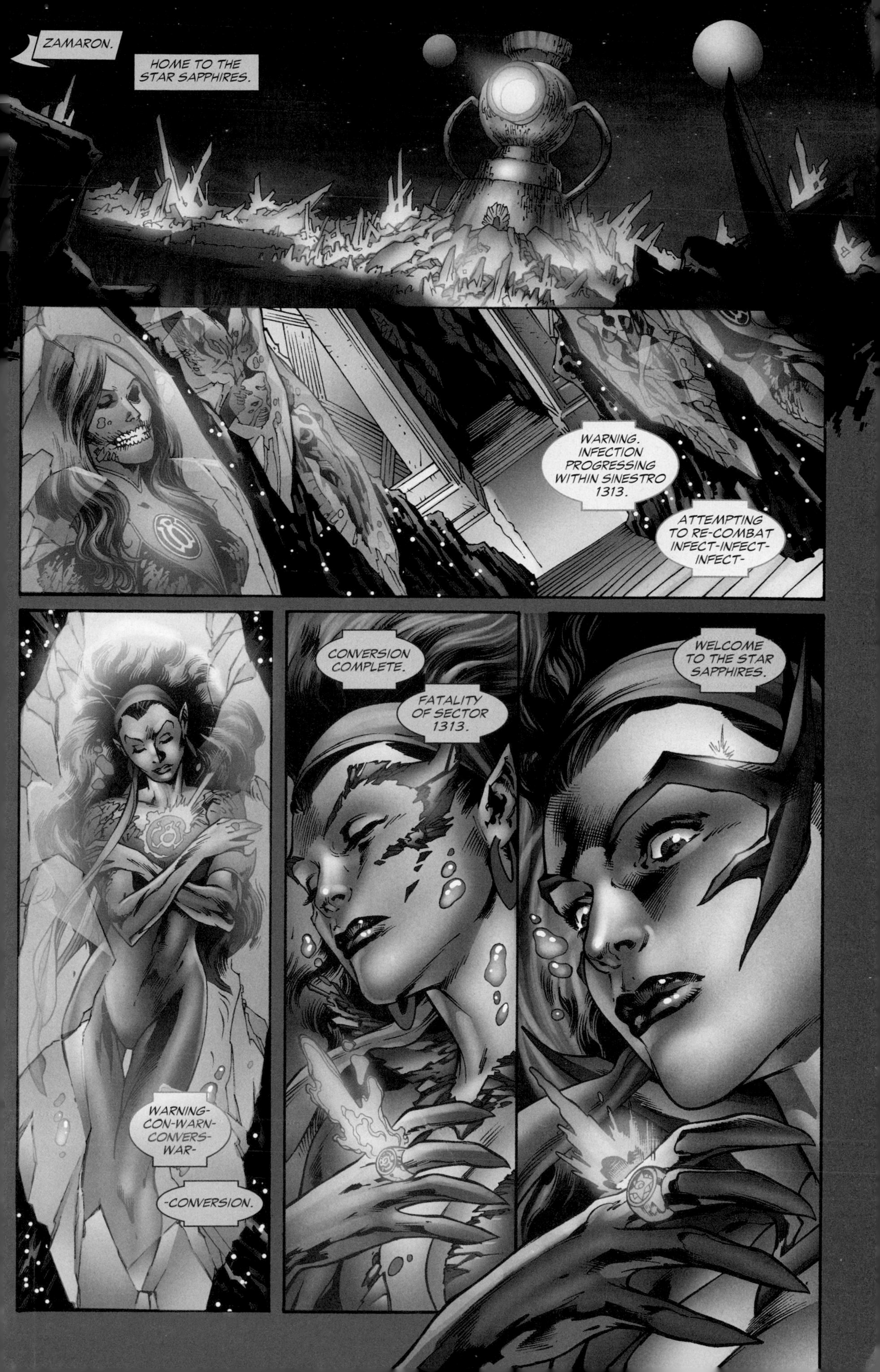
ZAMARON.
HOME TO THE STAR SAPPHIRES.
WARNING. INFECTION PROGRESSING WITHIN SINESTRO 1313.
ATTEMPTING TO RE-COMBAT INFECT-INFECT-INFECT-
WARNING-CON-WARN-CONVERS-WAR-
-CONVERSION.
CONVERSION COMPLETE.
FATALITY OF SECTOR 1313.
WELCOME TO THE STAR SAPPHIRES.

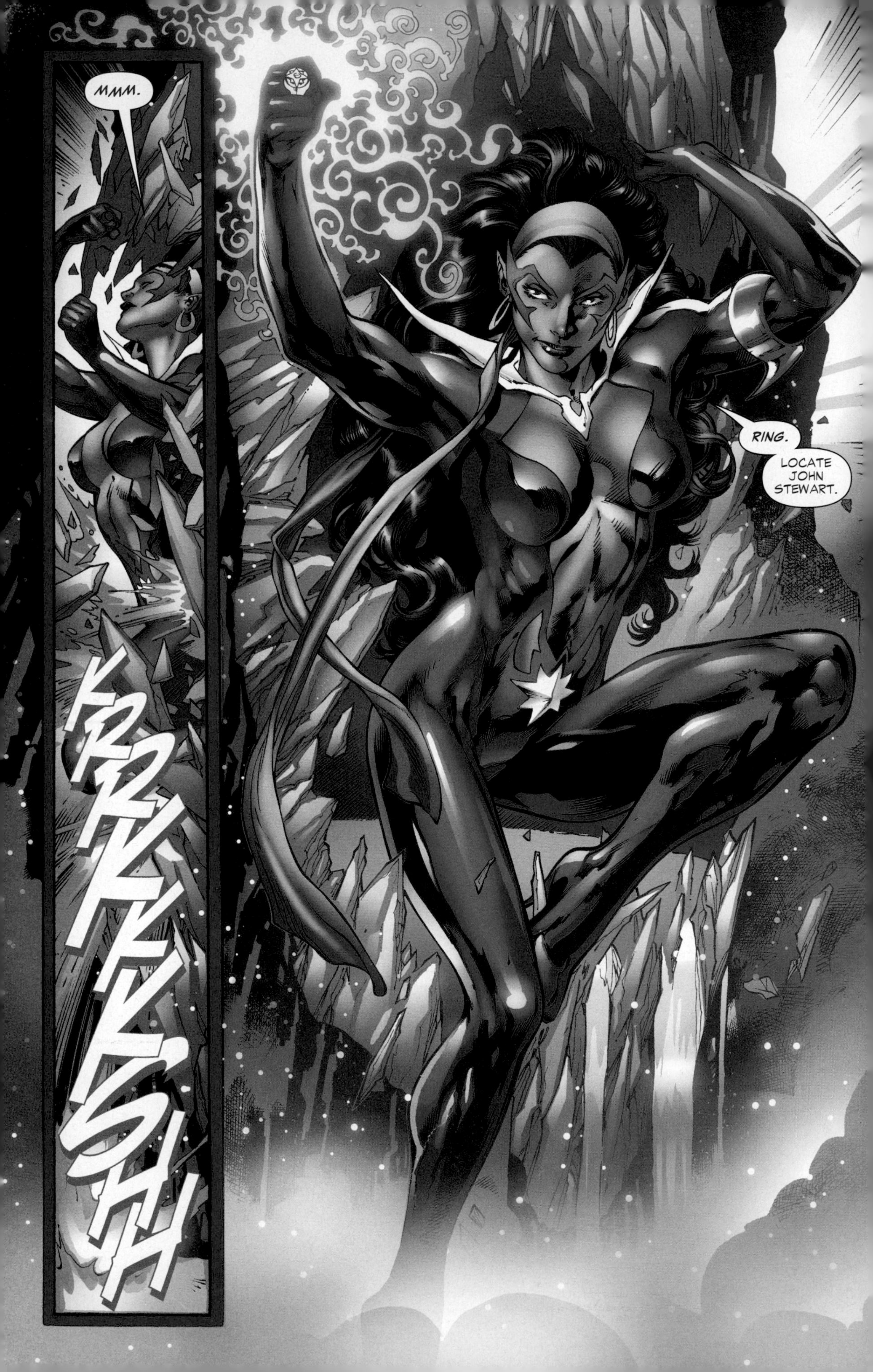
MMM.
KRRKKKSHH
RING.
LOCATE JOHN STEWART.

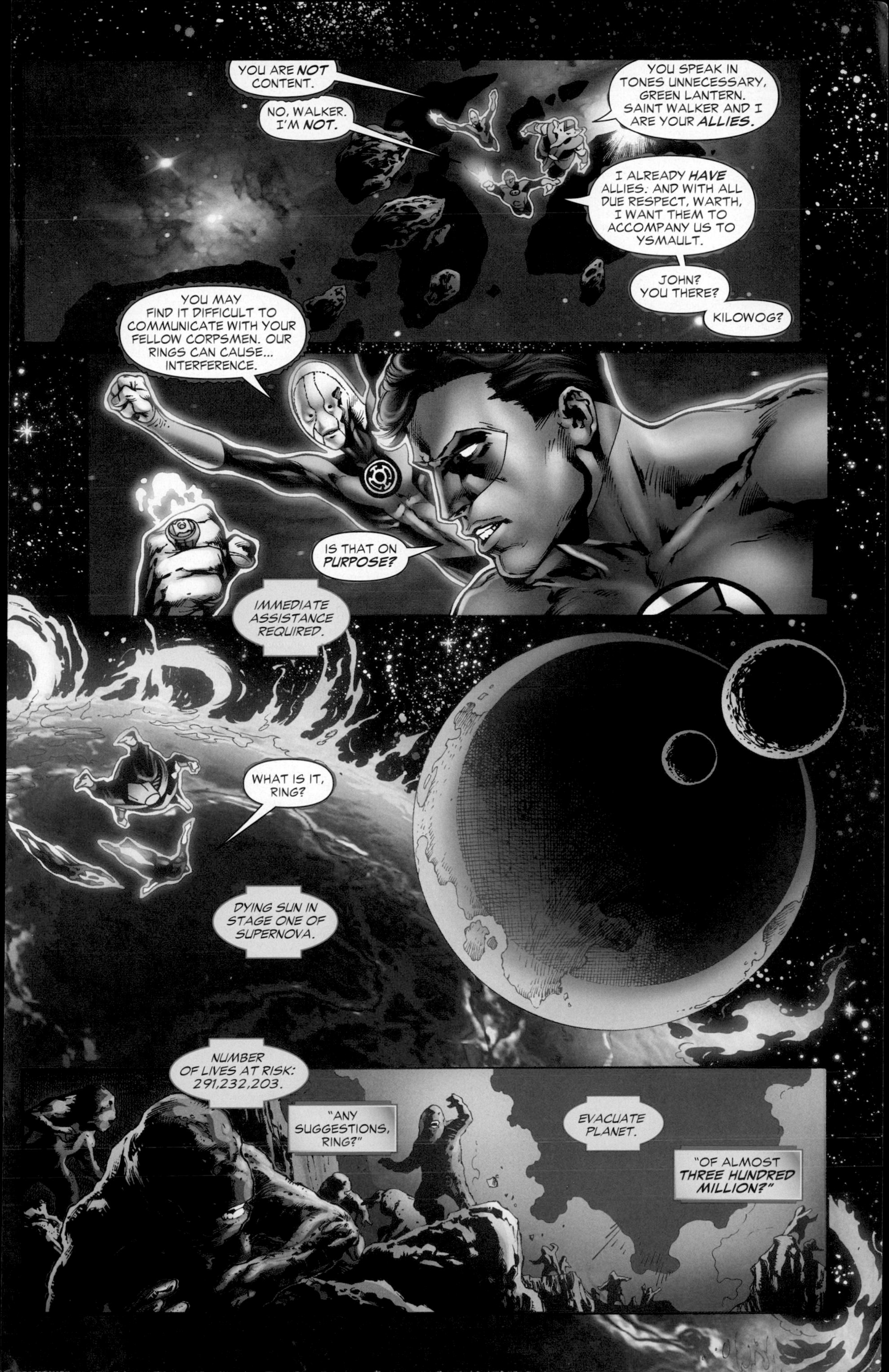
YOU ARE NOT CONTENT.
NO, WALKER. I'M NOT.
YOU SPEAK IN TONES UNNECESSARY, GREEN LANTERN. SAINT WALKER AND I ARE YOUR ALLIES.
I ALREADY HAVE ALLIES. AND WITH ALL DUE RESPECT, WARTH, I WANT THEM TO ACCOMPANY US TO YSMAULT.
JOHN? YOU THERE?
KILOWOG?
YOU MAY FIND IT DIFFICULT TO COMMUNICATE WITH YOUR FELLOW CORPSMEN. OUR RINGS CAN CAUSE... INTERFERENCE.
IS THAT ON PURPOSE?
IMMEDIATE ASSISTANCE REQUIRED.
WHAT IS IT, RING?
DYING SUN IN STAGE ONE OF SUPERNOVA.
NUMBER OF LIVES AT RISK: 291,232,203.
"ANY SUGGESTIONS, RING?"
EVACUATE PLANET.
"OF ALMOST THREE HUNDRED MILLION?"

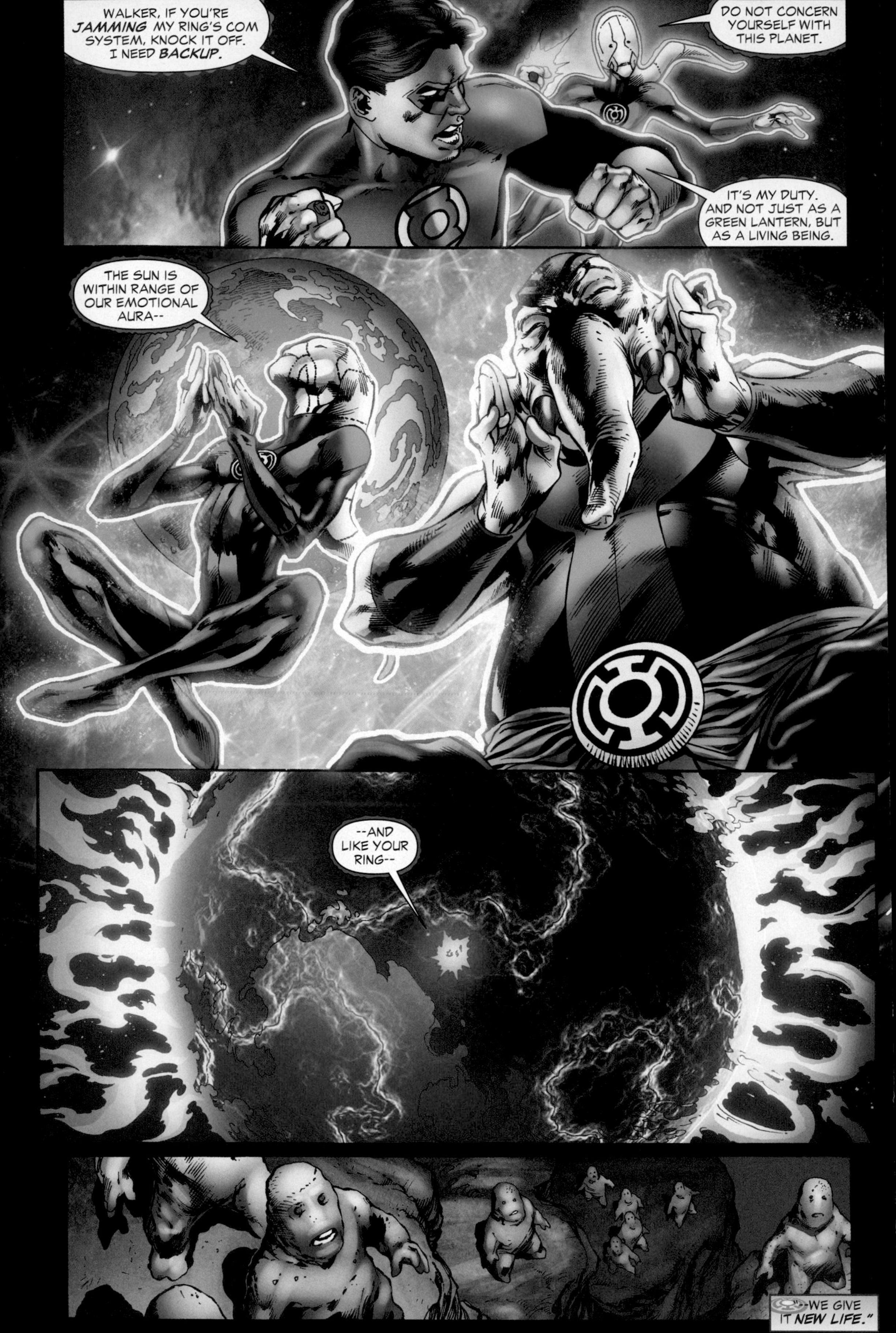
WALKER, IF YOU'RE JAMMING MY RING'S COM SYSTEM, KNOCK IT OFF. I NEED BACKUP.
DO NOT CONCERN YOURSELF WITH THIS PLANET.
IT'S MY DUTY. AND NOT JUST AS A GREEN LANTERN, BUT AS A LIVING BEING.
THE SUN IS WITHIN RANGE OF OUR EMOTIONAL AURA--
--AND LIKE YOUR RING--
--WE GIVE IT NEW LIFE."

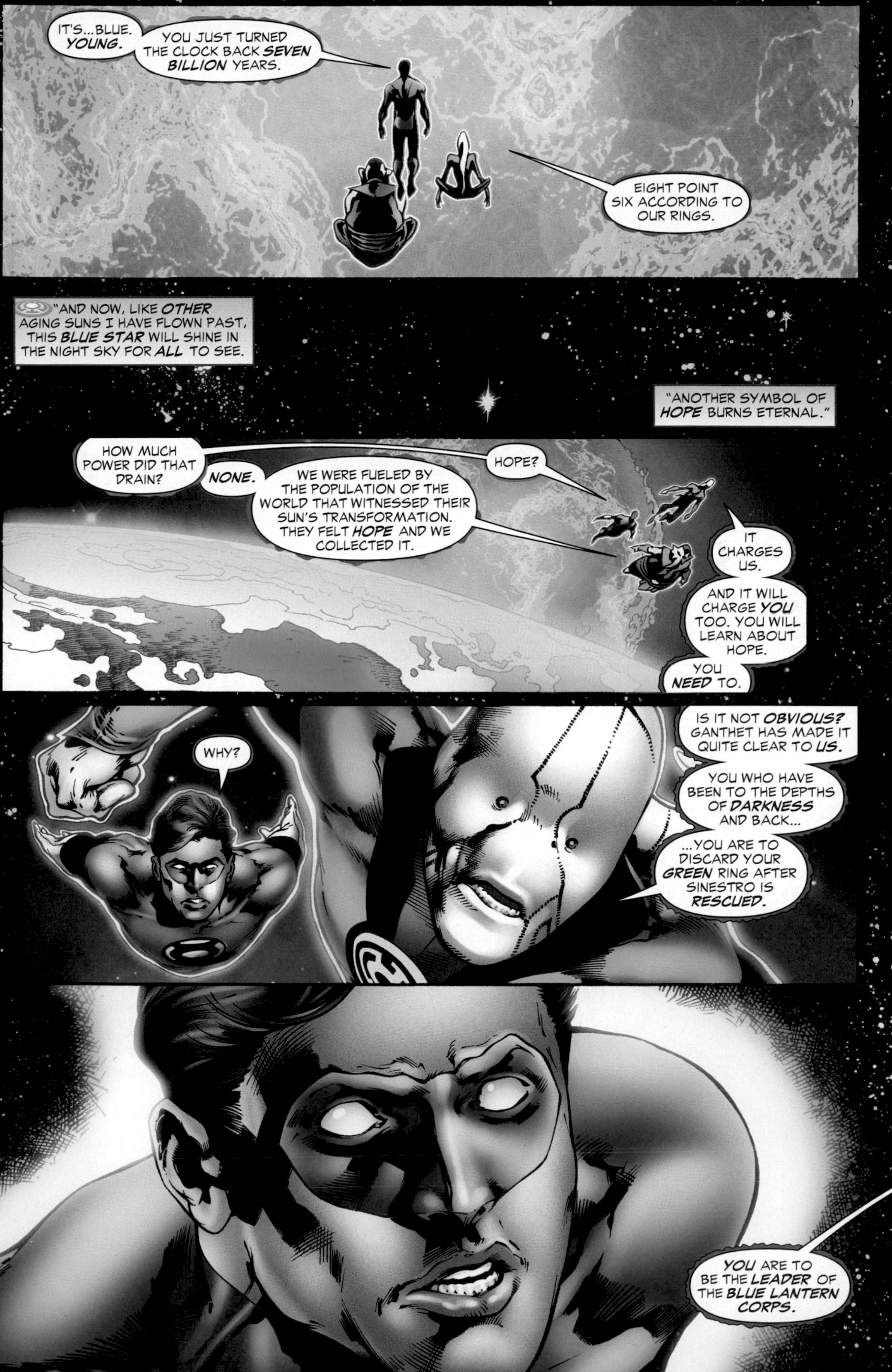
IT'S...BLUE. YOUNG.
YOU JUST TURNED THE CLOCK BACK SEVEN BILLION YEARS.
EIGHT POINT SIX ACCORDING TO OUR RINGS.
"AND NOW, LIKE OTHER AGING SUNS I HAVE FLOWN PAST, THIS BLUE STAR WILL SHINE IN THE NIGHT SKY FOR ALL TO SEE.
"ANOTHER SYMBOL OF HOPE BURNS ETERNAL."
HOW MUCH POWER DID THAT DRAIN?
HOPE?
NONE.
WE WERE FUELED BY THE POPULATION OF THE WORLD THAT WITNESSED THEIR SUN'S TRANSFORMATION. THEY FELT HOPE AND WE COLLECTED IT.
IT CHARGES US.
AND IT WILL CHARGE YOU TOO. YOU WILL LEARN ABOUT HOPE.
YOU NEED TO.
WHY?
IS IT NOT OBVIOUS? GANTHET HAS MADE IT QUITE CLEAR TO US.
YOU WHO HAVE BEEN TO THE DEPTHS OF DARKNESS AND BACK...
...YOU ARE TO DISCARD YOUR GREEN RING AFTER SINESTRO IS RESCUED.
YOU ARE TO BE THE LEADER OF THE BLUE LANTERN CORPS.

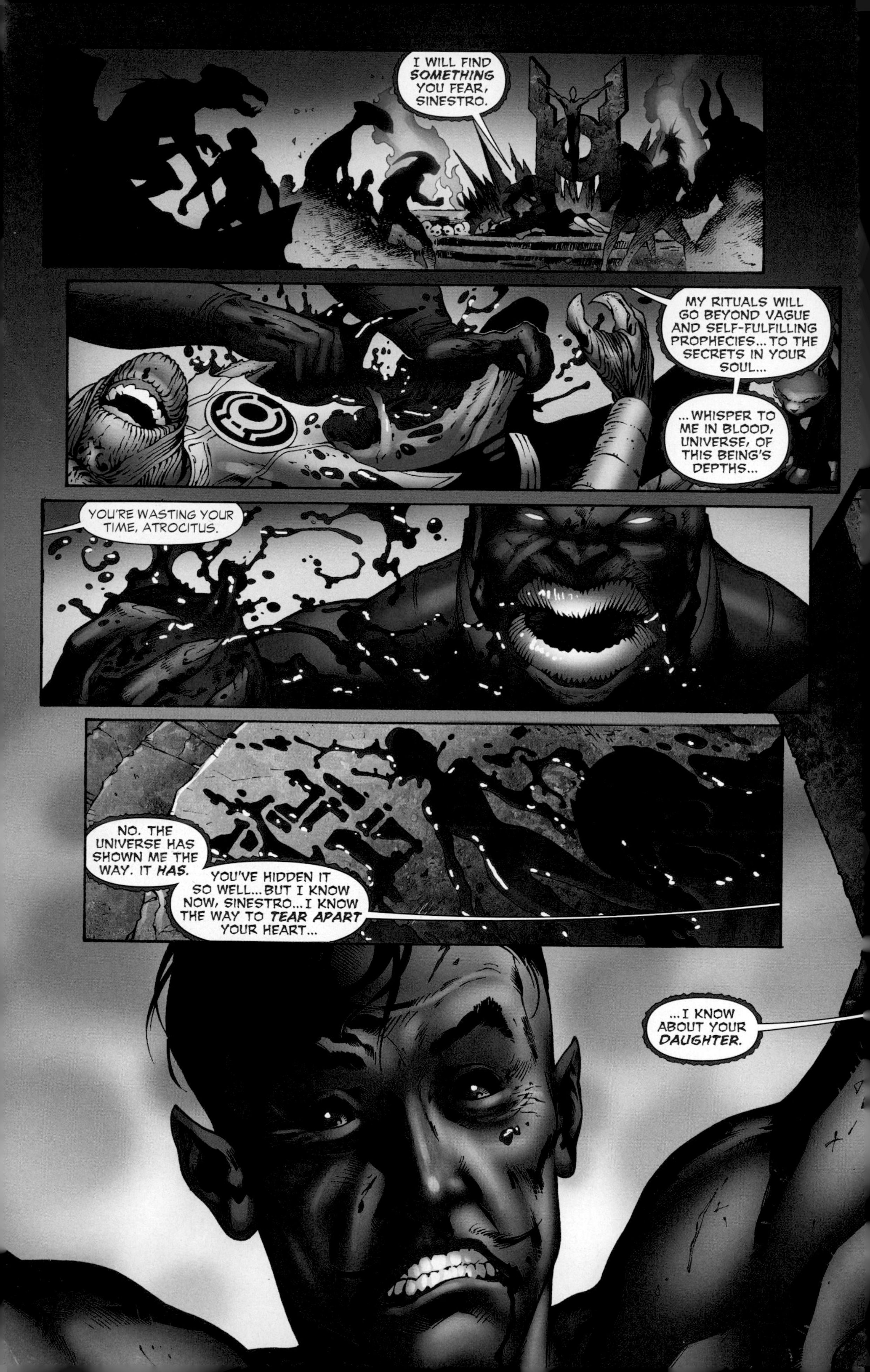
I WILL FIND SOMETHING YOU FEAR, SINESTRO.
MY RITUALS WILL GO BEYOND VAGUE AND SELF-FULFILLING PROPHECIES... TO THE SECRETS IN YOUR SOUL...
...WHISPER TO ME IN BLOOD, UNIVERSE, OF THIS BEING'S DEPTHS...
YOU'RE WASTING YOUR TIME, ATROCITUS.
NO. THE UNIVERSE HAS SHOWN ME THE WAY. IT HAS.
YOU'VE HIDDEN IT SO WELL... BUT I KNOW NOW, SINESTRO... I KNOW THE WAY TO TEAR APART YOUR HEART...
...I KNOW ABOUT YOUR DAUGHTER.

GREEN LANTERN 37 Cover by Shane Davis, Sandra Hope and Nei Ruffino

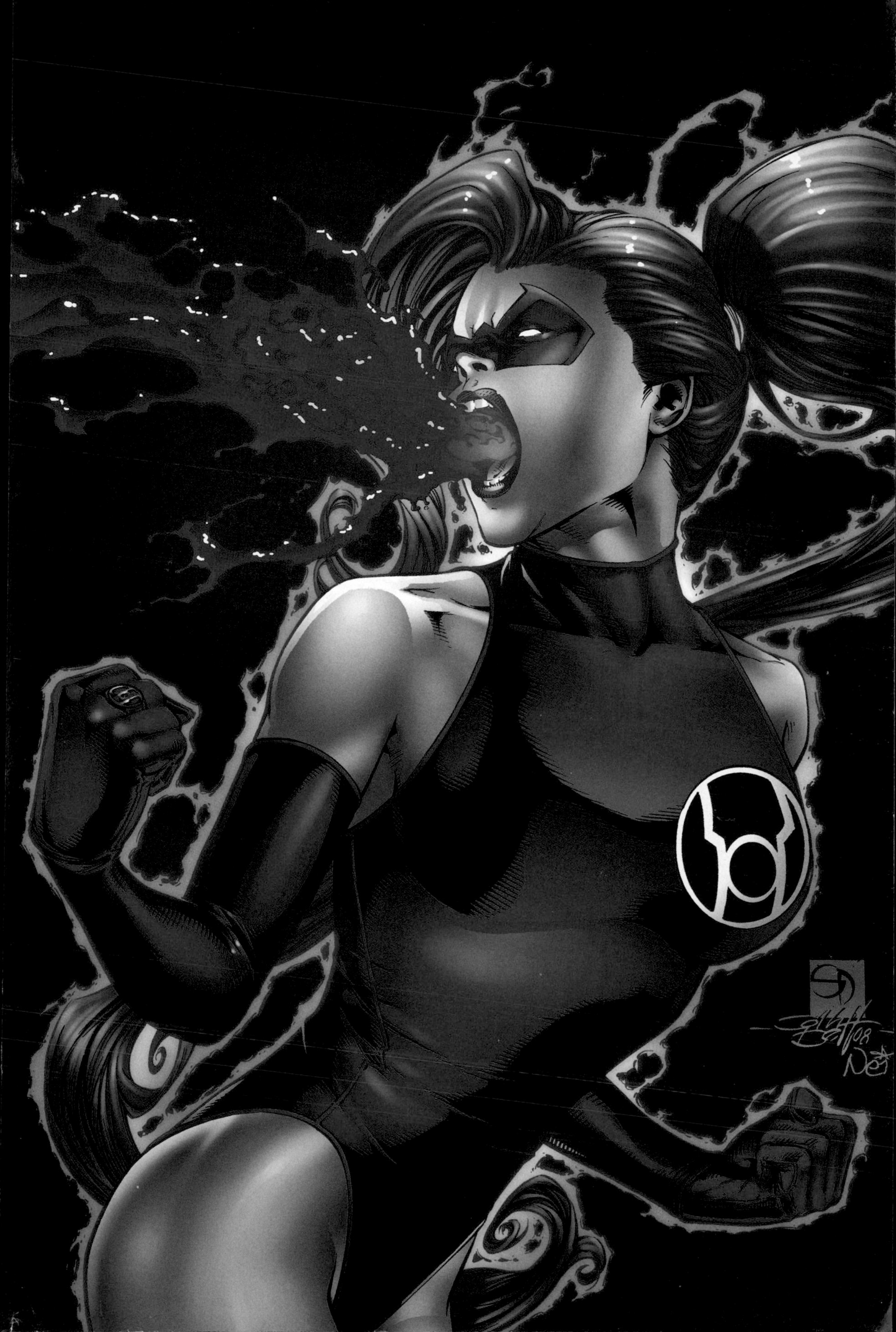

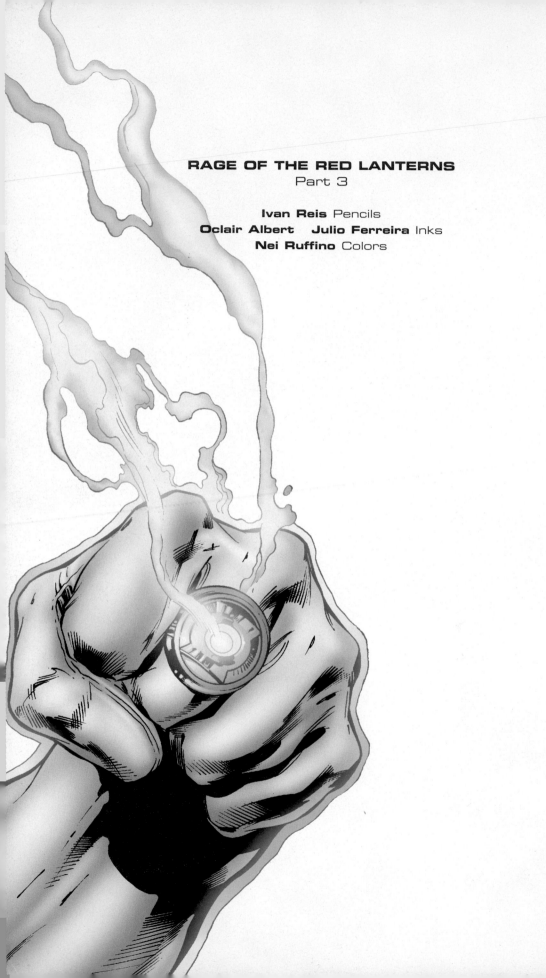

RAGE OF THE RED LANTERNS
Part 3

Ivan Reis Pencils
Oclair Albert   **Julio Ferreira** Inks
Nei Ruffino Colors

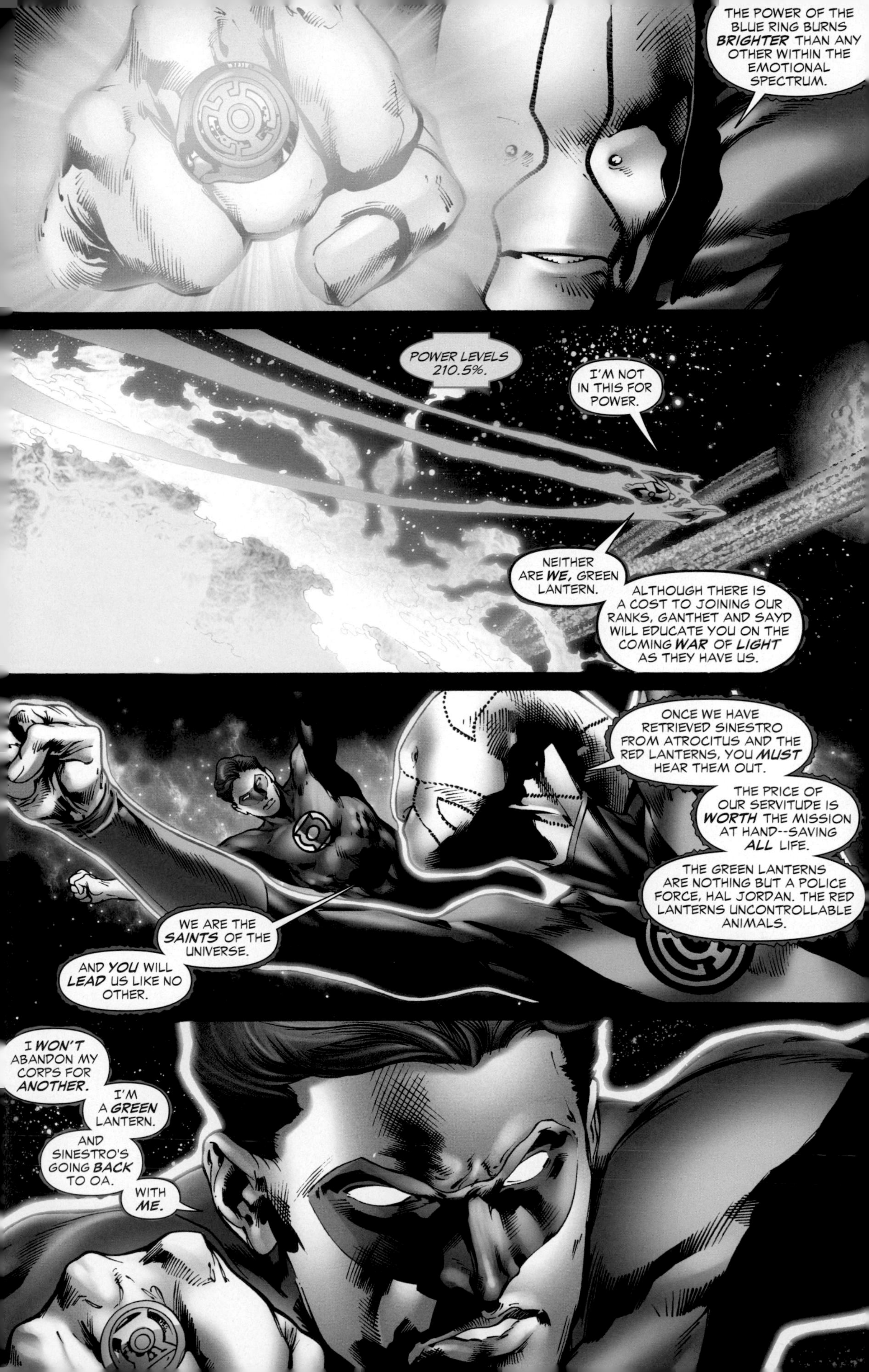
THE POWER OF THE BLUE RING BURNS BRIGHTER THAN ANY OTHER WITHIN THE EMOTIONAL SPECTRUM.
POWER LEVELS 210.5%.
I'M NOT IN THIS FOR POWER.
NEITHER ARE WE, GREEN LANTERN.
ALTHOUGH THERE IS A COST TO JOINING OUR RANKS, GANTHET AND SAYD WILL EDUCATE YOU ON THE COMING WAR OF LIGHT AS THEY HAVE US.
ONCE WE HAVE RETRIEVED SINESTRO FROM ATROCITUS AND THE RED LANTERNS, YOU MUST HEAR THEM OUT.
THE PRICE OF OUR SERVITUDE IS WORTH THE MISSION AT HAND--SAVING ALL LIFE.
THE GREEN LANTERNS ARE NOTHING BUT A POLICE FORCE, HAL JORDAN. THE RED LANTERNS UNCONTROLLABLE ANIMALS.
WE ARE THE SAINTS OF THE UNIVERSE.
AND YOU WILL LEAD US LIKE NO OTHER.
I WON'T ABANDON MY CORPS FOR ANOTHER.
I'M A GREEN LANTERN.
AND SINESTRO'S GOING BACK TO OA.
WITH ME.

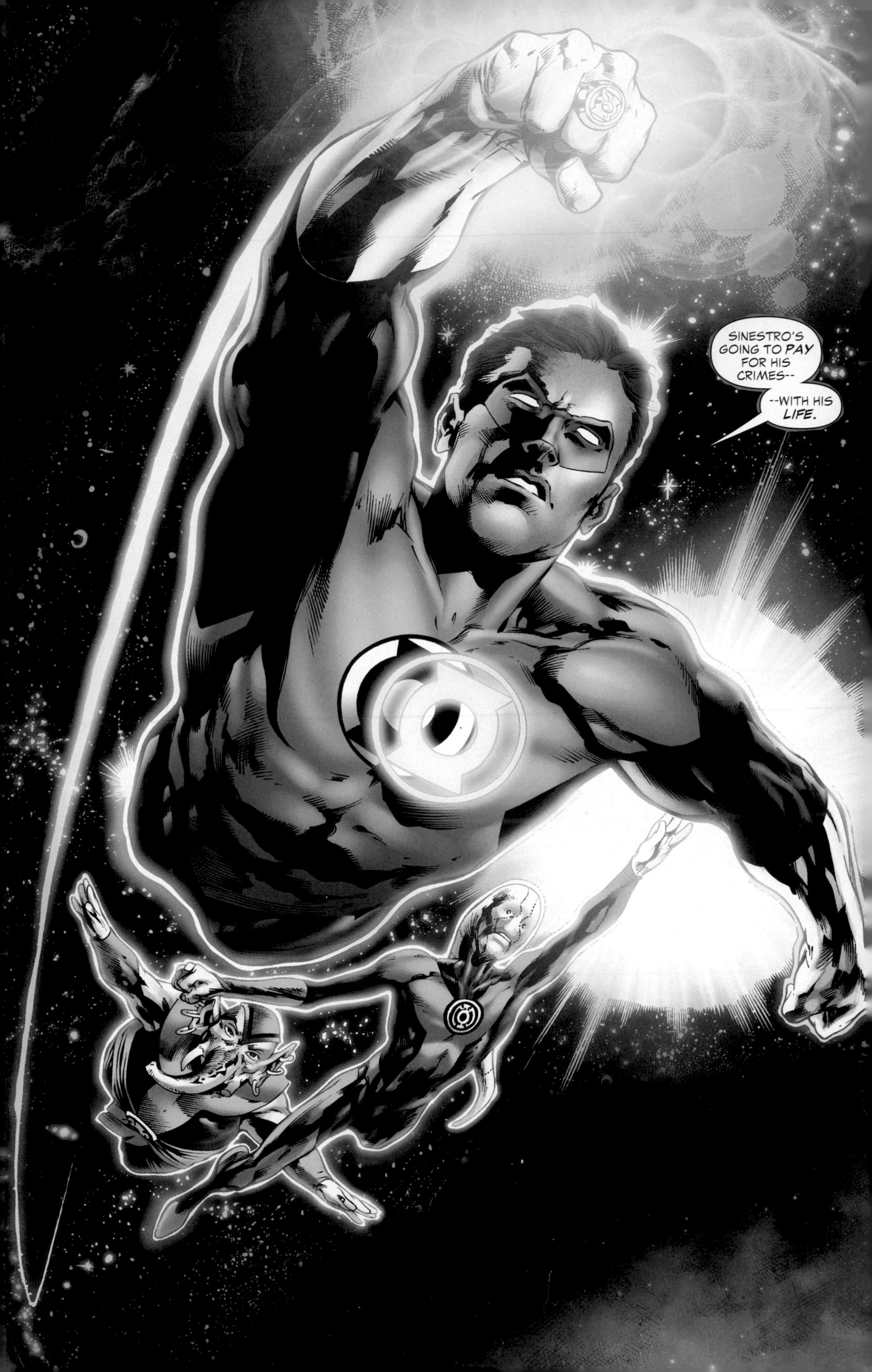
SINESTRO'S GOING TO PAY FOR HIS CRIMES--
--WITH HIS LIFE.

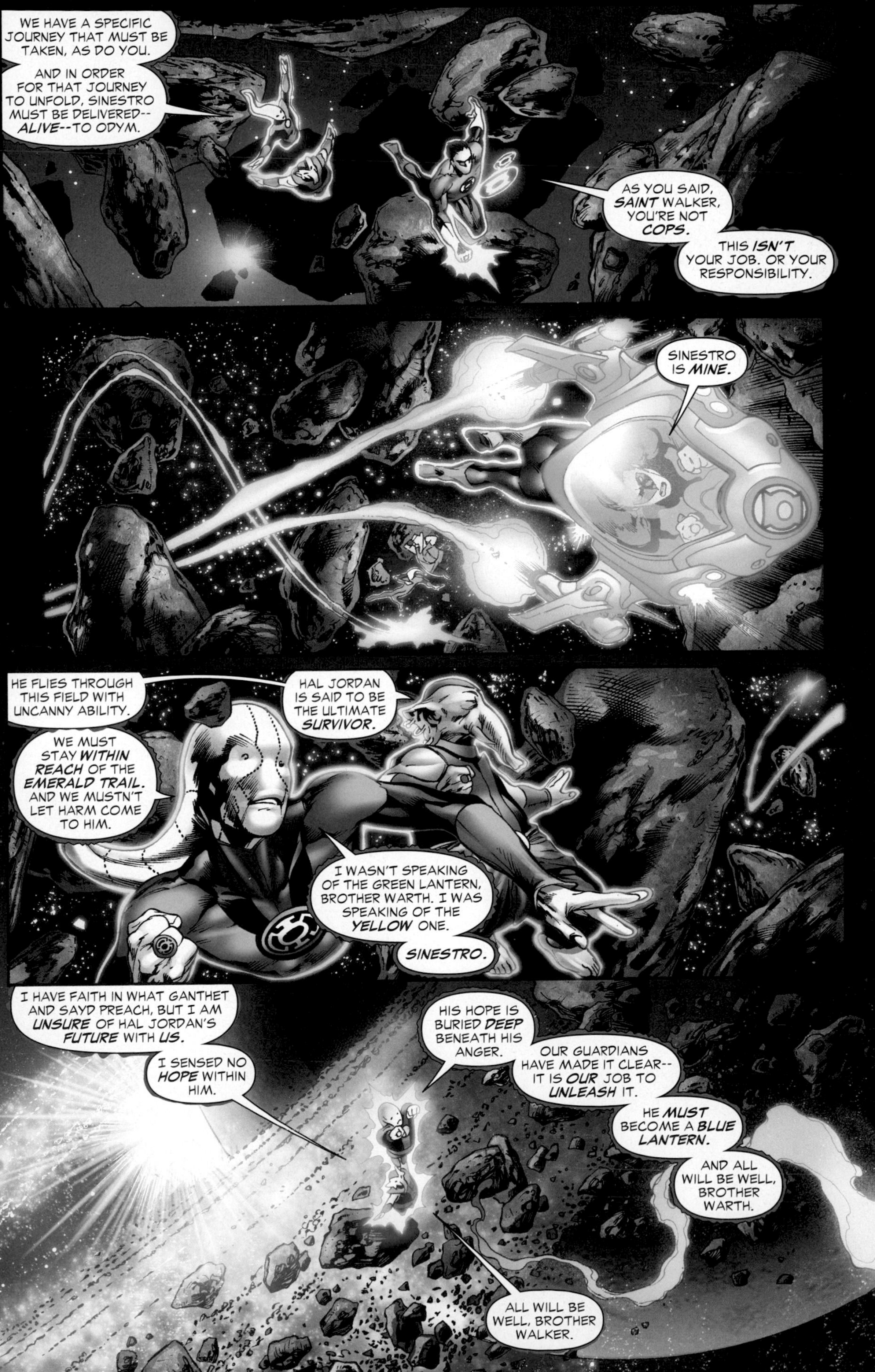

WE HAVE A SPECIFIC JOURNEY THAT MUST BE TAKEN, AS DO YOU.
AND IN ORDER FOR THAT JOURNEY TO UNFOLD, SINESTRO MUST BE DELIVERED-- ALIVE--TO ODYM.
AS YOU SAID, SAINT WALKER, YOU'RE NOT COPS.
THIS ISN'T YOUR JOB. OR YOUR RESPONSIBILITY.
SINESTRO IS MINE.
HE FLIES THROUGH THIS FIELD WITH UNCANNY ABILITY.
HAL JORDAN IS SAID TO BE THE ULTIMATE SURVIVOR.
WE MUST STAY WITHIN REACH OF THE EMERALD TRAIL. AND WE MUSTN'T LET HARM COME TO HIM.
I WASN'T SPEAKING OF THE GREEN LANTERN, BROTHER WARTH. I WAS SPEAKING OF THE YELLOW ONE.
SINESTRO.
I HAVE FAITH IN WHAT GANTHET AND SAYD PREACH, BUT I AM UNSURE OF HAL JORDAN'S FUTURE WITH US.
I SENSED NO HOPE WITHIN HIM.
HIS HOPE IS BURIED DEEP BENEATH HIS ANGER.
OUR GUARDIANS HAVE MADE IT CLEAR-- IT IS OUR JOB TO UNLEASH IT.
HE MUST BECOME A BLUE LANTERN.
AND ALL WILL BE WELL, BROTHER WARTH.
ALL WILL BE WELL, BROTHER WALKER.

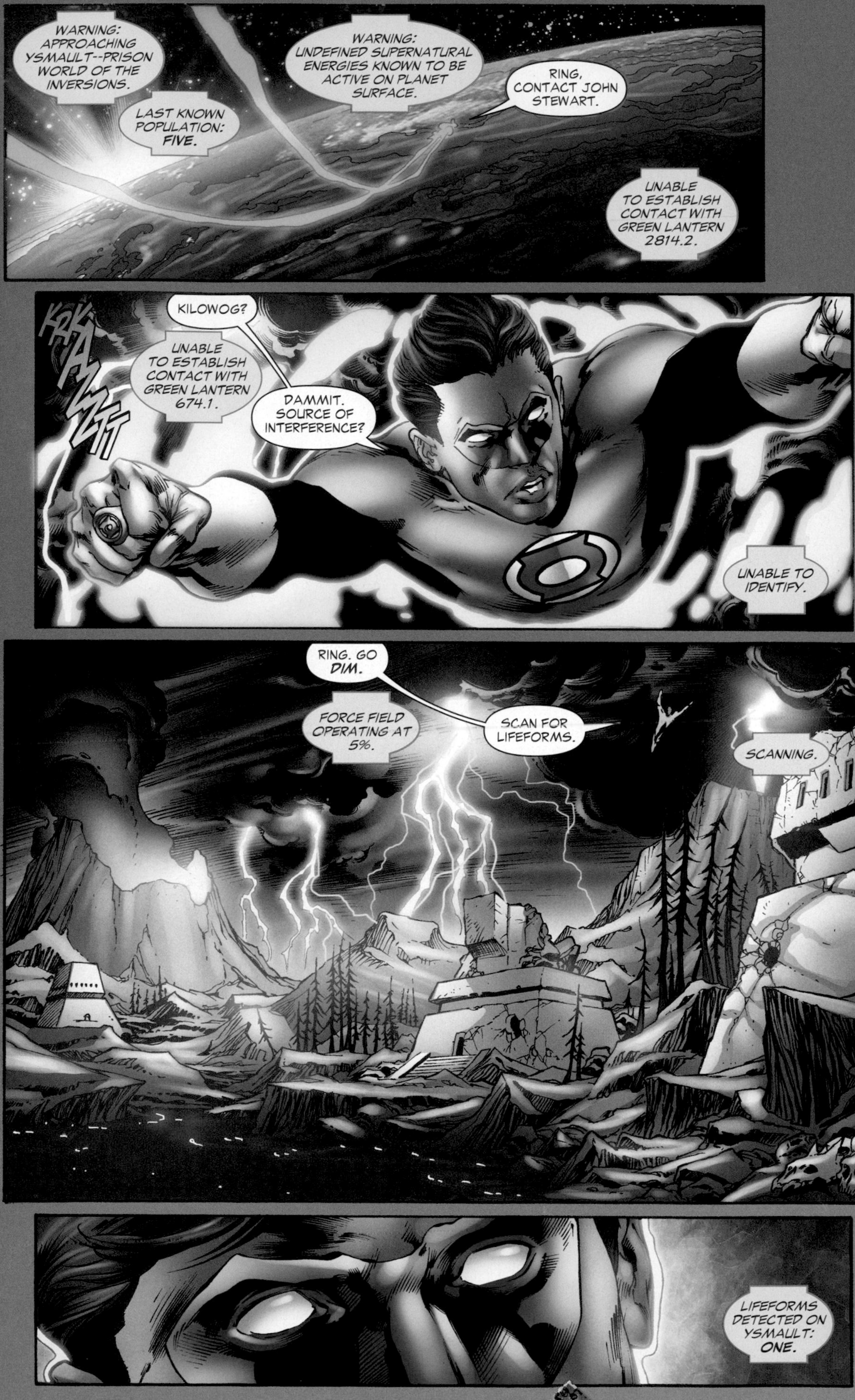
WARNING: APPROACHING YSMAULT--PRISON WORLD OF THE INVERSIONS.
LAST KNOWN POPULATION: FIVE.
WARNING: UNDEFINED SUPERNATURAL ENERGIES KNOWN TO BE ACTIVE ON PLANET SURFACE.
RING, CONTACT JOHN STEWART.
UNABLE TO ESTABLISH CONTACT WITH GREEN LANTERN 2814.2.
KRKAZZTT
KILOWOG?
UNABLE TO ESTABLISH CONTACT WITH GREEN LANTERN 674.1.
DAMMIT. SOURCE OF INTERFERENCE?
UNABLE TO IDENTIFY.
RING. GO DIM.
FORCE FIELD OPERATING AT 5%.
SCAN FOR LIFEFORMS.
SCANNING.
LIFEFORMS DETECTED ON YSMAULT: ONE.

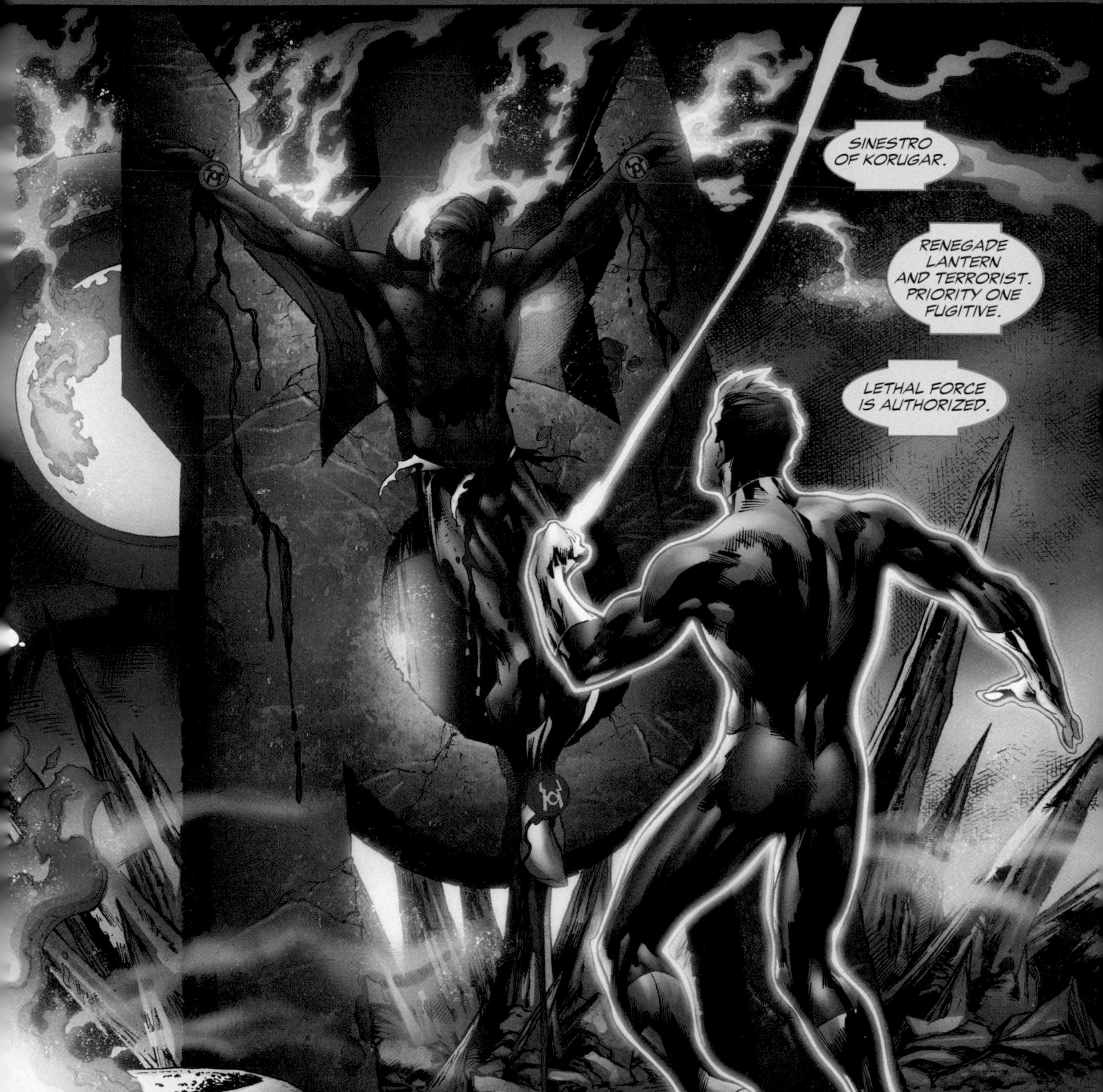
SINESTRO OF KORUGAR.
RENEGADE LANTERN AND TERRORIST. PRIORITY ONE FUGITIVE.
LETHAL FORCE IS AUTHORIZED.
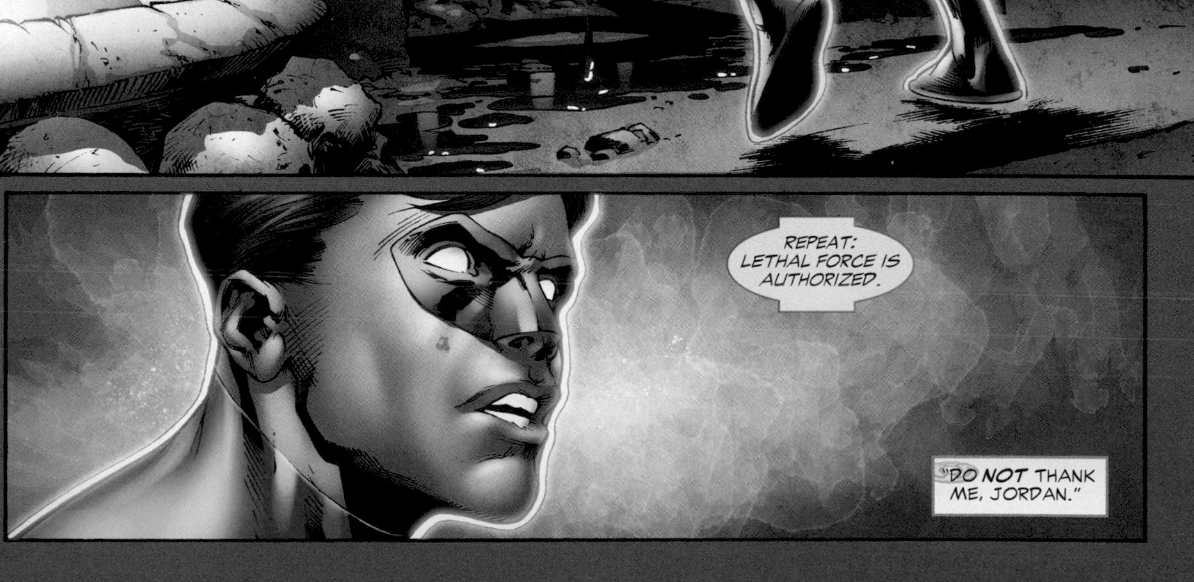
REPEAT: LETHAL FORCE IS AUTHORIZED.
"DO NOT THANK ME, JORDAN."

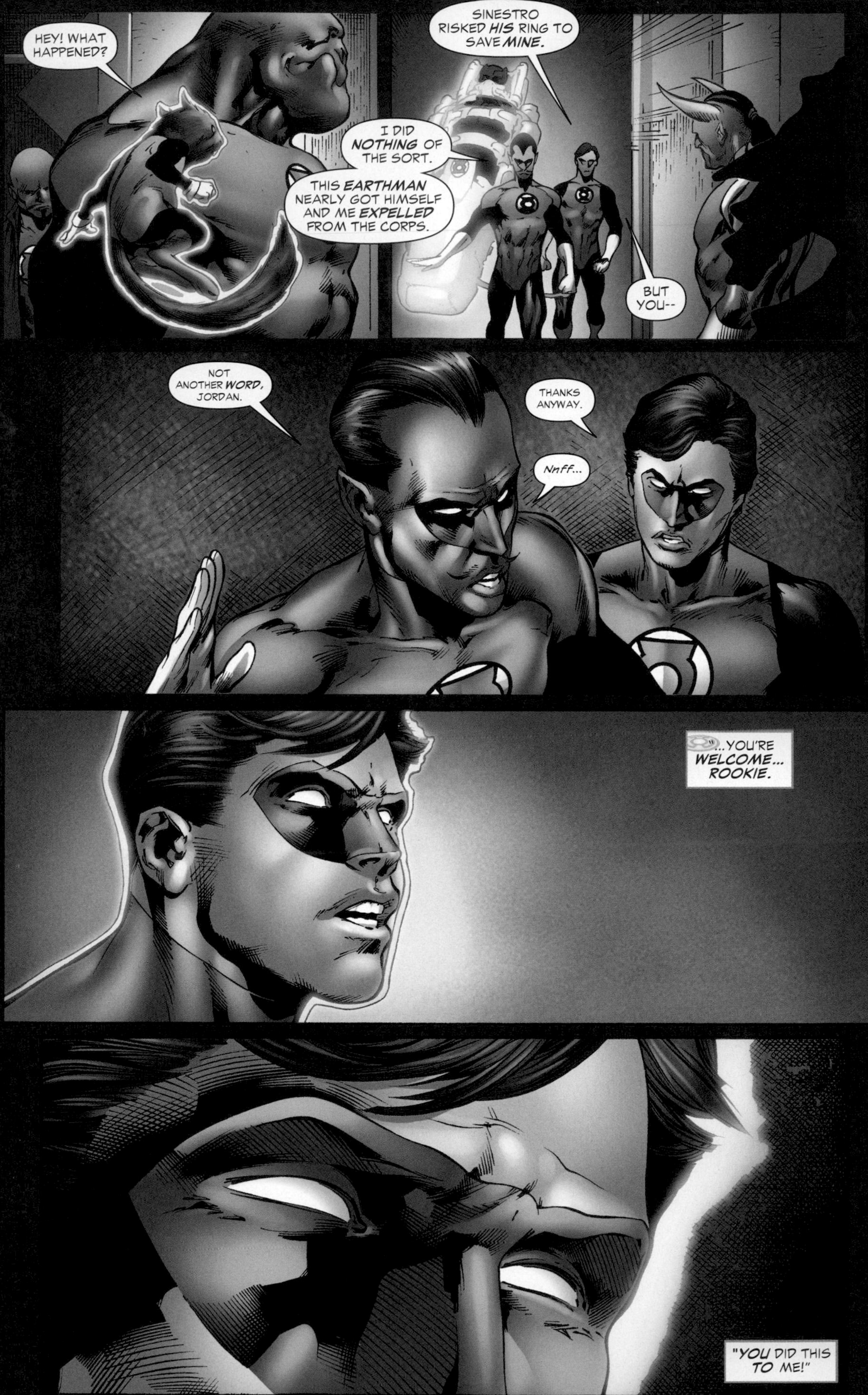
HEY! WHAT HAPPENED?
SINESTRO RISKED HIS RING TO SAVE MINE.
I DID NOTHING OF THE SORT.
THIS EARTHMAN NEARLY GOT HIMSELF AND ME EXPELLED FROM THE CORPS.
BUT YOU--
NOT ANOTHER WORD, JORDAN.
THANKS ANYWAY.
Nnff...
...YOU'RE WELCOME... ROOKIE.
"YOU DID THIS TO ME!"

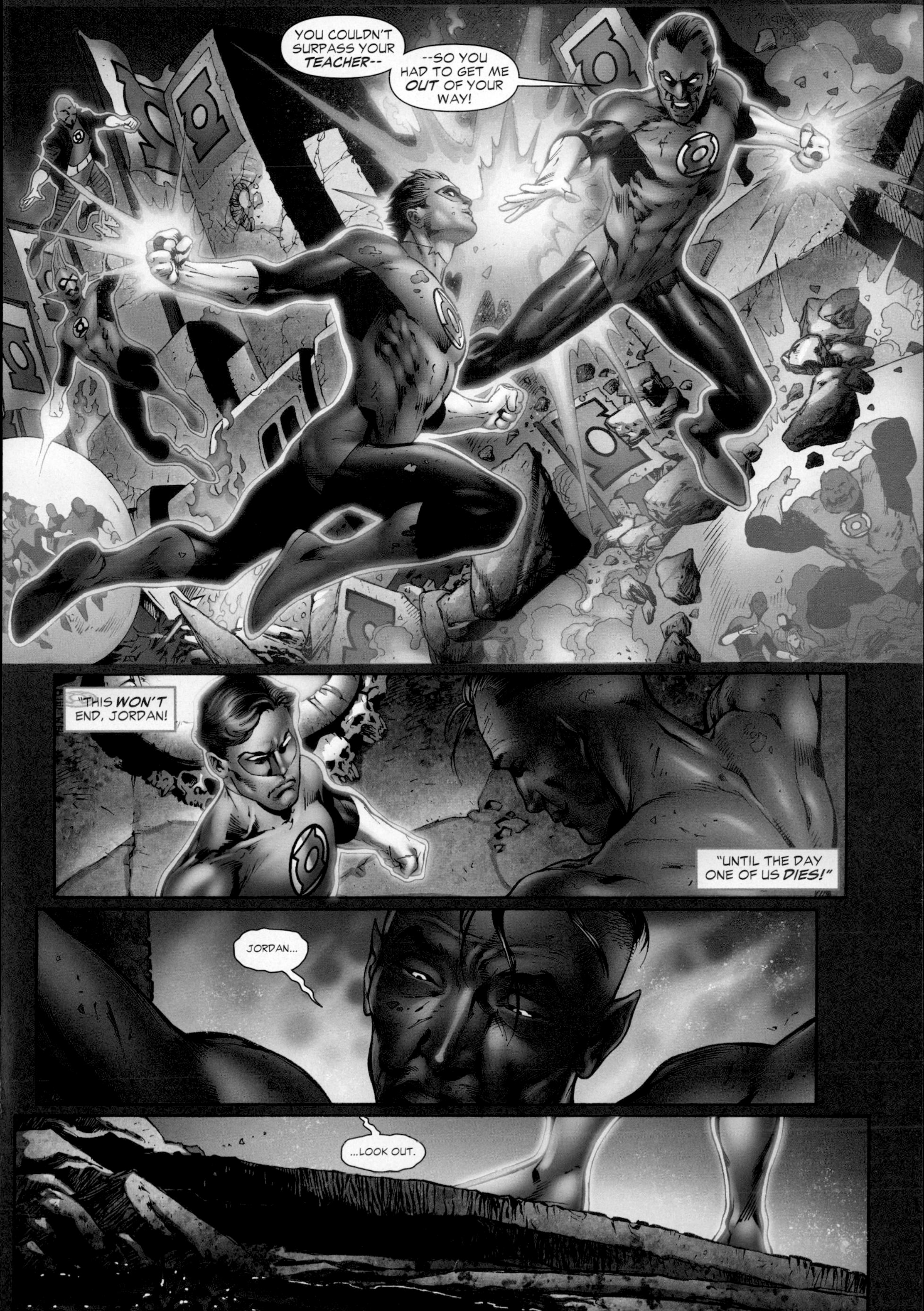
YOU COULDN'T SURPASS YOUR TEACHER--
--SO YOU HAD TO GET ME OUT OF YOUR WAY!
"THIS WON'T END, JORDAN!
"UNTIL THE DAY ONE OF US DIES!"
JORDAN...
...LOOK OUT.

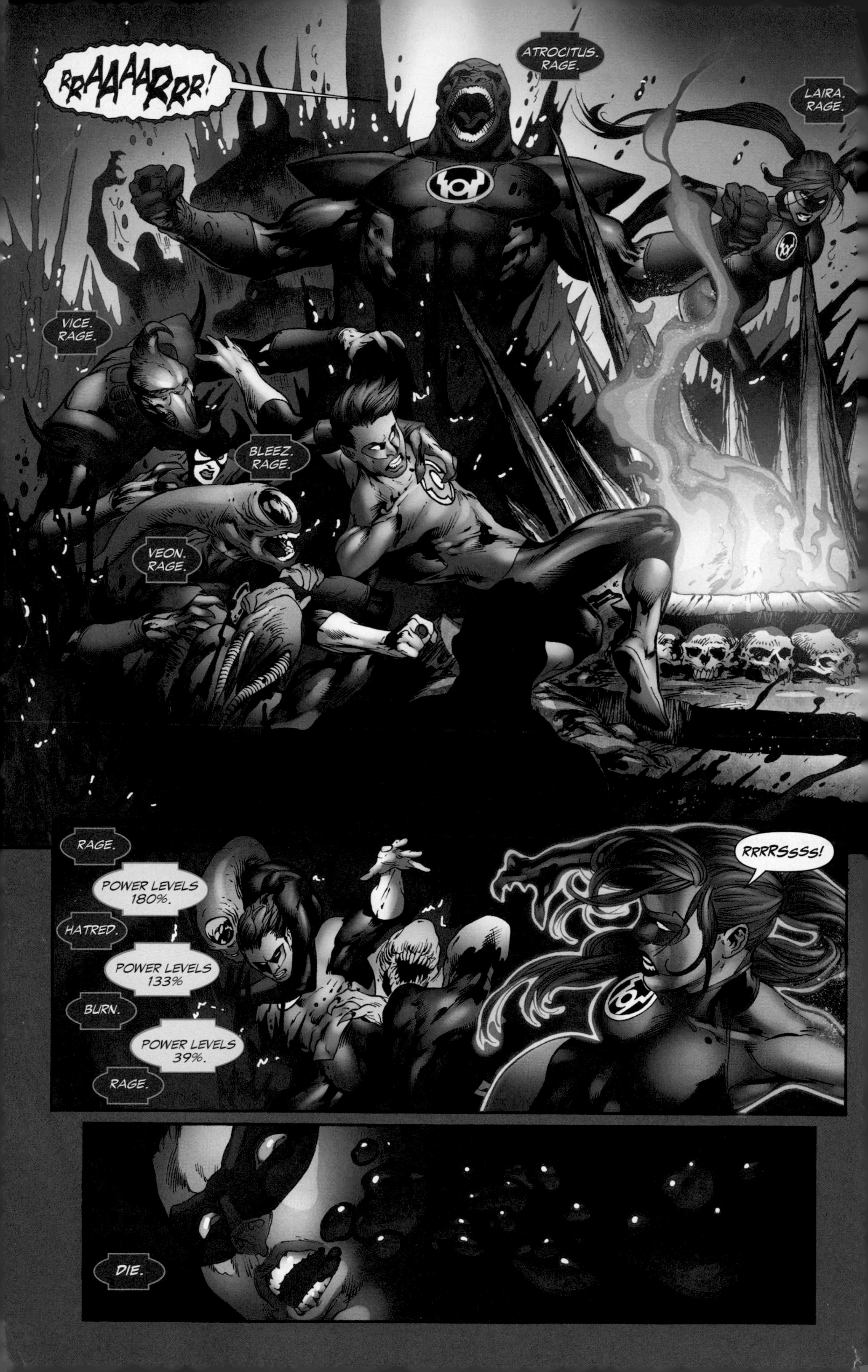
RRAAAARRR!
ATROCITUS. RAGE.
LAIRA. RAGE.
VICE. RAGE.
BLEEZ. RAGE.
VEON. RAGE.
RAGE.
POWER LEVELS 180%.
HATRED.
POWER LEVELS 133%
BURN.
POWER LEVELS 39%.
RAGE.
RRRRSSSS!
DIE.

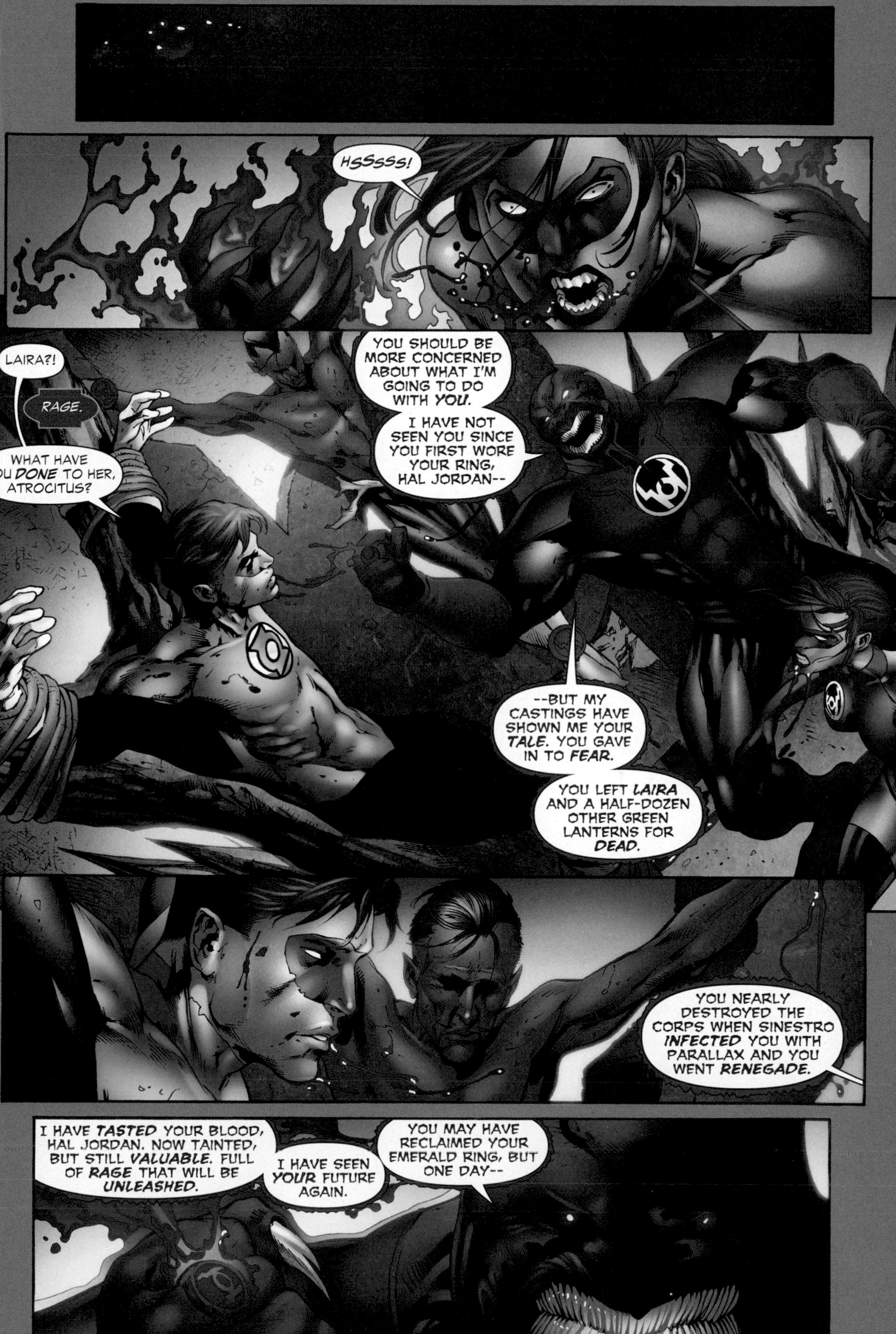
HSSSSS!
LAIRA?!
RAGE.
WHAT HAVE YOU DONE TO HER, ATROCITUS?
YOU SHOULD BE MORE CONCERNED ABOUT WHAT I'M GOING TO DO WITH YOU.
I HAVE NOT SEEN YOU SINCE YOU FIRST WORE YOUR RING, HAL JORDAN--
--BUT MY CASTINGS HAVE SHOWN ME YOUR TALE. YOU GAVE IN TO FEAR.
YOU LEFT LAIRA AND A HALF-DOZEN OTHER GREEN LANTERNS FOR DEAD.
YOU NEARLY DESTROYED THE CORPS WHEN SINESTRO INFECTED YOU WITH PARALLAX AND YOU WENT RENEGADE.
I HAVE TASTED YOUR BLOOD, HAL JORDAN. NOW TAINTED, BUT STILL VALUABLE. FULL OF RAGE THAT WILL BE UNLEASHED.
I HAVE SEEN YOUR FUTURE AGAIN.
YOU MAY HAVE RECLAIMED YOUR EMERALD RING, BUT ONE DAY--

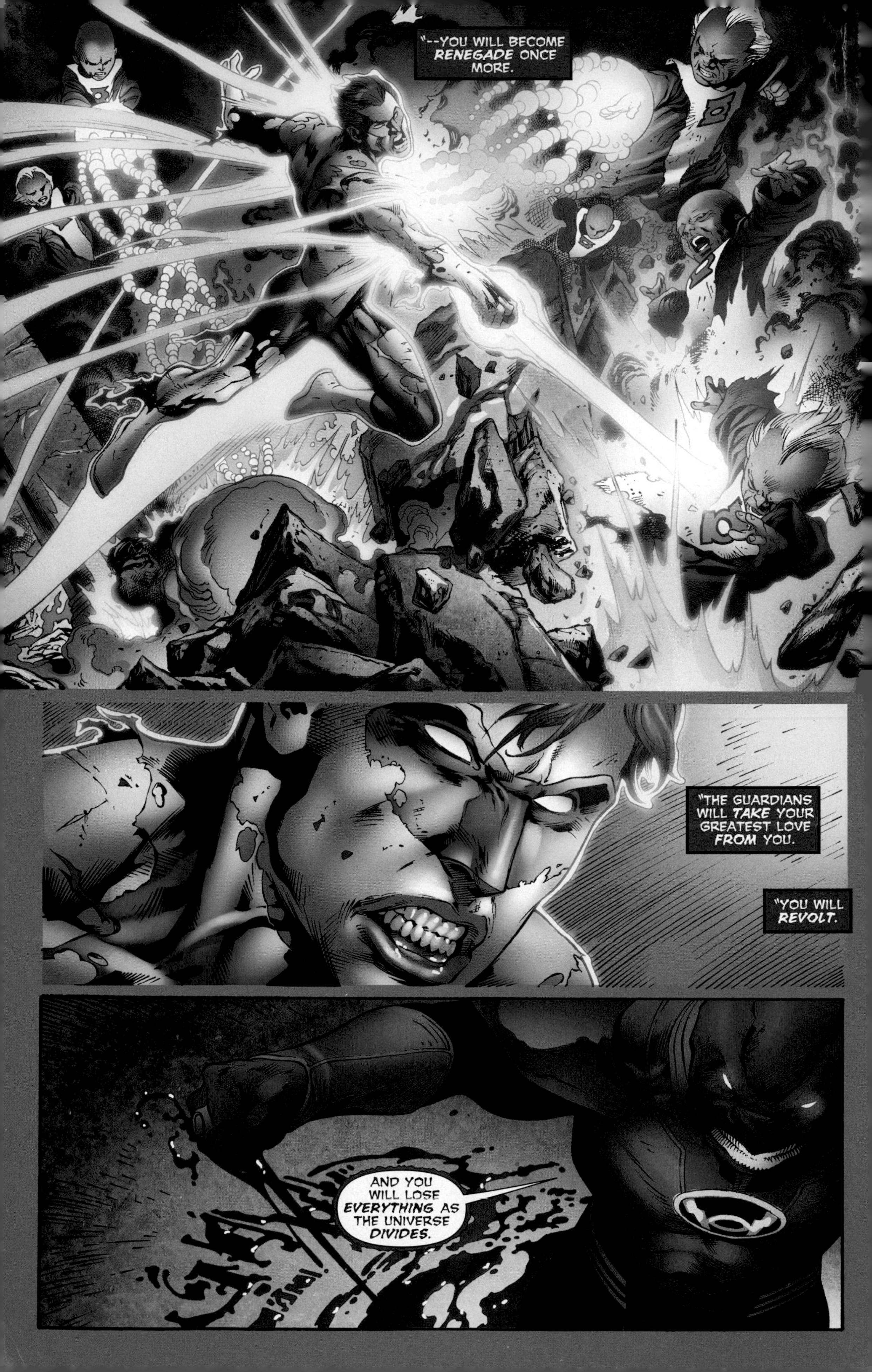
"--YOU WILL BECOME RENEGADE ONCE MORE.
"THE GUARDIANS WILL TAKE YOUR GREATEST LOVE FROM YOU.
"YOU WILL REVOLT.
AND YOU WILL LOSE EVERYTHING AS THE UNIVERSE DIVIDES.

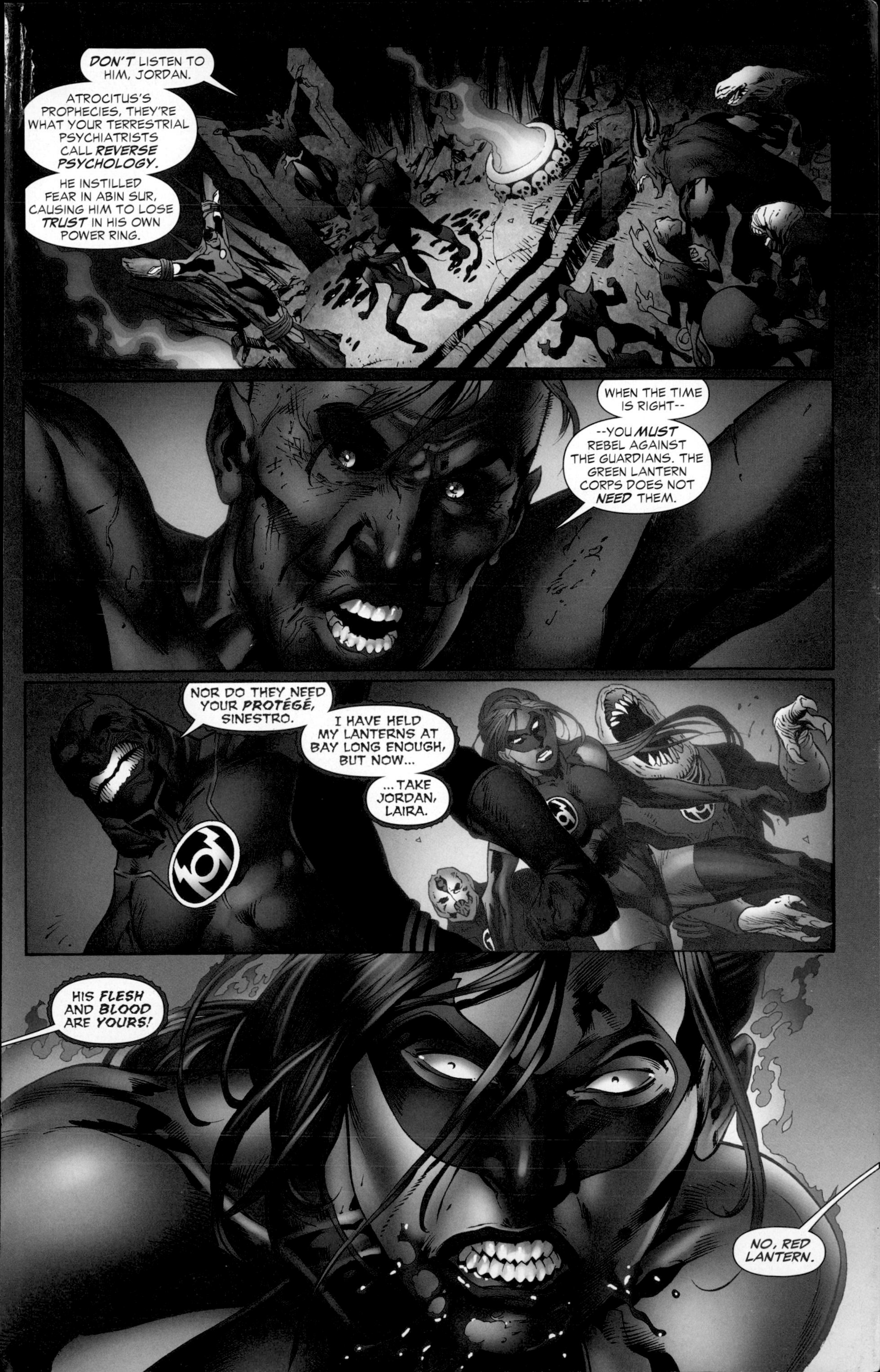

DON'T LISTEN TO HIM, JORDAN.
ATROCITUS'S PROPHECIES, THEY'RE WHAT YOUR TERRESTRIAL PSYCHIATRISTS CALL REVERSE PSYCHOLOGY.
HE INSTILLED FEAR IN ABIN SUR, CAUSING HIM TO LOSE TRUST IN HIS OWN POWER RING.
WHEN THE TIME IS RIGHT--
--YOU MUST REBEL AGAINST THE GUARDIANS. THE GREEN LANTERN CORPS DOES NOT NEED THEM.
NOR DO THEY NEED YOUR PROTÉGÉ, SINESTRO.
I HAVE HELD MY LANTERNS AT BAY LONG ENOUGH, BUT NOW...
...TAKE JORDAN, LAIRA.
HIS FLESH AND BLOOD ARE YOURS!
NO, RED LANTERN.

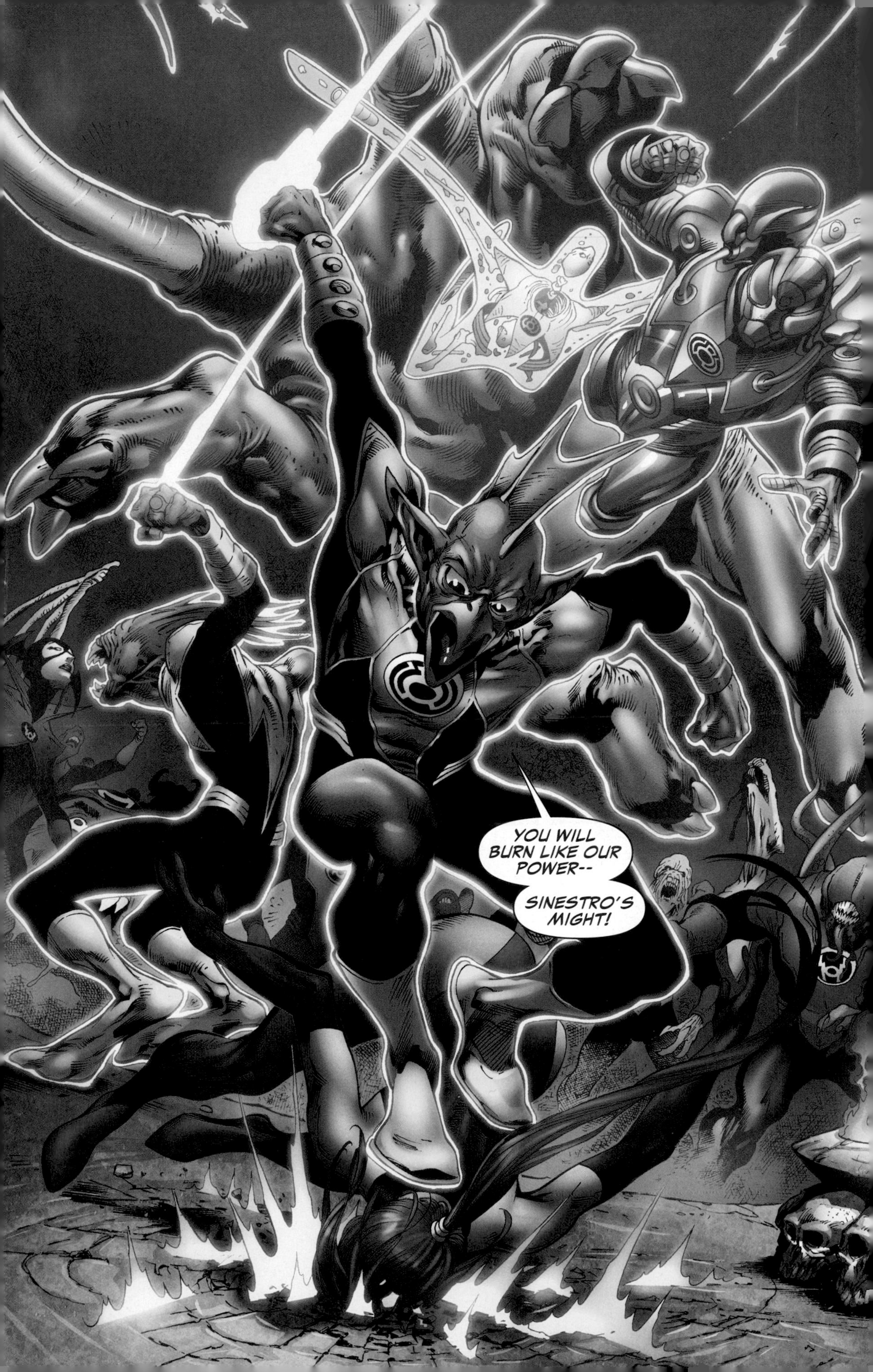
YOU WILL BURN LIKE OUR POWER--
SINESTRO'S MIGHT!

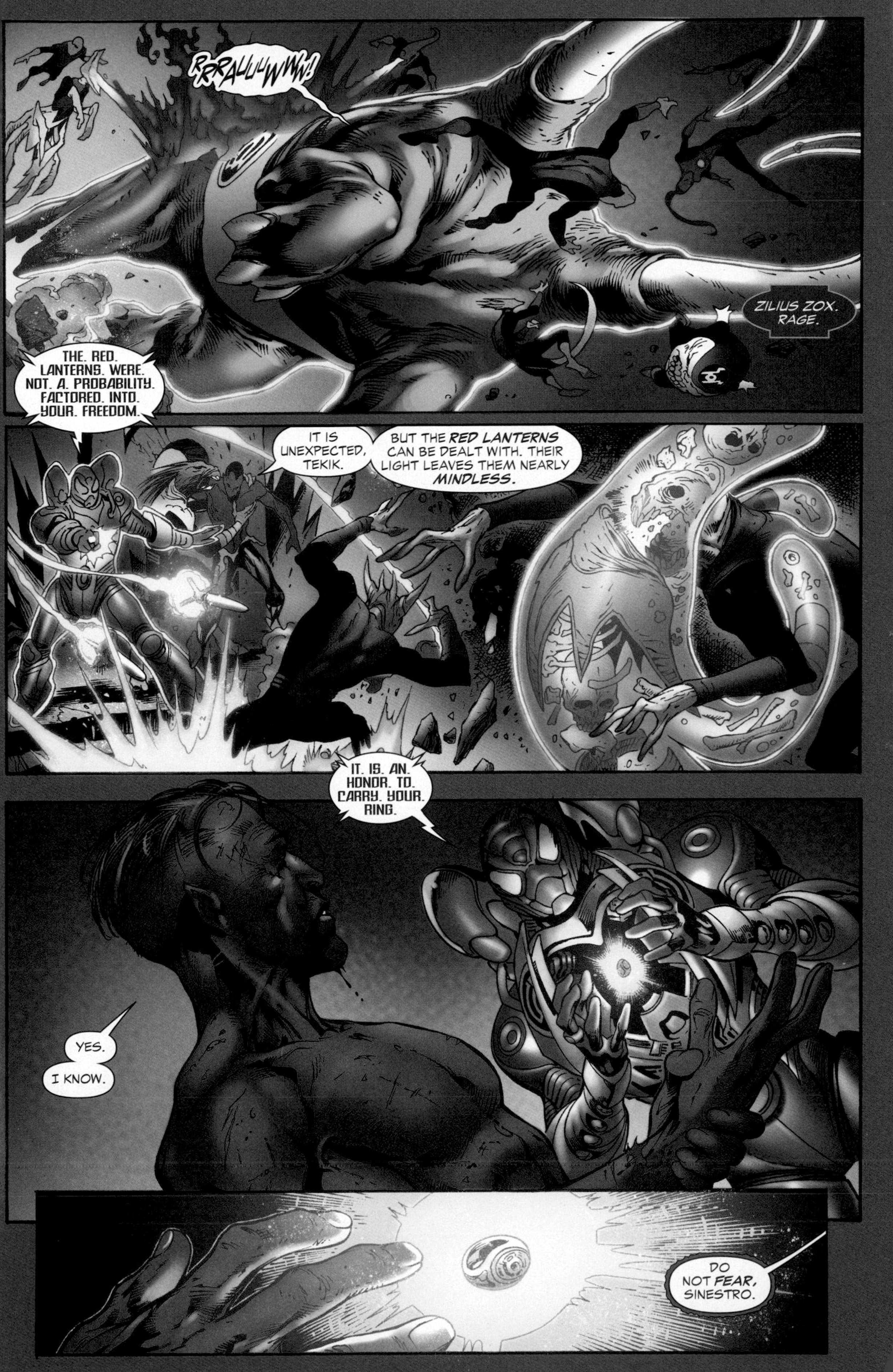
RRRAULUWW!
ZILIUS ZOX. RAGE.
THE. RED. LANTERNS. WERE. NOT. A. PROBABILITY. FACTORED. INTO. YOUR. FREEDOM.
IT IS UNEXPECTED, TEKIK.
BUT THE RED LANTERNS CAN BE DEALT WITH. THEIR LIGHT LEAVES THEM NEARLY MINDLESS.
IT. IS. AN. HONOR. TO. CARRY. YOUR. RING.
YES.
I KNOW.
DO NOT FEAR, SINESTRO.

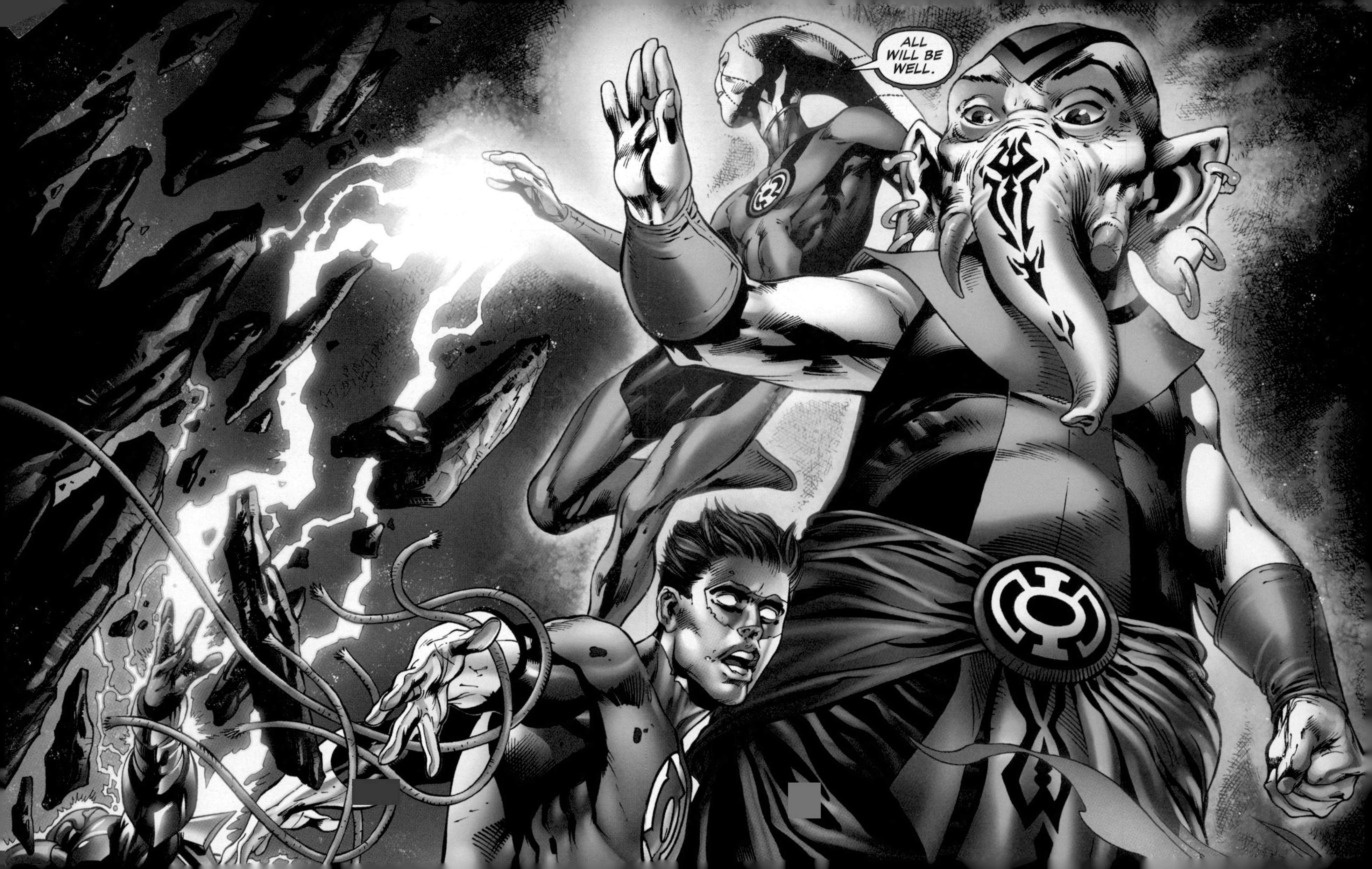
ALL WILL BE WELL.

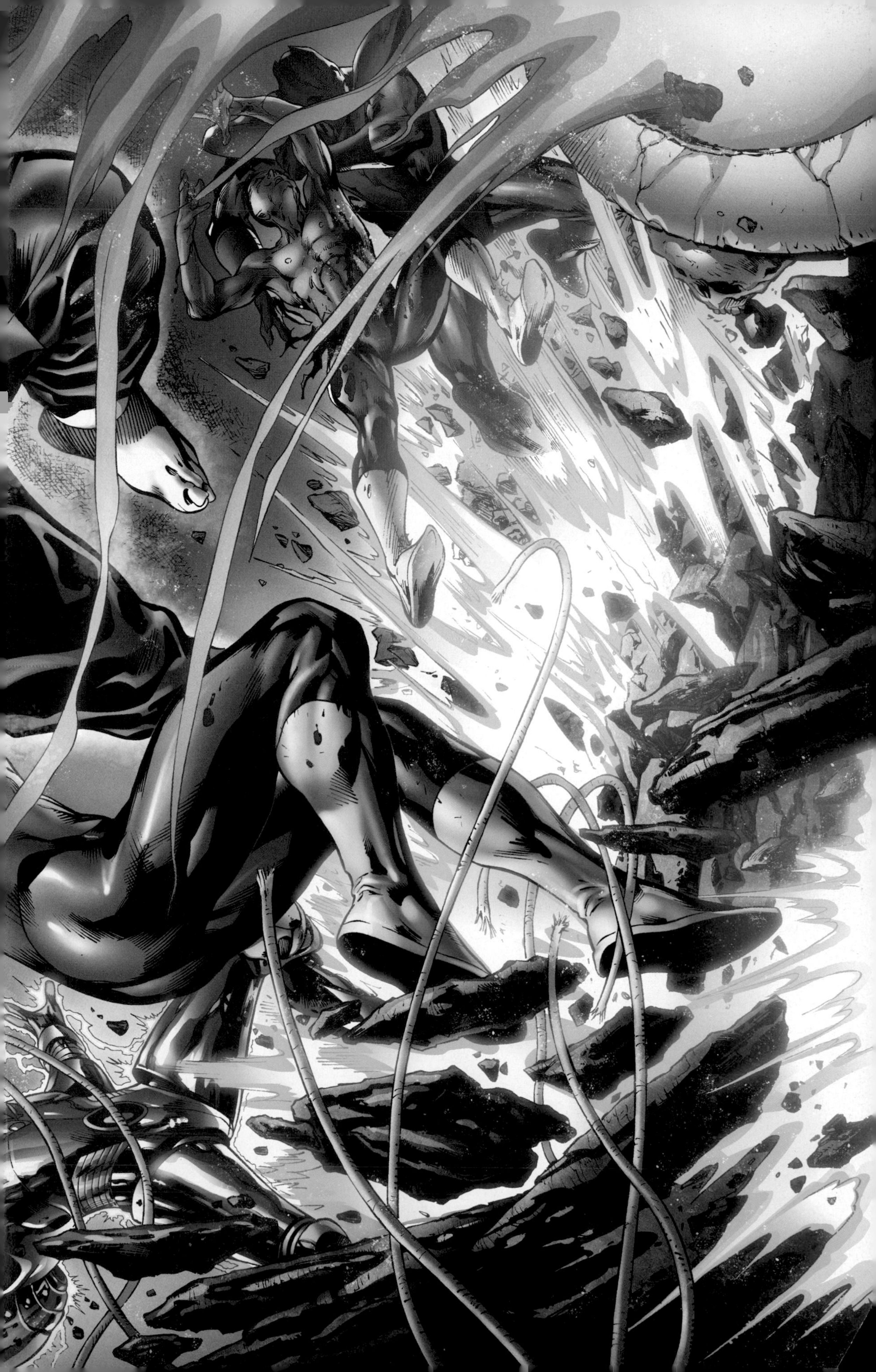

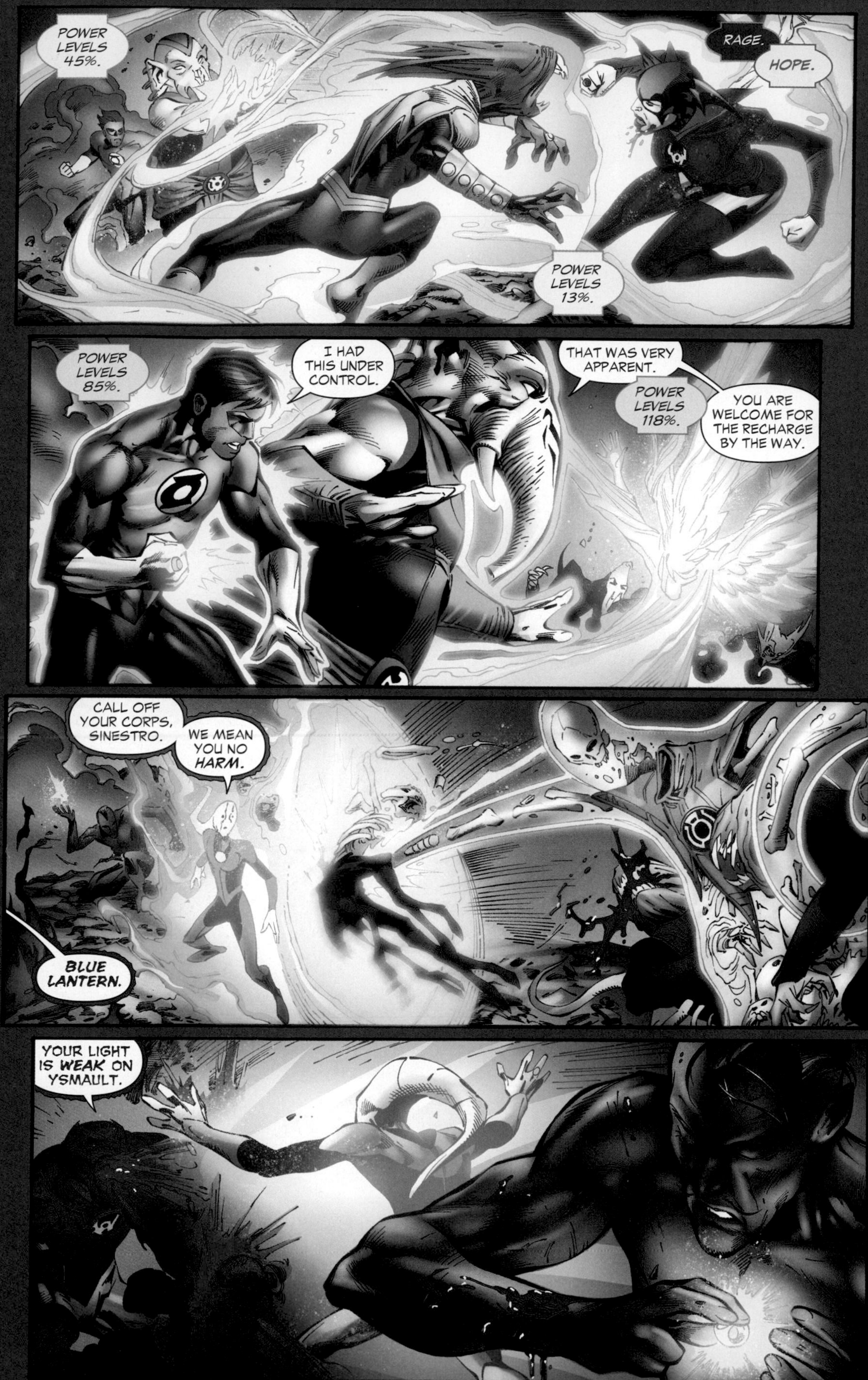
POWER LEVELS 45%.
RAGE.
HOPE.
POWER LEVELS 13%.
POWER LEVELS 85%.
I HAD THIS UNDER CONTROL.
THAT WAS VERY APPARENT.
POWER LEVELS 118%.
YOU ARE WELCOME FOR THE RECHARGE BY THE WAY.
CALL OFF YOUR CORPS, SINESTRO.
WE MEAN YOU NO HARM.
BLUE LANTERN.
YOUR LIGHT IS WEAK ON YSMAULT.

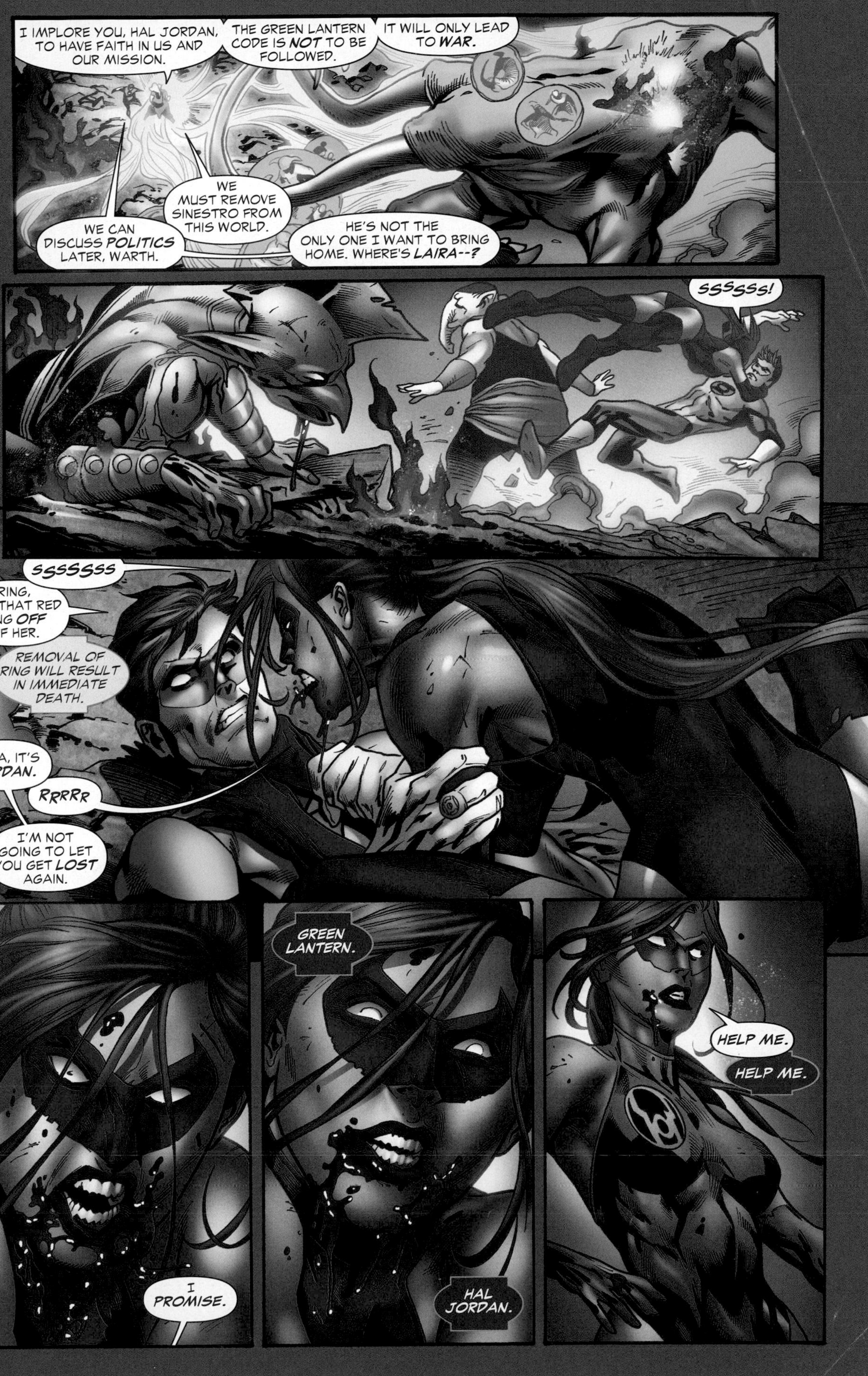
I IMPLORE YOU, HAL JORDAN, TO HAVE FAITH IN US AND OUR MISSION.
THE GREEN LANTERN CODE IS NOT TO BE FOLLOWED.
IT WILL ONLY LEAD TO WAR.
WE MUST REMOVE SINESTRO FROM THIS WORLD.
WE CAN DISCUSS POLITICS LATER, WARTH.
HE'S NOT THE ONLY ONE I WANT TO BRING HOME. WHERE'S LAIRA--?
SSSSSS!
SSSSSSS
RING, GET THAT RED RING OFF OF HER.
REMOVAL OF RING WILL RESULT IN IMMEDIATE DEATH.
LAIRA, IT'S JORDAN.
RRRRR
I'M NOT GOING TO LET YOU GET LOST AGAIN.
I PROMISE.
GREEN LANTERN.
HAL JORDAN.
HELP ME.
HELP ME.

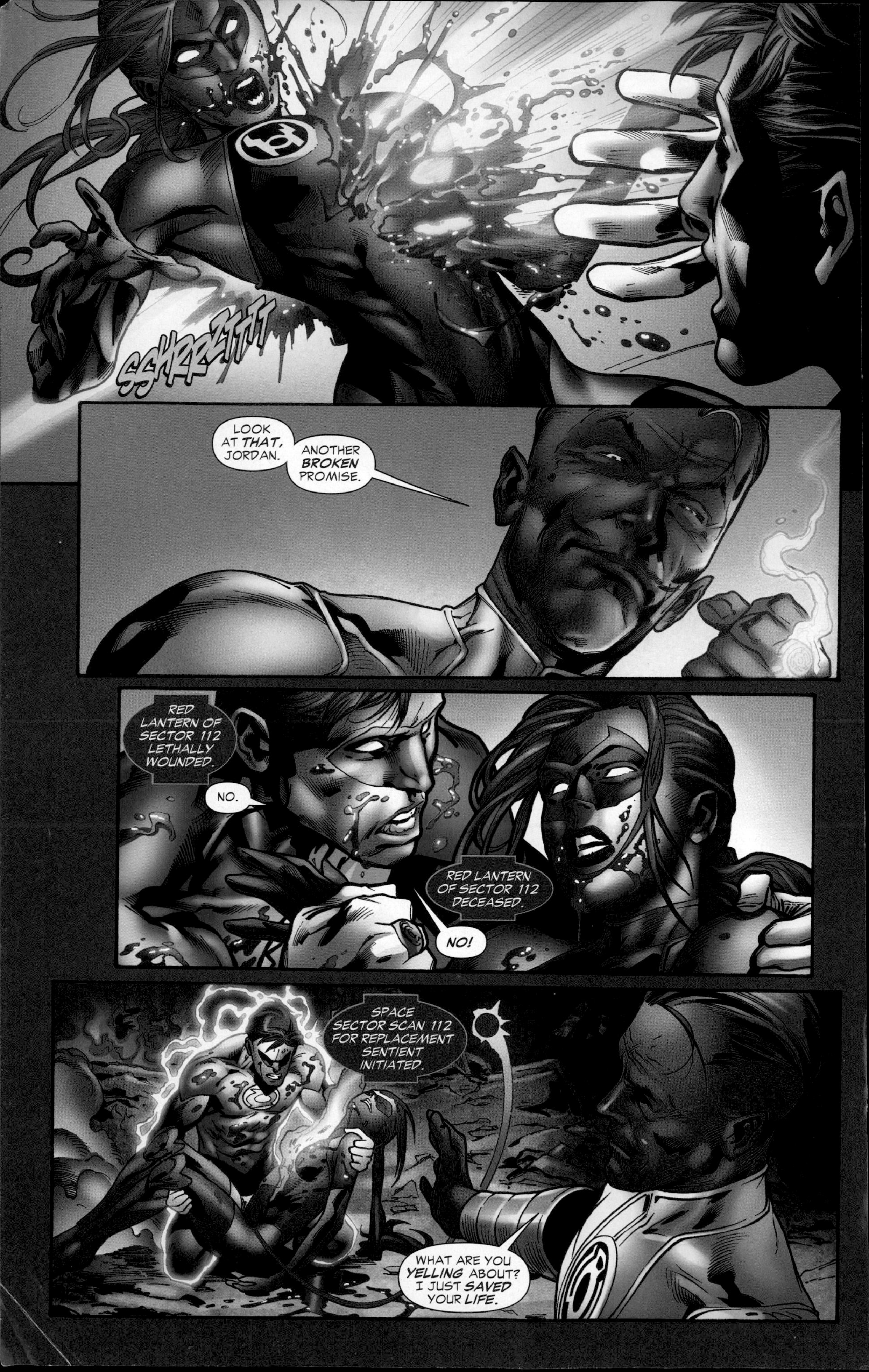
SSHRRZTTTT
LOOK AT THAT, JORDAN.
ANOTHER BROKEN PROMISE.
RED LANTERN OF SECTOR 112 LETHALLY WOUNDED.
NO.
RED LANTERN OF SECTOR 112 DECEASED.
NO!
SPACE SECTOR SCAN 112 FOR REPLACEMENT SENTIENT INITIATED.
WHAT ARE YOU YELLING ABOUT? I JUST SAVED YOUR LIFE.

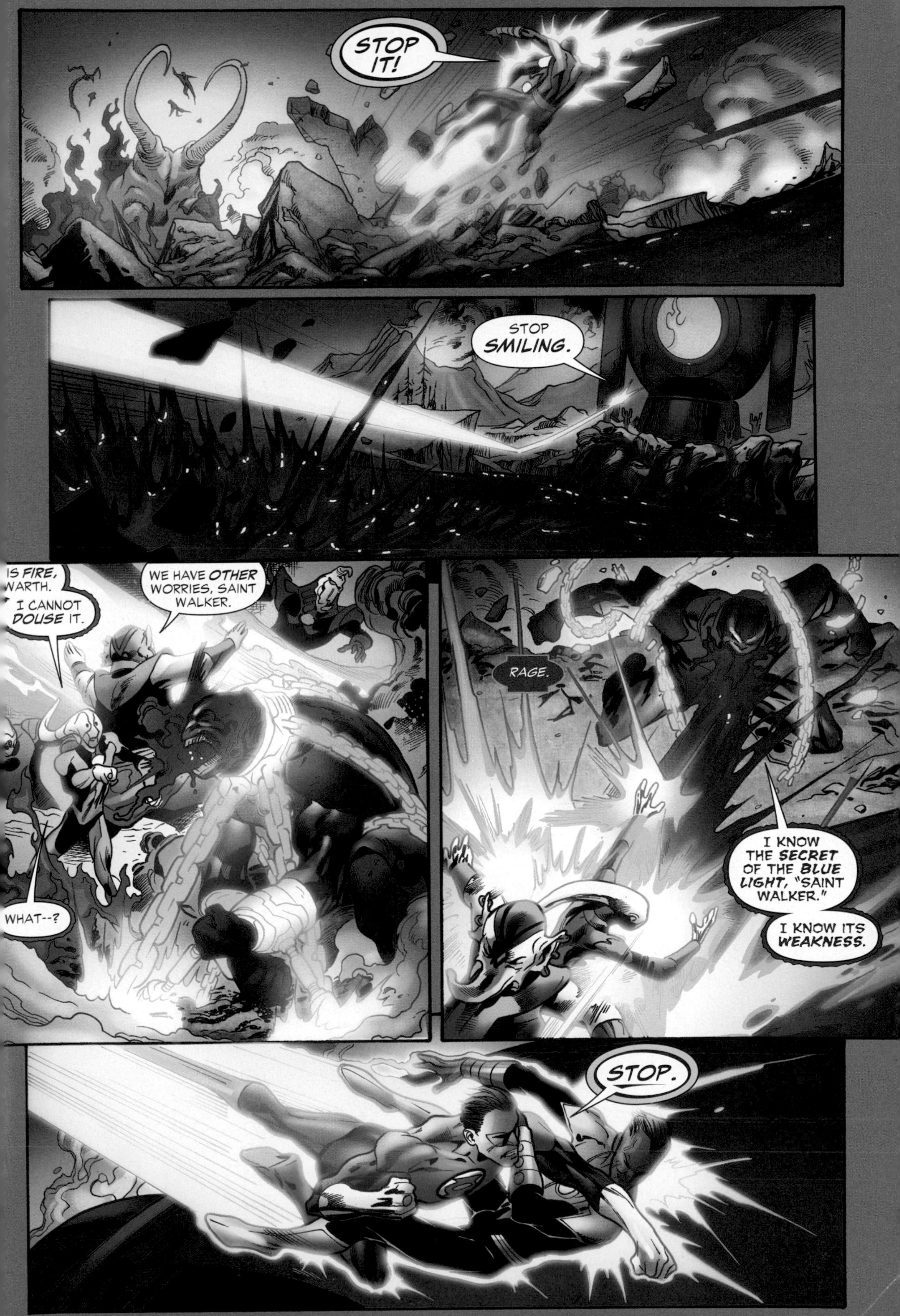
STOP IT!
STOP SMILING.
IS FIRE, WARTH. I CANNOT DOUSE IT.
WE HAVE OTHER WORRIES, SAINT WALKER.
WHAT--?
RAGE.
I KNOW THE SECRET OF THE BLUE LIGHT, "SAINT WALKER."
I KNOW ITS WEAKNESS.
STOP.

LETHAL FORCE HAS BEEN ENABLED.

AUTHORIZATION CONFIRMED. AWAITING VERBAL COMMAND.

GREEN LANTERN!

NO.

IT'S GONE ON LONG *ENOUGH*, WALKER!

HE'S KILLED *TOO* MANY.

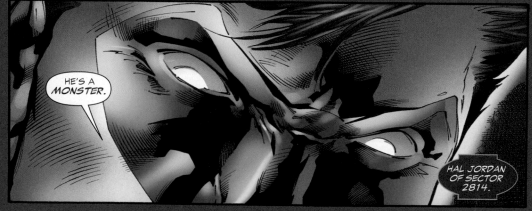

HE'S A MONSTER.

HAL JORDAN OF SECTOR 2814.

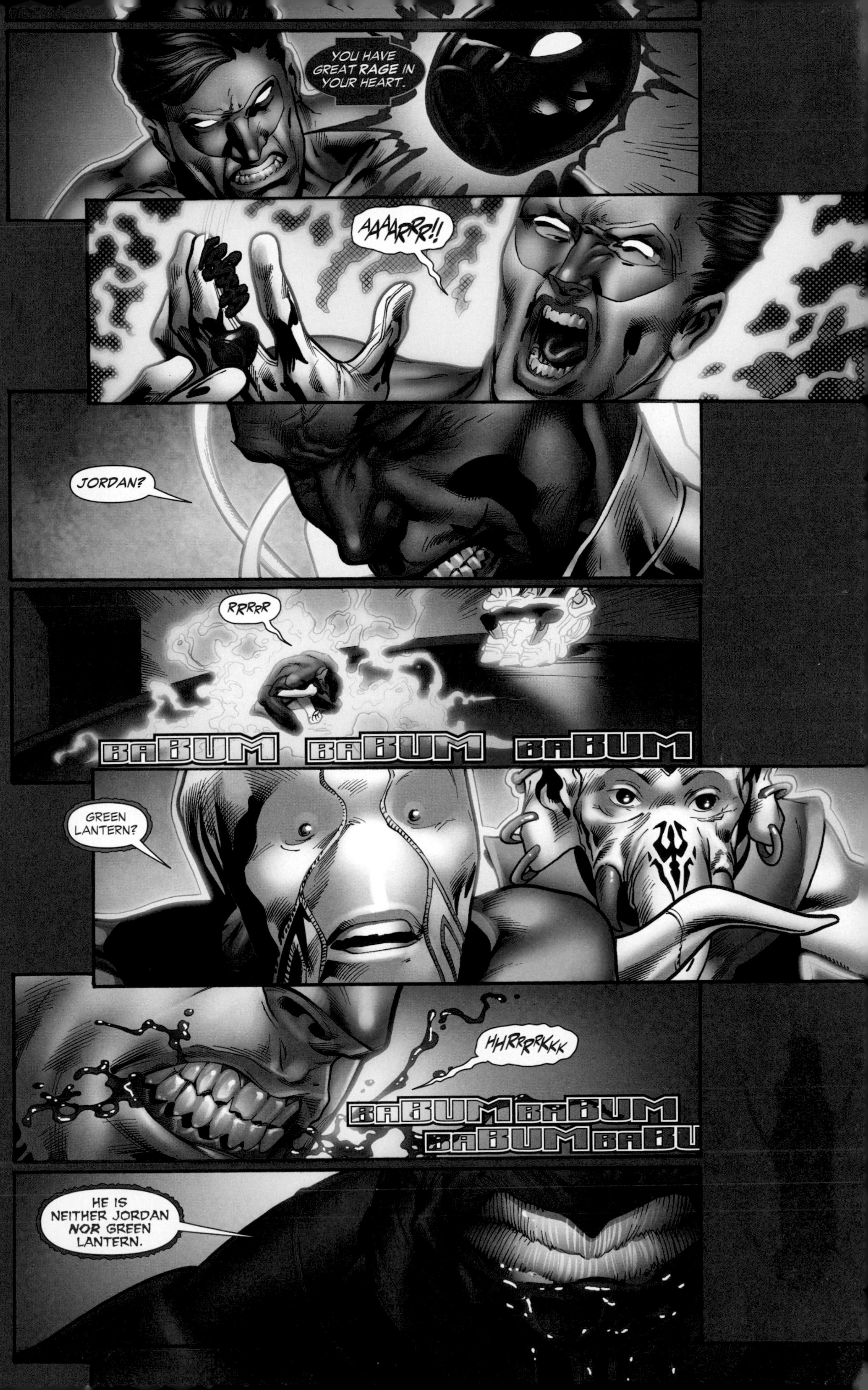
YOU HAVE GREAT RAGE IN YOUR HEART.
AAAARRR!!
JORDAN?
RRRRR
BABUM BABUM BABUM
GREEN LANTERN?
HHRRRKKK
BABUM BABUM BABUM BABU
HE IS NEITHER JORDAN NOR GREEN LANTERN.

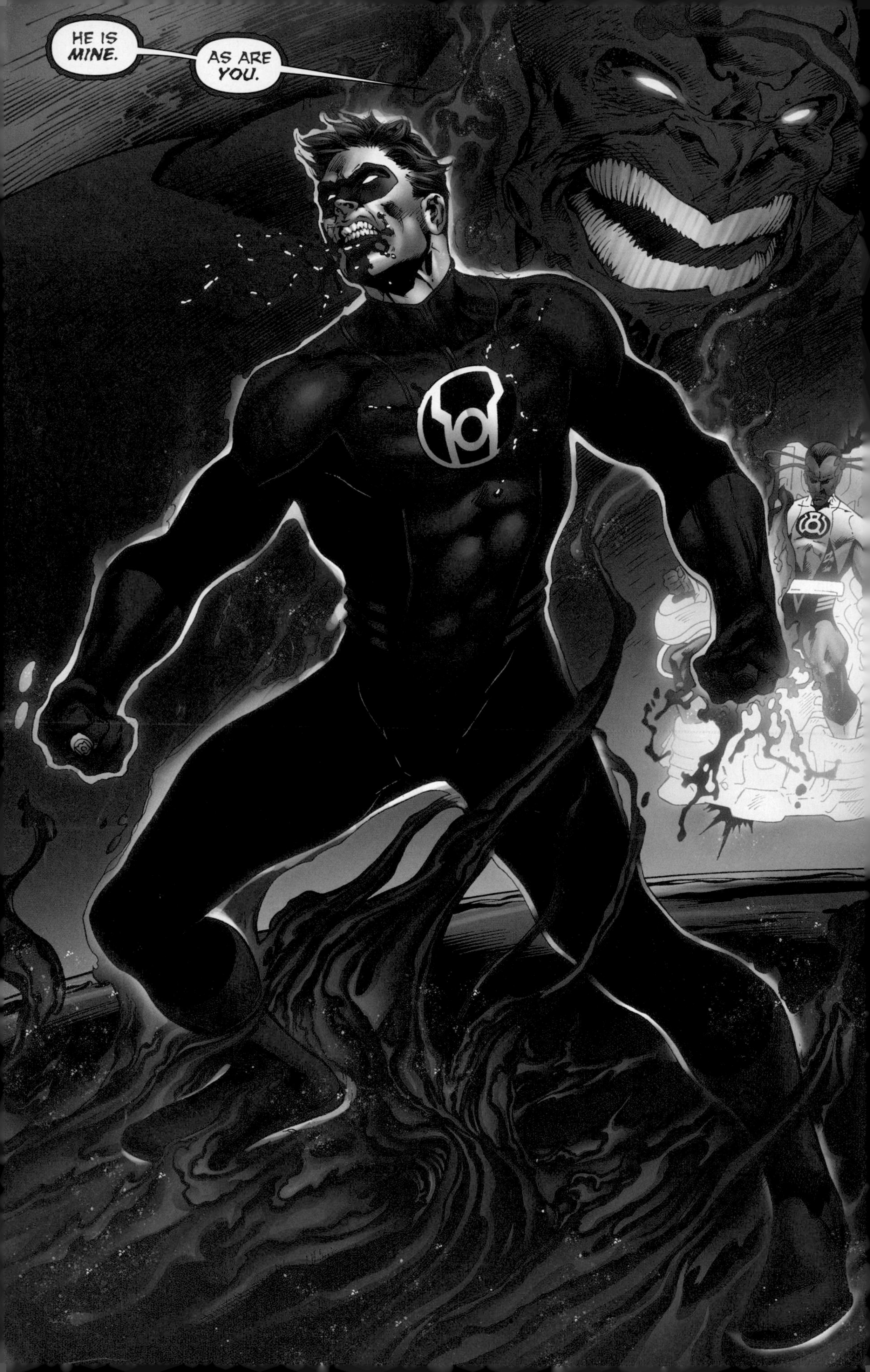
HE IS MINE.
AS ARE YOU.

GREEN LANTERN 38 Cover by Shane Davis, Sandra Hope and Nei Ruffino

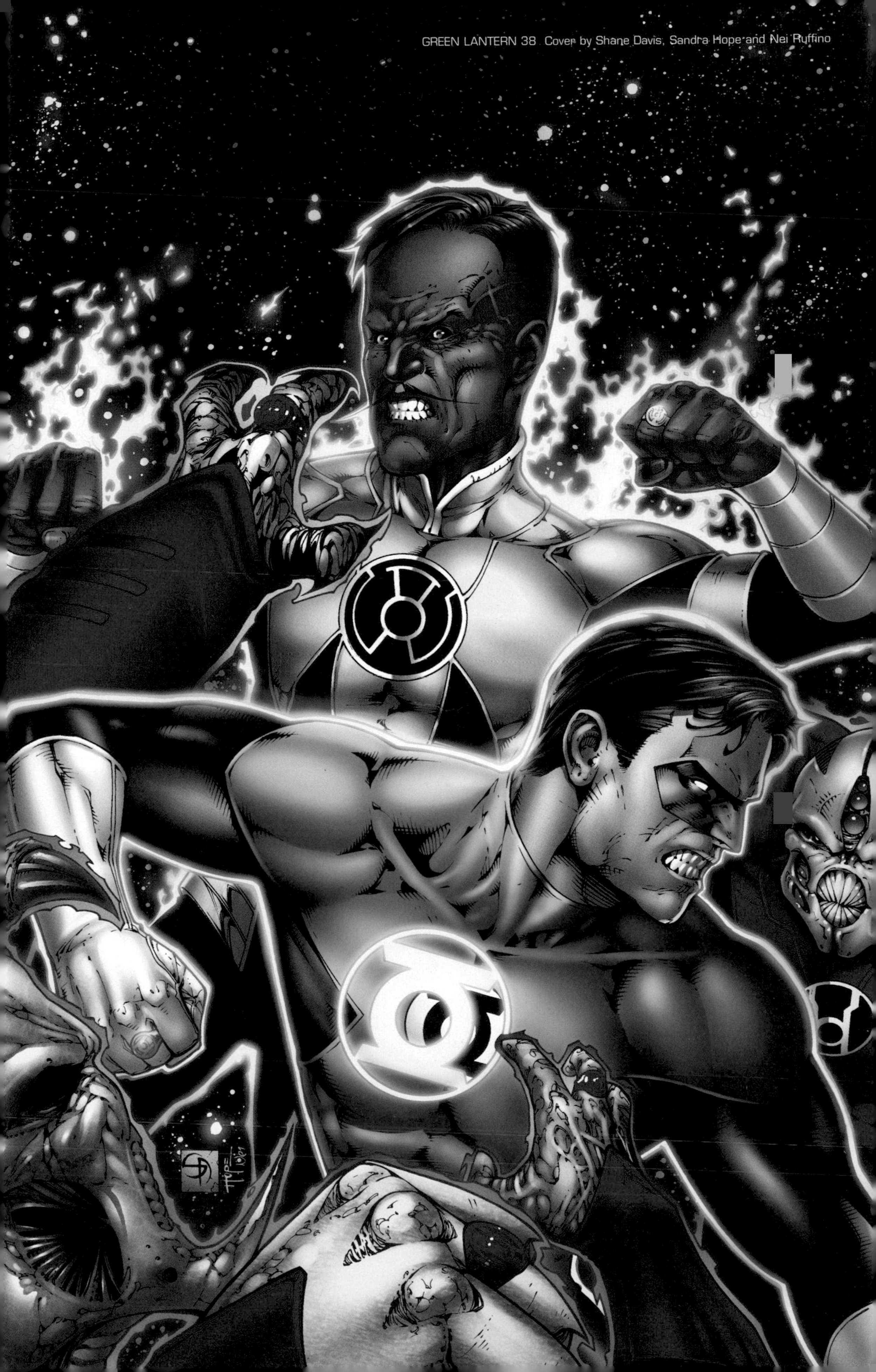

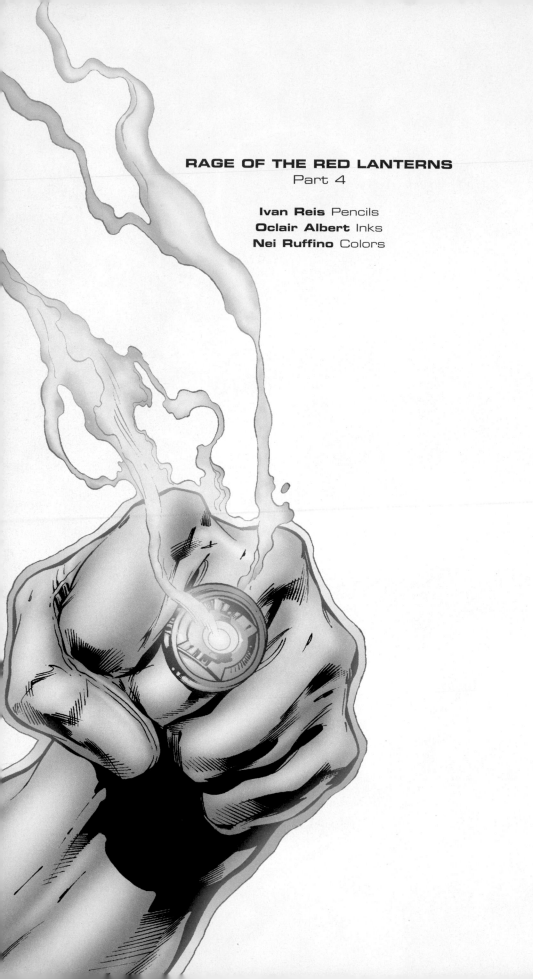

RAGE OF THE RED LANTERNS
Part 4

Ivan Reis Pencils
Oclair Albert Inks
Nei Ruffino Colors

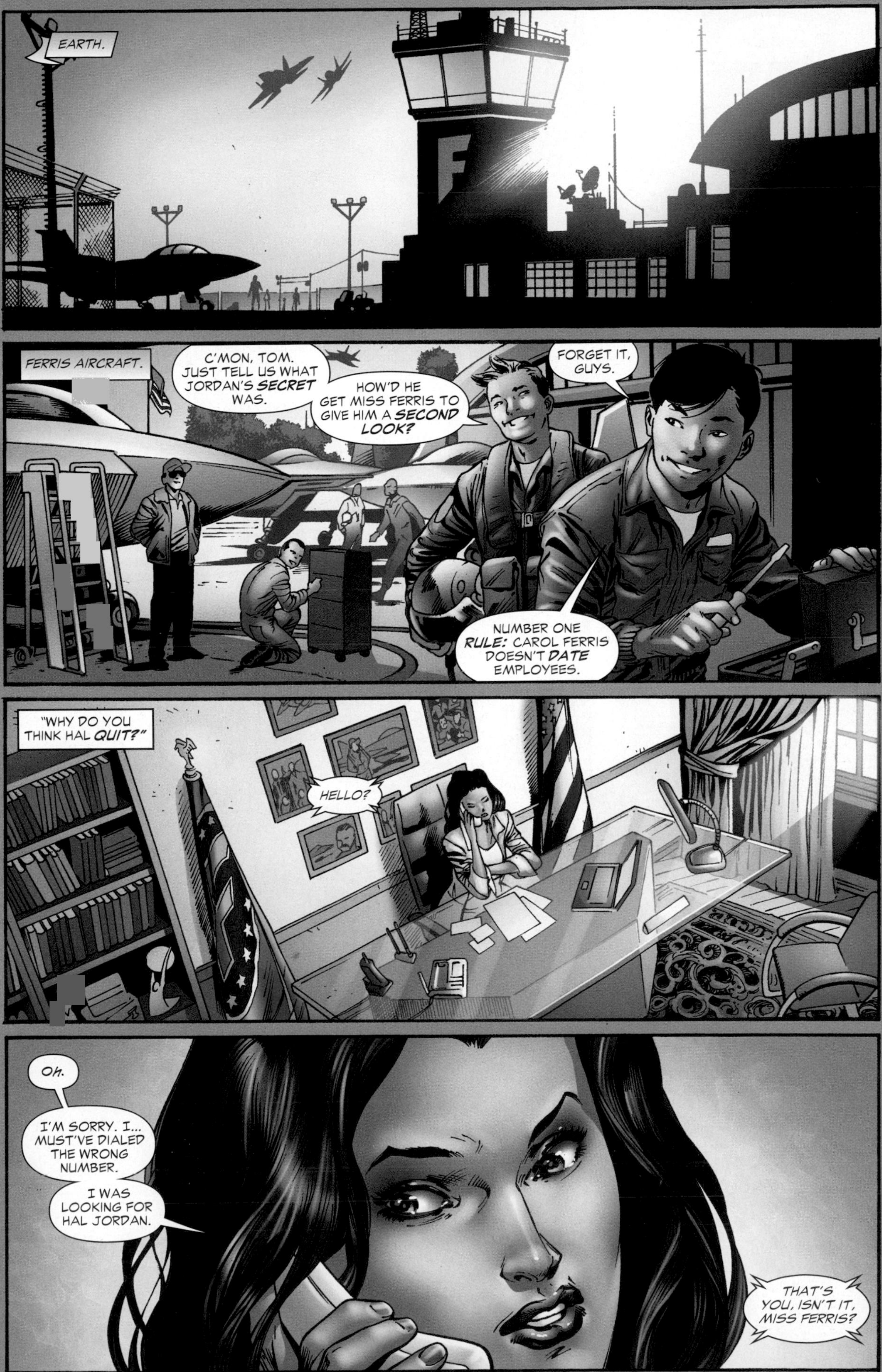
EARTH.
FERRIS AIRCRAFT.
C'MON, TOM. JUST TELL US WHAT JORDAN'S SECRET WAS.
HOW'D HE GET MISS FERRIS TO GIVE HIM A SECOND LOOK?
FORGET IT, GUYS.
NUMBER ONE RULE: CAROL FERRIS DOESN'T DATE EMPLOYEES.
"WHY DO YOU THINK HAL QUIT?"
HELLO?
Oh.
I'M SORRY. I... MUST'VE DIALED THE WRONG NUMBER.
I WAS LOOKING FOR HAL JORDAN.
THAT'S YOU, ISN'T IT, MISS FERRIS?

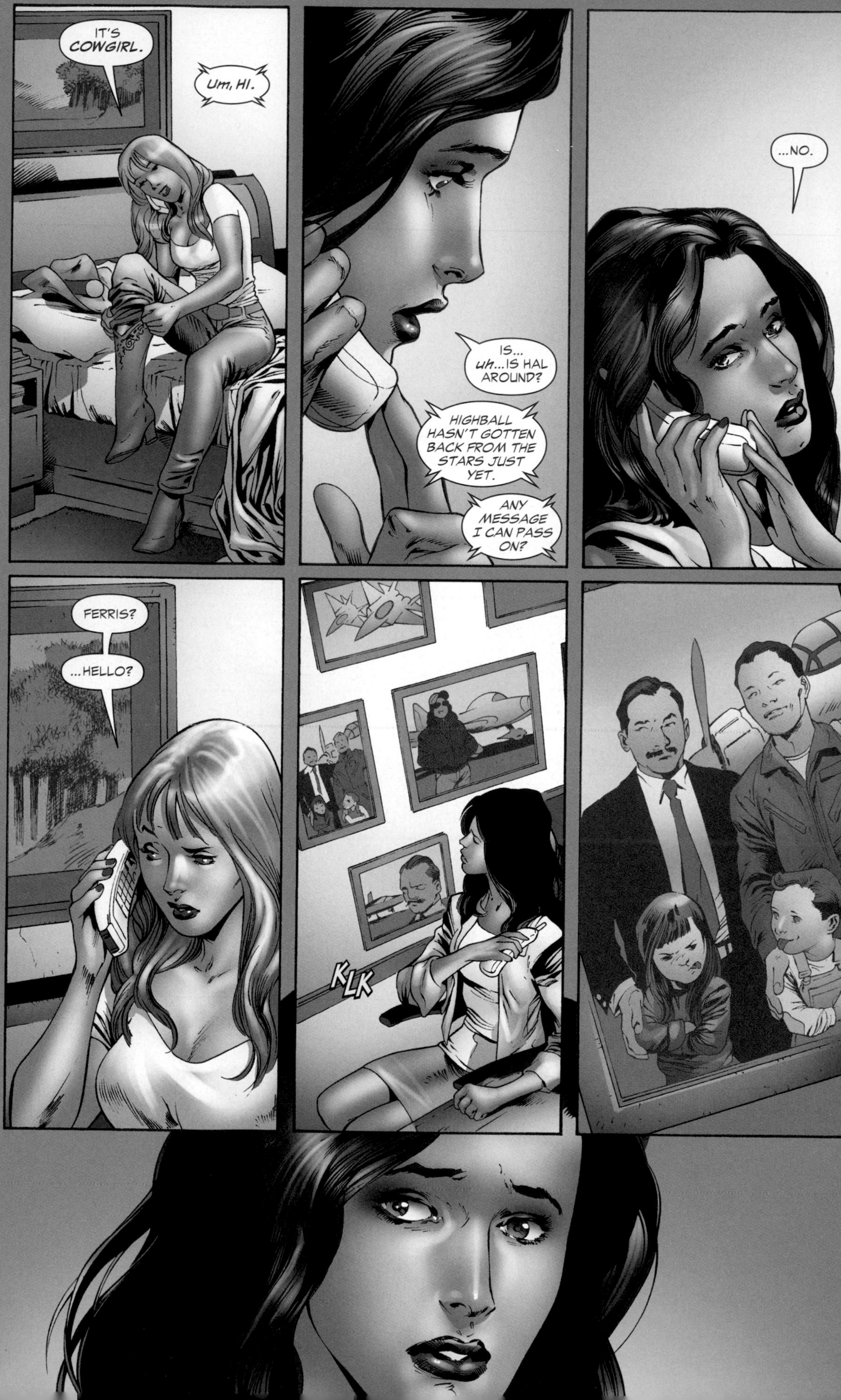
IT'S COWGIRL.
Um, HI.
IS... uh...IS HAL AROUND?
HIGHBALL HASN'T GOTTEN BACK FROM THE STARS JUST YET.
ANY MESSAGE I CAN PASS ON?
...NO.
FERRIS?
...HELLO?
KLK

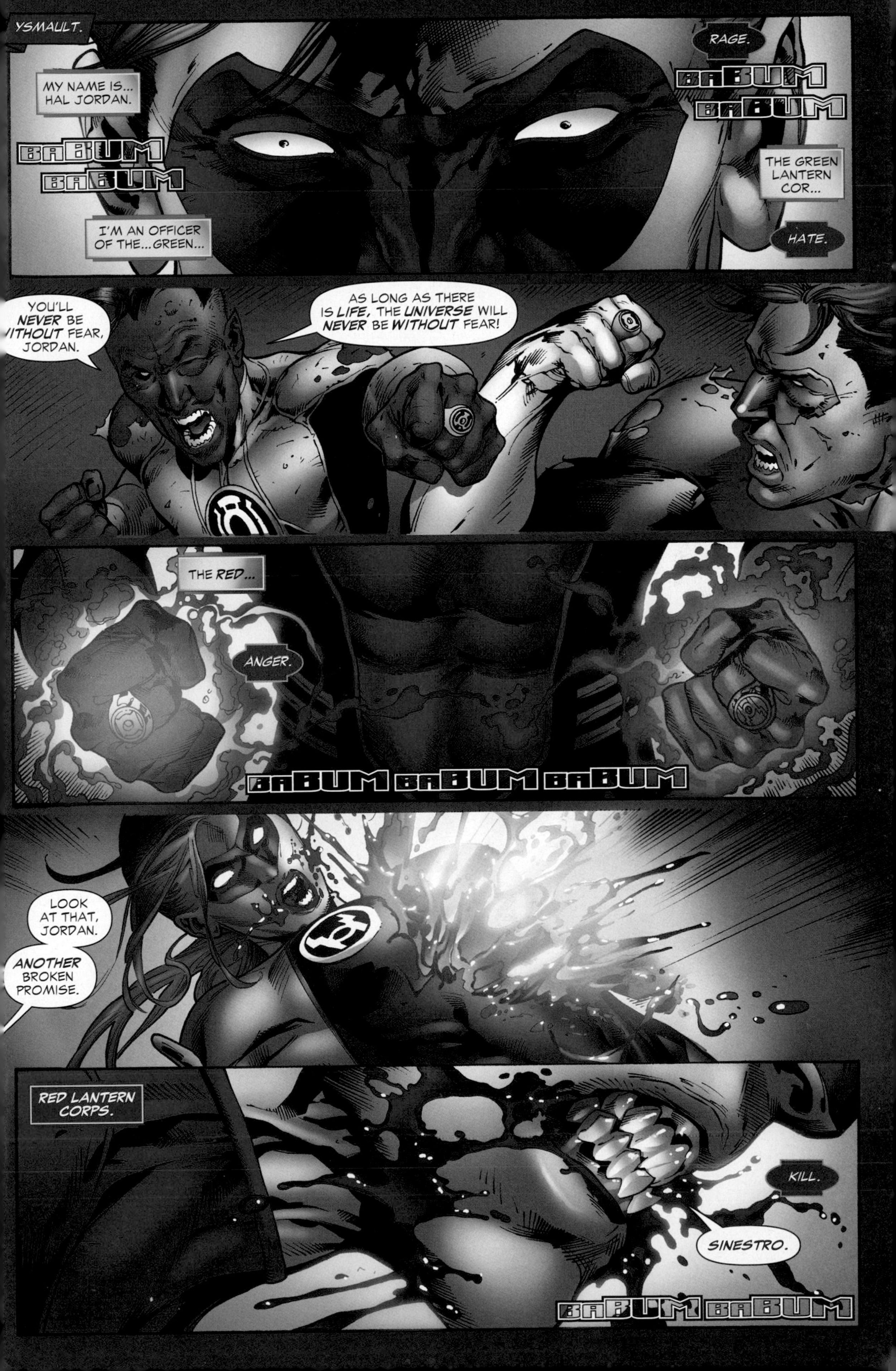
YSMAULT.
MY NAME IS... HAL JORDAN.
BABUM BABUM
I'M AN OFFICER OF THE...GREEN...
RAGE.
BABUM BABUM
THE GREEN LANTERN COR...
HATE.
YOU'LL NEVER BE WITHOUT FEAR, JORDAN.
AS LONG AS THERE IS LIFE, THE UNIVERSE WILL NEVER BE WITHOUT FEAR!
THE RED...
ANGER.
BABUM BABUM BABUM
LOOK AT THAT, JORDAN.
ANOTHER BROKEN PROMISE.
RED LANTERN CORPS.
KILL.
SINESTRO.
BABUM BABUM

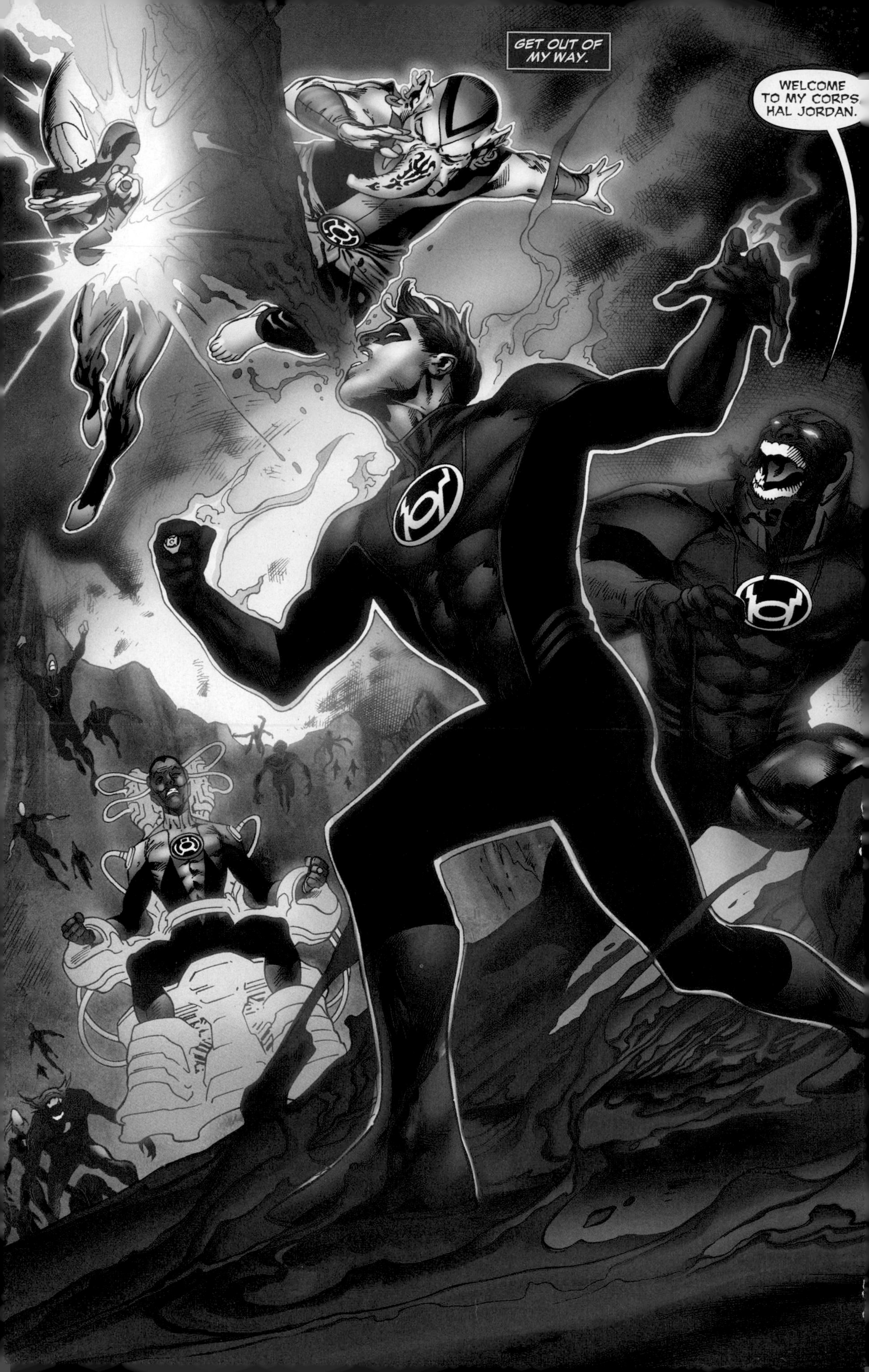
GET OUT OF MY WAY.
WELCOME TO MY CORPS, HAL JORDAN.

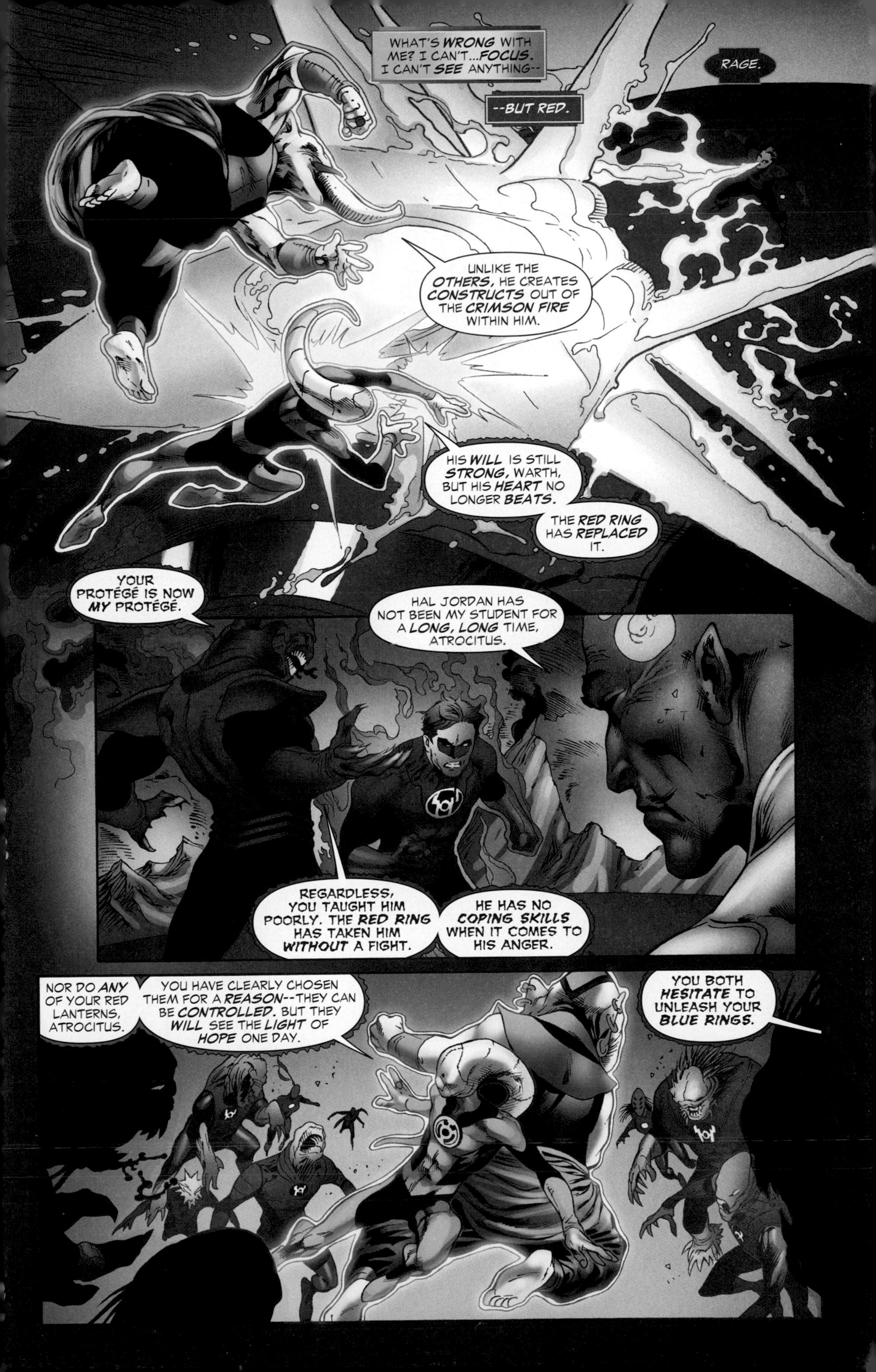
WHAT'S WRONG WITH ME? I CAN'T...FOCUS. I CAN'T SEE ANYTHING--
RAGE.
--BUT RED.
UNLIKE THE OTHERS, HE CREATES CONSTRUCTS OUT OF THE CRIMSON FIRE WITHIN HIM.
HIS WILL IS STILL STRONG, WARTH, BUT HIS HEART NO LONGER BEATS.
THE RED RING HAS REPLACED IT.
YOUR PROTÉGÉ IS NOW MY PROTÉGÉ.
HAL JORDAN HAS NOT BEEN MY STUDENT FOR A LONG, LONG TIME, ATROCITUS.
REGARDLESS, YOU TAUGHT HIM POORLY. THE RED RING HAS TAKEN HIM WITHOUT A FIGHT.
HE HAS NO COPING SKILLS WHEN IT COMES TO HIS ANGER.
NOR DO ANY OF YOUR RED LANTERNS, ATROCITUS.
YOU HAVE CLEARLY CHOSEN THEM FOR A REASON--THEY CAN BE CONTROLLED. BUT THEY WILL SEE THE LIGHT OF HOPE ONE DAY.
YOU BOTH HESITATE TO UNLEASH YOUR BLUE RINGS.

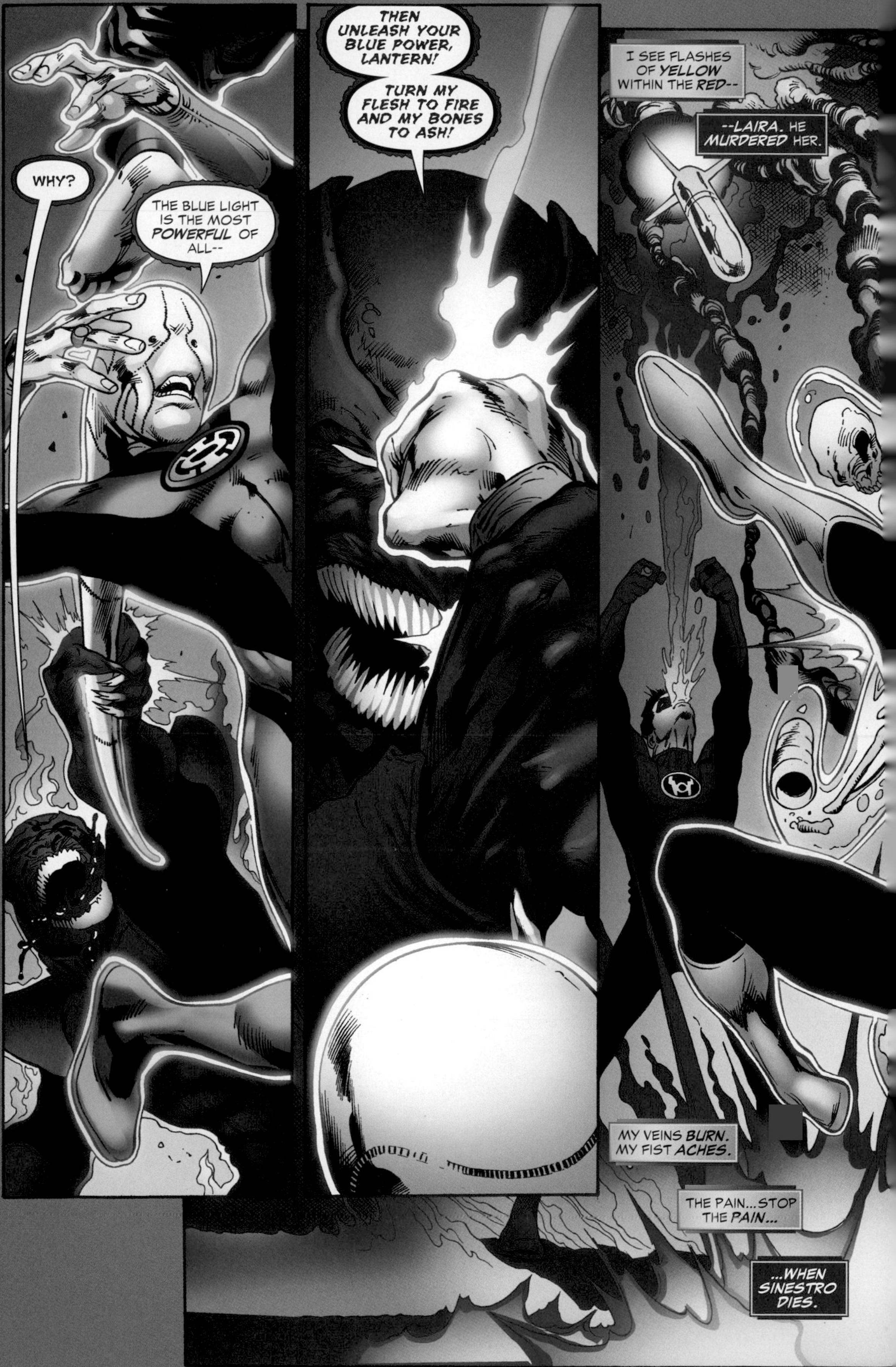
WHY?
THE BLUE LIGHT IS THE MOST POWERFUL OF ALL--
THEN UNLEASH YOUR BLUE POWER, LANTERN!
TURN MY FLESH TO FIRE AND MY BONES TO ASH!
I SEE FLASHES OF YELLOW WITHIN THE RED--
--LAIRA. HE MURDERED HER.
MY VEINS BURN. MY FIST ACHES.
THE PAIN...STOP THE PAIN...
...WHEN SINESTRO DIES.

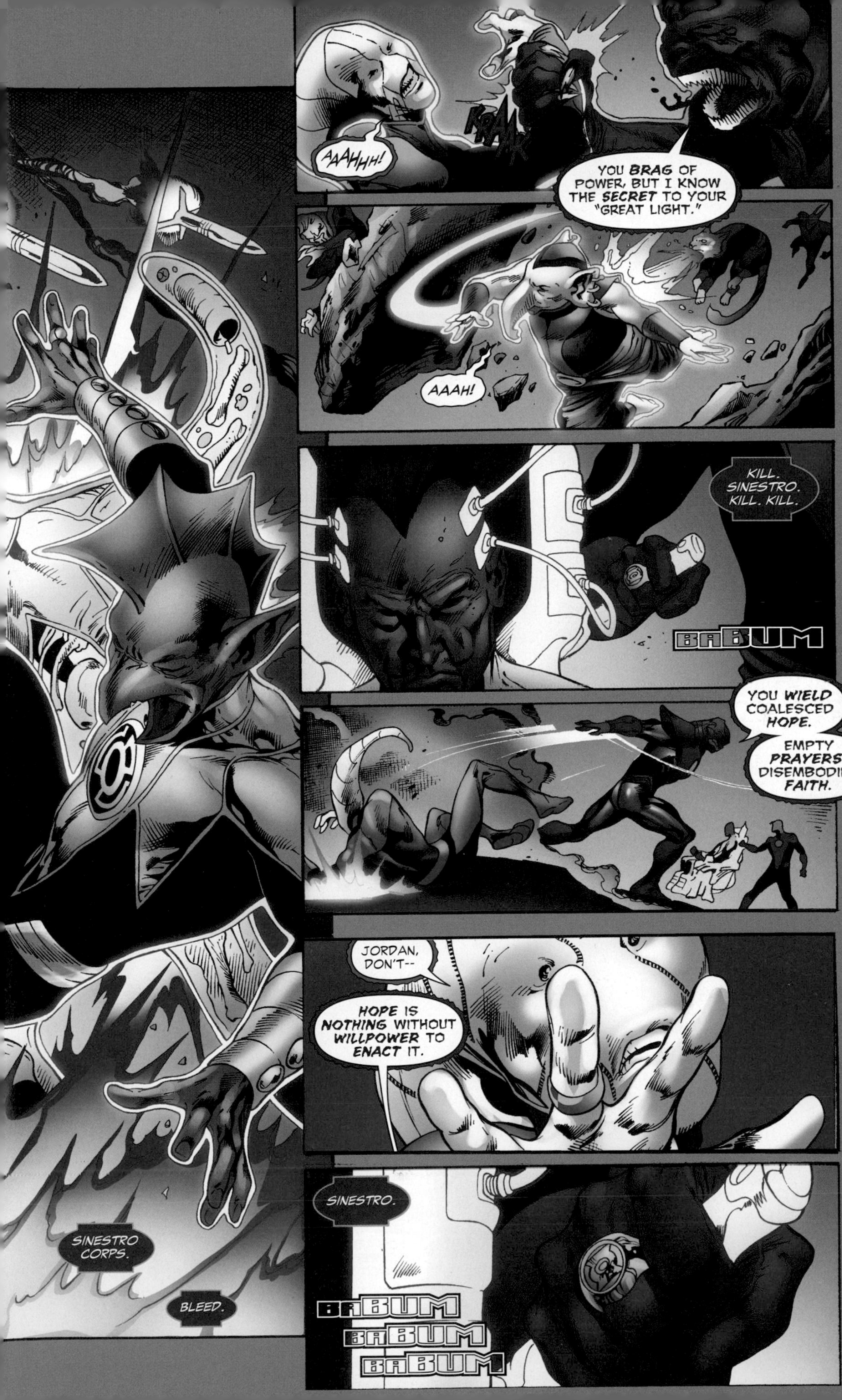
AAAHHH!
KRAAK
YOU BRAG OF POWER, BUT I KNOW THE SECRET TO YOUR "GREAT LIGHT."
AAAH!
KILL. SINESTRO. KILL. KILL.
BABUM
YOU WIELD COALESCED HOPE.
EMPTY PRAYERS. DISEMBODIED FAITH.
JORDAN, DON'T--
HOPE IS NOTHING WITHOUT WILLPOWER TO ENACT IT.
SINESTRO.
SINESTRO CORPS.
BLEED.
BABUM
BABUM
BABUM

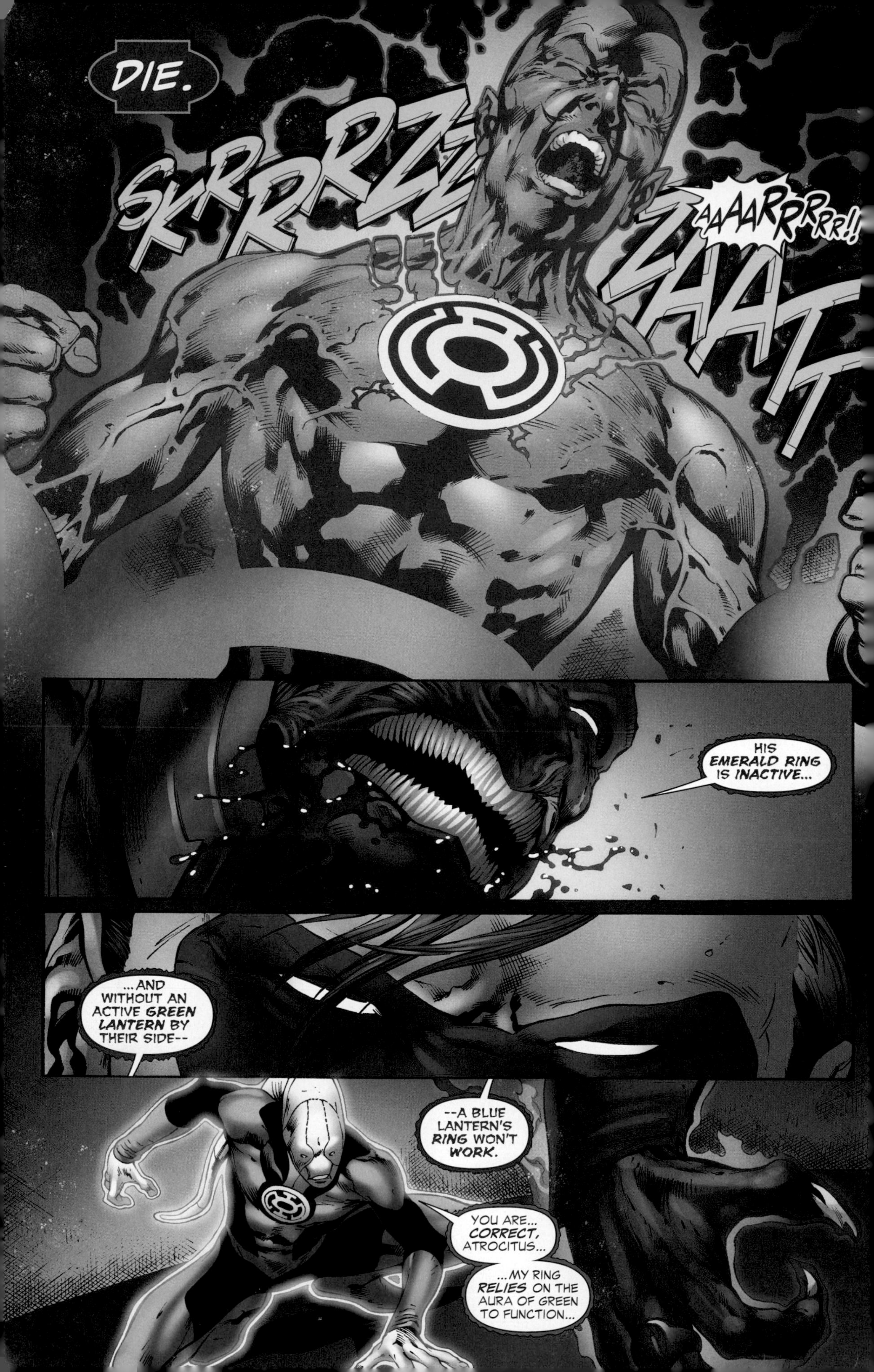
DIE.
SKRRRZZ
ZZAAT
AAAARRRRR!!
HIS EMERALD RING IS INACTIVE...
...AND WITHOUT AN ACTIVE GREEN LANTERN BY THEIR SIDE--
--A BLUE LANTERN'S RING WON'T WORK.
YOU ARE... CORRECT, ATROCITUS...
...MY RING RELIES ON THE AURA OF GREEN TO FUNCTION...

...BUT THAT DOES NOT MAKE ME HOPELESS.

ALL WILL BE WELL.

RAGE.

HAL JORDAN OF SPACE SECTOR 2814.

I DO NOT KNOW IF YOU HAVE *GREAT HOPE* IN YOUR *HEART*--

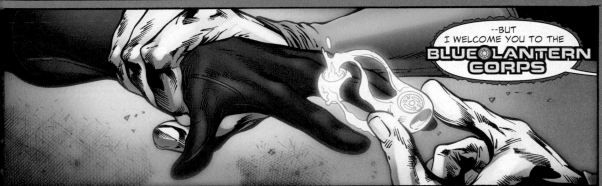

--BUT I WELCOME YOU TO THE BLUE LANTERN CORPS

KRRKOOMM

RED RING INFESTATION DETECTED.

CELLULAR CLEANSING IN PROCESS.

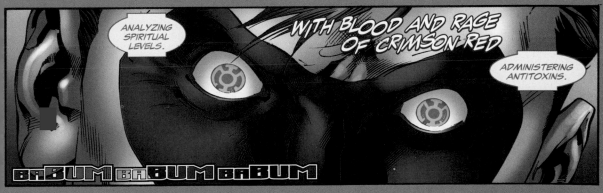

ANALYZING SPIRITUAL LEVELS.

WITH BLOOD AND RAGE OF CRIMSON RED

ADMINISTERING ANTITOXINS.

BABUM BABUM BABUM

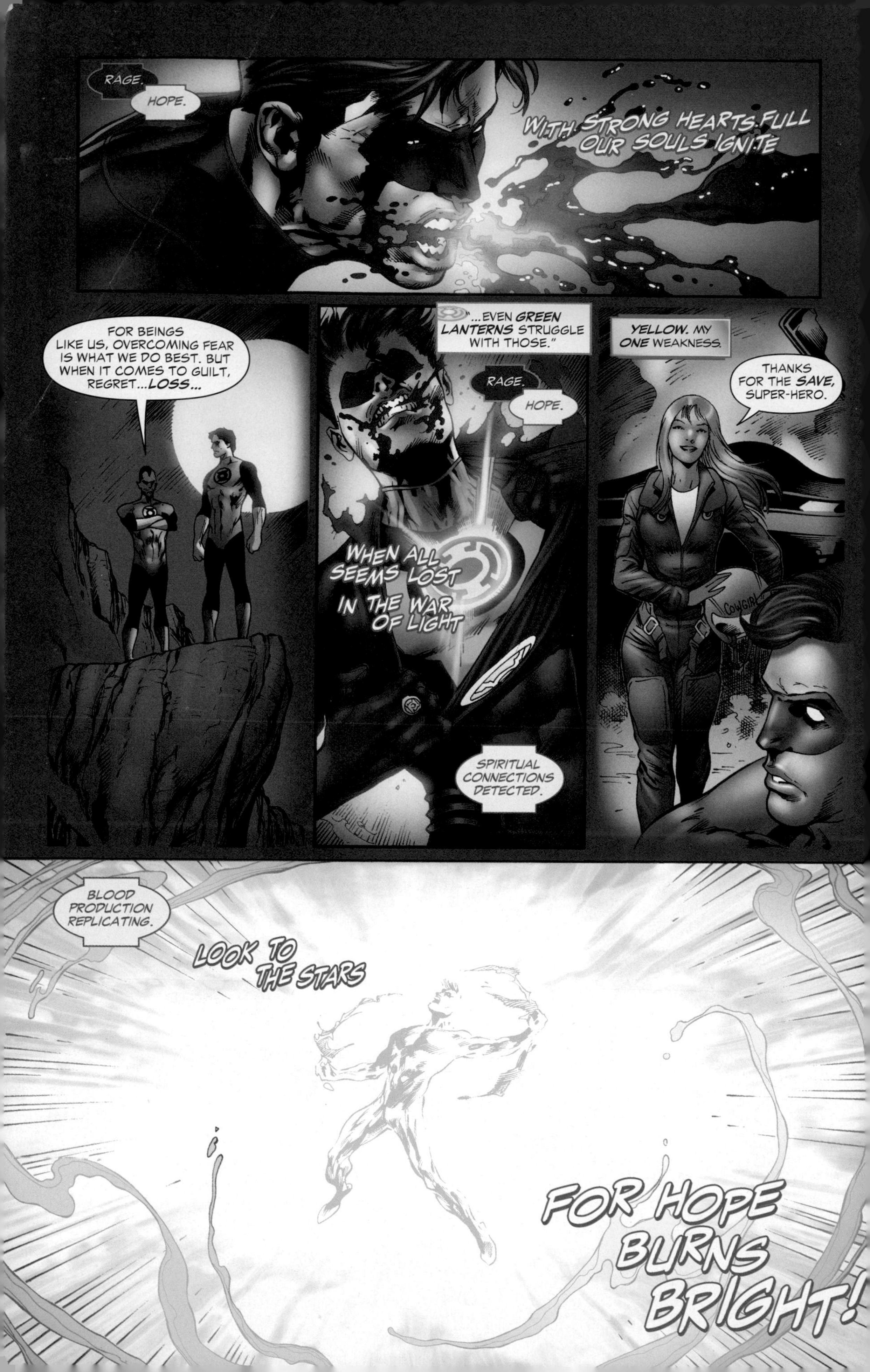
RAGE.
HOPE.
WITH STRONG HEARTS FULL OUR SOULS IGNITE
FOR BEINGS LIKE US, OVERCOMING FEAR IS WHAT WE DO BEST. BUT WHEN IT COMES TO GUILT, REGRET...LOSS...
"...EVEN GREEN LANTERNS STRUGGLE WITH THOSE."
RAGE.
HOPE.
WHEN ALL SEEMS LOST IN THE WAR OF LIGHT
SPIRITUAL CONNECTIONS DETECTED.
YELLOW. MY ONE WEAKNESS.
THANKS FOR THE SAVE, SUPER-HERO.
COWGIRL
BLOOD PRODUCTION REPLICATING.
LOOK TO THE STARS
FOR HOPE BURNS BRIGHT!

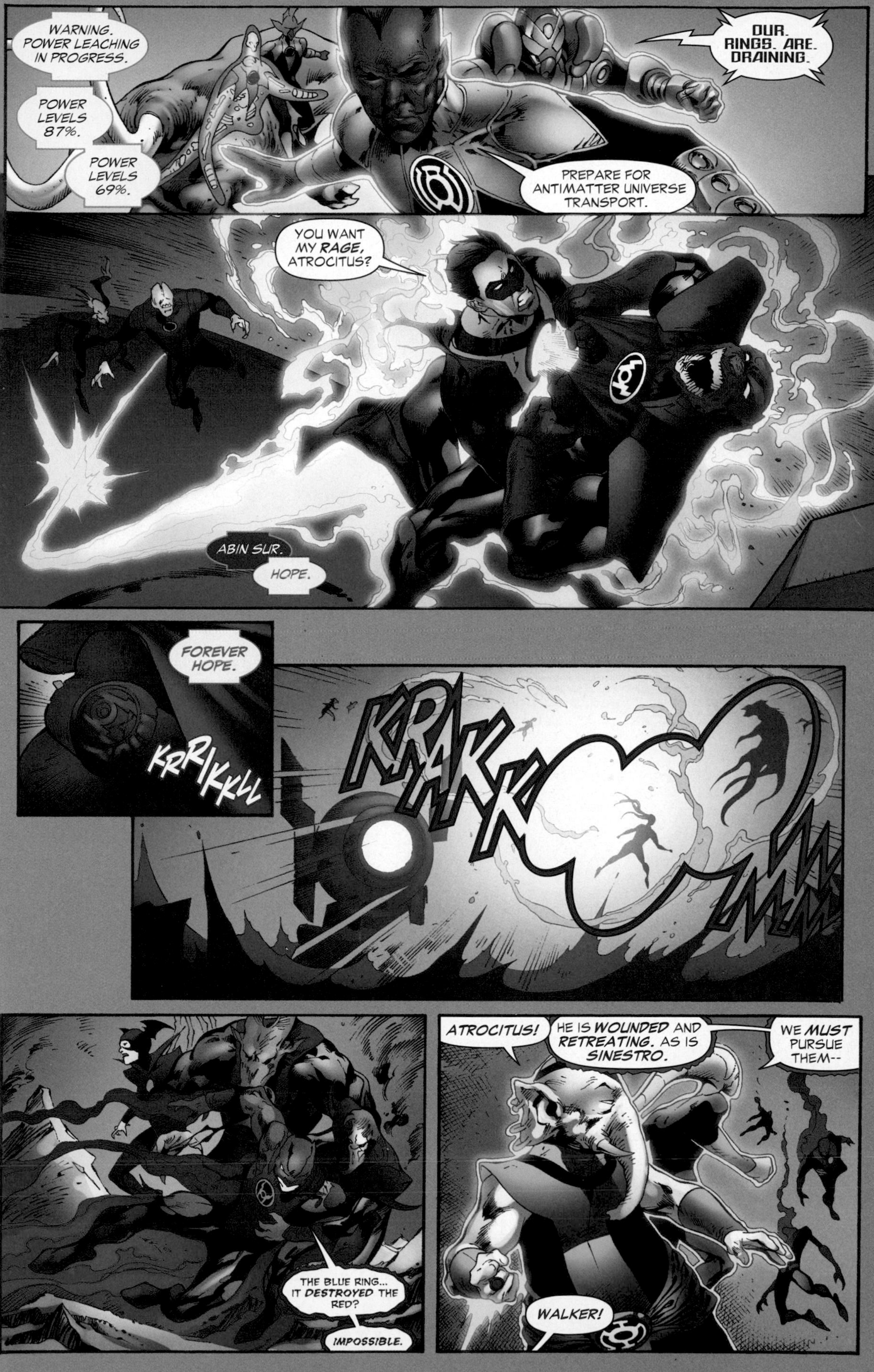
WARNING. POWER LEACHING IN PROGRESS.
POWER LEVELS 87%.
POWER LEVELS 69%.
OUR. RINGS. ARE. DRAINING.
PREPARE FOR ANTIMATTER UNIVERSE TRANSPORT.
YOU WANT MY RAGE, ATROCITUS?
ABIN SUR.
HOPE.
FOREVER HOPE.
KRRIKKLL
KRAKK
THE BLUE RING... IT DESTROYED THE RED?
IMPOSSIBLE.
ATROCITUS!
HE IS WOUNDED AND RETREATING. AS IS SINESTRO.
WE MUST PURSUE THEM--
WALKER!

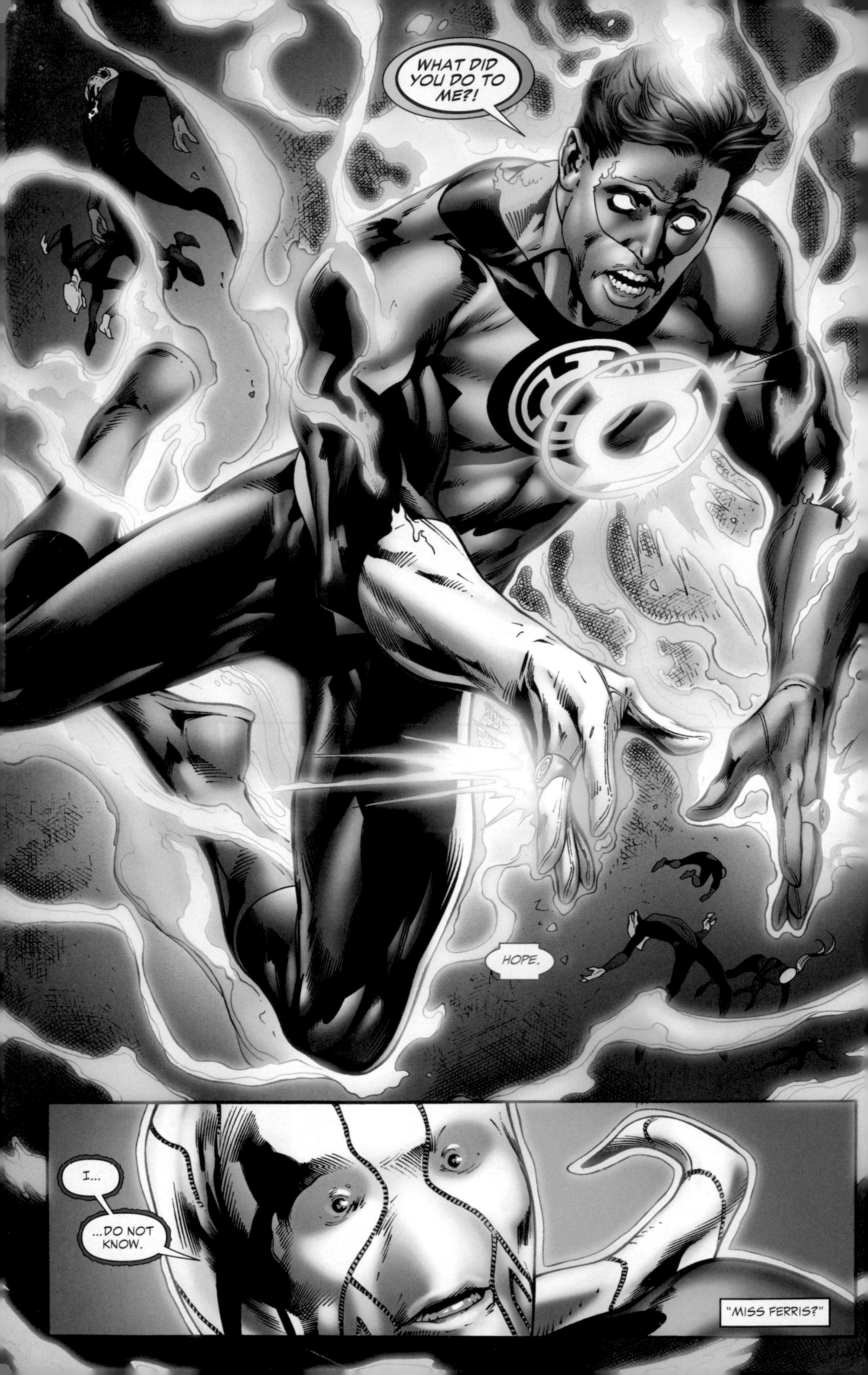
WHAT DID YOU DO TO ME?!
HOPE.
I...
...DO NOT KNOW.
"MISS FERRIS?"

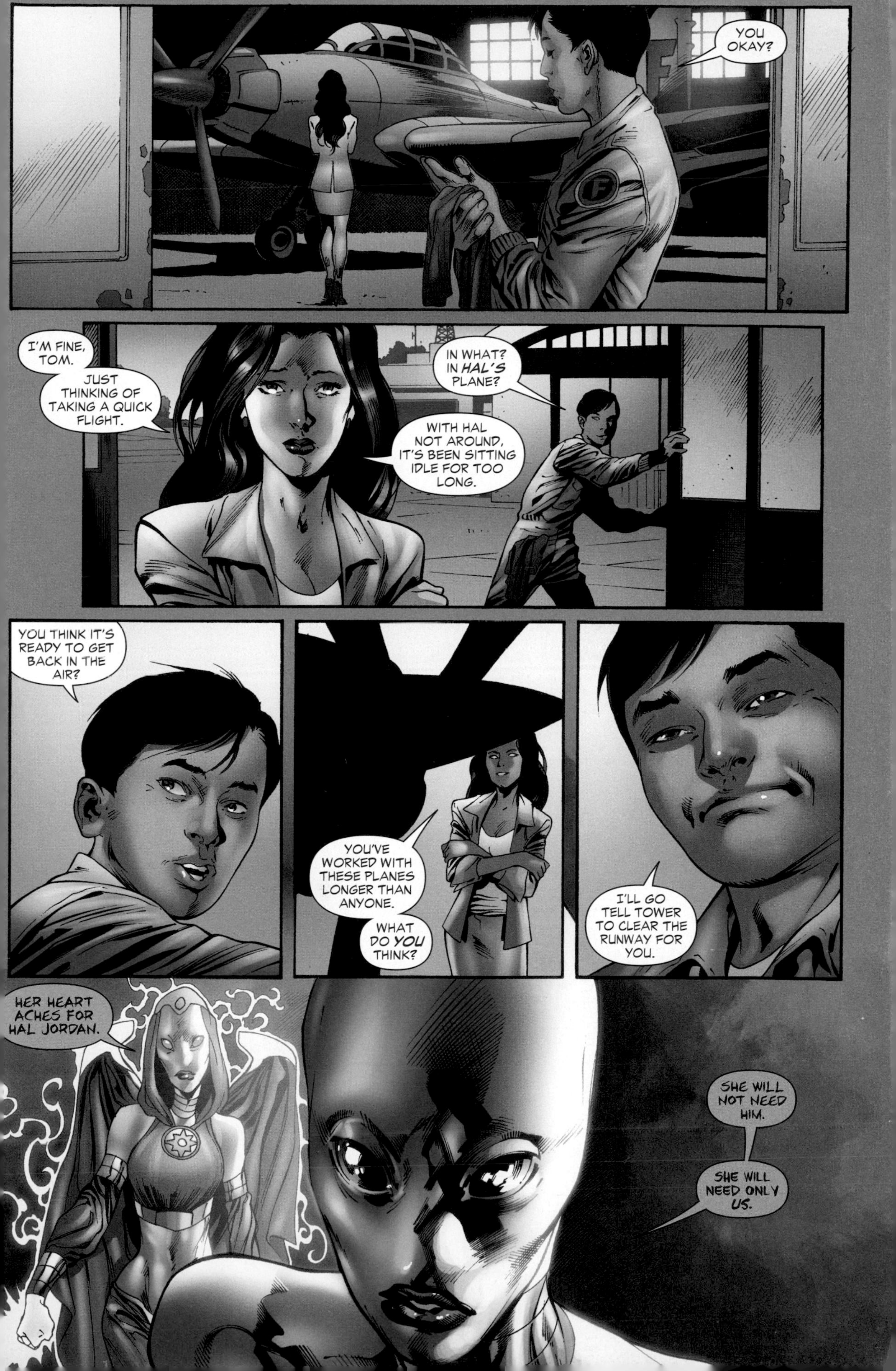
YOU OKAY?
I'M FINE, TOM.
JUST THINKING OF TAKING A QUICK FLIGHT.
IN WHAT? IN HAL'S PLANE?
WITH HAL NOT AROUND, IT'S BEEN SITTING IDLE FOR TOO LONG.
YOU THINK IT'S READY TO GET BACK IN THE AIR?
YOU'VE WORKED WITH THESE PLANES LONGER THAN ANYONE.
WHAT DO YOU THINK?
I'LL GO TELL TOWER TO CLEAR THE RUNWAY FOR YOU.
HER HEART ACHES FOR HAL JORDAN.
SHE WILL NOT NEED HIM.
SHE WILL NEED ONLY US.

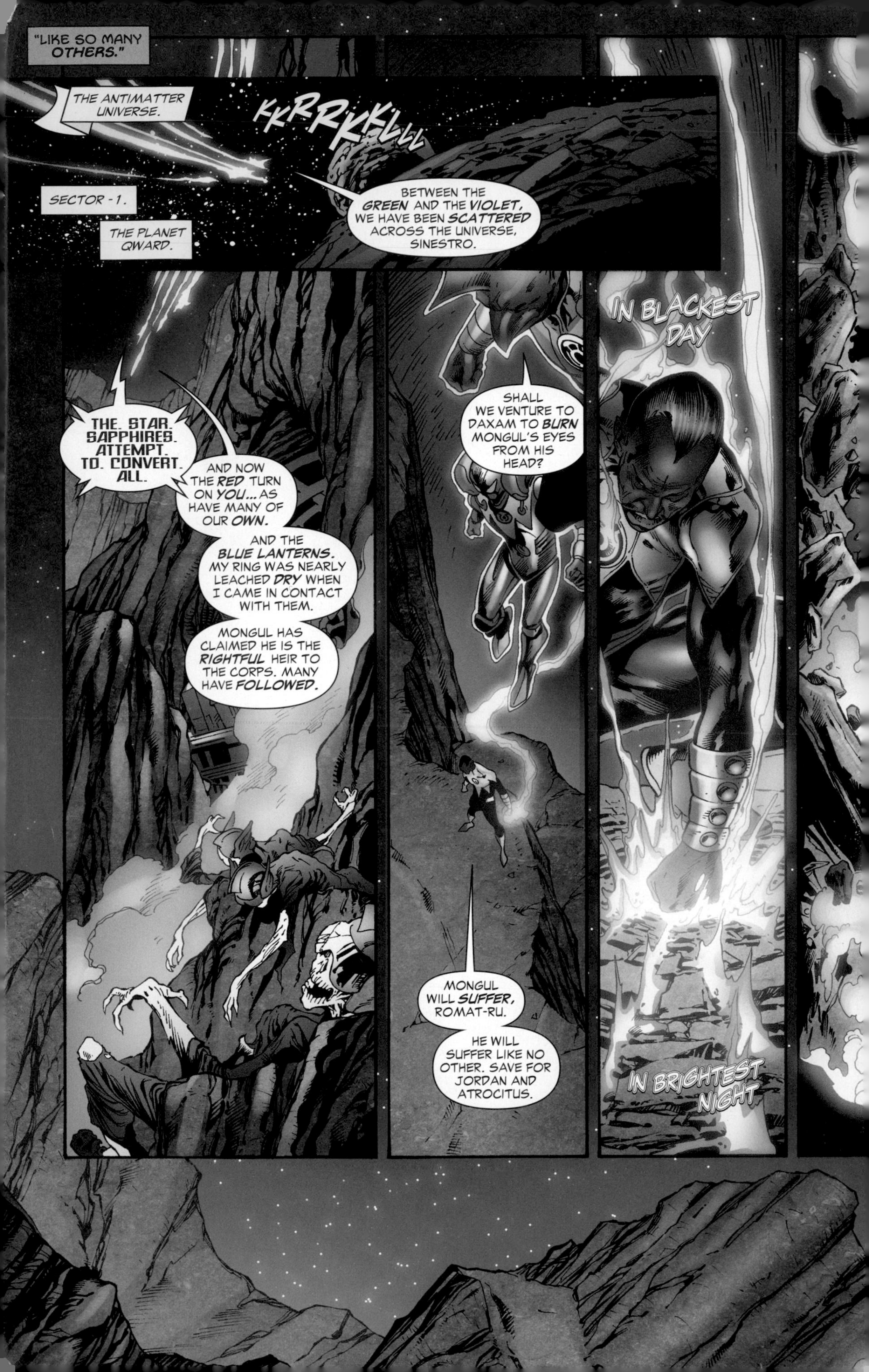
"LIKE SO MANY OTHERS."
THE ANTIMATTER UNIVERSE.
KKRRKKLLL
SECTOR -1.
THE PLANET QWARD.
BETWEEN THE GREEN AND THE VIOLET, WE HAVE BEEN SCATTERED ACROSS THE UNIVERSE, SINESTRO.
THE. STAR. SAPPHIRES. ATTEMPT. TO. CONVERT. ALL.
AND NOW THE RED TURN ON YOU... AS HAVE MANY OF OUR OWN.
AND THE BLUE LANTERNS. MY RING WAS NEARLY LEACHED DRY WHEN I CAME IN CONTACT WITH THEM.
MONGUL HAS CLAIMED HE IS THE RIGHTFUL HEIR TO THE CORPS. MANY HAVE FOLLOWED.
SHALL WE VENTURE TO DAXAM TO BURN MONGUL'S EYES FROM HIS HEAD?
MONGUL WILL SUFFER, ROMAT-RU.
HE WILL SUFFER LIKE NO OTHER. SAVE FOR JORDAN AND ATROCITUS.
IN BLACKEST DAY
IN BRIGHTEST NIGHT

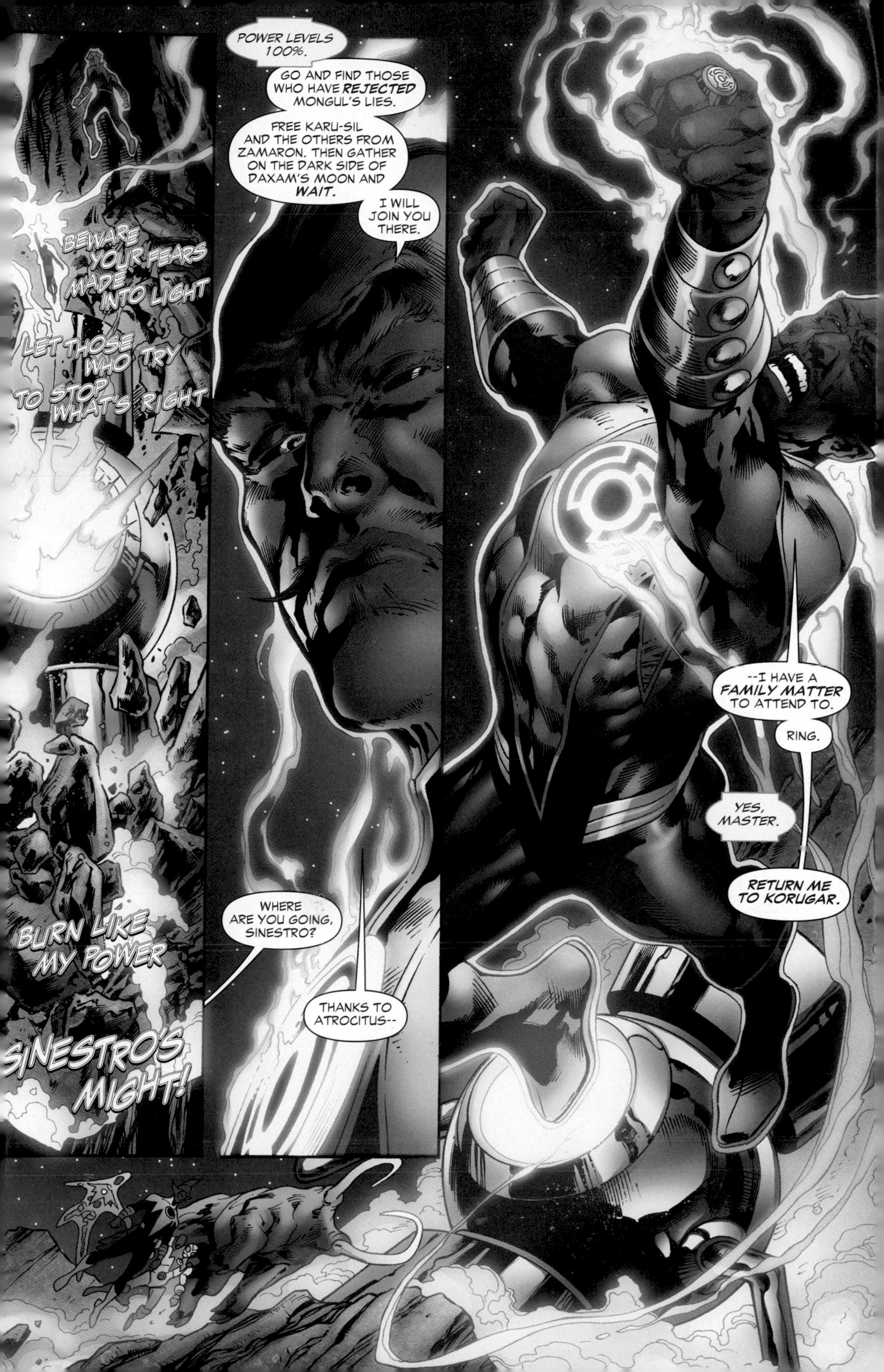
BEWARE YOUR FEARS MADE INTO LIGHT
LET THOSE WHO TRY TO STOP WHAT'S RIGHT
BURN LIKE MY POWER
SINESTRO'S MIGHT!
POWER LEVELS 100%.
GO AND FIND THOSE WHO HAVE REJECTED MONGUL'S LIES.
FREE KARU-SIL AND THE OTHERS FROM ZAMARON. THEN GATHER ON THE DARK SIDE OF DAXAM'S MOON AND WAIT.
I WILL JOIN YOU THERE.
WHERE ARE YOU GOING, SINESTRO?
THANKS TO ATROCITUS--
--I HAVE A FAMILY MATTER TO ATTEND TO.
RING.
YES, MASTER.
RETURN ME TO KORUGAR.

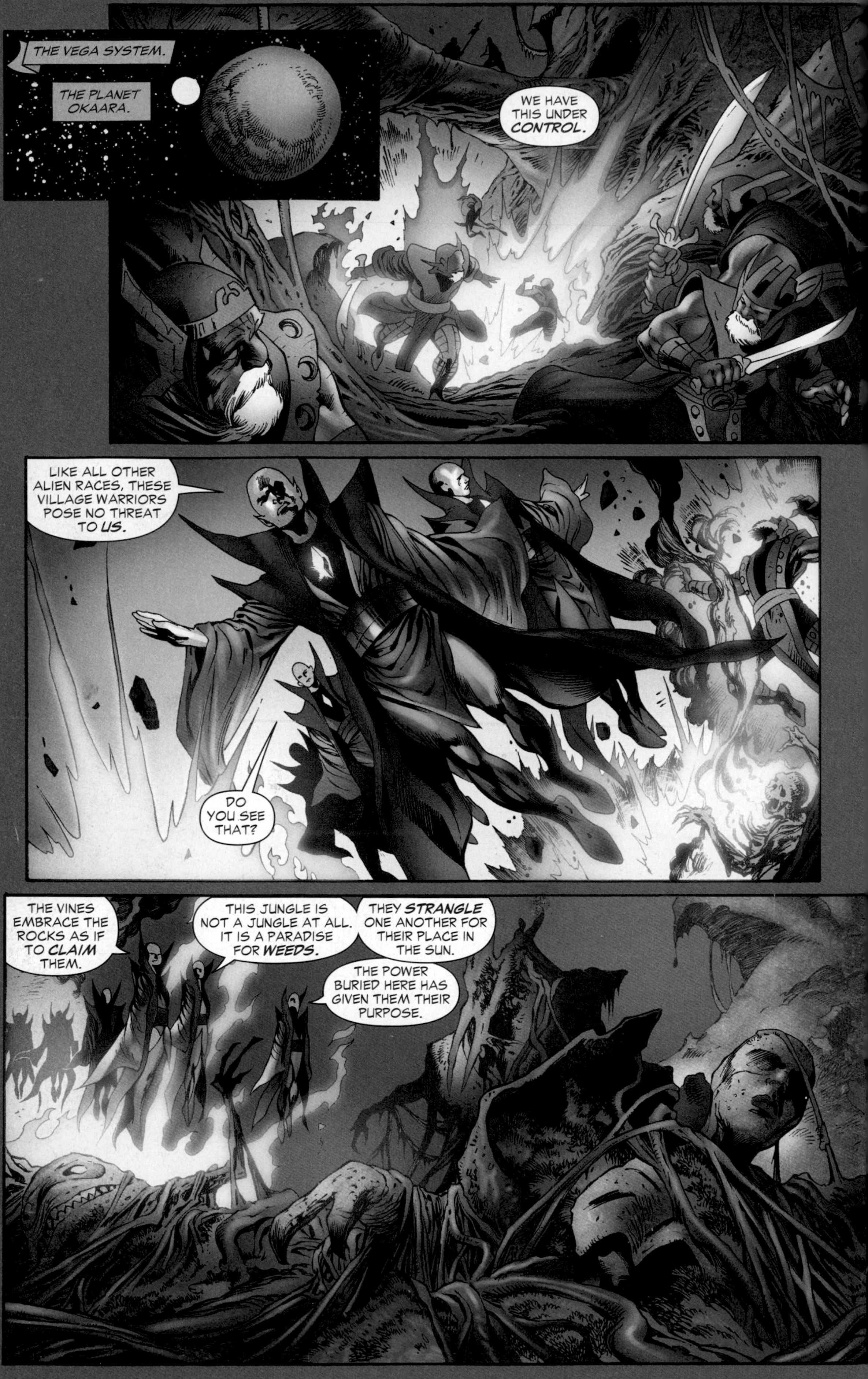
THE VEGA SYSTEM.
THE PLANET OKAARA.
WE HAVE THIS UNDER CONTROL.
LIKE ALL OTHER ALIEN RACES, THESE VILLAGE WARRIORS POSE NO THREAT TO US.
DO YOU SEE THAT?
THE VINES EMBRACE THE ROCKS AS IF TO CLAIM THEM.
THIS JUNGLE IS NOT A JUNGLE AT ALL. IT IS A PARADISE FOR WEEDS.
THEY STRANGLE ONE ANOTHER FOR THEIR PLACE IN THE SUN.
THE POWER BURIED HERE HAS GIVEN THEM THEIR PURPOSE.

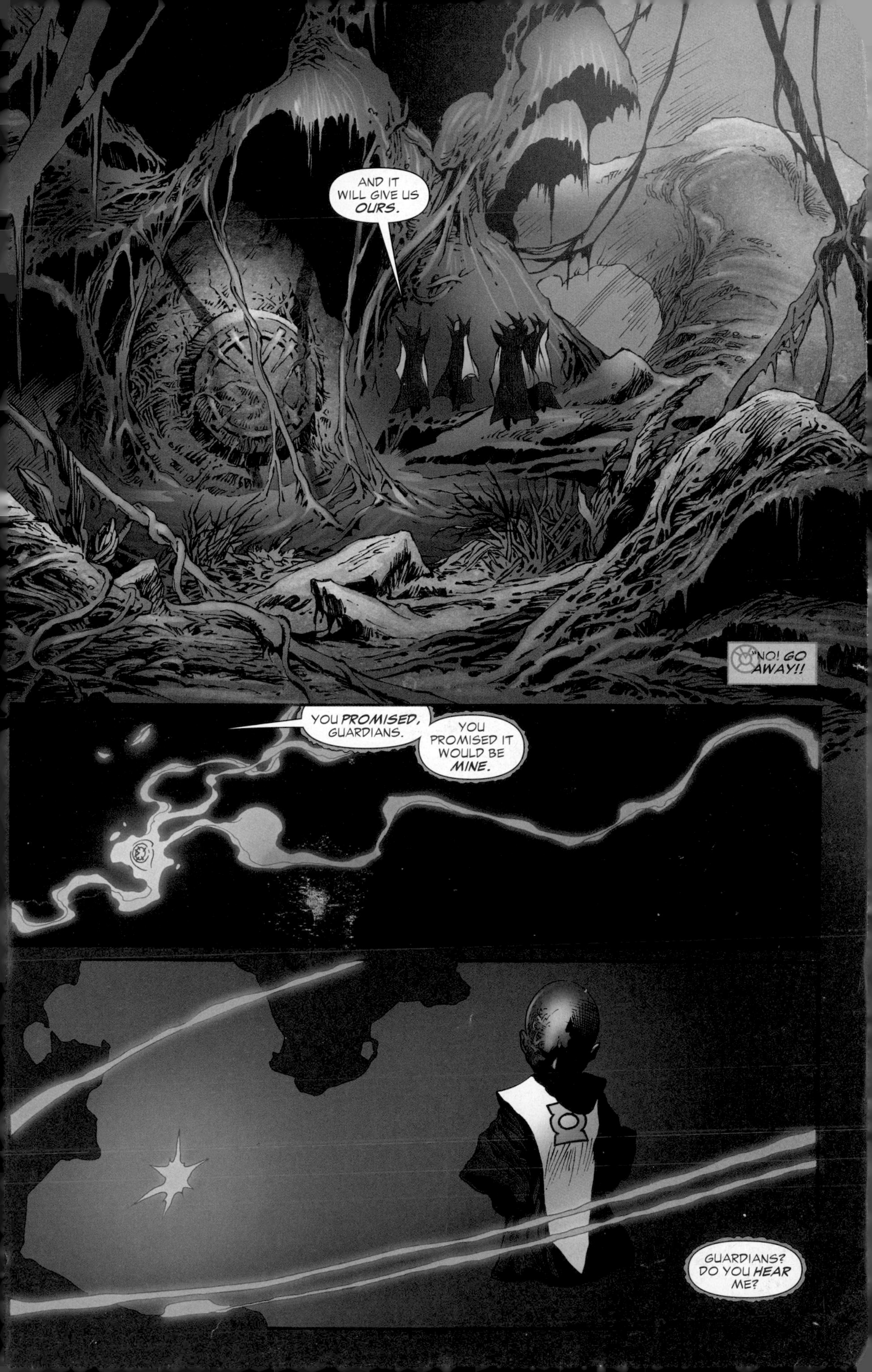
AND IT WILL GIVE US OURS.
"NO! GO AWAY!!
YOU PROMISED, GUARDIANS.
YOU PROMISED IT WOULD BE MINE.
GUARDIANS? DO YOU HEAR ME?

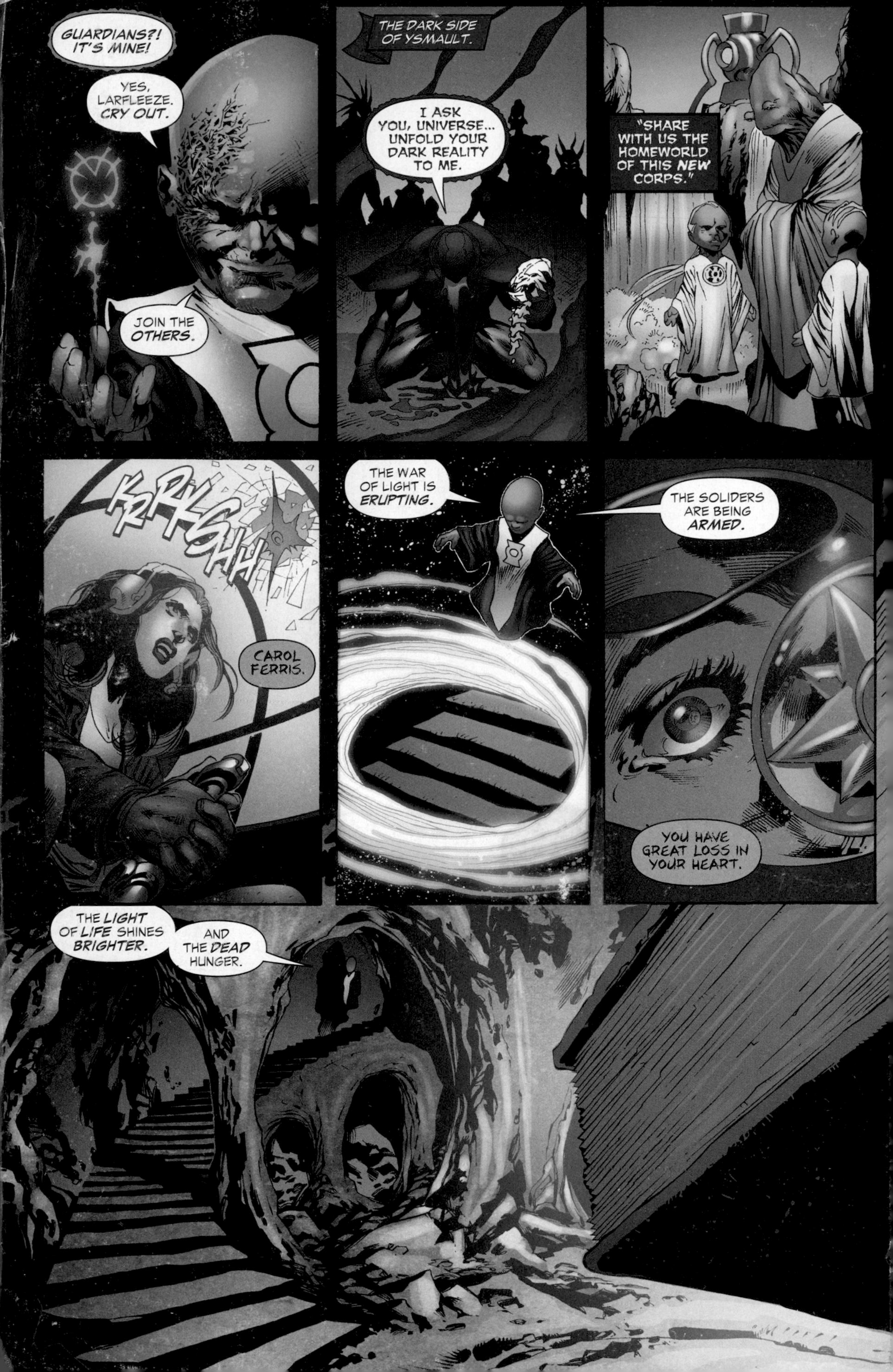
GUARDIANS?! IT'S MINE!
YES, LARFLEEZE. CRY OUT.
JOIN THE OTHERS.
THE DARK SIDE OF YSMAULT.
I ASK YOU, UNIVERSE... UNFOLD YOUR DARK REALITY TO ME.
"SHARE WITH US THE HOMEWORLD OF THIS NEW CORPS."
KRRKSHH
CAROL FERRIS.
THE WAR OF LIGHT IS ERUPTING.
THE SOLIDERS ARE BEING ARMED.
YOU HAVE GREAT LOSS IN YOUR HEART.
THE LIGHT OF LIFE SHINES BRIGHTER.
AND THE DEAD HUNGER.